Wal

# The Professional Housekeeper

## Fourth Edition

Madelin Schneider
Georgina Tucker
Mary Scoviak

**JOHN WILEY & SONS, INC.**

New York • Chichester • Weinheim • Brisbane • Singapore • Toronto

**Library of Congress Cataloging-in-Publication Data**

Schneider, Madelin.
   The professional housekeeper / Madelin Schneider, Georgina Tucker,
Mary Scoviak.—4th ed.
     p.    cm.
   Includes bibliographical references and index.
   ISBN 0-471-29193-5 (cloth : alk. paper)
   1. Hotel housekeeping.  I. Tucker, Georgina.  II. Scoviak-Lerner,
Mary.  III. Title.
TX928.S33  1998
648—dc21                            98-16187
                                             CIP

Printed in the United States of America.

10  9  8  7  6  5  4  3  2  1

# Dedication

*This book is dedicated to the great professional housekeepers of today and to the imaginative students who will expand the definition of "greatness" in the future.*

# Contents

# Preface

The changing face of the housekeeping profession and the lodging industry are the basis for changes in this fourth edition of *The Professional Housekeeper*. New lodging products, new markets, and new cleaning techniques are redefining the roles and responsibilities of the executive housekeeper.

What has not changed about the profession or *The Professional Housekeeper* is the need to understand the basics of managing a department and cleaning a property. Although the executive housekeeper is spending far more time managing than cleaning, he or she must have an in-depth practical understanding of the cleaning tasks that must be done, how long it takes to do them, and what equipment and supplies work best for each task. The professional housekeeper still needs to understand the basic design elements of the property, how to care for them and which will look best over the long term. There is also the need to understand co-workers in the department as well as in the hotel. The professional housekeeper must be a good manager and a good listener—often serving as a conduit in a work environment in which guests can afford to pay $250 a night for a room and the person who cleans that room makes little more than minimum wage.

The professional housekeeper's job continues to evolve and expand. To address this, *The Professional Housekeeper*, fourth edition, adds an ever tighter focus on management. New material will help future housekeepers prepare for a wide range of management challenges, from managing ethnic diversity and improving relations with unions to budgeting and maximizing technology. Key issues such as managing staff are covered in more depth because few issues have greater bearing on the success of the department. Finance also takes center stage in the housekeeping profession, and this too is reflected in the new content of *The Professional Housekeeper*. The various aspects of the housekeep-ing profession are put into a financial perspective, underscoring the importance of weighing decisions against both quality and the bottom line.

Much of the material added to this edition was hardly thought of when the third edition went to press: Issues such as bloodborne pathogens and other biohazards, e-mail and robotic cleaners. Professional housekeepers must address these concerns as part of managing their department. They must write health and safety plans, serve as experts in risk management, and train employees in how to protect themselves against viral and bacterial contamination. They must learn to accomplish these tasks without adversely affecting the environment around them and, someday, learn to do so at under-sea hotels or on the moon. Like the housekeepers themselves, the educational tools that help to train them must continue to change and innovate.

A new structure and new art program have been introduced to make this book easier to use. The number of chapters has been halved and subject matter condensed into cohesive chapters. For the first time, the book includes pedagogy that serves as a springboard to learning. From bold and defined key terms to an outline of chapter objectives and a summary, each chapter is equipped with learning tools that benefit both professor and student. Review questions reinforce key concepts. Critical thinking questions ask the students to put themselves in the role of the professional housekeeper and tackle the many challenges of this exciting profession. The pages also have a more streamlined look. Computer-generated forms and figures have taken the place of the standard, pre-printed forms of a decade ago. The photos provide a contemporary view of the interiors and equipment used in hotels today.

No resource, however rich, can prepare anyone fully for the roles and responsibilities of the house-

**viii    Preface**

keeping profession. How far the profession will evolve really depends on the skills of the people who enter it. Better trained and better educated than ever before, the professional housekeepers of tomorrow will continue to find better ways to manage and to redefine what standards of excellence really mean.

## ACKNOWLEDGMENTS

Like housekeeping, this book is a marvelous cooperative effort involving the talents of professional housekeepers from around the world, general managers from many properties, corporate hoteliers and experts in fields ranging from interior design to executive search to safety/security. Particular thanks go to Historic Hotels of America, Grand Heritage Hotels, Holiday Inn Worldwide, Choice Hotels International and its sister company, Manor Care Hotels, Marriott Hotels & Resorts, Westin Hotels and Resorts, Inter-Continental Hotels, Hyatt Hotels Corporation, Wyndham Hotels and Resorts, Hilton International, Radisson Hotels International, the American Hotel and Motel Association and the International Executive Housekeeper's Association.

These resources provided the essential and comprehensive information that makes this book a vital tool. The ever-supportive editorial experts at John Wiley & Sons, Inc. gave these ideas shape and form, refining them and using their own "best practices" to make the finished book as useful as possible to students and professors alike. Thanks are due, too, to the behind-the-scenes support team—researcher Robert Lerner and proofreader Oriana Lerner.

# The Professional Housekeeper

# 1

# Housekeeping: The Scope of the Lodging Industry

## Chapter Objectives

The first steps in building a career as a professional housekeeper are to:

- Develop an understanding of the importance of the housekeeping department
- Develop an understanding of the lodging industry
- Develop an understanding of the market-driven trends that are reshaping the lodging industry and their impact on housekeeping operations
- Develop an understanding of the housekeeping demands of different segments of the lodging industry, whether full-service or limited-service, all-suite or extended-stay properties
- Develop an understanding of the housekeeping demands of different categories of hotels, from economy to deluxe
- Develop an understanding of the impact of different ownership and management structures on the housekeeping department

Housekeeping is the heart of the lodging industry. Hotels, motels, and inns around the world can succeed without ballrooms, meeting rooms, swimming pools, or even restaurants. But the one thing every successful lodging establishment must have, regardless of its size, location, or industry segment, is clean rooms. Room sales generally drive 70 percent or more of the revenues generated by lodging establishments (see Table 1.1). Without a well-managed housekeeping department, there would be no rooms to sell.

The need for quality-oriented, efficient housekeeping is the link that unites the highly diverse hospitality industry. Luxury hotels, bed and breakfast inns, motels, cruiseships, and casino hotels have different styles of design and operations. Yet, they all have housekeeping departments that are challenged to provide clean, neat, attractive interior spaces that will help make first-time guests into loyal, long-term customers.

The housekeeping profession continues to evolve to meet changing guest demand and the changing profile of lodging establishments. Professional housekeepers manage housekeeping operations for the celebrity guests of deluxe boutique hotels, sail around the world on cruiseships that may hold thousands of passengers, and oversee housekeeping departments at multi-market resorts that cater to conference groups one day and families the next. They work in lodging establishments in small towns, major cities and secluded resort destinations. Some even work at the White House, embassies or other official residences of heads of states (see Tales of the Trade 1.1). With the experience gained as the business manager of a multi-million-dollar department with complex budgeting and staffing challenges, the professional housekeeper is highly marketable in any job market in virtually any area of the world.

## Tales of the Trade 1.1
### The Executive Housekeeper At the White House

Shirley Bender was a young, divorced mother of two young children when she took the job as sec-

**TABLE 1.1**   *The U.S. Hotel Market—Source of Total Revenue*

| Upper | % Room | % Food/beverage | % Telephone | % Other |
|---|---|---|---|---|
| Luxury Hotels | 66.9 | 26.3 | 2.7 | 4.1 |
| Upscale Hotels | 67.3 | 26.9 | 2.5 | 3.3 |
| **Middle** | **% Room** | **% Food/beverage** | **% Telephone** | **% Other** |
| Mid-Priced Hotels | 77.5 | 17.5 | 2.4 | 2.6 |
| **Lower** | **% Room** | **% Food/beverage** | **% Telephone** | **% Other** |
| Economy | 80.6 | 13.5 | 2.4 | 3.5 |
| Budget | 94.5 | 0 | 2.8 | 2.7 |

*Source:* Smith Travel Research, June 1995.

retary for the chief engineer of the Ritz-Carlton Hotel in Boston, Massachusetts. By the time she retired, she had served as executive housekeeper of the White House for nearly a decade.

Bender is proof of how far intelligence, work ethic, and professionalism can take a member of the housekeeping profession. While at the Ritz-Carlton in Boston, Massachusetts, she applied for and was hired as the executive housekeeper. She took classes in hospitality management at Boston University and joined the National Executive Housekeepers Association (NEHA—now IEHA). Weighing the need to support her family, provide a good environment for her children, and expand her own expertise, Bender took charge of her career. She learned to care for antiques and provide gracious service to guests while executive housekeeper at the Williamsburg Lodge in the preserved colonial city of Williamsburg, Virginia. She broadened her education with courses in food and beverage and accounting. She helped found chapters of NEHA. She was on the pre-opening team of a hotel in Tampa, Florida, and learned city center housekeeping at an upscale, 1,000-room hotel in St. Louis, Missouri. Bender had just left a position at a resort hotel in Texas when her mother told her about an ad in a Tampa newspaper for an executive housekeeper at the White House.

"I sent off a letter of application, but I kept on looking for other jobs. I thought I had nothing to lose in applying. Several months later, I got the call from the White House inviting me to interview," says Bender.

Bender's extensive housekeeping experience in upscale and luxury hotels, her knowledge of antiques gained at Williamsburg, her NEHA certification, her education, and her commitment to the profession as evidenced through her active involvement in NEHA proved to be impressive credentials. After months of background checks, she was offered the post as executive housekeeper of the White House.

Her broad duties ranged from preparing for and cleaning up after public tours which bring millions of people through the public areas each year, to coordinating special events with the state department and hosting celebrity guests. She and her staff of 18, all of whom had also passed intensive background checks by the Federal Bureau of Investigation, cared for some of the most precious pieces of American history.

"One of the more challenging aspects was obtaining replacements for the interior design elements. Perhaps the hardest of all was finding the white linen damask linens used during the Nixon administration. The kinds of mills that made them were going out of business, even in Ireland, but we finally did find a company to make them. The hand embroidery was done in Portugal. I also had to review all the interior design elements manufacturers wanted to donate. Some were acceptable; some definitely were not," comments Bender.

Bender, a frequent speaker to industry and civic groups, says the challenges of White House housekeeping were mainly logistical: the quick changes needed to transform the public areas from a sightseeing destination for millions to the sedate setting for a press conference or diplomatic visit; scheduling deep cleaning at times that do not interfere with the White House activities; and making sure guests' needs are met. Flexibility is the key. The Nixons were more formal, she says; the Fords and Carters more informal. Her staff cleaned up after family pets as well as heads of state. Her experiences ranged from watching awed entertainer Sammy Davis, Jr. call his mother to say he was actually staying in the Lincoln bedroom to seeing that much-loved teddy bears belonging to Queen Elizabeth's children were not disturbed when beds were made.

From Bender's point of view, working in hotel housekeeping departments was far more "political" than being at the White House. "I've always enjoyed people and I've always enjoyed a challenge. That makes housekeeping a good profession for me. No two days are ever the same. I never could have stood some repetitive job. But there are challenges, including the internal politics of a hotel," she says.

## THE IMPORTANCE OF HOUSEKEEPING

"Housekeeping is the toughest job in the lodging business. Housekeepers are heros. It is a constant battle for the executive housekeeper who has to motivate staff; and the staff who has to clean up after guests. Without housekeeping, we'd have nothing to sell," says Craig Hunt, a 24-year industry veteran who has worked his way up through the ranks "from the washing up" to become president of Holiday Inn International, based at the company's suburban Atlanta headquarters.

Housekeeping is a business function in the lodging industry, and the professional housekeeper is a true business manager. His or her decisions are executive decisions regarding staffing and scheduling, payroll, purchasing, daily operations, and cost controls. The entire property depends on the smooth, efficient management of the housekeeping department.

The housekeeping department has two prime functions: providing clean interiors in order to increase sales, and protecting the owner's investment in the property's interiors. It is the executive housekeeper's responsibility to make sure these goals are met on time, on budget, and at the highest possible levels of quality.

### Housekeeping as a Business-Building Tool

The housekeeping department does not generate sales directly, as do the food and beverage (F&B) department and the sales department. Yet its performance is one of the most critical factors in driving sales for rooms and other services the property offers.

In survey after survey, the traveling public rates cleanliness as a key factor in deciding whether to return to a property. A dirty room is cited as one of the main reasons guests choose *not* to return. Competition for guests is fierce and shows no signs of abating. Each property needs every competitive edge it can get. No general manager wants to see the property's loyal customer base pirated away because the rooms were not cleaned properly.

The importance of housekeeping activities goes beyond providing clean guest rooms to sell. Restaurants, meeting rooms, and function space bring enhanced revenue to the property. What meeting planner would plan a lucrative association gala in a dirty banquet hall? Lackluster housekeeping is one of the biggest obstacles to generating and delivering revenues.

### Protecting the Owner's Investment

Upscale hotels can cost from $50 million to $100 million to build. Even with the cost of the building's architecture and the land factored out, a guest room can represent an investment of tens of thousands of dollars or even $150,000 for very luxurious rooms or suites. It is the executive housekeeper's job to protect this investment and maximize the life expectancy of all interior design elements by developing effective cleaning practices and training staff to carry out these practices efficiently.

Working with maintenance and engineering, the housekeeping department ensures that the property's interiors continue to look and operate like new as long as possible. Effective housekeeping practices combined with a sound renovation program enable a property to evolve to meet guest demand without unnecessary spending.

### Overview of the Lodging Industry

The first step in launching a successful career as a professional housekeeper is to understand the lodging industry and the role the professional housekeeper and the housekeeping department play in it. Part of the thriving service sector, the lodging industry continues to expand, and the opportunities for professional housekeepers are expanding with it.

The **lodging industry** is a broad term that covers all types of home-away-from-home sleeping accommodations, from the three-room bed and breakfast inn—which is also the owner's home, to small, chain-operated roadside motels, YMCAs and YWCAs, elegant small hotels in city centers, and idyllic resorts, to business hotels in gateway cities and giant casino hotels with more than 2,000 guest rooms. Cruise ships are seagoing hotels. Properties that combine traditional hotel functions with residential components, such as apartments or condominiums, also belong within the parameters of the lodging industry. Senior living centers, colleges, universities, and even some country clubs and athletic clubs also provide their own kind of home-away-from-home accommodations.

This book focuses on the skills professional housekeepers will need to succeed in the lodging industry (exclusive of such specialized facilities as hospitals and prisons) and presents an in-depth picture of both the unique opportunities and challenges it affords.

Professional housekeepers need to understand the entire spectrum of the lodging industry for several reasons:

- To assess their career opportunities
- To understand how guests' needs and demands affect housekeeping operations
- To understand the competitive nature of the industry, and how competition influences both services and performance standards
- To understand how the category of the hotel defines performance standards

## A Brief History of the Lodging Industry

The first time a wandering human sought and was given temporary shelter in the cave of another tribe, the hospitality industry was born. In the Christmas story, two famous travelers, Mary and Joseph, spent the night in a stable because there was "no room at the inn." Perhaps the oldest hotels still in existence can be seen at Pompeii in southern Italy, where the eruption of Mt. Vesuvius buried the town under hot lava and preserved numerous buildings almost intact. The first innkeepers' guild was formed in Florence, Italy in 1282. What many claim to be the oldest inn still standing in the

United States is a stone house in Guildford, Connecticut, built in 1640 (see Figures 1.1a and 1.1b).

However, it was the introduction of the passenger-carrying stagecoach in England in 1658 that sparked a new age for the lodging industry. Inns, or taverns as they were called, sprang up along every coach route to provide overnight hospitality to the seventeenth-century forerunners of today's truly mobile society.

Railroads later replaced the stagecoaches, only to be largely replaced themselves by cars zooming down interstate highways and air travel. Each development in transportation changed where travelers needed to go to do business or wanted to go for their holidays. Shifts in accessible modes of transportation have created boom towns and ghost towns across countries throughout the world.

Faster transportation also meant more people were willing, able, and could afford to travel to more places. The affluent could idle away a week, a month, or even a season at a small but growing number of posh hotels. City Hotel in Baltimore, built by David Barnum in 1826, is usually ranked as the United States' *first grande luxe* property. Within 30 years, pampering resorts for the rich were springing up around the country, from properties such as the Mountain House (now Mohonk Mountain House in New York's Catskill Mountains) to The Spring House (now Greenbrier in White Sulphur Springs, West Virginia; see Figure 1.2) and, in 1887, the Hotel del Coronado, a Victorian wonder on California's Coronado Peninsula.

Although North America had its first lodging "chain" in 1769 when Father Junipero Serra set up a series of missions one day's journey apart along 600 miles of road in California (see Figure 1.3), development of the multi-unit lodging chain, in which each hotel or motel operates under the same brand name, did not really begin until the twentieth century. American hotel tycoon Ellsworth Statler entered the field in 1901. By the time of his death in 1928, he had built Statler hotels in six major cities, as well the 2,200-room Pennsylvania Hotel in New York. In 1954, his widow sold the 10-unit Statler chain to Hilton Hotels for $111 million. Ernest Henderson, who built Sheraton into one of the world's largest and most international hotel chains; Conrad Hilton, who engineered the growth of Hilton Hotels; and Kemmons Wilson, who founded Holiday Inns in 1952, are among those who transformed the lodging industry into one of the most economically influential industries in the world.

*(a)*                                                                           *(b)*

**Figure 1.1**   *(a) The hotel industry in the United States traces its history back to the early colonial period when travelers enjoyed hospitality at structures such as this stone house dating from 1640. (Courtesy of the Henry Whitfield State Museum, Guilford, Connecticut) (b) With its well-preserved Great Hall, the Whitfield house may be the oldest inn still standing in the United States. (Courtesy of the Whitfield State Museum, Guilford, Connecticut)*

**Figure 1.2**   *By the mid- to late 1880s, the rich were enjoying getaways at pampering resorts such as The Greenbrier (then called The Spring House) in White Sulphur Springs, West Virginia. (Courtesy of The Greenbrier, a CSX Resort)*

**Figure 1.3** *America's first lodging chain was established as early as 1769 by Father Junipero Serra, who set up a series of missions one day's journey apart along the 600-mile El Camino Real (the King's Road) in California. Food and lodging were provided to all who requested them in these 21 self-contained communities. Shown here is the Mission San Carlos Borromeo in Carmel, California.*

## TODAY'S U.S. LODGING INDUSTRY

Housekeepers considering a career in the lodging industry are entering a powerful and diverse industry. The American Hotel & Motel Association (AH&MA), based in Washington, D.C., estimates there are more than 45,000 properties with 3.4 million guest rooms in the United States alone. These U.S. hotels and motels generate sales of more than $66 billion a year and employ more than 1.56 million people full- and part-time.

Although the information age is changing hotel operations, the lodging industry remains labor intensive—even at the management level. The U.S. Department of Labor projects the total number of people employed in the U.S. lodging industry will increase from 1.56 million in the mid-1990s to 2.2 million by 2005. AH&MA points out that these 637,000 additional jobs would place the lodging industry tenth among 40 major employment classifications in terms of creating new jobs. The lodging industry would tie for eighth (with agriculture) in terms of the rate of increase in jobs—40.5 percent. An important statistic for job-seeking students is that roughly one of out every 10 jobs in the lodging industry is managerial.

The travel and tourism industry, which includes the hotel industry, accounts for 6 percent of the United States' gross annual product, making it the third largest industry in the United States be-hind auto sales and retail food sales. Travel and tourism is the largest employer in 11 states, and among the top three in 34 states. The industry also leads the nation in employment of women and minorities. Over the past decade, travel industry employment has grown 43.9 percent, more than twice the growth rate for all other U.S. industries.

## THE INTERNATIONAL LODGING INDUSTRY

The hospitality industry is an important economic force in countries around the world. *Into the New Millennium,* a white paper on the global hospitality industry by the Paris-based International Hotel Association, estimates total revenues for the world's more than 300,000 hotels at nearly $250 billion. (Some of the world's largest hotel companies are listed in Tables 1.2 and 1.3.)

This contributes significantly to the economic clout of the worldwide travel and tourism industry. The World Tourism Organization (WTO), based in Madrid, reports that international tourism receipts reached $372 billion in 1995, exclusive of international transport fares. This marked 7.2 percent growth over the previous year's totals. Travel and tourism is among the top five revenue and foreign exchange generators in many countries around the globe. It is also one of the world's major employers, and one of the few that can continue to engineer job growth.

The travel and tourism industry is a growth industry internationally. More and more people travel each year. People start to travel at a younger age, and continue to travel longer. Traditional travel markets such as London, Paris, and Hong Kong share center stage with rising young markets in Bombay, Ho Chi Minh City, Kuala Lumpur, and Singapore (see Figure 1.4). Hotel development is resurgent in Latin America, while renovation is the order of the day in Europe. Adventure travelers, looking for beyond-the-ordinary experiences deep in jungles or high on mountains, are pushing the travel and tourism industry to new areas. Anywhere people travel, which means virtually anywhere on the globe, could be a target for hotel development and a potential job opportunity for professional housekeepers.

## TYPES OF LODGING ESTABLISHMENTS

With the vast array of lodging types, often referred to as lodging **segments** or **products,** the professional housekeeper can easily find a property that suits his or her career goals, management style, and even personal interests. Before making a career decision, professional housekeepers should become familiar with the basic segments in the lodging industry.

The lodging industry includes both hotels and motels. A **hotel** is a lodging establishment in which guest rooms are accessed from the interior. Generally, a hotel is expected to provide services in addition to accommodations, the most common being food service. A **motel** is literally defined as "a hotel for motorists." Initially, motels provided guest rooms with access to exterior corridors on upper floors and directly to the parking area on the ground floor. Now, for safety and security reasons, few properties of any kind are built with exterior corridors. The differences between hotels and motels today lie more in their target guest market and pricing. Hotels are more upscale and offer more services than limited-service motels.

New lodging products **come on line,** a common industry term for openings, each year to meet customer demand. The basic categories (see Figure 1.5) of lodging now include:

**TABLE 1.2** *The World's Largest Corporate Hotel Chains*

| Rank 1996 1995 | Corporate chain Headquarters | Rooms 1996 1995 | Hotels 1996 1995 |
|---|---|---|---|
| **1** | **HFS Inc.** | **490,000** | **5,300** |
| 1 | Parsippany, NJ USA | 509,500 | 5,430 |
| **2** | **Holiday Inn Worldwide** | **386,323** | **2,260** |
| 2 | Atlanta, GA USA | 369,738 | 2,096 |
| **3** | **Best Western International** | **295,305** | **3,654** |
| 3 | Phoenix, AZ USA | 282,062 | 3,462 |
| **4** | **Accor** | **279,145** | **2,465** |
| 4 | Evry, France | 268,256 | 2,378 |
| **5** | **Choice Hotels International** | **271,812** | **3,197** |
| 5 | Silver Spring, MD USA | 249,926 | 2,902 |
| **6** | **Marriott International** | **251,425** | **1,268** |
| 6 | Washington, D.C. USA | 198,000 | 976 |
| **7** | **ITT Sheraton Corp.** | **130,528** | **413** |
| 7 | Boston, MA USA | 129,201 | 414 |
| **8** | **Promus Cos.** | **105,930** | **809** |
| 9 | Memphis, TN USA | 88,117 | 669 |
| **9** | **Hilton Hotels Corp.** | **101,000** | **245** |
| 8 | Beverly Hills, CA USA | 90,879 | 219 |
| **10** | **Carlson Hospitality Worldwide** | **91,177** | **437** |
| 10 | Minneapolis, MN USA | 84,607 | 383 |
| **11** | **Hyatt Hotels/Hyatt International** | **80,598** | **176** |
| 11 | Chicago, IL USA | 79,483 | 172 |
| **12** | **Inter-Continental Hotels** | **69,632** | **193** |
| 12 | London, England | 61,610 | 179 |
| **13** | **Hilton International** | **51,305** | **160** |
| 13 | Watford, England | 52,063 | 161 |
| **14** | **Grupo Sol Meliá** | **47,371** | **203** |
| 15 | Palma de Mallorca, Spain | 46,825 | 185 |
| **15** | **Forté Hotels** | **46,847** | **259** |
| 14 | London, England | 49,183 | 270 |
| **16** | **Doubletree Hotels** | **43,555** | **166** |
| 21 | Phoenix, AZ USA | 28,501 | 105 |
| **17** | **Westin Hotels & Resorts** | **42,897** | **97** |
| 18 | Seattle, WA USA | 40,074 | 82 |
| **18** | **Club Méditerranée SA** | **37,906** | **133** |
| 16 | Paris, France | 45,104 | 147 |

*TABLE 1.2*   (Continued)

| Rank 1996 1995 | Corporate chain Headquarters | Rooms 1996 1995 | Hotels 1996 1995 |
|---|---|---|---|
| 19 / 19 | Société du Louvre / Paris, France | 36,059 / 32,926 | 567 / 511 |
| 20 / 20 | La Quinta Inns / San Antonio, TX USA | 32,096 / 30,000 | 249 / 240 |
| 21 / 23 | Red Roof Inns / Hilliard, OH USA | 28,000 / 26,135 | 248 / 231 |
| 22 / 22 | Prince Hotels Inc. / Tokyo, Japan | 26,643 / 26,235 | 86 / 85 |
| 23 / 24 | Tokyu Hotel Group / Tokyo, Japan | 23,130 / 21,870 | 109 / 84 |
| 24 / 25 | Circus Circus / Las Vegas, NV USA | 19,585 / 20,754 | 16 / 17 |
| 25 / 30 | Walt Disney Co. / Burbank, CA USA | 19,415 / 16,163 | 18 / 13 |
| 26 / 28 | Nikko Hotels International / Tokyo, Japan | 18,632 / 16,726 | 49 / 42 |
| 27 / 27 | Wyndham Hotels & Resorts / Dallas, TX USA | 18,413 / 17,196 | 72 / 65 |
| 28 / 42 | Park Plaza Int'l Hotels & Resorts / Scottsdale, AZ USA | 17,722 / 12,722 | 131 / 77 |
| 29 / 26 | Hotels & Compagnie / Les Ulis, France | 17,579 / 17,391 | 342 / 340 |
| 30 / 31 | Fujita Kanko Inc. / Tokyo, Japan | 17,234 / 15,941 | 75 / 70 |
| 31 / 36 | Shangri-La Hotels & Resorts / Hong Kong | 16,985 / 14,646 | 34 / 30 |
| 32 / 29 | Scandic Hotels AB / Stockholm, Sweden | 16,000 / 16,400 | 98 / 101 |
| 33 / 41 | Riu Hotels Group / Playa de Palma, Mallorca, Spain | 15,896 / 12,889 | 63 / 53 |
| 34 / 32 | Omni Hotels / Corpus Christi, TX USA | 15,184 / 15,728 | 41 / 38 |
| 35 / 47 | ANA Hotels / Tokyo, Japan | 15,031 / 12,128 | 43 / 38 |
| 36 / 33 | Hospitality International / Tucker, GA USA | 14,665 / 15,366 | 259 / 269 |
| 37 / 44 | Budgetel Inns / Milwaukee, WI USA | 14,367 / 12,613 | 137 / 120 |
| 38 / 34 | Husa Hotels Group / Barcelona, Spain | 14,000 / 15,354 | 177 / 182 |

*TABLE 1.2*   (Continued)

| Rank 1996 1995 | Corporate chain Headquarters | Rooms 1996 1995 | Hotels 1996 1995 |
|---|---|---|---|
| 39 / 39 | Thistle Hotels Plc / Leeds, England | 13,574 / 13,556 | 100 / 100 |
| 40 / 35 | Dusit Thani/ Kempinski / Bangkok, Thailand | 13,208 / 11,648 | 55 / 49 |
| 41 / 40 | Southern Pacific Hotels Corp. / St. Leonards, Australia | 12,816 / 13,187 | 74 / 77 |
| 42 / 46 | Occidental Hotels / Madrid, Spain | 12,806 / 12,432 | 52 / 56 |
| 43 / 43 | Four Seasons Hotels Inc. / Toronto, Ontario, Canada | 11,900 / 12,663 | 37 / 37 |
| 44 / 38 | Queens Moat Houses Hotels / Romford, Essex, England | 11,626 / 14,092 | 91 / 122 |
| 45 / — | Robinson Club GmbH / Hannover, Germany | 11,416 / — | 24 / — |
| 46 / 48 | Canadian Pacific Hotels / Toronto, Ontario, Canada | 11,139 / 10,536 | 26 / 25 |
| 47 / 50 | National 9 Inns / Salt Lake City, UT USA | 10,822 / 10,420 | 182 / 181 |
| 48 / 51 | Ritz-Carlton Hotel Co. / Atlanta, GA USA | 10,682 / 10,311 | 33 / 31 |
| 49 / 45 | Maritim Hotels / Bad Salzuflen, Germany | 10,520 / 12,517 | 41 / 41 |
| 50 / 59 | ShoLodge / Gallatin, TN USA | 10,417 / 8,884 | 100 / 83 |

Note: Rankings are based on total rooms open as of Dec. 31, 1996.
*HOTELS* estimate.
(—) Not ranked in previous report.
*Hotels*, July 1997.

- Deluxe
- Upscale
- Mid-tier
- Economy, limited-service
- All-suite

**TABLE 1.3** *The World's Largest Independent Management Companies*

| Rank 1996 1995 | Management company Headquarters | Rooms 1996 1995 | Hotels 1996 1995 |
|---|---|---|---|
| **1** | **Doubletree Hotels Corp.** | **56,144** | **242** |
| 3 | Phoenix, AZ USA | 23,974 | 86 |
| **2** | **Interstate Hotels Corp.** | **43,178** | **212** |
| 2 | Pittsburgh, PA USA | 35,492 | 153 |
| **3** | **Richfield Hospitality Services** | **38,745** | **132** |
| 1 | Englewood, CO USA | 37,268 | 134 |
| **4** | **Starwood Lodging** | **20,350** | **75** |
| 29 | Los Angeles, CA USA | 7,802 | 34 |
| **5** | **Barrington Hotels & Resorts Int'l** | **19,290** | **48** |
| — | Fort Lauderdale, FL USA | — | — |
| **6** | **Carnival Hotels & Resorts** | **18,196** | **78** |
| 5 | Miami, FL USA | 17,000 | 65 |
| **7** | **Queens Moat Houses Plc** | **17,092** | **127** |
| 4 | Romford, England | 19,675 | 154 |
| **8** | **CDL Hotels** | **15,782** | **61** |
| 20 | Singapore | 9,985 | 46 |
| **9** | **UniHost Corp.** | **15,122** | **136** |
| 14 | Belleville, Ontario, Canada | 10,555 | 119 |
| **10** | **Prime Hospitality Corp.** | **14,617** | **103** |
| 7 | Fairfield, NJ USA | 13,443 | 93 |
| **11** | **Tharaldson Enterprises** | **14,190** | **224** |
| 9 | Fargo, ND USA | 11,143 | 182 |
| **12** | **Westmont Hospitality Group Inc.** | **12,043** | **63** |
| 30 | Houston, TX USA | 7,590 | 46 |
| **13** | **Servico Inc.** | **11,663** | **60** |
| 11 | West Palm Beach, FL USA | 11,000 | 57 |
| **14** | **Southern Sun Hotels** | **11,628** | **63** |
| 16 | Johannesburg, South Africa | 10,500 | 60 |
| **15** | **Remington Hotel Corp.** | **11,596** | **70** |
| 8 | Dallas, TX USA | 11,741 | 70 |
| **16** | **Ocean Hospitalities Inc.** | **11,537** | **65** |
| 12 | Portsmouth, NH USA | 10,964 | 63 |
| **17** | **American General Hospitality** | **11,500** | **64** |
| 6 | Dallas, TX USA | 14,381 | 80 |
| **18** | **Motels of America Inc.** | **11,185** | **135** |
| 13 | Des Plaines, IL USA | 10,573 | 124 |
| **19** | **Columbia Sussex Corporation** | **11,072** | **46** |
| 10 | Fort Mitchell, KY USA | 11,072 | 46 |
| **20** | **Winegardner & Hammons Inc.** | **10,697** | **51** |
| 15 | Cincinnati, OH USA | 10,553 | 51 |
| **21** | **John Q. Hammons Hotels** | **10,658** | **43** |
| 17 | Springfield, MO USA | 10,464 | 42 |
| **22** | **Grupo Posadas Management** | **10,204** | **45** |
| 23 | Mexico City, Mexico | 9,504 | 39 |
| **23** | **Gencom American Hospitality** | **10,172** | **39** |
| 28 | Houston, TX USA | 7,902 | 33 |
| **24** | **CapStar Hotels** | **9,712** | **47** |
| 25 | Washington, D.C. USA | 9,096 | 50 |
| **25** | **Bristol Hotel Management Co.** | **9,684** | **38** |
| 19 | Dallas, TX USA | 10,020 | 38 |
| **26** | **Beck Summit Hotel Mgmt Group** | **9,100** | **60** |
| 22 | Boca Raton, FL USA | 9,519 | 65 |
| **27** | **Kokusai Kogyo Hotel Mgmt** | **9,069** | **31** |
| 24 | Tokyo, Japan | 9,354 | 36 |
| **28** | **Lane Hospitality** | **8,082** | **37** |
| 21 | Northbrook, IL USA | 9,913 | 55 |
| **29** | **Sage Hospitality Resources Inc.** | **8,068** | **54** |
| 27 | Denver, CO USA | 8,000 | 55 |
| **30** | **Tishman Hotel Corp.** | **7,874** | **13** |
| — | New York, NY USA | — | — |
| **31** | **Hostmark Management Group** | **7,665** | **36** |
| 26 | Rolling Meadows, IL USA | 8,571 | 42 |
| **32** | **Amerihost Properties Inc.** | **6,448** | **72** |
| 33 | Des Plaines, IL USA | 5,979 | 59 |
| **33** | **Impac Hotel Group** | **6,396** | **35** |
| 67 | Atlanta, GA USA | 3,337 | 18 |

***TABLE 1.3***   *(Continued)*

| Rank 1996 1995 | Management company Headquarters | Rooms 1996 1995 | Hotels 1996 1995 |
|---|---|---|---|
| **34** | **Shaner Hotel Group** | **6,214** | **52** |
| 41 | State College, PA USA | 4,965 | 42 |
| **35** | **Boyd Gaming Corp.** | **6,140** | **8** |
| 39 | Las Vegas, NV USA | 5,225 | 10 |
| **36** | **Horizon Hotels Ltd.** | **6,038** | **31** |
| 37 | Eatontown, NJ USA | 5,776 | 30 |
| **37** | **Destination Hotels/ Resorts** | **5,700** | **34** |
| — | Englewood, CA USA | — | — |
| **38** | **Tollman-Hundley Hotels** | **5,567** | **22** |
| 31 | Hopewell Junction, NY USA | 7,100 | 31 |
| **39** | **WestCoast Hotels** | **5,536** | **26** |
| 44 | Seattle, WA USA | 4,694 | 22 |
| **40** | **Aztar Corporation** | **5,249** | **4** |
| 49 | Phoenix, AZ USA | 4,427 | 3 |
| **41** | **Ramkota Companies** | **5,192** | **39** |
| 45 | Sioux Falls, SD USA | 4,690 | 35 |
| **42** | **Davidson Hotel Company** | **5,109** | **23** |
| 52 | Memphis, TN USA | 4,293 | 20 |
| **43** | **Kahler Corp.** | **5,082** | **16** |
| 40 | Rochester, MN USA | 5,119 | 22 |
| **44** | **Signature Hospitality Resources** | **5,030** | **18** |
| 43 | Denver, CO USA | 4,750 | 14 |
| **45** | **White Lodging Services** | **4,987** | **43** |
| 60 | Merrillville, IN USA | 3,550 | 30 |
| **46** | **Capitol Hotel Group** | **4,963** | **16** |
| 36 | Rockville, MD USA | 5,780 | 20 |
| **47** | **H.I. Development Corp.** | **4,878** | **33** |
| 18 | Tampa, FL USA | 10,090 | 104 |
| **48** | **Tamar Inns Inc.** | **4,848** | **6** |
| 42 | Orlando, FL USA | 4,847 | 6 |
| **49** | **Trigild Corporation** | **4,475** | **40** |
| 46 | San Diego, CA USA | 4,548 | 46 |
| **50** | **Windsor Hospitality Group** | **4,238** | **18** |
| 63 | Los Angeles, CA USA | 3,513 | 15 |

Note: Rankings are based on total rooms open as of Dec. 31, 1996.
*HOTELS* estimate.
(—) Not ranked in previous report.
***Source:*** *Hotels,* July 1997.

- Extended-stay
- Resorts and time-share
- Inns

### Deluxe Hotels

Deluxe hotels are the most challenging in terms of maintaining standards. This category includes the most elite hotels of the world (see, for example, Figure 1.6). They represent the largest investment in architecture, interior design and, frequently, real estate. Some recent deluxe hotels have been rumored to cost $1 billion, exclusive of land. Because of the high level of guest expectations, these hotels feature the best furnishings, fixtures, and even linens available.

Generally, these top-of-the-line hotels also command top room rates, frequently $250 a night or more. Their genteel clientele values impeccable service, demands privacy, and is willing to pay for these comforts. In Europe, where these deluxe hotels are often referred to as **five-star,** luxury properties must provide an extensive range of services to earn and maintain their top ratings. Some areas of the world allow for more flexibility, but few hotels can hope to earn deluxe status without a full list of standard hotel services. Bell staff, 24-hour room service, in-room fax and computer hookups if not the machines themselves, two or three in-room telephones, in-room entertainment centers, fitness facilities, and business centers are expected at this level.

In order to provide the necessary, personalized service, deluxe hotels are usually fairly small—less than 300 rooms—though there are exceptions. Very small, elegant hotels are referred to as **boutique hotels** and usually have the individualized, stylish flair of their fashion industry counterparts.

*Advantages:* Executive housekeepers in these properties share in the glamour and excitement of working amidst this kind of monied and/or famous clientele. For professional housekeepers at deluxe properties, there is a great deal of prestige connected with this type of position as well as commensurate compensation. Exceptional, well-qualified professional housekeepers are sought out for these positions.

*Challenges:* The sophisticated guests of these hotels, as well as the hotel managers, expect flawless service. The executive housekeeper is under constant pressure not only to meet but to anticipate guests' needs. Also, these are frequently among the most difficult properties to clean because easy-to-clean vinyls and synthetics would not meet quality

***Figure 1.4*** *Deluxe hotels, including the venerable Raffles Hotel in Singapore, boast top-quality design elements. Executive housekeepers must know how to clean and care for customized or even one-of-a-kind elements. (Courtesy of the Singapore Tourist Board)*

standards. Instead, the housekeeping department must find ways to maintain one-of-a-kind designer furnishings and expensive fabrics.

Job growth in this sector is limited because the guest market for these hotels is so small. Some estimate the target client market for deluxe hotels at less than 5 percent of the travel market; some say, realistically, it is less than 1 percent. Real estate and development costs have restricted development of five-star or deluxe hotels in many markets in the United States. However, in Asia, luxury hotel development is booming.

## Upscale Hotels

Upscale hotels, also referred to as **four-star** hotels, commercial hotels, or business-class hotels, provide the traditional menu of hotel services, includ-

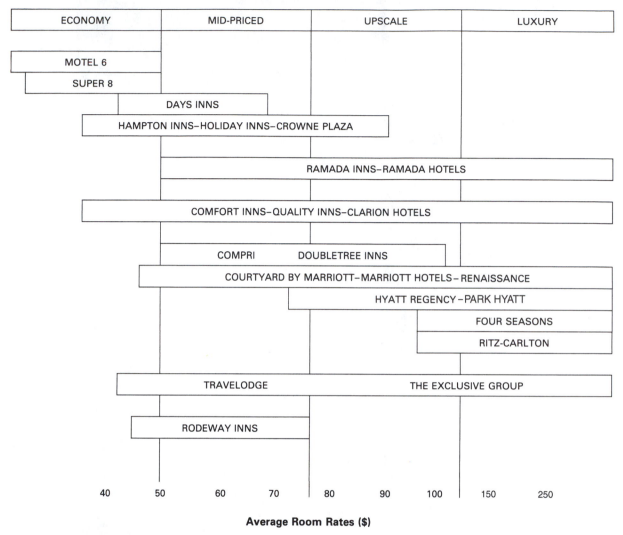

**SEGMENTATION COMPARISONS**

**Figure 1.5**  *This diagram shows the relative prices of the different segments of the various hotel chains. Those that belong to the same companies are on one line across the diagram. The room rates in the luxury chains at the far right can go higher than the $250 shown; in New York City, for example, only a few mid-tier rooms are available for under $150.*

ing food service on premise as well as new amenities such as business centers, private meeting rooms, and functional fitness centers. Upscale business hotels have in-room hookups for computers and fax and may offer a two-line phone or more than one in-room phone. Corporate business travelers represent the main client base for these hotels and rely on them to provide a high level of standardized services. These business-oriented hotels generally range from 300-room properties that market primarily to **frequent individual travelers** (FITs) to the 1,000-room and 2,000-room mega-

hotels that primarily service the meetings and convention market.

*Advantages:* Executive housekeepers of four-star hotels frequently have the opportunity to broaden their management skills and operational expertise. Salaries reflect the high degree of professionalism required to run a large department. Though not designer originals, these properties feature good quality furnishings and fixtures that have a long life expectancy if cared for properly. The interior design elements are more standardized, making replacement easier as well.

**Figure 1.6**  *Guests paying hundreds of dollars a night to stay at top-rated deluxe hotels such as New York City's famous Plaza Hotel expect flawless service from all departments, including housekeeping. (Courtesy of The Plaza Hotel, New York)*

*Challenges:* The main pressure on the housekeeping department in this sector is efficiency. One thousand people may be checking out while an equal number are checking in. The housekeeping department must return rooms to inventory to be "resold" as quickly as possible, without sacrificing quality.

New opportunities in the four-star market most likely will be found in second-tier cities such as San Diego, California or Portland, Oregon that are emerging as bases for corporate development as well as regional convention business.

## Mid-tier Hotels and Motels

Experts say this is the sector with the most potential for near-term expansion. It also is the sector undergoing the most rapid change. Kemmons Wilson rolled out Holiday Inns primarily to meet the demands of traveling families for clean, comfortable, affordable rooms. In the last three decades, both corporations cutting back on travel expenses and families who want a guarantee of a clean room are building market demand for these **three-star** properties. Renovation is rampant in this sector, where many core properties are now more than 30 years old. Most are still full-service and include food service on the premises, as well as a small function room and, often, a swimming pool.

New mid-tier properties look and operate differently than their predecessors. The list of amenities is becoming more individualized. Holiday Inn recently rolled out its KidSuites℠, which creates a room within a room. Using a partition or actual full walls, this new room type provides a separate sleeping area for children, complete with their own beds, television, and even a small work area, and another sleeping area for adults. They can be **new build,** which means newly constructed, or **retrofitted,** which means installed in an existing space. Hilton's new Garden Inns brings the in-room office concept from the upscale sector to the mid-tier—complete with working desks with two-line phones and dataports and an in-room microwave (see Tales of the Trade 1.2).

## Tales of the Trade 1.2
### New Products' Impact on Housekeeping

Development of Holiday Inns' KidSuites concept underscores how much impact the hotel product has on housekeeping. Since a second fully equipped sleeping area was added to each of the KidSuites℠, these rooms could no longer be assigned as a single room. James Olson, the general manager of the Holiday Inn Sunspree resort in Lake Buena Vista, Florida, who developed KidSuites℠ along with owner Terri Whaples, worked with the executive housekeeper to set new quotas. "We had various attendants clean the space and analyzed how long, on average, it would take to clean this room within a room. From that we developed the procedures that worked best and were able to determine the suites would be equivalent to 1.5 rooms," says Olson.

Some other problems discovered during the labor analysis: the need for nonskid stools so attendants could reach the top bunk; finding sheets for the bunk beds, since standard twins were too large; and finding a way to easily dis-

tinguish the sheets in the linen supply room. The hotel's seamstresses were trained to make the sheets, and the hotel opted for colored sheets that easily stood out from the standard sheet supply.

*Advantages:* Less experienced professional housekeepers have an opportunity to rise quickly to the executive housekeeper's position. Larger mid-tier properties and those that are part of major chains offer solid managerial experience, as well as job growth opportunities. The advantage for the housekeeping department is that most of the surfaces in these properties are easy to clean and durable. Salaries at these properties are in a median range, unless the property is very large.

*Challenges:* The housekeeping department must work with the necessary speed to service business travelers who stay only one night, as well as mid-sized groups who may stay three days. Families frequently require extra beds, bedding, and towels. Their rooms may require extra time to clean—as when a family of four has eaten one or two meals a day in the room. Executive housekeepers in mid-tier properties must find flexible solutions for meeting these cleaning challenges without exceeding the labor budget.

## Economy/Limited-Service Properties

Guests who stay at economy properties do not expect elaborate furnishings or fixtures, but they do expect a clean room and an affordable room rate (see Figure 1.7). According to AH&MA, *average* room rates in the United States stand at nearly $64. Several chains in the upper-tier economy properties charge $40 or more per night.

Economy properties' rates have come a long way from the $6 to $8 a night room rates that first attracted budget-conscious travelers several decades ago, but economy properties are also providing more value-for-money services. Since on-premise food service is not considered essential at economy properties, money that would have been invested in kitchens and restaurants can be spent on upgrading both design and amenities in the guest rooms. At the upper end of this segment, guest rooms are beginning to include small work desks and even in-room coffee or tea makers. Functionality is the main directive, but the look is far more welcoming and residential than it once was.

**Figure 1.7** *Durable, easy-to-clean surfaces reduce cleaning time in economy hotel chains such as Fairfield Inn by Marriott. However, standards of cleanliness and hygiene still apply. (Courtesy of Marriott Hotels and Resorts, Washington, D.C.)*

These **two-star** properties have a mixed market of business travelers and families. Stays are usually fairly short, except in resort markets.

*Advantages:* Many economy properties still offer room attendants the opportunity to rise quickly to the position of executive housekeeper. They provide on-the-job managerial training that could open up opportunities for further advancement. An advantage for some is that executive housekeepers in economy properties generally work only the day shift. With no-frills rooms and an emphasis on durability, these properties are generally easy to clean.

*Challenges:* In very small or independently owned properties, the executive housekeeper may be a room attendant who is assigned both cleaning and managerial tasks. The pay is generally low—sometimes only a higher hourly rate than that paid the other room attendants.

## All-Suite Hotels

All-suite hotels are exactly what their name implies. Instead of the traditional guest room, these prop-erties sell suites which include a living/dining area, separate sleeping area, bathroom, and some type of kitchenette. These hotels are designed for executives and families who need and will pay for dedicated living/work space and a separate sleeping area. Initially, these properties had only a pastry-and-coffee continental breakfast, no restaurants, no fitness facilities, and no meeting rooms. The new generation of all-suites tends to provide a full menu of guest services, from recreational and fitness amenities to full conference and meeting rooms.

Newer concepts have brought about some minor adjustments to keep rates in line and increase profitability. Instead of actual walls between the living and sleeping areas, some have only solid dividers. Instead of a kitchenette, some properties provide a microwave and a mini-refrigerator. What has not changed is that, even with the addition of food service, fitness facilities, or meeting space, 80 percent of the property's area is still devoted to space for the suites, as opposed to 50 to 60 percent for guest rooms in standard full-service properties.

Size of the suites and the long list of amenities have made all-suites among the most popular lodging choices among business and leisure travelers.

*Advantages:* The longer average length of stay, three nights to a week versus the usual 1.1 nights, means fewer check-out suites each day, which reduces cleaning time. All-suites can be found in all market sectors, and salaries and experience requirements for executive housekeepers vary accordingly.

*Challenges:* The primary disadvantage is that there is more space and equipment to clean. There is also more furniture and equipment to replace during renovation.

## Extended-Stay Properties

Extended-stay properties take the all-suite concept one step further. Designed primarily for business travelers who spend several months in a destination, extended-stay properties are far more like apartments than guest rooms. They provide real cooking facilities—not just microwaves, ample living/working areas, and one or two bedrooms. They also look more like home than their traditional hotel counterparts, with residential furnishings and a greater variety of seating and decorative accents.

An alternative being offered in some city centers, particularly in the Middle East and Asia, is to combine traditional hotels with serviced apartments. They target international business travelers who may be assigned to a location for a year or less and may even be with their families—too long a time to be confined in a traditional hotel room, but too short a time to require the commitment of buying or renting a home. Most of the extended-stay concepts were in the upscale range, but now companies such as Marriott are rolling out lower-priced options (see Figures 1.8a and 1.8b).

*Advantages:* The long stay means less pressure to clean rooms on tight deadlines. It also allows for more predictability in scheduling and workload.

*Challenges:* Although executive housekeepers do not face the time pressures they would in an upscale hotel, they must find ways to work around the schedules of long-term guests, clean a space that is being "lived in" rather than "visited," and keep guests satisfied over a longer time.

## Resorts and Time-share

Located in some of the most beautiful places on earth, resorts generally offer a less harried environment in which to work. They cover the gamut from the serene elegance of individual villas along a pristine beach to ski lodges in the mountains, championship golf resorts, spa hotels, and aging, two-story motels a few blocks from a small lake. They can provide the utmost in seclusion or, as in casino hotels, 24-hour-a-day activity.

Time-share has resurfaced as a major trend, and many name-brand operators are getting into this fast-growing market. **Time-share** enables a traveler to buy a block of time either at a specific property or group of properties for a certain amount of money. For a $15,000 upfront payment, a person may be able to "buy" a 52nd, or one week's stay, at a condominium in a property anywhere in the world that the company operates. This condo will be reserved for the buyer's use during a certain time each year for a specified number of years. Time-share units must be cleaned regularly, whether they are occupied or not. Some new projects now combine traditional hotel space with time-share units in the same building.

*Advantages:* The setting itself may be a considerable advantage. Usually, stays are longer and booked farther in advance, which makes scheduling easier. Occupancy is also more predictable than in highly transient business hotels. Some resorts benefit from the fact that they are the area's only major employer and, thus, have a ready supply of labor. Most upscale resorts require highly experienced executive housekeepers who can address cleaning challenges ranging from outdoor balconies to spas.

*Challenges:* Nature frequently poses one of the biggest challenges for the executive housekeeper in resorts. Mold, mildew, sun, sand, or snow cause myriad problems with cleaning and maintaining guest rooms and public areas of resorts. Some resorts are quite remote and must not only find workers from other areas but must sometimes provide housing as well.

## Inns

As a lodging segment, an inn generally refers to a small bed-and-breakfast property or a relatively small, low-rise property—often with historic significance. In Europe, these properties cover the range of lodging categories from plain yet functional rooms above a pub or tavern to elegantly restored country homes. Spain has converted some of its treasured historic buildings into *paradores*, or inns, to preserve and bring new life to these landmark structures (see Figures 1.9a and 1.9b). In the

(a)

**Figure 1.8** *(a) While executive housekeepers in extended-stay properties do not have the time pressure of heavy check-ins and check-outs each day, they do face greater challenges in terms of the variety of fixtures and furnishings used in the residential-style accommodations. (Courtesy of Residence Inns by Marriott)*

United States, too, *inns* focus on different categories. However, the trend has been for both bed-and-breakfast properties and historic properties to move more into the upper tiers.

*Advantages:* These small inns, especially the smaller bed-and-breakfast operations, offer entrepreneurial opportunities—as well as a charming environment in which to work. They also can be less formal, with guests treated more like visitors in a home.

*Challenges:* Maintaining the antique and signature furnishings may be a constant challenge. Also, few of the smaller inns can afford to provide either salary or benefits comparable to larger and/or chain-affiliated properties.

## Casino Hotels

Casino operations on both land and water are in the midst of a development boom. Although this trend cannot last indefinitely, it does present an at-

tractive "destination" for groups attending conferences or trade shows or leisure travelers.

*Advantages:* For some professional housekeepers, the complexity and vitality of these operations is highly appealing. For others, the major draw is that some casinos offer some of the highest paying jobs in the housekeeping profession.

*Challenges:* Gaming is virtually an around-the-clock activity, forcing the housekeeping department to work under time pressures even on the graveyard shift. The volume of foot traffic, combined with heavy usage, requires constant vigilance from the housekeeping department (see Figure 1.10).

## Cruise Ships

Cruising is the fastest growing sector of the travel market according to *Meetings & Conventions* magazine. The Cruise Line International Association reports passenger totals have been growing 7 to 10 percent a year in recent years. Based on that, pas-

### Address

Timog Avenue corner Tomas Morato Avenue,
Quezon City, Philippines
Tel.: (632) 9278001 or 4110116 Fax: (632) 9230562 / 9207881

### Location

Situated within the entertainment and commercial hub of
Quezon City. With easy access to the various historical and
cultural points of interest in the metropolis.

### Transportation

| From | Distance | Time | By |
|---|---|---|---|
| International Airport | 30 kms | 40 min. | Car |
| Domestic Airport | 27 kms | 35 min. | Car |
| SM City (North Edsa) | 3 kms | 5 min. | Car |
| Celebrity Sports Plaza | 8 kms | 20 min. | Car |
| Quezon Circle | 3.5 kms | 5 min. | Car |
| University of the Philippines | 5.5 kms | 15 min. | Car |

### Accommodation

12-storey, newly-built, full-service condominium hotel
complex featuring studio, as well as 1 and 2 bedroom suites.
All rooms are equipped with complete living, dining and
kitchen facilities.

Courtesy Century Imperial Palace Suites,
Quezon City, Philippines

### Features

- Refrigerator, stove, dining/kitchenware in all rooms
- IDD Telephones
- Outdoor Swimming Pool
- Health Club

### Food & Beverage Facilities

- Food and beverage outlets are located within the complex
- Discounts available at Fu-Lin Gardens; Padis Point; Racks, Brew Brothers, Annabels, Luigis, Alfredo's, Red's Cafe, Icings, Steaktown, Tamarind Grill, Gene's Bistro, Casa Marcos, Mobius.
- Room Service

### Banquet and Meeting Facilities

- Conference suite for meetings and seminars.

### Services

- Multilingual hotel staff
- Business Center with secretarial, photocopying, and facsimile services
- Multilingual satellite television
- Daily and monthly rates
- Foreign currency exchange
- Laundry and valet services
- Carpark
- Reservations for other Century International Hotels

*(b)*

**Figure 1.8** *(b) New concepts pose new opportunities and challenges for the house-keeping department. The Century Imperial Palace Suites is a full-service condominium hotel. The studios and one- and two-bedroom suites all feature complete living, dining, and kitchen facilities. (Courtesy of Century Imperial Palace Suites, Quezon City, Philippines)*

*(a)*

*(b)*

**Figure 1.9** *(a) For executive housekeepers who work in the historic inns of the Spanish paradores, the workplace can literally be a castle. Historic workplaces provide unique challenges and rewards. (Courtesy of The Paradores, Madrid, Spain) (b) Executive housekeepers who work in historic properties such as this parador must be expert in maintaining and preserving antiques and aged surfaces. (Courtesy of The Paradores, Madrid, Spain)*

senger totals are expected to jump from 4.8 million in 1994 to an estimated 8 million by the year 2000. Dozens of new cruise ships are under construction in shipyards worldwide.

Hotel companies such as Radisson Hotels International, based in Minneapolis, are crossing over to diversify their business base. Sonesta and ITT Sheraton, both based in Boston, and several other hotel companies already operate cruise ships on the Nile. Aboard ship, lodging and food service are managed much like their competitors on land. All cruise operations require a knowledgeable professional housekeeper (see Figure 1.11).

*Advantages:* The predetermined level of occupancy eases scheduling and inventory problems experienced by professional housekeepers in landside hotels where check-ins and check-outs are unpredictable. Also, staffing is set prior to sailing, which eliminates worries about finding and keeping staff. These are jobs for experienced housekeepers. Salaries vary with the line and category of the ship.

*Challenges:* Cruise ships have a set of unique challenges, ranging from variable water quality in

port to storms. Unlike land-based operations, staff cannot go "home" at night, underscoring the need for excellent human resources skills on the part of the executive housekeeper.

## Residential Facilities and Clubs

Universities and colleges, senior living centers, conference centers and city clubs or athletic clubs all provide accommodations and all require a professionally run housekeeping department. Of these three sectors, the senior living center sector is the fastest growing. Hotel companies such as a Marriott International sister company are crossing over to manage senior living centers.

Housekeeping plays a different role in each of these sectors. Students generally clean their own rooms. The college or university housekeeping department's responsibilities are concentrated in public areas, which may range from student lounges to "halls" that host glittering social functions. The role of the housekeeping department differs among senior living centers, depending on the management and residents' needs. Conference centers host tran-

**Figure 1.10** *Casino hotels pose some of the toughest housekeeping challenges. The MGM Grand's executive housekeeper must oversee the cleaning of the hotel's 5,000 rooms, as well as its miles of public space. (Courtesy of the MGM Grand Hotel, Las Vegas, Nevada)*

sient guests; clubs may have transient and long-stay accommodations. While the responsibilities of housekeeping may differ from day to day in these sectors, the professional housekeeper in all of these sectors still has the primary responsibility for keeping interiors flawlessly clean and protecting the owner's investment in the building's interiors (see Figures 1.12a and 1.12b).

*Advantages:* Because of the residential component in many of these facilities, the workload is fairly predictable, as are the hours. Also, especially in the case of senior living centers, there are a growing number of job opportunities.

*Challenges:* Trying to please residents every day, year round can be a difficult assignment. Though salaries are improving, they generally lag behind the hotel sector.

## Ownership and Management Structures

Simply because a property says Hilton, Sheraton, or Holiday Inn on the door does not guarantee it is owned or even managed by one of these compa-

nies. Before deciding on a position, the professional housekeeper should investigate the ownership and management structure of the property. Some aspects of these different structures have a significant bearing on housekeeping policies (see Table 1.4).

It is important for professional housekeepers to understand these structures for several reasons:

1. Some franchise or management companies have well-defined procedures and policies. These policies determine a broad range of issues from setting acceptable standards for furnishings and fixtures to how often revenue reports must be provided to the owner. Some management companies also set down policies on staff size and management styles.

2. Independent properties usually offer maximum flexibility in responding to the property's unique challenges and opportunities. Properties affiliated with reservation services or managed by regional or national companies may have to uphold certain standards regarding interior design ele-

**Figure 1.11**  *Predictable occupancy and staffing levels are just two of the advantages that attract experienced housekeepers to the fast-growing cruise industry. (Courtesy of Carnival Cruise Lines, Miami, Florida; Ships Registry: Liberia and Panama)*

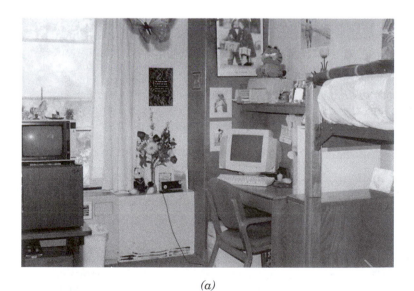

(a)

(b)

**Figure 1.12**  *(a–b) Executive housekeepers at university dormitories and other residential facilities generally benefit from a more standardized work week and fairly steady levels of occupancy. (Courtesy of Indiana University, Bloomington, Indiana)*

***TABLE 1.4*** *Ownership/Management Structures*

| Ownership or management structure | Characteristics | Examples |
|---|---|---|
| Independent property | Property bears no branded name and follows its own, individualized approach to operations | The Greenbrier in West Virginia; The Hotel del Coronado in California; The Imperial, Tokyo; The Ritz, Paris. |
| Chain-operated, company-owned property | Property bears the brand name of its chain; company ownership requires compliance with all of the chain's policies and programs. | Chains such as Hong Kong's Shangri-La prefer to own and operate; other companies such as Washington, D.C.-based Marriott have a small core of company-owned hotels. |
| Managed property | An owner "hires" a lodging chain or company specializing in lodging management to manage the property professionally in return for a management fee and, perhaps, overrides; however, the owner still owns the real estate and reserves the right to review the management firm's decisions and performance. | Inter-Continental, based in London; Seattle-based Westin; Marriott, based in Washington, D.C.; Boston-based Sheraton; Chicago-based Hyatt are a few examples of management companies. |
| Franchised property | In return for an upfront investment and annual fees, the franchisee, the person who buys a franchise, is permitted to use the name of a major chain, such as Holiday Inn, and share in the chain's reservation service and other support services. Franchisees must maintain basic standards, but are not required to participate in all programs offered by the franchisor. | Some of the world's biggest franchisors are HFS, based in Parsippany, New Jersey; Choice Hotels, Silver Spring, Maryland; Holiday Inn, Atlanta; Radisson, Minneapolis; Sheraton, Boston; and Hilton Hotels Corp., Beverly Hills, California. Some upscale chains also franchise or license the use of their brand name. |
| Affiliated properties and consortia members | Properties wishing to keep their own identity may join a consortia or reservation service, which may also offer central purchasing capabilities and marketing support. In many cases, certain standards must be met to belong to the consortia. Other properties associate themselves with major chains, not through branding but by buying into the chain's reservation service. | Leading Hotels of the World, New York City; Preferred Hotels, Chicago; and SRS, Frankfurt, Germany, all provide these types of services. Niche-driven companies such as Historic Hotels of America, Washington, D.C., provide services to members that share specific segments or other features. |

Different ownership and management structures directly influence how properties are run, what kinds of design and service standards must be maintained and, sometimes, even what thickness the wallpaper must be. All these factors help the executive housekeeper define the goals for the housekeeping department.

ments, cleanliness, and service. Some even have inspections; if properties do not pass, they must leave the system.

3. Properties managed by outside companies or chains, or franchised properties, offer more career mobility, in terms of the sheer volume and variety of positions available as well as location.

Some provide international opportunities. Chains that are **segmented,** with brands in various sectors of the lodging market, enable professional housekeepers to gain experience at different sizes and categories of properties.

4. Chain-affiliated hotels, and those affiliated with marketing services, usually share **best prac-**

**tices,** the optimal process for accomplishing a task, among their members. Professional housekeepers and other department heads share ideas and learn from their colleagues. Most organizations are moving away from the philosophy that there is only one solution for a problem and are giving their department heads more decision-making power.

The property's ownership and management structures affect both the demands made on and support given to the housekeeping department.

## SUMMARY

A century ago, the lodging industry offered few choices. A small group of properties pampered rich travelers with fine decor and finer services, the rest provided a place to sleep and not much else. Modes of travel have changed. Guests' demands have changed. And the lodging industry has changed in response. The need to provide clean rooms and interior spaces has made housekeeping the single most important department in any lodging establishment.

As head of this vital department, the professional housekeeper plays a key role in the success, or failure, of the property. Some of the must-have knowledge for the housekeepers of tomorrow includes:

- Where lodging industry growth will be
- The impact of each lodging segment on housekeeping
- The impact of different categories of lodging on housekeeping

- How different management structures impact housekeeping practices and policies
- The trends that are shaping the industry in the United States and around the world

## Review Questions

1. Name the basic segments of the lodging industry.
2. What is the difference between a hotel and a motel?
3. Discuss the impact of different ownership and management structures on the housekeeping department.
4. Why is the housekeeping department important to a lodging operation?
5. What is a franchise?
6. What is a consortia, and how may membership affect the housekeeping department?
7. How important is the lodging industry to the U.S. economy?
8. What are the primary functions of the housekeeping department?

## Critical Thinking Questions

1. What questions should one ask about the property when applying for a position as an executive housekeeper?
2. Discuss the pros and cons of working in a traditional hotel versus a cruise ship of the same category.
3. Discuss the pros and cons of working in a deluxe boutique hotel versus a mid-tier property.

# 2

# Key Roles and Responsibilities of the Professional Housekeeper

## Chapter Objectives

To maximize his or her performance, as well the department's performance, the professional house-keeper must:

- Understand the property's management structure
- Understand where the housekeeping department fits into the property's management structure
- Work within the property's management philosophy to motivate staff and maximize perform-ance
- Fulfill the managerial and technical requirements of professional housekeeping
- Communicate effectively with department staff members
- Communicate effectively with other departments
- Create an efficient organizational structure for the department

The executive housekeeper has one of the most complex managerial roles in any lodging establish-ment. Not only does the executive housekeeper manage what is typically the property's largest de-partment and one of its largest departmental budg-ets, he or she also oversees a 24-hour-a-day depart-ment that must perform as effectively on the **graveyard shift,** which typically runs from mid-night to 8 A.M., as it does during peak day-time ac-tivity.

It is the executive housekeeper's responsibility to coordinate all the varied activities assigned to the housekeeping department and to maximize the performance of the individuals who work within the department. As the manager of what is fre-quently a six-figure if not multi-million-dollar budget, the executive housekeeper must under-stand cost controls and the property's financial goals. He or she must be able to create a sound budget and operate the department within these budgetary guidelines. Technical expertise regarding cleaning practices, human resources management, and purchasing expertise are all part of the skills required of an executive housekeeper.

Executive housekeepers not only play a lead-ership role in their own department, they are key departmental managers in the property and gen-erally sit on the property's **executive committee,** the primary decision-making body for the property. They work with the other department heads and general manager in helping the property realize its financial goals.

## THE HIERARCHY OF THE PROPERTY

To understand fully the role and responsibilities of the professional housekeeper, it is first necessary to see how housekeeping fits into the overall property operations. The housekeeping department interacts with all other departments in the property. Each employee in the housekeeping department, from the executive housekeeper to the **attendants** who clean the property, relies on information provided by staff members in other departments. Such communication requires the cooperation of everyone who works in, or services, the property—and ultimately helps to create a satisfactory stay for guests.

Hotels and motels are organized into **departments** or **divisions.** Each department or division is responsible for a particular operational function or functions. Divisions are typically broader in scope. For example, most larger properties have a **rooms division,** which includes several departments such as the front office and housekeeping.

Departments are then broken down further by specialized functions. For example, the housekeeping department may be subdivided organizationally into cleaning functions and laundry functions. The breakdown differs with the size and category of the property. A mid-size or larger property usually would have the following:

- **Rooms division,** which includes reception where guests may check in and out (either in person or electronically), the switchboard or **private branch exchange** (PBX), concierge staff, bell staff, parking and doormen—that is, all sections that deal directly with guests, from the initial greeting to totaling their bills (called **folios**) just prior to check-out. In an increasing number of properties, the reservations department is part of the rooms division rather than a separate department. The **reservations department** handles individual reservations and also fields inquiries about rooms rates, room availability, and services. In most properties, the housekeeping department is part of the rooms division.
- **Food and beverage (F&B) department,** which includes all food-service operations such as the restaurants and lounges. This department may also include catering/banqueting in a small property. If the property does substantial function business, catering/banqueting would be a separate department.
- **Sales and marketing department,** which analyzes the property's market base, devises a marketing plan for reaching potential customers, and sells to and books reservations and functions for group business and key corporate clients.
- **Accounting department,** which tracks all incoming revenue and outgoing cash. In a large hotel, accounting may actually be a division that incorporates the purchasing department.

- **Engineering and maintenance department,** which maintains most of the equipment and machinery on the property and keeps it in working order. This department also may clean and maintain the swimming pool and pool deck area, as well as some or all parts of the grounds.
- **Security department,** which addresses concerns ranging from handling hazardous waste to securing the building against bomb threats and protecting the privacy of celebrity guests. This department is also responsible for the safety of guests and staff, and their belongings. Lost-and-found may be handled by housekeeping or security, or may be a shared responsibility.
- **Human resources department,** which oversees all matters relating to staff, from recruiting and hiring, to setting salary ranges and benefits. This department also develops policies for dismissal or retirement.

Each one of these departments has an impact on the housekeeping department. Understanding their functions helps the professional housekeeper anticipate the impact of other departments and better plan how to address their needs.

## Understanding the Chain of Command

It is not only important to understand what each department does, but to understand who does what in each department. The executive housekeeper must work closely with other department heads. He or she must be able to communicate effectively with managerial colleagues, find ways to cooperate in order to improve overall operations, and deal with problems constructively.

The chain of command for the property is usually outlined in an **organizational chart.** The organizational chart tracks the chain of responsibility for every job title in the property (see Figures 2.1a and 2.1b). In doing so, the chart also gives an overview of where employees fit into the organization of the property and defines the lines of communication. Organizational charts are tailored to fit the needs of each property. The following are typical titles and responsibilities:

*General manager.* If the property is part of a chain or multi-unit management company, the top of the organizational chart may be a chairman of the board, chief executive officer (CEO), president, or managing director who is miles—even continents—away. At the property level, the general manager, who occasionally may hold some title in

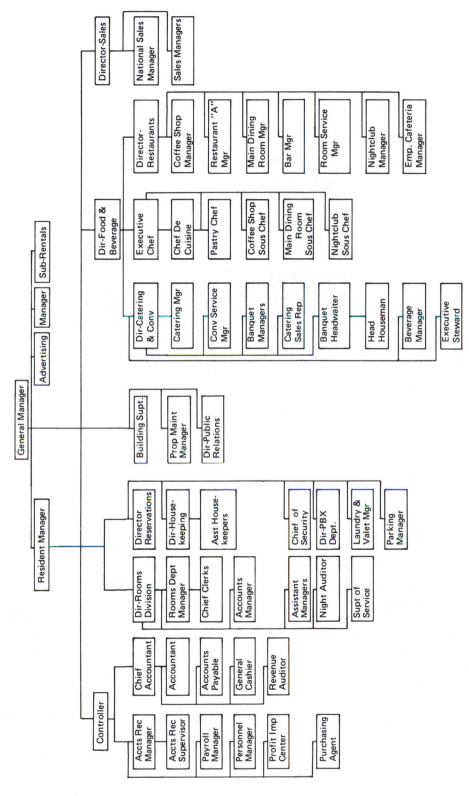

**Figure 2.1** (a) An organizational chart for a large hotel (500–1,500 rooms). Note that some housemen are under the director of conventions and catering while others are, with room attendants, under the assistant housekeepers (see Figure 2.1b).

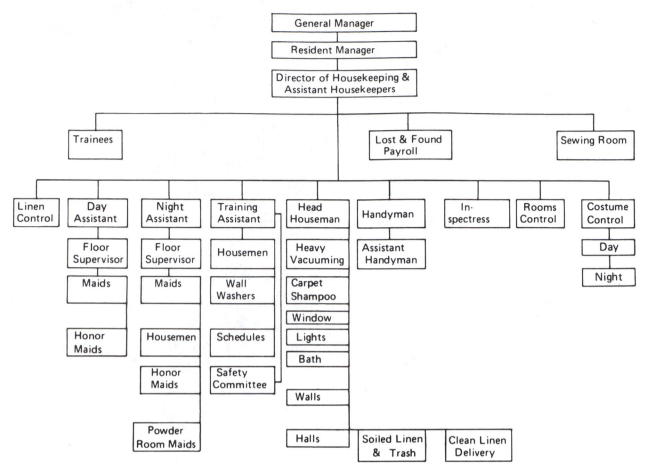

**Figure 2.1** (b) An organizational chart of the housekeeping department in a large hotel (a detailed part of Figure 2.1a).

the corporation such as regional manager or vice president of the property, is at the top of the organizational pyramid.

The general manager has the ultimate decision-making power for the property, thereby setting the tone and management style for the property. He or she sets policy for the property, oversees all operations, and makes sure that any corporate mandates are carried out. The general manager is responsible for the property's day-to-day performance as well as its long-term ability to meet its financial goals, and also has final approval power over budgets and spending requests. The good manager also assumes ultimate responsibility for making certain that the needs of both guests and staff are anticipated and met. All departments or divisions report to the general manager.

**Assistant manager.** In a larger or upscale hotel, the second in command under the general manager is the resident manager, executive assistant man-

ager, or senior assistant manager. These titles are actually interchangeable, depending on the size of the property. It is the role of this second in command to take over the general manager's duties when he or she is off-property and to be closely involved in making sure day-to-day operations go smoothly. Although this person works closely with the general manager and would have a thorough understanding of the property's performance goals, responsibilities focus more on maintaining operational standards than setting policy or defining longer term financial goals.

At smaller properties, the assistant manager typically works the eight-hour night shift starting at 3 P.M. or 4 P.M. This shift provides ample opportunity to build managerial skills and improve skills in handling guest requests.

**Director of rooms.** Larger and more upscale properties may also have a director of rooms or a rooms division manager. The manager of the rooms division is responsible for the smooth and efficient operation of the front office and, typically, housekeeping. In some properties, the executive housekeeper reports to the rooms division manager. In others, because of the size and importance of housekeeping, the executive housekeeper reports directly to the general manager, even if other aspects of housekeeping such as budgeting fall under the rooms division function.

**F&B director.** The F&B director is responsible for all of the management aspects of food-service operations, from optimizing the efficiency of the waitstaff to deciding on themes for restaurants and lounges. Large hotels may also have a banqueting or catering manager whose job it is to manage all aspects of function business, from special requests for an elephant or two to liven up a convention's last-night gala, to elegant food service for glittering social functions. This differs from property to property.

**Controller.** The financial aspects of the property may be overseen by a night auditor in an economy property or an entire accounting department in a larger or upscale hotel. The **controller** is the head of the accounting department and monitors all financial activities of the property. In most larger properties, the controller will have an active role in budgeting.

**The director of purchasing.** This person usually answers to the controller. Some properties are moving toward systems in which department heads do their own purchasing, subject to the general manager's or controller's approval. Others have directors of purchasing. Still others are centralizing purchasing functions at corporate headquarters.

**Department heads.** Some properties have a director of housekeeping whose responsibilities include more managerial functions and less management of day-to-day housekeeping operations. Most housekeeping departments are headed by an executive housekeeper, whose role is both managerial and technical. The director of maintenance or engineering may also be called building superintendent. Other managers usually are referred to as directors of their departments. Department heads have direct, day-to-day responsibility for managing their departments and making sure all assigned tasks are completed. They manage the staff and oversee the inventory of products and supplies that staff members need to do their job. Department

heads also have responsibility for writing budgets, analyzing costs, and preparing labor and cost forecasts. They have ultimate responsibility for hiring and firing decisions regarding departmental staff and setting departmental policies, with the general manager's approval.

Except in very small properties, most department heads have assistants. In housekeeping, if the top title is director of housekeeping, the next in command would be the executive housekeeper. If executive housekeeper is the top title, the next in command would be an executive assistant or, simply, assistant housekeeper. The primary duty of the second in command who works the same shift as the superior is to oversee operational functions and help with departmental management. Those who work the overnight shift or graveyard shift usually have more decision-making power and generally report to the department head, either by submitting a written report or by reporting verbally at the end of their shift.

**Mid-level management.** The most vulnerable layer of management during staff cutbacks, mid-level managers in the hospitality industry usually have hands-on responsibility for making sure each day's assignments are completed and that the quality of the work is up to standard. **Supervisory staff** is part of the housekeeping department's mid-level management.

**Front-line employees.** The backbone of any organization, the front line or, simply, line employees, do most of the basic work that must be done each day. In the lodging industry, this ranges from the room attendants who clean guest rooms to the front desk staff, bartenders, restaurant waitstaff, and some of the kitchen staff.

## MANAGEMENT STYLES

Each executive housekeeper puts the individual stamp of his or her personality on the job. However, in a broad sense, the procedures and programs the professional housekeeper uses to manage staff and the department must fit with the management philosophy of the property. Executive housekeepers should be familiar with some basic management approaches.

**Decentralized versus centralized management.** Some properties use a **decentralized** approach in which staff members are given as much decision-making power as their job function, areas of responsibility, and training permit. Usually, decentralized organizations have fewer layers of management and fewer mid-level managers. Room attendants who are **self-supervising,** which means they are given the responsibility for "inspecting" their own work and releasing the cleaned room for sale, are an example of a highly decentralized management structure (see Chapter 3).

In the **centralized** management style, decisions come from the top down. Department heads and supervisory personnel hold most of the decision-making power. Any problems are reported to a superior who then deals with them.

Decentralization is the current trend in the United States. With most companies looking for ways to cut or control labor costs, efforts are being made to make each employee more responsible and responsive. However, some executive housekeepers still prefer a centralized management approach. Centralized management can work well for housekeeping departments whose primary labor market speaks little English or comes from a culture in which line employees typically are given little responsibility. Decentralizing decision-making power in these cases needs to be a more gradual process and requires a thorough training program.

*Administrative theory.* This management approach looks at the larger picture. It involves planning for the organization as a whole. This approach is most useful when looking for ways to create more efficient work relations between groups or departments and for setting property-wide goals. Administrative theory considers such key issues as how the property is organized, how its managers manage, and how its departments work together and coordinate their functions.

*Scientific management.* Using more of a bottom-to-top approach, this type of management approach centers on improving the productivity of each worker, using scientific methods of training and development. It stresses cooperation between managers and workers.

The scientific method can be highly useful in the problem-solving process, says Ronald Cribbet of the Ron Cribbet Group, Green Valley, Nevada. It is a matter of: plan, do, study, and act. According to Cribbet, planning requires identifying the problem, analyzing the problem, identifying possible solutions, and selecting a solution/plan and action. The "do" phase requires implementation of the solution. Studying means testing the solution and measuring the results. The final phase involves

"acting" on a workable solution by making it a standard procedure. "Then you start all over again," advises Cribbet. Scientific management can be combined with other systems for effective results.

*Empowerment and participative management.* **Empowerment** is the most popular trend in the hospitality industry. It means each employee is "empowered," or literally given the authority to make decisions and take action that will resolve problems or improve performance. Rather than simply carrying out orders, employees must analyze whether existing procedures are reaping maximum rewards and what could be done better. If a guest complains that a room attendant failed to provide clean towels, the empowered attendant not only provides clean towels but tries to turn the guest's negative experience into a positive one. In some properties, the empowered attendant not only apologizes to the guest for any inconvenience but may also authorize delivery of a fruit plate or other small complementary item on behalf of the property's management. This is known as a **compensatory service event.** Empowerment brings home the message that each employee is responsible for guest satisfaction.

**Participative management techniques** encourage employee participation in diverse aspects of decision making. Employees are encouraged to suggest ways in which to improve productivity and performance. They are involved in assessing their work environment. Usually, employees work in groups to engender a spirit of cooperation.

*Total quality management.* Some companies used total quality management (TQM) as a means toward an end of "zero defects." However, this approach missed the mark. As the Ron Cribbet Group points out, TQM stresses that quality leadership starts with satisfying the customer. The goal is to have everyone in the organization become "obsessed" with quality.

"Dr. Edward Demming, the American who developed this management approach and introduced it to the Japanese in the 1950s, hated the phrase total quality management. His concept focused on continuous improvement," explains Cribbet. Improvement in processes translates into improvement in productivity and, adds Cribbet, improvements in profitability.

*Systems management.* "Everything the organization does is a series of processes and systems. Management must understand that its job is to improve the system in which the employee works by developing systems and managing systems. The potential to eliminate mistakes and errors lies mostly in improving the systems through which work is done, not in changing the workers," says Cribbet. Some key points to remember in systems management, according to Cribbet, are:

- Every employee in the system must understand how what they do affects the system and its processes
- All processes have variation. The aim is to reduce variation in processes so that standards and productivity are constantly improved
- Employees are subject to the systems manager's setup, which means management must work continuously to improve these systems
- Processes must be designed and redesigned to improve quality

Technology is an important tool in creating the necessary documentation for a systems management approach because the effectiveness of the system is under constant study. It speeds up such necessary measurements as statistical analysis and makes it easier to view results in different ways.

*Re-engineering.* Properties with inflexible management approaches pay a high price during economic downturns. Re-engineering is a management approach that enables companies to constantly redesign and re-invent processes and priorities according to market demand and the economic climate.

Most properties borrow aspects from all of these management approaches, adding whatever is necessary to meet their own needs. Scientific approaches can be blended successfully with participative management, TQM, or even systems approaches. The goal for the executive housekeeper, as a manager, is to create a management environment in which staff can succeed.

### Scope of the Professional Housekeeper's Role

"In the past, too many general managers underestimated the value of the executive housekeeper," says Kevin Cameron, general manager of the 111-room Radisson Airport Hotel, a Johnson and Wales University Educational Facility in Providence, Rhode Island. The executive housekeeper is responsible for keeping all interiors clean and neat in appearance and ensuring that all this work is done in a cost-efficient way that meets the property's standards. Like all other managers, the professional housekeeper is expected to understand the property's financial goals and implement departmental programs that will help achieve them. Clean, well-maintained rooms are a goal for any housekeeping department, but today the department's success is also measured against the bottom line.

As a department head, the executive housekeeper is part of the management team. An expected part of the professional housekeeper's job is to find effective ways to cooperate and communicate with these other departments.

## MANAGERIAL RESPONSIBILITIES

One veteran hotelier defines the executive housekeeper's role this way: "When you don't know who to call, you call the executive housekeeper." Dedicated housekeepers throughout the world agree that defining the role and responsibilities of the professional housekeeper is no simple task. Except at very small economy properties of less than 100 rooms in the United States and, perhaps, less than 50 rooms in other countries, where the title of executive housekeeper may be given to an hourly employee, the job of the professional housekeeper requires at least basic knowledge of the following:

- Operations management, including technical expertise in regard to cleaning practices, cleaning supplies and equipment
- Labor management, including recruiting, training, and retaining staff, and solving day-to-day personnel problems
- Financial management and cost controls
- Leadership skills, including interdepartmental communication skills
- Safety and security, including what is necessary to comply with federal, state, and local safety codes
- Laundry management (if there is an on-premise laundry) or expertise in working with a contract service (if there is no on-premise laundry)
- Computer skills and expertise in other aspects of technology, in order to apply the power of technology to controlling costs, increasing efficiency, and monitoring inventory
- Interior design elements
- Chemistry as it pertains to cleaning agents and compounds
- Union regulations, if the department is unionized
- Guest relations

- Purchasing, whether the housekeeping department purchases directly or simply provides specifications to the purchasing director
- Effective practices for negotiating contracts with, and working with, contract cleaning services

Each new guest demand expands the list of skills the professional housekeeper must develop. Housekeepers now must understand environmentally friendly cleaning practices. They must make sure no-smoking rooms remain smoke free, and that low-allergen rooms are cleaned properly. Some have had to become expert in preserving fine antiques; others care for space-age structures and high-tech design elements.

In the same day, the professional housekeeper may be looking for ways to save an extra 2 percent on overall costs, looking at fabric samples to be used for renovation, and looking for three extra cribs. The range of skills required of a professional housekeeper makes the position unique within the property. The wide gamut of specialized knowledge required to accomplish a variety of tasks makes professional housekeeping challenging but stimulating. As any executive housekeeper will point out, no two work days are ever the same.

"As the director of housekeeping, I am responsible for the cleanliness of all areas of the hotel except the kitchens and the meeting rooms. I oversee cleaning, uniform controls, lost and found, the in-house laundry and pool maintenance. Typically, I work 10-hour days. Fortunately, this work is something I really enjoy. The housekeeping department has always been the underdog. I like changing that perception," says David Green, director of housekeeping for the elegant, 491-room Renaissance Hotel, Cleveland, Ohio.

## Operations Management

At its most elementary level, professional housekeeping requires technical knowledge of how to clean and maintain the property, which means having a working knowledge of:

- cleaning supplies
- cleaning equipment
- proper cleaning practices and methods

## Ensuring Proper Cleaning Practices

There is no question that the role of professional housekeeper is becoming more managerial and less technical. However, a housekeeping manager who has *no* technical knowledge is at a real disadvantage in running the department efficiently. Even seemingly simple cleaning tasks are not simple at all. Cleaning ranges from routine dusting and vacuuming to degreasing vents in kitchens, removing gum and grime from elevators, and washing crystal chandeliers valued at $50,000 or more. The professional housekeeper is not expected to climb a ladder and clean the crystal, but the executive housekeeper who knows the basics of how to do it will be in the best position to determine what chemicals will work best and how many labor hours should be required for the job. "As executive housekeeper, I have to know how a room or a public area is supposed to be cleaned because I need to be able to explain to the room attendant what is wrong and how it should be corrected," says Ed Conaway, the veteran executive housekeeper at the historic U.S. Grant Hotel in San Diego, California.

The executive housekeeper must make sure that all areas of the property are clean, properly maintained, and neat in appearance. He or she also is expected to find ways to maximize the life expectancy of interior design elements by keeping them looking good and functioning properly as long as possible.

## Managing Inventory and Supplies

The executive housekeeper must provide staff members with the proper tools and supplies so that they can do their jobs properly. Product knowledge is important, since the executive housekeeper either buys supplies and equipment or advises the director of purchasing on what to buy.

The executive housekeeper also coordinates all aspects of inventory to ensure that the supplies and equipment are ready and waiting for the attendants, not vice versa. Inventory controls are another important part of the executive housekeeper's job. He or she must know what to buy, how much to buy, and what price to pay.

## Contract Cleaning Services

Some housekeeping departments do not have the budget or staff expertise to do certain specialty cleaning functions. Executive housekeepers hire **contract cleaning services,** off-premise cleaning services, to do the work. As part of his or her responsibility, the executive housekeeper has to find firms to do the work, obtain bids, award a contract, write out work assignments, and track the company's performance.

## Human Resources Management

Managing staff is a primary responsibility for executive housekeepers, who must develop the expertise to meet ongoing staffing challenges and build a strong team that will work together to meet property-wide goals.

Executive housekeepers must acquire expertise in such areas as recruiting, hiring, training, and motivating staff. Although portions of these functions will be delegated to other staff or experts in the field, it remains the executive housekeeper's responsibility to create a satisfying work environment and a successful department.

## Financial Management

Being a manager means being able to meet financial goals. As head of what is typically the property's most labor intensive department with one of the largest budgets, the executive housekeeper plays a major role in the property's financial well-being. The executive housekeeper's main goal is controlling expenses and finding efficiencies in both operations and purchasing.

Budgeting is an important facet of the professional housekeeper's managerial role. In larger mid-tier and most upscale properties, the executive housekeeper will be expected to create an annual budget that lays down the financial constraints within which the department should function.

Professional housekeepers must understand cost monitoring procedures. They must be able to use various forecasting tools to anticipate cost overruns, analyze demand, and make adjustments before a cash-flow crisis arises. Managing the housekeeping department effectively also requires an understanding of business projections and economic trends. All executive housekeepers must expect their department's performance to be measured against the bottom line.

## Guest Satisfaction

The housekeeping department's responsibility does not end with cleaning. Professional housekeepers are responsible for guest satisfaction, whether making sure that special requests for items such as extra pillows or hair dryers are met, or scheduling public area cleaning so as to minimize disturbance to guests. The executive housekeeper also plays a role in the guests' safety and security. This means monitoring staff to prevent theft and working with the security department to ensure that lost-and-found articles are returned to their owners.

## Working with Other Departments

Executive housekeepers are a critical link between the housekeeping department and other departments. Information from the night clerk's or night auditor's report, confirmation of check-outs and special requests noted by the front desk staff, advisories of group check-ins from the sales staff, and requests for special color napkins for functions all must be handled by the housekeeping staff.

The front desk and sales departments provide housekeeping with essential information on how many rooms to clean and when clean rooms will be needed for guests checking in. Housekeeping, maintenance, and security also work together closely.

Without ready cooperation from maintenance and engineering, repairs will not be made and rooms will be out of inventory longer than necessary. Though lost-and-found is the most direct link between housekeeping and security, the executive housekeeper and chief of security also coordinate their activities when a **VIP (very important person),** political leader, or celebrity plans a stay at the property.

A strong working relationship with the director of purchasing is also essential to a smoothly run housekeeping operation. The executive housekeeper's expertise will be vital in directing the purchasing department to seek out and get bids for the equipment and supplies that will best satisfy the needs of the housekeeping department and guests.

Like any other department head, the executive housekeeper works closely with the general manager, who not only conveys the overall goals of the property, but discusses major changes, from planned renovation to the introduction of a new computer system. During the weekly executive committee meetings, the general manager will discuss occupancy for the upcoming week and any major new programs that departmental managers must implement. The executive housekeeper should keep the general manager well apprised of departmental successes and needs so that when budget time comes, there will be no surprises—for either side.

## Leadership Skills

The executive housekeeper must be a leader. It has been documented repeatedly that entry-level housekeeping workers feel a maximum sense of security when they have confidence in the decision-making abilities of a strong person with proven leadership skills.

The most successful leader is a people-oriented person who can motivate, innovate, and use automation. An effective leader should be flexible with regard to business requirements as well as requests from personnel. Executive housekeepers must also know when to permit a valued employee to leave to pick up a sick child from school, and when to say "no" to personal requests. Learning to evaluate each situation, whether in terms of human resources or departmental workload, is a valuable asset to managers who hope to lead by example. A hard-working manager who is consistent, fair, and strong will earn the respect and cooperation of the staff.

## Educational Requirements

The skills required of an executive housekeeper are changing as the job evolves. Research done as recently as the early 1990s showed that executive housekeepers averaged a little over 13 years of education. This profile will be very different in the near future. "Executive housekeepers will no longer be individuals who have come up through the ranks from the attendant's job. They will probably have a degree and, in the United States, it is likely they will have to be certified or registered at some point. There will be less emphasis on knowing how machinery works and more on managing," says Beth Risinger, head of the International Executive Housekeepers Association (IEHA), Westerville, Ohio.

Registration is the higher of the two designations. It requires completion of a bachelor's degree from an accredited university or college, as well as specific coursework that addresses both the managerial and technical sides of housekeeping. Certification requires a high school diploma or the equivalent and completion of coursework on housekeeping, either through self-study or through a collegiate program. Certification or registration through IEHA and AH&MA also involves passing an exam. Certification needs to be renewed biennially. At this point, New York State requires certification and other legislatures are considering it. However, this may affect professional housekeepers in the health care field before those in the lodging industry.

In addition to growing core professional skills, executive housekeepers also benefit from knowledge of fields ranging from chemistry to interior design. In the housekeeping department, no skill is wasted.

## Chemistry and Microbiology

The executive housekeeper benefits from a basic knowledge of chemistry. This is essential to understanding how to handle chemicals safely and how to remove stains. As a department head, the executive housekeeper has to know which products can be mixed safely and which products can be used to treat stains effectively.

Microbiology has become an important aspect of housekeeping. Not only does the executive housekeeper need to eliminate pests, he or she also needs to address the added challenge of limiting transmittal of bloodborne pathogens such as the AIDS virus or hepatitis B—two major concerns of both staff and guests.

## Interior Design

Executive housekeepers must familiarize themselves with the basic concepts of interior design. Knowing the basics of how interior design elements are made is essential to caring for them properly. Frequently, the executive housekeeper is asked to comment on materials, furnishings, and fixtures that will be used for a renovation.

## Laws and Regulations

Aided by the property's legal counsel and, for labor issues, the human resources department, the executive housekeeper needs to understand the legal and legislative guidelines that affect operations. The two most basic include legislation that prohibits discrimination in hiring and promotion, and the health and safety regulations set forth by the Occupational Health & Safety Administration (OSHA). But professional housekeepers also must keep abreast of changing codes and local, county, and state regulations, such as those covering proper disposal of cleaning chemicals or necessary protective gear for employees.

## Management Functions

If the executive housekeeper does not have a strong background in property management, he or she should take extra classes in this area. Property management helps the executive housekeeper see where the department fits into the overall operation of the property. Many front office skills, from report analysis to accounting, are valuable in the housekeeping department as tools to streamline operations.

Since labor management is so critical to the department's success, classes in psychology, training, and staff motivation are beneficial. Foreign language classes may also be beneficial for the manager of a culturally diverse staff. Some companies offer tuition reimbursement for continuing education that enhances the manager's skills. Some associations, such as IEHA, may have financing programs available to spread the cost over a year or more. Scholarships may be available as well.

## CAREER PATHS

The title of executive housekeeper is a career goal for some; others find jobs ranging from attendant to assistant housekeeper both satisfying and stimulating. Experience in the housekeeping department can be a stepping stone to property management. Career opportunities are diverse in terms of property size, location, and segment.

Some executive housekeepers find the right job early in their careers. Others make moves throughout their careers to advance their careers or gain skills in different types of lodging operations. Executive housekeepers who tire of the pressures of managing housekeeping operations in a 1,000-room city center hotel can look for opportunities at a rambling, slower paced resort hotel in the mountains or at a beach. Others may prefer the high-end intimacy of a 50-room boutique hotel with a discerning clientele. Still others may turn to cruise ship or casino operations.

Possibilities for upward mobility are also increasing, as are opportunities in related fields. The problem-solving skills and managerial experience of the executive housekeeper are always in demand.

### Opportunities within the Property

**Director of housekeeping.** This position, currently available only in larger or more upscale operations, carries broad managerial responsibility. Frequently, the director of housekeeping has an executive housekeeper or highly trained executive assistant who is responsible for day-to-day opera-

tions. This frees the director of housekeeping to address planning issues, from long-term budgeting and renovation to environmental and maintenance issues. This is the next logical step up the career ladder for the executive housekeeper who does not want to leave the housekeeping profession but does want to expand his or her other managerial expertise (see Tales of the Trade 2.1).

---

### Tales of the Trade 2.1
### Building a Career in Housekeeping

Susan King, director of housekeeping and laundry for the elegant, 440-room Charleston Place Hotel in Charleston, South Carolina, took a fairly typical route to reaching one of the profession's top jobs in a hotel that has earned recognition from rating guides as well as consumer publications. King studied hotel and institutional management and received her associate's degree from a two-year college. Her internship was in the purchasing department at a four-star hotel. "I really felt I needed to become well-rounded, so I started my career at the front desk, then was promoted to supervisor," says King.

She joined the housekeeping department as executive assistant. "I was very fortunate in my career path at different hotels. I was able to learn some great approaches to training and technology while I was working with Hyatt, for example. I've learned different approaches to inventory and purchasing. In this position at this hotel, I am able to be involved in implementing computer systems and trying out new approaches to increasing productivity and managing," says King.

---

**General manager; rooms division manager.** As lodging companies finally acknowledge the role of the executive housekeeper as a true manager, more opportunities are opening up within the property. Managerial experience in housekeeping is becoming a viable stepping stone to positions such as rooms division manager or front office management, according to Stephen J. Renard, head of Renard International, an international personnel search firm based in Toronto, Ontario, Canada.

Industry executives agree. "Housekeeping is indeed the heart of the hotel. Every general manager should have a complete understanding of housekeeping. We now have two general managers who came from the housekeeping department, and we're looking to begin training two or three more," says Jonathan Schade, vice president of operations for Manor Care Hotels, Silver Spring, Maryland.

Several major lodging chains now regularly scout their property-level housekeeping department for general manager trainees. They acknowledge that few staff members are in a better position to direct operations than those who have managed the housekeeping department effectively and efficiently. Renard points out that, more and more, general managers are coming from the rooms division or marketing, not through the traditional food and beverage route.

## Opportunities at Corporate Headquarters

Although lodging companies are streamlining and downsizing their headquarters, there remain some selected opportunities for professional housekeepers. Skills gained in the housekeeping department are beneficial in positions in corporate-level operations management. These experts frequently travel throughout the company's or chain's properties advising rooms division managers and executive housekeepers on issues from training to best practices and cost savings. On-the-job experience gained over a number of years is a must for any professional housekeeper aspiring to this kind of position.

Executive housekeepers may be able to create a career path at a smaller company. As some regional management companies grow, their executives see a need to standardize operations. A top-performing executive housekeeper at one property may be chosen to develop and maintain company-wide housekeeping practices. He or she may still have responsibility for day-to-day operations at one hotel, but may be given budget for more executive assistants or more highly paid assistants to cover times when he or she must visit other properties. The experience gained in developing these programs and applying them to various types and sizes of operations can lay the foundation for further advancement at larger companies or in related fields.

## Career Paths in Related Industries

Lodging itself is only one avenue for career advancement. Adjunct fields provide other opportunities for professional housekeepers who want to try a new type of operation or broaden their skills. Most experts in the industry say housekeeping

management skills easily cross over from lodging to cruise ships, university residence halls, and senior living centers. The exception is in the health care field. Professional housekeepers who want to shift to careers in hospitals or hospice facilities would benefit from additional training and further education in chemistry and microbiology.

*Cruise ships.* This may be one of the easier crossover fields to try. Generally, the executive housekeeper signs a contract providing for four months of work, then two months off. Barring some unforeseen occurrence, such as a damaging storm or flood, the executive housekeeper knows before sailing exactly what will be required. The staff is already under contract; the occupancy is fixed and all supplies and equipment already purchased. Overseeing housekeeping on cruise ships also has its own unique set of challenges, from technical problems with water quality to handling personnel problems that arise among staff members who cannot "go home" each night. The other problem is that, despite industry growth, the dozens of cruise ships constructed each year in no way keep pace with the myriad openings in the lodging industry.

"What we look for in an executive housekeeper is someone who has already had experience at least as an assistant and has several years of experience in an upscale or luxury hotel," says Othmar Hehli, director, operations, for Radisson Seven Seas Cruises.

*Casinos.* These round-the-clock operations are demanding, but frequently financially rewarding. One of the highest paid professional housekeepers in the United States works in a large casino/hotel complex and commands a salary of more than $160,000—a salary that reflects the demands on and expertise required of a department head in a highly complicated, multimillion-dollar business.

*Universities and colleges.* Predictability may be an advantage for some professional housekeepers. Hours are more regular for executive housekeepers on campuses, and the range of FF&E is generally far more limited than in the lodging industry. Occupancy is fixed, unless a student drops out. Advancement prospects are above average, though initial salaries may be lower than in the hotel industry. Housekeeping supervisors may be promoted to positions as housing managers or residence hall directors. In a few instances, housekeepers have even risen to positions as presidents of universities.

***Senior living centers.*** Professional housekeepers who hope to stay in the senior living center field may want to pursue positions in companies with multiple facilities. Some of those with multiple facilities offer more competitive salaries and a broader range of career movement. Another option in this field is the residence hotels that have both apartment and hotel components, or the new, very upmarket villa-like compounds being designed exclusively for senior living. These types of centers involve a wide range of housekeeping skills, including training attendants to care for residents' own furnishings and artwork.

## Other Opportunities

Savvy professional housekeepers can parlay their experience into jobs in various fields. Museums, national and state parks (some of which operate their own lodging facilities), landmark buildings, and even the White House, all need executive housekeepers. Professional housekeepers can combine an interest in the environment with a position at a property in a national park. Some historic homes and landmark buildings allow housekeepers or maintenance engineers to live on-site while maintaining the structure.

In some cases, the entrepreneurial executive housekeeper may be able to build his or her skills into permanent and profitable self-employment. Former executive housekeepers have set up their own contract cleaning firms, some of which work for their former employers. Others have put their technical and managerial skills to work as owners of small bed and breakfast inns or franchisees of major chains.

Training is another avenue open to executive housekeepers. Should other legislators deem certification or registration necessary, executive housekeepers may find new careers in "train the trainer" programs. They may also be able to move into compliance training for OSHA or other regulations, or join consulting firms that specialize in this area. Teaching at the university level is an option, either for full-time or part-time employment.

Some professional housekeepers may cross over into the fast-expanding hospital field. This book does not address hospital housekeeping because it differs substantially from lodging industry housekeeping. The problems and systems are both different, as is the medical environment.

This variety of career opportunities not only ensures that the professional housekeeper has ample latitude in finding a job that suits his or her personality, interests, and management style, but also that there will always be job openings. If one industry sector is flagging, another may be burgeoning.

## Salary Trends

Salaries for professional housekeepers have been improving in recent years. Renard predicts future increases in base pay for executive housekeepers will be evolutionary rather than revolutionary. Some no-frills economy properties that retain the executive housekeeper's title likely will continue paying only an hourly rate plus a small premium for running the department. But in larger operations, either in the lodging industry or related fields, executive housekeepers' salaries will continue to improve gradually and reflect their status as department heads (see Table 2.1).

## SUMMARY

Arguably the most innovative managers in the hospitality industry, professional housekeepers have diverse and challenging responsibilities. They must be first-rate managers with a sound understanding of the basics of cleaning and preventive maintenance. They must understand and meet the needs of both their staff members and the property's guests. The close working relationship between housekeeping and all other departments within the property makes the executive housekeeper a pivotal decision maker.

As many housekeepers point out, the roles and responsibilities of the professional housekeeper continue to expand. In the future, all maintenance, security, and traditional housekeeping functions may be under their management. For the present, professional housekeepers need to understand these basics:

- The proper chain of command within the property
- Management philosophies
- Organizational charts
- Staffing tables

**TABLE 2.1** *Salaries for Executive Housekeeper*

| Rooms | # of properties | Avg # of rooms | # of incumbents/ % receiving bonus | Quartile analysis | | | |
|---|---|---|---|---|---|---|---|
| | | | | 25th | 50th | 75th | Average |
| FIRST CLASS Salary | | | | | | | |
| 0 to 250 | 67 | 150 | 90 | $22,400 | $25,700 | $30,000 | $26,900 |
| 251 to 350 | 34 | 300 | 38 | $27,000 | $32,100 | $37,100 | $32,300 |
| 351 to 500 | 23 | 430 | 26 | $34,800 | $39,900 | $48,100 | $41,400 |
| 501+ | 14 | 870 | 16 | $36,500 | $42,000 | $51,500 | $45,500 |
| All Rooms | 138 | 310 | 170 | $25,000 | $31,200 | $37,700 | $32,600 |
| Bonus | | | | | | | |
| 0 to 250 | 21 | 150 | 24.4% | $500 | $1,500 | $2,800 | $1,900 |
| 251 to 350 | 5 | 280 | 13.2% | $800 | $2,000 | $3,000 | $2,000 |
| 351 to 500 | 8 | 440 | 30.8% | $1,200 | $2,600 | $4,600 | $3,500 |
| 501+ | 5 | 660 | 31.3% | $1,400 | $3,400 | $5,000 | $3,400 |
| All Rooms | 39 | 290 | 23.5% | $800 | $1,500 | $3,400 | $2,500 |
| STANDARD Salary | | | | | | | |
| 0 to 150 | 35 | 110 | 67 | $18,000 | $22,000 | $25,000 | $22,400 |
| 151 to 250 | 28 | 190 | 28 | $20,300 | $24,200 | $25,000 | $23,700 |
| 251 to 300 | 11 | 300 | 14 | $20,300 | $24,000 | $32,500 | $25,800 |
| 351+ | 12 | 530 | 12 | $25,800 | $31,300 | $37,100 | $30,800 |
| All Rooms | 86 | 220 | 121 | $19,600 | $24,000 | $28,400 | $24,500 |
| Bonus | | | | | | | |
| 0 to 150 | 14 | 110 | 26.9% | $500 | $600 | $1,000 | $1,000 |
| 151 to 250 | 4 | 190 | 14.3% | — | — | — | $2,000 |
| 251 to 350 | 2 | 290 | 14.3% | — | — | — | — |
| 351+ | 2 | 660 | 16.7% | — | — | — | — |
| All Rooms | 22 | 190 | 21.5% | $500 | $900 | $2,400 | $1,700 |
| SUITES Salary | | | | | | | |
| 0 to 100 | 7 | 60 | 7 | $20,000 | $20,000 | $21,500 | $20,500 |
| 101 to 225 | 13 | 170 | 16 | $19,000 | $21,000 | $23,000 | $21,600 |
| 226+ | 6 | 270 | 16 | $27,000 | $27,200 | $27,600 | $27,200 |
| All Rooms | 26 | 160 | 39 | $20,000 | $21,400 | $26,200 | $22,600 |
| Bonus | | | | | | | |
| 0 to 100 | 4 | 50 | 57.1% | — | — | — | $800 |
| 101 to 225 | 6 | 150 | 56.3% | $400 | $1,000 | $1,900 | $1,300 |
| 226+ | 2 | 300 | 12.5% | — | — | — | — |
| All Rooms | 12 | 140 | 38.5% | $500 | $1,200 | $1,600 | $1,600 |

***TABLE 2.1***   *(Continued)*

| Rooms | # of properties | Avg # of rooms | # of incumbents/ % receiving bonus | Quartile analysis | | | |
|---|---|---|---|---|---|---|---|
| | | | | 25th | 50th | 75th | Average |
| **ECONOMY** Salary | | | | | | | |
| 0 to 100 | 12 | 60 | 13 | $11,800 | $12,700 | $15,200 | $13,200 |
| 101 to 175 | 15 | 130 | 30 | $15,500 | $17,100 | $21,700 | $18,200 |
| 176+ | 10 | 220 | 10 | $17,700 | $19,100 | $21,600 | $19,900 |
| All Rooms | 37 | 130 | 53 | $13,200 | $17,000 | $20,700 | $17,100 |
| Bonus | | | | | | | |
| 0 to 100 | 2 | 70 | 15.4% | — | — | — | — |
| 101 to 175 | 5 | 130 | 46.7% | $400 | $1,200 | $1,900 | $1,500 |
| 176+ | 2 | 230 | 20.0% | — | — | — | — |
| All Rooms | 9 | 140 | 34.0% | $300 | $1,200 | $2,800 | $1,600 |

Salaries reflect the increasing responsibilities of and demands made on executive housekeepers. Deluxe, or larger, more complex properties provide the highest salaries.
***Source:*** American Hotel & Motel Association (AH&MA), Annual Salaries and Hourly Wages, 1995.

- Technical requirements of the executive housekeeper's job
- Intradepartmental and interdepartmental communication

## Review Questions

1. Name the key departments of a hotel and describe their functions.
2. What is the executive committee and what is its prime function?
3. What is the difference between a department and a division?
4. Define the primary responsibilities of the executive housekeeper's job.
5. What is decentralized management?
6. What is an organizational plan?
7. What is Total Quality Management?

8. What is empowerment?
9. What is participative management?

## Critical Thinking Questions

1. An executive housekeeper has a choice between a position that offers a higher salary and may require relocation to a sister property within a year and a local position that pays less but affords job security in the local market. Discuss the pros and cons of each offer.
2. Discuss the advantages and disadvantages of having the executive housekeeper report to the rooms division manager rather than directly to the general manager.
3. An assistant manager eager to gain experience is making decisions usually reserved for the executive housekeeper. As a leader and manager, how could the executive housekeeper address this situation?

# 3

# Effective Staffing and Scheduling

## Chapter Objectives

Human resources management is one of the biggest challenges executive housekeepers face. To build an effective, efficient staff, the executive housekeeper must:

- Define staffing needs
- Define duties relating to each position
- Identify skills required for each position
- Identify and reach local sources of labor
- Interview effectively
- Hire the best person for the job
- Schedule effectively to control labor costs and maximize performance

The executive housekeeper manages what is usually the largest staff of any single department in the property. The housekeeping department's labor force accounts for 35 percent to 40 percent of the total staff of a large hotel or casino hotel, and as much as 50 percent of the staff in a limited-service economy property. The labor-intensive nature of housekeeping is not likely to change in the near term. No amount of computer programming can take the place of the hard-working housekeeping staff.

Building an effective staff starts with determining what duties staff must perform and how many staff members it will take to accomplish the assigned tasks. The property's size, location, market sector, and clientele all influence staff organization.

The next step involves finding the right people for the jobs. Creativity in recruiting is essential, as

is selectivity in hiring. Though these factors can build extra time into the hiring process, they pay off in terms of increased staff productivity and better departmental performance. Hiring the right person for the right job also reduces **staff turnover,** which refers to changes in staffing as people quit or resign. For some executive housekeepers keeping turnover among room attendants as *low* as 70 percent per year is a goal; 100 percent turnover may be the reality.

Turnover is costly. Each employee who leaves costs the hotel $2,000 or more because of the investment in training. The cost goes up significantly for experienced employees who have accumulated vacation, sick days, and profit sharing or retirement fund benefits. Not only is turnover costly monetarily; there is a ripple effect in terms of lost efficiency while a new employee is recruited and trained and there is often a decline in morale as well.

Once hired, new employees must become productive staff members as quickly as possible. Efficient scheduling optimizes labor hours and contributes to the smooth operation of the department. It also functions as a key cost control measure.

## STAFFING THE HOUSEKEEPING DEPARTMENT

An organizational plan is the basis for an efficient, professional housekeeping department. The goals in writing this plan are: (1) to show the lines of authority and how responsibility is distributed; and 2) to show staff members where they fit into the overall organization and how they might move up.

More than one executive housekeeper puts the guest at the top of the organizational chart, with attendants in the next tier down. This reminds the attendants how much the satisfaction of their ultimate "boss"—the guest—depends on their performance.

The organizational plan for each property will be slightly different depending on the property's needs. The plan should be flexible enough to allow for adding or subtracting personnel as occupancy fluctuates. Once the organizational plan determines what positions are needed, the executive housekeeper must calculate how many workers will be needed in each position.

## Who Does What in Housekeeping

The main responsibilities of the executive housekeeper or director of housekeeping and the housekeeping assistants were outlined in Chapter 2. Other job titles within the housekeeping department include:

**Room attendant.** Formerly called a "maid," the room attendant is responsible for cleaning the guest rooms. He or she reports the need for any repairs in the guest room, any damage by staff or guests, and any suspected theft of hotel or motel property.

**Public area/house attendant.** The public area attendant, sometimes referred to as a **lobby attendant,** cleans the **public spaces** of the property; that is, all areas used by the guests inside the property other than the guest rooms. He or she also is assigned **back-of-the-house** areas, the areas used by employees—from the employee locker rooms to service corridors, service elevators, and offices. The only exceptions may be swimming pools, fitness facilities, areas where trash is stored, and loading docks, which are cleaned by the maintenance staff. The F&B department usually is responsible for cleaning kitchens. The audio-visual department maintains the technical aspects of areas such as business centers and meeting or function space. Typical duties for house attendants include keeping public areas clean and neat and, in the case of public restrooms, sanitary.

**House attendant; houseman.** This title is usually reserved for public area staff assigned to do tasks other than routine cleaning. Typically, these are the staff members (both male and female) who clean carpets, wash walls, remove trash and recycling,

care for floors and clean high, hard-to-reach areas. House attendants may work as **linen runners** whose main job is to take soiled linens from the guestroom floors and transport clean linen, as needed, to the room attendants on the floors.

**Inspector.** An inspector checks the quality of the work done and makes sure the assigned tasks are completed. He or she discusses any oversights or other problems with the attendants, making sure the problem is remedied. Inspectors are assigned to guest rooms and public areas. Larger in-house laundries may also have an inspector specifically for the laundry.

**Supervisor.** This title carries with it managerial responsibilities. The supervisor may write work assignments for attendants, issue supplies, conduct brief morning meetings to discuss assignments and policy changes with attendants, and serve as a conduit for instructions from the executive housekeeper. Supervisors are responsible for seeing to it that their crews of attendants complete their assignments properly. They also relay work orders to maintenance and communicate with the front desk regarding any special instructions for guest rooms not already noted on the assignment sheets. Technical expertise is essential, since supervisors may be called on to clean in a staffing crunch. The head house attendant is the primary supervisor for the property's house attendants.

**Laundry attendant.** The laundry attendant sorts dirty linens, operates all laundry equipment, and readies the clean linen for distribution.

**Linen/uniform attendant.** The linen room attendant makes sure linen inventories are adequate, that all linen is accounted for each day, and that the amount of clean linen needed for the upcoming shift is ready and waiting for the attendants. He or she also checks linen for tears or stains.

The uniform attendant organizes the uniform room, making sure that all employees have clean uniforms available, issues uniforms, and ascertains that all component parts of each uniform are accounted for. He or she also checks uniforms for tears and stains and oversees uniform inventory.

**Laundry manager.** The laundry manager is responsible for all laundry operations. He or she makes sure that the laundry is operating efficiently, that special requests are handled promptly, that all equipment is in good repair, that safety/health codes are enforced, and that the property is being supplied with bed linens, towels, and table linens as needed. A key staff member, the laundry manager reports directly to the executive housekeeper.

**Seamstress.** The seamstress fabricates a variety of items, from draperies to bed coverings and uniforms. He or she also is responsible for mending and repairing fabric items.

**Clerical staff.** In additional to the traditional duties of answering phones and relaying messages, the office clerk or administrative assistant should be able to enter and retrieve data on a computer and assist with other matters regarding office operations.

**Specialists.** Staff positions reflect property needs. A large casino hotel may need a manager specifically for the public areas. Historic hotels and some deluxe properties have upholsterers on staff, as well as experts in furniture maintenance and repair.

## Calculating Labor Needs

**Right-sizing** is a key term in today's lodging industry. It means staffing properties with the "right" number of people to provide the necessary levels of service while keeping labor costs in line. Executive housekeepers must find this right size for their departments.

Staffing is based on the number of labor hours needed to accomplish the department's workload. Staffing tables such as the one shown in Table 3.1, developed for a 2,832-room hotel, show not only how many people are needed, but also what the costs will be for the labor. This table also shows the critical impact of occupancy on staffing.

Numbers on paper are only guidelines. The professional housekeeper needs enough technical knowledge about cleaning to determine how to adjust the guidelines. Other factors to consider include:

- The number and size of rooms and overall square footage of the property
- The complexity of the design and architecture. For example, a lobby with only two contemporary sofas and an accent table requires far less time to clean than one of similar size with antique chairs, intricately carved tables, and numerous decorative elements (see Figure 3.1).
- The category of the property. Upscale and luxury properties are more time-consuming to clean be-

cause they have more different types of surfaces, furnishings, and fixtures.
- The employees' capabilities. An experienced, efficient department may be able to cut staff requirements by a half position or even a full position.

Executive housekeepers should conduct a **time and motion study,** which calculates how long it takes, on average, to perform a certain task. After looking at all these factors, quotas can be set. A **quota** is the number of rooms or areas of the property an attendant is expected to clean during one shift. Quotas, occupancy projections, and a labor budget provide the framework for staffing the department.

## Time and Motion Study

A time and motion study is helpful in calculating staffing levels. To do a time and motion study, several staff members clean the same guest room. Their movements are studied and clocked. The results are compared and an analysis is made on how long it takes on average to clean the space. From this, best practices can be defined, adapted, and implemented. If these best practices are used by everyone, performance will be more standardized and more predictable.

## Quotas

Setting quotas depends on both staff structure and property type. In a full-service hotel, a room attendant is expected to clean 14 to 18 rooms a day. This number is based on the following arithmetic:

Each room takes 18 to 30 minutes to clean, and

$$14 \text{ rooms} \times 30 \text{ minutes} = 420 \text{ minutes}$$

roughly seven working hours. Using an eight-hour shift, this leaves a half hour for lunch and two 15-minute breaks. So, 15 to 21 full-time room attendants would be needed to clean a full-service, 300-room property. The category of the hotel also affects quotas (see Table 3.1).

Inspectors or supervisors can spot check 30 to 50 guest rooms a day. The exact room count depends on how detailed the inspections must be. Supervisors oversee the work of up to seven attendants on a particular floor or in several room sections, each of which has 13 to 20 guest rooms. The amount of managerial responsibility and number of technical assignments must be taken into account when setting staffing levels for supervisors.

**Figure 3.1** *Not all lobbies are created equal in terms of cleaning requirements. Rich detailing adds a sense of elegance, but also increases the number of staff hours required to clean the space properly. (Courtesy of The Plaza Hotel, New York)*

However, not every guest room is occupied every night so quotas must be weighed against occupancy before determining how much staff is needed.

Quotas for public space supervisors and public space attendants are based on a certain amount of square footage or an area of the property. Formulae must be developed for house attendants as well and should be based on time and motion studies.

An executive housekeeper may require one or sometimes two assistants during the day shift if the property's operation is complex and the staff is

**TABLE 3.1** *Time Spent On Room Cleaning*

| Hotel size | Hotel type | Number of rooms cleaned per day | Number of minutes per room |
|---|---|---|---|
| 92 rooms | Five-star, with custom furnishings | 9 | 50 |
| 100 rooms | No-frills economy | 20 | 23 |
| 500 rooms | Four-star, standard furnishings | 17 | 27 |
| 435 rooms | Five-star landmark | 13–14 | 32–35 |
| 200 suites | Upscale, all-suite | 11–14 | 32–40 |
| 150 residences | Extended-stay | 9 | 50 |

large. Mega-hotels with 1,500 rooms or more, and casino hotels, may require a manager for each major activity within the housekeeping department to keep all operations running smoothly. That may mean five day-shift managers, each with two supervisory assistants. A night assistant housekeeper will be needed to manage the night staff in a property that provides extensive night service. Some properties also have an assistant housekeeper on the graveyard shift to oversee late night and early morning cleaning and work with off-premise services that do specialized cleaning.

Laundry staffing depends on the size and amount of equipment and how much of the work is automated. A 700-room hotel may require 25 full-time employees; a mini-laundry can be operated by one or two employees. But there is only one executive housekeeper and he or she must coordinate the work of all the other staff.

## Finding the Right Staff

Success in staffing begins with recruiting. The first step toward finding the ideal staff is to determine what work needs to be done and what skills the candidate needs to accomplish this work. These functions and skills are defined in two separate documents: **a job description** and a **job specification.**

A job description is a detailed report of all the functions that must be performed by an employee and the manner in which they must be performed (see Figure 3.2). The job description for a room attendant, for example, could include an overview of cleaning responsibilities, reporting duties and, perhaps, expectations regarding confidentiality and security.

A job specification clearly spells out the minimum requirements that must be met by an applicant (see Figure 3.3). For example, a job description for a room attendant should include standard job specifications, ranging from the physical ability to clean a certain number of rooms per shift to a basic understanding of English or a certain level of education or experience.

Job descriptions and job specifications should be as specific as possible. Pointing out which skills are essential and which are desirable can narrow the field of applicants. In a five-star luxury hotel, prior experience in cleaning hotel guest rooms and guest relations training may be highly desirable. For a hotel with a staff that includes two or three major cultural groups, fluency in a second language may be an important skill. At a small property, rudimentary knowledge of carpentry or painting may be a plus.

## Tapping Resources On-Property

The high turnover that characterizes the hospitality industry puts constant pressure on the executive housekeeper to find a ready supply of new workers. Referrals from current employees represent one of the best and most cost-effective avenues for recruiting. The property's human resources department also should have a ready file of applicants suitable for positions in the housekeeping department.

## Encouraging Staff Referrals

Whether present staff includes college students seeking extra income or self-supporting heads of households, current employees frequently have access to a ready labor pool of friends and family (see Figure 3.4). The advantage to recruiting by referral is that current employees understand precisely what the job entails, both the day-to-day difficulties and rewards of working in the housekeeping department. Current employees are likely to weigh referrals carefully since they will have to work with the person they refer.

Executive housekeepers can encourage referrals in several ways:

- Posting notices about openings in employee areas
- Talking with employees on an informal basis and stressing the benefits of having an efficient, fully staffed department
- Providing monetary or nonmonetary incentives for referrals

Incentives have become a key tool in generating referrals. These incentives should reflect the hiring market. In tight labor markets, the biggest problem may be finding anyone interested in an entry-level job. One solution is to offer a **lump-sum bonus** (a cash payment over and above the earned hourly wage paid all at one time) to the person who refers the prospective employee as soon as the referral is hired. Such bonuses average $25 to $50. Finding workers for difficult jobs or less desirable shifts may require a higher incentive, perhaps as much as $100. If attracting new hires and retaining them are dual problems, the bonus may be structured so that the staff member receives $50 when the new employee begins work and another $50 if the new hire stays 60 days.

***TABLE 3.2***  *Staffing Table*
*Staffing needs vary with occupancy, especially for line employees. Note how the average days worked by an attendant climb with occupancy.*

| Rooms occupied | | Dir. hskpg. | Asst. dir. hskpg. | Exectve. hskeeper. | Asst. exectve. | Shift supv. | Trning. spclst. | Admin. asst. | Secrtry. | Pyrol. clerk | Control clerks | Status clerk | Inspctrs. days | Gst. rm. attndts. days |
|---|---|---|---|---|---|---|---|---|---|---|---|---|---|---|
| From | To | | | | | | | | | | | | | |
| 1849 | 1862 | 5.71 | 5.71 | 5.71 | 11.43 | 17.14 | 5.71 | 5.71 | 5.71 | 17.14 | 11.42 | 62.86 | 136 | 1064 |
| 1863 | 1876 | 5.71 | 5.71 | 5.71 | 11.43 | 17.14 | 5.71 | 5.71 | 5.71 | 17.14 | 11.42 | 62.86 | 144 | 1072 |
| 1877 | 1890 | 5.71 | 5.71 | 5.71 | 11.43 | 17.14 | 5.71 | 5.71 | 5.71 | 17.14 | 11.42 | 62.86 | 144 | 1080 |
| 1891 | 1904 | 5.71 | 5.71 | 5.71 | 11.43 | 17.14 | 5.71 | 5.71 | 5.71 | 17.14 | 11.42 | 62.86 | 144 | 1088 |
| 1905 | 1918 | 5.71 | 5.71 | 5.71 | 11.43 | 17.14 | 5.71 | 5.71 | 5.71 | 17.14 | 11.42 | 62.86 | 144 | 1096 |
| 1919 | 1932 | 5.71 | 5.71 | 5.71 | 11.43 | 17.14 | 5.71 | 5.71 | 5.71 | 17.14 | 11.42 | 62.86 | 144 | 1104 |
| 1933 | 1946 | 5.71 | 5.71 | 5.71 | 11.43 | 17.14 | 5.71 | 5.71 | 5.71 | 17.14 | 11.42 | 62.86 | 144 | 1112 |
| 1947 | 1960 | 5.71 | 5.71 | 5.71 | 11.43 | 17.14 | 5.71 | 5.71 | 5.71 | 17.14 | 11.42 | 62.86 | 144 | 1120 |
| 1961 | 1974 | 5.71 | 5.71 | 5.71 | 11.43 | 17.14 | 5.71 | 5.71 | 5.71 | 17.14 | 11.42 | 62.86 | 144 | 1128 |
| 1975 | 1988 | 5.71 | 5.71 | 5.71 | 11.43 | 17.14 | 5.71 | 5.71 | 5.71 | 17.14 | 11.42 | 62.86 | 152 | 1130 |
| 1989 | 2002 | 5.71 | 5.71 | 5.71 | 11.43 | 17.14 | 5.71 | 5.71 | 5.71 | 17.14 | 11.42 | 62.86 | 152 | 1144 |
| 2003 | 2016 | 5.71 | 5.71 | 5.71 | 11.43 | 17.14 | 5.71 | 5.71 | 5.71 | 17.14 | 11.42 | 62.86 | 152 | 1152 |
| 2017 | 2030 | 5.71 | 5.71 | 5.71 | 11.43 | 17.14 | 5.71 | 5.71 | 5.71 | 17.14 | 11.42 | 62.86 | 152 | 1160 |
| 2031 | 2044 | 5.71 | 5.71 | 5.71 | 11.43 | 17.14 | 5.71 | 5.71 | 5.71 | 17.14 | 11.42 | 62.86 | 152 | 1168 |
| 2045 | 2058 | 5.71 | 5.71 | 5.71 | 11.43 | 17.14 | 5.71 | 5.71 | 5.71 | 17.14 | 11.42 | 62.86 | 152 | 1176 |
| 2059 | 2072 | 5.71 | 5.71 | 5.71 | 11.43 | 17.14 | 5.71 | 5.71 | 5.71 | 17.14 | 11.42 | 62.86 | 152 | 1184 |
| 2073 | 2086 | 5.71 | 5.71 | 5.71 | 11.43 | 17.14 | 5.71 | 5.71 | 5.71 | 17.14 | 11.42 | 62.86 | 152 | 1192 |
| 2087 | 2100 | 5.71 | 5.71 | 5.71 | 11.43 | 17.14 | 5.71 | 5.71 | 5.71 | 17.14 | 11.42 | 62.86 | 160 | 1200 |
| 2101 | 2114 | 5.71 | 5.71 | 5.71 | 11.43 | 17.14 | 5.71 | 5.71 | 5.71 | 17.14 | 11.42 | 62.86 | 160 | 1208 |
| 2115 | 2128 | 5.71 | 5.71 | 5.71 | 11.43 | 17.14 | 5.71 | 5.71 | 5.71 | 17.14 | 11.42 | 62.86 | 160 | 1216 |
| 2129 | 2142 | 5.71 | 5.71 | 5.71 | 11.43 | 17.14 | 5.71 | 5.71 | 5.71 | 17.14 | 11.42 | 62.86 | 160 | 1224 |
| 2143 | 2156 | 5.71 | 5.71 | 5.71 | 11.43 | 17.14 | 5.71 | 5.71 | 5.71 | 17.14 | 11.42 | 62.86 | 160 | 1232 |
| 2157 | 2170 | 5.71 | 5.71 | 5.71 | 11.43 | 17.14 | 5.71 | 5.71 | 5.71 | 17.14 | 11.42 | 62.86 | 160 | 1240 |
| 2171 | 2184 | 5.71 | 5.71 | 5.71 | 11.43 | 17.14 | 5.71 | 5.71 | 5.71 | 17.14 | 11.42 | 62.86 | 160 | 1248 |
| 2185 | 2198 | 5.71 | 5.71 | 5.71 | 11.43 | 17.14 | 5.71 | 5.71 | 5.71 | 17.14 | 11.42 | 62.86 | 160 | 1258 |
| 2199 | 2212 | 5.71 | 5.71 | 5.71 | 11.43 | 17.14 | 5.71 | 5.71 | 5.71 | 17.14 | 11.42 | 62.86 | 168 | 1264 |
| 2213 | 2226 | 5.71 | 5.71 | 5.71 | 11.43 | 17.14 | 5.71 | 5.71 | 5.71 | 17.14 | 11.42 | 62.86 | 168 | 1272 |
| 2227 | 2240 | 5.71 | 5.71 | 5.71 | 11.43 | 17.14 | 5.71 | 5.71 | 5.71 | 17.14 | 11.42 | 62.86 | 168 | 1280 |
| 2241 | 2254 | 5.71 | 5.71 | 5.71 | 11.43 | 17.14 | 5.71 | 5.71 | 5.71 | 17.14 | 11.42 | 62.86 | 168 | 1288 |
| 2255 | 2268 | 5.71 | 5.71 | 5.71 | 11.43 | 17.14 | 5.71 | 5.71 | 5.71 | 17.14 | 11.42 | 62.86 | 168 | 1296 |
| 2269 | 2282 | 5.71 | 5.71 | 5.71 | 11.43 | 17.14 | 5.71 | 5.71 | 5.71 | 17.14 | 11.42 | 62.86 | 168 | 1304 |
| 2283 | 2296 | 5.71 | 5.71 | 5.71 | 11.43 | 17.14 | 5.71 | 5.71 | 5.71 | 17.14 | 11.42 | 62.86 | 168 | 1312 |
| 2297 | 2310 | 5.71 | 5.71 | 5.71 | 11.43 | 17.14 | 5.71 | 5.71 | 5.71 | 17.14 | 11.42 | 62.86 | 168 | 1320 |

**Source:** Courtesy of Bally's, Las Vegas, Nevada.

## Human Resources' Role in Recruiting

The hotel's human resources department is another source of prospective employees. Though the human resources department is more likely to keep files on candidates for supervisory or managerial positions, the executive housekeeper can work with the director of human resources to find ways to attract applications for entry-level positions as well (see Tricks of the Trade 3.1).

### Tricks of the Trade 3.1
### Building a Bigger Labor Pool

*The Problem:* Competition for entry level workers is high, and the labor pool is shrinking.
*The Solution:* Regular, well-publicized job fairs or open houses can bring large numbers of prospective employees to the property. Some properties accept applications on a certain day of each week. The human resources department pre-screens applicants to find out who may be best suited to housekeeping. One veteran housekeeper convinced a local university interested in

| Inspctrs. swing | Gst. rm. attndts. swing | Inspctrs. grave | Gst. rm. attndts. grave | Shampoo persons | Utility persons days | Floor hseprsn. days | Utility persons swing | Floor hseprsn. swing | Utility persons grave | Floor hseprsn grave | Seamers | Working hskeeper | General cleaning | Dept. total |
|---|---|---|---|---|---|---|---|---|---|---|---|---|---|---|
| 24 | 56 | 8 | 24 | 74.29 | 125.71 | 148.71 | 5.71 | 57.14 | 5.71 | 11.43 | 17.14 | 11.43 | 32 | 1,956 |
| 24 | 56 | 8 | 24 | 74.29 | 125.71 | 148.71 | 5.71 | 57.14 | 5.71 | 11.43 | 17.14 | 11.43 | 32 | 1,972 |
| 24 | 56 | 8 | 24 | 74.29 | 125.71 | 148.71 | 5.71 | 57.14 | 5.71 | 11.43 | 17.14 | 11.43 | 32 | 1,980 |
| 24 | 56 | 8 | 24 | 74.29 | 125.71 | 148.71 | 5.71 | 57.14 | 5.71 | 11.43 | 17.14 | 11.43 | 32 | 1,988 |
| 24 | 56 | 8 | 24 | 74.29 | 125.71 | 148.71 | 5.71 | 57.14 | 5.71 | 11.43 | 17.14 | 11.43 | 32 | 1,996 |
| 24 | 56 | 8 | 24 | 74.29 | 125.71 | 148.71 | 5.71 | 57.14 | 5.71 | 11.43 | 17.14 | 11.43 | 32 | 2,004 |
| 24 | 56 | 8 | 24 | 74.29 | 125.71 | 148.71 | 5.71 | 57.14 | 5.71 | 11.43 | 17.14 | 11.43 | 32 | 2,012 |
| 24 | 56 | 8 | 24 | 74.29 | 125.71 | 148.71 | 5.71 | 57.14 | 5.71 | 11.43 | 17.14 | 11.43 | 32 | 2,020 |
| 24 | 56 | 8 | 24 | 74.29 | 125.71 | 148.71 | 5.71 | 57.14 | 5.71 | 11.43 | 17.14 | 11.43 | 32 | 2,028 |
| 24 | 56 | 8 | 24 | 74.29 | 125.71 | 148.71 | 5.71 | 57.14 | 5.71 | 11.43 | 17.14 | 11.43 | 32 | 2,044 |
| 24 | 56 | 8 | 24 | 74.29 | 125.71 | 148.71 | 5.71 | 57.14 | 5.71 | 11.43 | 17.14 | 11.43 | 32 | 2,052 |
| 24 | 56 | 8 | 24 | 74.29 | 125.71 | 148.71 | 5.71 | 57.14 | 5.71 | 11.43 | 17.14 | 11.43 | 32 | 2,060 |
| 24 | 56 | 8 | 24 | 74.29 | 125.71 | 148.71 | 5.71 | 57.14 | 5.71 | 11.43 | 17.14 | 11.43 | 32 | 2,068 |
| 24 | 56 | 8 | 24 | 74.29 | 125.71 | 148.71 | 5.71 | 57.14 | 5.71 | 11.43 | 17.14 | 11.43 | 32 | 2,076 |
| 24 | 56 | 8 | 24 | 74.29 | 125.71 | 148.71 | 5.71 | 57.14 | 5.71 | 11.43 | 17.14 | 11.43 | 32 | 2,084 |
| 24 | 56 | 8 | 24 | 74.29 | 125.71 | 148.71 | 5.71 | 57.14 | 5.71 | 11.43 | 17.14 | 11.43 | 32 | 2,092 |
| 24 | 56 | 8 | 24 | 74.29 | 125.71 | 148.71 | 5.71 | 57.14 | 5.71 | 11.43 | 17.14 | 11.43 | 32 | 2,100 |
| 24 | 56 | 8 | 24 | 74.29 | 125.71 | 148.71 | 5.71 | 57.14 | 5.71 | 11.43 | 17.14 | 11.43 | 32 | 2,116 |
| 24 | 64 | 8 | 24 | 74.29 | 125.71 | 148.71 | 5.71 | 57.14 | 5.71 | 11.43 | 17.14 | 11.43 | 32 | 2,132 |
| 24 | 64 | 8 | 24 | 74.29 | 125.71 | 148.71 | 5.71 | 57.14 | 5.71 | 11.43 | 17.14 | 11.43 | 32 | 2,140 |
| 24 | 64 | 8 | 24 | 74.29 | 125.71 | 148.71 | 5.71 | 57.14 | 5.71 | 11.43 | 17.14 | 11.43 | 32 | 2,148 |
| 24 | 64 | 8 | 24 | 74.29 | 125.71 | 148.71 | 5.71 | 57.14 | 5.71 | 11.43 | 17.14 | 11.43 | 32 | 2,156 |
| 24 | 64 | 8 | 24 | 74.29 | 125.71 | 148.71 | 5.71 | 57.14 | 5.71 | 11.43 | 17.14 | 11.43 | 32 | 2,164 |
| 24 | 64 | 8 | 24 | 74.29 | 125.71 | 148.71 | 5.71 | 57.14 | 5.71 | 11.43 | 17.14 | 11.43 | 32 | 2,172 |
| 24 | 64 | 8 | 24 | 74.29 | 125.71 | 148.71 | 5.71 | 57.14 | 5.71 | 11.43 | 17.14 | 11.43 | 32 | 2,180 |
| 24 | 64 | 8 | 24 | 74.29 | 125.71 | 148.71 | 5.71 | 57.14 | 5.71 | 11.43 | 17.14 | 11.43 | 32 | 2,196 |
| 24 | 64 | 8 | 24 | 74.29 | 125.71 | 148.71 | 5.71 | 57.14 | 5.71 | 11.43 | 17.14 | 11.43 | 32 | 2,204 |
| 24 | 64 | 8 | 24 | 74.29 | 125.71 | 148.71 | 5.71 | 57.14 | 5.71 | 11.43 | 17.14 | 11.43 | 32 | 2,212 |
| 24 | 64 | 8 | 24 | 74.29 | 125.71 | 148.71 | 5.71 | 57.14 | 5.71 | 11.43 | 17.14 | 11.43 | 32 | 2,220 |
| 24 | 64 | 8 | 24 | 74.29 | 125.71 | 148.71 | 5.71 | 57.14 | 5.71 | 11.43 | 17.14 | 11.43 | 32 | 2,228 |
| 24 | 64 | 8 | 24 | 74.29 | 125.71 | 148.71 | 5.71 | 57.14 | 5.71 | 11.43 | 17.14 | 11.43 | 32 | 2,236 |
| 24 | 64 | 8 | 24 | 74.29 | 125.71 | 148.71 | 5.71 | 57.14 | 5.71 | 11.43 | 17.14 | 11.43 | 32 | 2,244 |
| 24 | 64 | 8 | 24 | 74.29 | 125.71 | 148.71 | 5.71 | 57.14 | 5.71 | 11.43 | 17.14 | 11.43 | 32 | 2,252 |

> starting a housekeeping course to allow her to conduct the class at the hotel where she worked. The result: a ready pool of talented, trained staff.

Recruiting staff for cruise ships is handled by the human resources department for the shipping line. Since cruise ship staffs may include people from 16 to 20 different countries, recruiting and hiring are coordinated by the corporate human resources department or the regional human resources department nearest the ship's home port or a combination, depending on the position to be filled. The executive housekeeper's role is to provide the human resources department with clear job descriptions and job specifications and to point out any past problems in hiring.

## Tapping Off-Premise Resources

Staff referrals are valuable tools in recruiting, but off-premise sources can be effective. Advertising reaches a large group of prospective employees. Executive housekeepers also focus on capitalizing on

---

**JOB DESCRIPTION**

*Title:* Linen controller
*Responsible to:* Director of housekeeping
**PURPOSE AND FUNCTION**
**A.** Control and coordinate the receiving of clean tablecloths and napkins and issue those linens requisitioned by the various food and beverage facilities within the hotel. The functions of this service are as follows:

1. Receiving linen several times throughout the day as it is processed by the laundry and delivered.
2. Inspection of linens for burns, tears, fading, etc., maintaining standards outlined to you with samples.
3. Stocking of linens on shelves according to size, color, and use for each food or beverage facility.
4. Issuing linen for only the amount requisitioned that day.
5. Communications with laundry manager for a specially requested quantity, color, or size linen that is in short supply or not available on the shelf when requested.
6. Issuing *only* the linens designated for each facility's use. *Remember:* Banquet department has priority on linens necessary for its use.

**B.** Adequately control, and give proper attention to, the issuance of linen to the housekeeping department. Failure to keep track of linens results in their misuse, damage, and disappearance, thus wasting time and money.

**C.** Remove all linens requiring repairs to the sewing room.

---

**Figure 3.2** *Typical job description for a linen controller.*

the growing number of under-utilized sections of the work force.

## Advertising

Local media such as newspapers and "shoppers" (weekly publications filled primarily with advertising) are good outlets for advertising most positions, with the possible exception of executive housekeeper or executive assistant. These more senior positions, especially at larger hotels, usually require the expertise of an executive search firm or help from the hotel chain's or management company's corporate human resources department. Ads should be clear and concise. They should define the available position, what the responsibilities are, what skills are required, and whom to contact to apply. If the budget allows, the ad should emphasize the benefits of working at the particular property rather than its competitors.

The decision on which medium to use depends on the location of the property. Daily or weekly newspapers draw better numbers of applicants in large urban areas. Free "shoppers" give regional coverage in some sprawling suburbs or rural regions. Campus publications can also generate good response. In some exotic resort settings, trade publications may be effective in attracting **expatriate** workers (workers from outside of that country).

## Reaching the Culturally Diverse Labor Market

Many housekeeping departments have multicultural staffs. For properties in larger cities and suburbs and in various parts of the United States and other countries worldwide, recruiting staff from diverse cultures is an operational way of life.

If most of the property's prospective labor pool speaks a different language but represents a fairly well established cultural community, ads should be placed in newspapers written in the appropriate language. A member of the housekeeping department fluent in the language should represent the property at job fairs that may be sponsored by community organizations or schools and community colleges with substantial student populations drawn from the particular cultural group.

For smaller cultural groups or new groups of immigrants, the executive housekeeper can contact

---

**JOB SPECIFICATION**

*Job Title:* Linen controller

*Number Employed:* 1

*Hours:* 7:30 A.M. to 3:30 P.M.; Monday to Friday

*Days Off:* 2 consecutive days in 7 days

*Vacation:* 1 week after 1 year, 2 weeks after 3 years

*Salary:* Union scale

*Extras:* Uniform furnished; 1 meal

*Working Conditions:* Pleasant

*Contact:* Employees of food and beverage, banquet, all other departments that use linens

*Supervisor:* Assistant housekeeper

*Type of Labor:* Unskilled

*Responsibility:* All food and beverage linens be in good condition

*Age Limits:* 20 years or older (see Physical Qualifications, below)

*Mental Qualifications:* Average; ability to follow instructions; alert

*Personality and Appearance:* Very pleasant; careful; neat

*Experience:* None required

*Education:* Able to read and write, speak, or understand Spanish or whichever second language is widespread in the area.

*Physical Qualifications:* Able to stand light, sustained physical activity— including frequent use of arms; able to lift moderate weight; good eyesight for examining fabrics for stains, snags, and holes and for stitching in linens.

---

**Figure 3.3** *A job specification for a linen controller. The job description explains the job that has to be done.*

the appropriate cultural, fraternal, or civic groups. Many will translate notices of employment opportunities at a low cost or no cost; some will even send translators to the property to help with training and the first days of work (see Tales of the Trade 3.1).

## Tales of the Trade 3.1
## Tapping New Sources of Labor

Newly arrived immigrants have long provided a ready work force for housekeeping departments. But tapping these labor pools can be challenging initially.

Kristine Hall, executive housekeeper of the 538-room Hyatt Regency Union Station in St. Louis, Missouri recently hired immigrants who fled war-torn Bosnia, adding them to a culturally mixed staff that includes African Americans, Vietnamese, and Mexican Americans.

The biggest problem was communication. Working through a group that was resettling Bosnian refugees, Hall found an interpreter who worked with the staff at the hotel for two weeks. The interpreter explained the basics of housekeeping.

"The rest was really show and tell. We would go to a rollaway, for example, and show the new Bosnian employees how to make it up. We had some signs translated, such as those indicating what to throw away. We had to make certain they understood our color coded chemical warnings and safety procedures. Other things were harder to communicate, such as whether someone could work an extra day. We would hold up a schedule and say 'off' or 'on'," Hall noted.

Some cultural differences were even more delicate to address. "When there are language barriers there are no delicate ways to discuss

MOHONK MOUNTAIN HOUSE welcomes your friends who are seeking employment. We can offer them a secure future and assist them in their personal growth and development. The applicants you refer will be given our personal attention in helping to meet their needs as well as ours. Just fill in the bottom half of this form and have the person you are referring attach it to their application for employment.

------------------------------------------------------------

Date: _____

To: Human Resources Department

    Please give your personal attention to the following

applicant, _____ who is interested in.

a position as _____.

                              Referred by:

                              _____

**Figure 3.4** *Staff referrals are an effective recruitment tool. Reminders such as this help encourage referrals.*

such issues as personal hygiene. We simply took the employee to the locker room, showed him or her the shower, showed him or her the soap and deodorant and tried to explain how to use them. We would give each a toothbrush and toothpaste. We tried to stress in simple terms that keeping personal grooming up to a certain standard was an expected part of the job," Hall added.

The extra effort has paid off, according to Hall. Through networking, the hotel has been able to tap a new supply of hard-working entry level employees and future managers. To make sure it continues to attract Bosnian employees and retains reliable workers already on staff, the hotel applied for and won a government grant to fund an English class on-property for the Bosnian workers.

## Recruitment Specialists

Executive search firms can be hired to recruit the several hundred employees needed for a new hotel or launch a search for one key staff member. Costs vary depending on the extent of the search and difficulty in filling the position. The advantage in hiring an expert is that these firms have in-depth knowledge of the labor pool and, given a set of clear, concise requirements, can minimize unnecessary time and expense in recruiting. Except in cases of newly built hotels, these firms' services are used most often for senior positions.

Both public and private employment offices can generate a steady supply of prospective workers. To maximize the benefit of these services, the executive housekeeper must provide clear descriptions of the job and clear parameters for the qualities and skills required, and require that candidates be well screened before being recommended for an interview at the hotel.

## The Internet

Technology has opened up new doors in the recruitment process. Electronic bulletin boards and on-line "chat rooms" link colleagues around the world. Using features with built-in privacy features, such as **electronic mail,** or E-mail, which leaves messages in the recipient's computer, professional housekeepers or human resource departments can selectively launch their own personnel search.

Corporate human resources departments also use technology to coordinate personnel management. When a position is vacant, the corporate human resources staff can shop the entire chain's personnel database to find the top candidates.

## Overlooked Sources of Prospective Employees

Growing competition for reliable, loyal workers means executive housekeepers must be more creative than ever before in developing steady sources of prospective employees. There are a number of under-utilized sources such as union offices, churches, charities, and senior citizens organizations that are frequently overlooked.

- Union offices can provide a ready source of labor for unionized properties or unionized positions within the property. Here, too, providing a precise job description and job specification will help discourage unqualified applicants from applying.
- Veterans' hospitals, churches, charitable institutions, living centers for those with mental or physical disabilities, fraternal organizations, and military bases are frequently overlooked sources of labor.
- Senior citizens and early retirees who can meet the physical requirements of housekeeping are emerging as a new labor pool. Older workers can bring much-needed expertise to jobs that range from seamstress to furniture preservation and repair. Targeting this group is fairly simple since most areas have both government-sponsored agencies and social organizations aimed at senior citizens.
- Women returning to the work force after having children and men and women looking for second jobs may be good sources of labor. Part-time positions or weekend work may be a major attraction for this growing labor pool.

## HIRING EFFECTIVELY

It is common for a new, luxury hotel in a large city such as Boston or Chicago to receive 5,000 or more applications prior to opening. But not everyone who applies is qualified. The human resources department and the housekeeping department work together to match the best candidates to the jobs.

The job application and interview processes are important tools in this search. The aim of both is to weed out undesirable candidates as quickly as possible and make sure the property is hiring the best people available.

## Working Effectively with Human Resources

Whether hiring a full staff for a new hotel or replacing one position, the human resources department is the starting point for the hiring process. The executive housekeeper can make this process more efficient by regularly updating job descriptions and job specifications.

The job application itself should help cull the field of applicants. If citizenship or eligibility to work in the country are prime issues, they should be addressed near the beginning of the application. Questions pertaining to an applicant's work history and one or two questions that require some thought and commentary can be placed on the back of the application.

In larger hotels, the human resources department may conduct initial interviews. The field of applicants is narrowed to two or three individuals. Their resumes and applications are passed on to the housekeeping department.

Finally, in-person interviews may be conducted by the executive housekeeper and/or the executive assistant or assistant housekeeper, or, in smaller properties, the resident manager. In larger properties, room attendants and housemen may be interviewed first by the assistant housekeeper. The assistant housekeeper may be authorized to hire. More typically, he or she will set up a separate interview for the best candidate with the executive housekeeper, who makes the final hiring decision.

## Becoming a Good Interviewer

The purpose of interviewing is to find the right person for the job. An ideal person is one who will perform up to expectations and who will stay in the job for a reasonable period of time. Key points to address:

- Throughout the interview, make sure that the applicant understands the position for which he or she is being interviewed.
- Show the applicants what their job would entail. As part of the interview process, take the applicant onto the guestroom floors of the property while room attendants are cleaning. This would allow him or her to see the conditions in which he or she would work, the uniform he or she would wear, and some of the supplies he or she

would use. Once on the guestroom floor, the interviewer could have a working room attendant demonstrate how to clean a room and briefly explain each step in proper cleaning procedures. If pertinent, the interviewee also could be taken through the public areas and any other indoor or outdoor spaces for which housekeeping is responsible. This walk-through may give an indication of whether the applicant would be able to keep up the pace. It is critical to present a realistic picture of the job. Many room attendants leave after several days or weeks claiming they had no idea the work would be so hard (see Tricks of the Trade 3.2).

- Stress the physical nature of attendants' work. Interviewers cannot legally question applicants about their health or stamina. Yet, it must be made clear that housekeeping requires physical endurance such as constant bending and lifting. Even supervisory staff may be called on to do hands-on cleaning when necessary.

---

**Tricks of the Trade 3.2**
**Interviewing Short-Cuts**

*The Problem:* Time constraints or the size of the property may make it impractical to take each applicant onto the hotel's guest floors.

*The Solution:* David Green, director of housekeeping for the 491-room Renaissance Hotel in Cleveland, Ohio uses a photo album to show prospective employees what a room attendant's job entails. He discusses photos ranging from a guest room with unmade beds and room service dishes strewn all over to a properly cleaned, luxury guest room. The album also includes photos of uniformed room attendants, so that applicants know what constitutes proper attire. At the end of the album is a job description. Green asks a veteran room attendant to sit in on the interview and aid in the interview process. "Our room attendants know what it takes to get the job done every day. They have a good sense of who will last," says Green.

---

The goal is to give the applicant as realistic a picture as possible of the job, the working atmosphere, and performance expectations. Stressing the toughest parts of the job helps to make sure attendants and managers are fully aware of the challenges and opportunities of professional house-keeping.

Work experience indicates the applicant's basic skill levels. Ideally, the applicant's resume shows how his or her career path has built the necessary skills to meet the demands of the position. The interviewer's questions should focus on how this work experience benefitted departmental performance. Applicants for entry-level positions may have no prior experience. The important thing to determine in these cases is whether the applicant has had good work habits at previous jobs.

Interviewing is a skill worth developing. Asking the right questions and learning how to listen to the replies are essential to effective hiring (see Tricks of the Trade 3.3).

---

**Tricks of the Trade 3.3**
**10 Rules for Improved Interviewing**

1. **Practice.** Work with the human resources department or another department manager with good interviewing skills to hone the necessary techniques.

2. **Be prepared.** Study the job specifications. Set aside ample time for the interview. There should be no interruptions. Schedule a translator if one is needed. If another department head or staff member would need to sit in on the interview, make these arrangements in advance to make sure the person will be free at the scheduled time.

3. **Find a private place.** The applicant will feel freer to talk if others are not listening. A quiet atmosphere such as a private office is preferable.

4. **Study the application.** Take time to read the application form to assess the applicant's work history and skills before asking any questions.

5. **Encourage the applicant to talk.** Steer clear of illegal questions or questions that are too personal. Standard questions include why the applicant is interested in this job; career goals; what has attracted the person to the housekeeping field; and questions about work experience.

6. **Ask questions that involve explanations.** Questions eliciting a "yes" or "no" answer do

not reveal much about the prospective employee. Neither do questions worded in such a way as to indicate what answer the interviewer wants to hear.

7. **Recheck dates on the application with the applicant.** Sometimes, when looking at the work history on the application, time gaps will be evident. By asking questions about these gaps (again, without reverting to illegal questions), the interviewer may find out a great deal that was not on the application.

8. **Give complete, honest, accurate information about the job and the company.** It is far better to undersell than oversell the position and the company.

9. **Evaluate and rate the applicant.** This is a difficult process that goes on in the interviewer's mind during the interview. There is no way to eliminate subjectivity. Most executive housekeepers admit that, too often, hiring is based on a "gut" reaction. Concentrate on facts and demonstrated performance.

10. **Avoid "crisis hiring,"** if at all possible. Unless the property faces a long-term staffing emergency, veteran housekeepers say it is preferable to schedule dependable, existing staff to work overtime rather than hiring someone whose qualifications or attitude toward work are questionable. This allows time to advertise the position again and allows more applications to be submitted. Few housekeepers have the luxury of waiting for the ideal staff member, but fewer still can afford to hire someone who cannot do the job.

---

## Evaluating Personality Traits

Working in the housekeeping department requires not only the physical skills to do the job but also the personality traits suited to this demanding work environment. From room attendants to the executive housekeeper, all department members must be able to deal satisfactorily with other staff members and guests. They must be able to handle the stress of a heavy workload and deal with the pressure of turning in a perfect performance every day. They must be able to accept constructive criticism well and use it to improve their performance. They also must cope with pressures that few employees experience: the possibility of being accused of stealing something from a guest room or the possibility of handling emergencies ranging from a fire in the hotel to a seriously ill guest.

The interviewer needs to ask questions that reveal how the applicant copes with pressure and how he or she views himself or herself. The answers to such questions help determine whether the applicant can interact effectively with departmental staff, the public, and other departments.

## Avoiding Illegal Questions

Any departmental staff members who conduct interviews should be well versed in what interview questions are illegal. The human resources director can provide a list of which questions to avoid. If the property does not have a human resources department, the executive housekeeper can contact the hotel chain or management company which manages the hotel, the state department of human rights, labor, or employment or the federal department of labor.

Discrimination is one of the most serious issues in hiring. Unfair employment practices carry substantial penalties. If a suit is filed, it may take several years for the case to be heard. In a worst-case scenario, should discrimination be proven, the hotel may be liable for reimbursement of the complainant's potential salary from the date of the complaint, payment of a state fine equal to that sum (depending on the state regulations), hiring the employee with a clear record, and payment of other expenses, including, of course, legal fees.

It is hard to become an expert in this area. The rule of thumb is that it is illegal to ask questions that limit, segregate, or classify prospective employees. Some basic guidelines are:

- An employer cannot fail to hire or refuse to hire an applicant solely on the basis of race, color, religion, sex, age, culture, disabilities, sexual preference (the extent of this issue is being reviewed by the courts), or national origin.

- An employer cannot classify employees in any way that would deprive them of employment opportunities or adversely affect their status as employees. It follows, then, that employees cannot be discharged or otherwise discriminated against on these bases, nor can they be limited or segregated.

- It is illegal to ask an applicant's attitudes toward unions. The interviewer is allowed to say whether union membership is mandatory for the position available. It is illegal to say that a certain position is currently nonunion and must remain nonunion. Questions regarding how to handle the issue of union membership should be discussed with the human resources department or a local office of the National Labor Relations Board.

- An applicant cannot be asked about his or her religious affiliation, church, or any holidays he or she may observe. The interviewer may not mention the religious beliefs of anyone in the organization. In rare instances, an applicant may ask the religious beliefs of staff or management. The proper response should be outlined in the hotel's policy manual.

- Employers may not ask the prospective employee to submit a photo until after he or she is hired. The employee's picture may be legally required after hiring if the property uses identification cards.

- Employers may not ask the applicant's marital status or whether the person has or intends to have children. Without mentioning these issues directly, the interviewer can stress that repeated tardiness and/or absenteeism are grounds for dismissal.

- It is illegal to ask about health problems.

Some issues are particularly complex. For example, if the applicant has been convicted of a crime, the interviewer may ask what the crime was, when and where it was committed, and what was the disposition of the case. It is illegal to ask whether the person has been arrested. Professional housekeepers need to master these complexities to make sure the property does not risk a costly lawsuit.

## The Right Questions on Citizenship

Cultural diversity among housekeeping staffs leads to questions regarding citizenship and work permits. It is legal to ask the applicant whether he or she is a citizen of the United States or, if not, whether he or she has the legal right to remain permanently in the United States.

This question is legally and financially crucial. Employers must be prepared to document whether employees are citizens or authorized aliens. Although some executive housekeepers admit it is tempting to hire without checking, especially when labor is tight, the risk is never worthwhile. Legislation regarding immigration control includes stiff fines for failure to comply, including fines of $1,000 to $10,000 for each unauthorized employee. If the interviewer has questions regarding this issue, he or she should contact the federal Immigration and Naturalization Service (INS) or the Department of Labor for a list of documents required for verification and other information. (see Appendix A). Any employee who is not a citizen must provide the necessary documentation.

The INS has launched an experimental program in Southern California that enables employers to check work authorizations via computer. The employer keys in certain required information, then sends it via computer modem to the immigration service. INS then flashes a message on the employer's computer that indicates that employment is authorized or that it is unable to verify work authorization.

### Clarifying Physical Requirements

Housekeeping is strenuous work. Without asking directly about the applicant's health, the interviewer must make it clear that lifting, twisting, and bending are part of the job. Showing the applicant what room attendants do and discussing a **job analysis,** which outlines how much time the employee spends doing different aspects of the job, helps to point out the physical requirements of housekeeping.

The kind of work done by the housekeeping department does not preclude hiring people with disabilities. Skills simply must be matched to responsibilities. **Team cleaning,** an approach to cleaning in which a task such as cleaning a guest room is done by a group of specialists, each with a separate function such as vacuuming or cleaning the bathroom, opens up a wide range of possibilities.

### Interviewing Non–English-Speaking Applicants

The executive housekeeper, executive assistant, or assistant housekeeper needs to learn at least the basics of the most prevalent second language. If that is not practical, a bilingual supervisor should be called in to help translate during interviews.

Even when using a translator, the executive housekeeper must maintain control of the interview. It is critical that the applicant understand what is being discussed in the interview and what is being asked on the application. It is inadvisable to hire staff members who do not have minimal

knowledge of English, or the mother tongue of the country. Staff members need to understand the language spoken by most of the guests and staff in order to respond quickly to their needs.

### Addressing Union Membership

The interviewer must make clear whether a position requires membership in a union. Although the interviewer may respond to questions regarding when employees have to join the union or how much membership in the union costs, a better course (to prevent legal problems) is to refer the person directly to the union office. Hotels in large cities, particularly New York, San Francisco, Boston, and Chicago, generally are unionized; most other hotels or motels are not (see Tricks of the Trade 3.4).

---

### Tricks of the Trade 3.4
### Working Smarter with Unions

Hotel companies are looking at new ways of working with unions that balance the unions' interests and those of the management and ownership. One option is to have a core of union employees who do key housekeeping tasks, such as cleaning the guest rooms. A janitorial service hired on contract provides the balance of the employees, including night cleaners and cleaners who do some special project cleaning. Union and nonunion employees have different work assignments clearly outlined in the union contract.

Communication is the key. New or newly rebranded hotels often invite union representatives to meet with management prior to opening—frequently at a luncheon or special welcoming event. Some housekeepers also discuss various options, such as team cleaning or cross-training, with union officials to determine what kinds of problems—if any—might arise.

---

Since contracts differ, the executive housekeeper should make sure the contract is reviewed by a legal expert before hiring an outside cleaning service. He or she should also ask the legal adviser whether **cross-training** is permitted under the terms of the contract. Cross-training enables employees to learn how to perform several jobs within their own department or in other departments.

Union membership for employees who work for cruise lines is handled somewhat differently than in hotels. The question of union membership depends on the country in which the ship is registered, and union agreements vary widely from country to country. Some ships are registered in countries that do not require union membership for cruise ship staff;

## Testing

Psychological testing and skills testing can be useful tools in screening applicants. At a small property, testing may be as simple as asking a prospective employee to sign his or her name or read and write room numbers, floor numbers, and dates. This basic process shows whether the employee understands enough of the language to carry out such basic but necessary functions.

However, most tests administered by larger hotels use standardized questions that reveal skill-oriented aptitude or behavioral tendencies. Tests for manual dexterity, mental ability, job aptitude, and job knowledge can help determine what the applicant can do. Psychological tests are designed to show personality traits that indicate what the person will do. Computerized "integrity tests" measure the applicant's attitudes towards subjects ranging from drug abuse to theft. An increasing number of hotels conduct tests to detect drug abuse.

Some types of tests can be illegal. Before conducting any testing, the executive housekeeper should contact the human resources department, the state department of employment, and/or the union office to find out what testing is permitted.

Aptitude-oriented results are only an indicator, because some people do not test well. Results should be weighed against the impression made during the personal interview and work history. How the applicant responds during the interview may indicate how well he or she can get along with and work with the other departmental staff and how well he or she performs in a high-pressure situation.

## Discussing Salary and Benefits

Human resources departments regularly check salary ranges at competitive properties to make sure their property's pay rates are attractive yet fair. The salary range should be included in the ad for the position. Most employers *request* a salary history along with a resume; some *require* it as part of the application procedure. The human resources department or executive housekeeper may use the preliminary interview to ask the applicant what an acceptable salary range would be. The goal is to find out whether the person's expectations are in line with the property's pay scale.

For entry-level positions, discussing salary and benefits is an expected part of second interviews or, in small properties, even first interviews. Starting salaries for inexperienced room attendants typically range from minimum wage or a base rate set by state law in some states to more than $7 an hour in some highly competitive urban markets. The interviewer can explain briefly any incentives the property offers for increasing the hourly rate, as well as the cycle of reviews and raises. The property's willingness to promote from within and promotion opportunities should be addressed.

For more senior staff positions, the discussion of salary usually is deferred until the final interview. A firm salary typically is not discussed until a job offer is made. Benefits can be a major attraction. Ranging from free hotel stays at other properties within the hotel chain or management company to valuable insurance and stock programs, benefits can be a major selling point for a property.

Benefits that could make an important difference in recruiting include: on-site child care, wellness programs for employees at the hotel's fitness facilities, or on-site training in a second language. Anything that sets the hotel apart from its competitors helps the property attract and retain the best staff available.

## Learning to Listen

A good interview involves a give and take of information. The interviewer should provide all necessary information the applicant needs to decide whether to accept the job. Likewise, the interviewer should gather all pertinent information needed to make a decision on whether to hire the applicant. Learning to listen is a critical skill in hiring. In particular, the interviewer should pay attention to the following:

- Listen to the types of questions the applicant asks. Is he or she more concerned with salary issues or vacations and days off? Does he or she ask about educational opportunities and promotion? For senior staff positions, where does the applicant hope to be in three to five years? For the executive housekeeper's job, why is the person seeking a job change and why is the person interested in this position?

- Listen to the comments he or she makes. Can this person work in a multicultural setting if that is an issue? Is the person generally negative? Does he or she complain about the workload of previous jobs?

Appearance is not always a good basis for evaluating an applicant; however, it may indicate whether the person is serious about the position and it also says something about the applicant's level of attention to detail. The minimum expectation is that the applicant should be neat and clean.

### Following Up and Verifying Information

The human resources department automatically will verify the information on the job application of a candidate likely to be hired. References should be checked. A call to a previous employer can verify work history.

The human resources department generally follows certain guidelines in questioning previous employers. Key questions include whether the person did work at that establishment, the dates of employment, job title, and whether the business would re-employ that person. That may be the only information that can be obtained, since most companies have strict policies about how to respond to such inquiries. For managerial jobs, the applicant's references should be contacted and asked about the person's leadership qualities and ability to motivate and manage staff and about any weaknesses or areas that would require improvement.

The executive housekeeper must communicate priorities to the human resources department. He or she should discuss whether the human resources department is recommending qualified applicants for second interviews, or if there are qualities or qualifications that are not being evaluated correctly. Problems in hiring should be tracked, as should information compiled from exit interviews, when people leave the company. This information can help resolve obstacles to hiring such as noncompetitive salaries, unrealistic working conditions, or lack of promotion opportunities.

### The First Day

Once the decision is made to hire a person, the application should be processed and the applicant should be notified when to report for work. Processing usually includes filling in a **bonding** application. Bonding means that the property essentially is putting up a "bond" to cover that person in case of theft. Insurance companies usually insist that room attendants and house attendants be bonded since housekeeping employees are in regular contact with guests' belongings.

A substantial part of the new hire's first morning is usually spent filling out paperwork, ranging from the bonding application to filling out tax forms or having a photo taken for an employee identification card. A management-level staff member in the human resources department or the executive housekeeper will confirm the salary for the position and explain the benefits offered by the company. An **orientation** session in the housekeeping department should be scheduled next. Orientation introduces the new employee to the physical layout of the property, the functions of various departments, and the job he or she will perform (see Tricks of the Trade 3.5).

---

**Tricks of the Trade 3.5**
**Easing the Orientation Process**

*The Problem:* Not all staff members who conduct orientation sessions cover the necessary material new hires should know.
*The Solution:* A clear, concise orientation checklist. Rita Genslé, executive housekeeper of the deluxe Inter-Continental in Miami, Florida, gives new hires a simple orientation checklist when they start their new jobs. All items on the list must be covered by department managers within the employee's first month of work and checked off. The completed form must be returned to the human resources department. She also provides employee manuals in both English and Spanish (see Figure 3.5).

---

As part of orientation, the new staff member should be shown the property, the areas in which he or she will work, and also, if applicable, the back-of-the-house employee locker rooms and employee cafeteria. If the property is large or the layout is complex, new employees should be given simple floor plans of all areas that are germane to the job.

HOTEL
INTER-CONTINENTAL
MIAMI

## DEPARTMENT ORIENTATION CHECKLIST

In order to ensure that all our employees receive all the important information needed for a successful start in their new job, it is necessary to complete this form for every new employee and have him/her return it to Human Resources within the first month of their employment.

_____ Department introductions.
_____ Purpose/function of the department.
_____ Chain of command/Supervisors.
_____ Overview of positions in the department.
_____ Responsibilities of each position.
_____ Job Description, Training.
_____ Tour of the department.
_____ Department policies and procedures
_____ Punching in and out
_____ Punctuality and attendance/calling in sick.
_____ Break periods.
_____ Evaluations and job performance.
_____ Fire/evacuation procedures and exits.(Employees and Guests)
_____ Use and location of fire extinguishers/pull stations.
_____ Emergency procedures (hurricane, blackout, robbery, illness)
_____ Reporting accidents and injuries.
_____ Reporting unsafe conditions.
_____ Bloodborne Pathogens procedures
_____ Housekeeping and safety (keeping the work area clean)
_____ Proper use of chemicals/Material Safety Data Sheets.
_____ Care and use of equipment/importance of using proper equipment.
_____ Handling guest complaints.
_____ Telephone courtesy.
_____ Taking messages/using beepers.
_____ Guest expectations (quality of service, courtesy, safety)
_____ Key control.
_____ Lost and found.
_____ Departmental Standards
_____ Other: _____

I acknowledge that I have been informed of the above mentioned items and that I am familiar with all department policies applicable to my position.

NAME      (please print)          HIRE DATE    DEPARTMENT

SIGNATURE                          DATE          MANAGER

**Figure 3.5** *Orientation lists should require tht all employees receive identical orientation. Checklists such as this one should be kept by department heads.*

## Employee Handbooks and Procedure Manuals

New employees should be given an employee handbook and procedural manual that covers the salient points of the property's policies and procedures. An **employee handbook** should provide information on:

- Use of the standardized or computerized time clock and provisions on overtime
- Policies on what constitutes the proper uniform, where employees must park, where they should enter the building
- Breaks and meal times

- The proper way to communicate with guests and other staff members
- Policies on use of hotel facilities (including whether room attendants can use the in-room radio, for example)
- Standards of conduct
- Safety procedures for employees and guests
- Policies regarding security and confidentiality for employees and guests
- Procedures for reporting and receiving treatment for on-the-job accidents
- Procedures for reporting tips/gratuities
- Employee leave and vacation
- Information about benefits
- Regulations regarding job performance, evaluation, promotions/job posting, disciplinary action, and termination or resignation

A **procedure manual** tells the employee exactly how to perform each step of his or her job. It is written in language that is easy to understand. A manual should be written for each position. The executive housekeeper should have a master manual, which includes procedure manuals for the entire department and all job descriptions.

The new employee should be shown where all equipment and supplies are stored and how to fill out any necessary forms regarding inventory controls. Any areas that are off limits or only accessible with special approval should be pointed out in the manual. Major points in the employee handbook and procedure manual should be stressed by the staff member responsible for training the new hire.

From the start, new employees should feel respected and valued. If possible, the executive housekeeper or the assistant (in a larger property) should schedule lunch with the new staff member. Talking in the informal setting of an employee lunch room opens up the lines of communication between the manager and new employee.

## SCHEDULING

Once the executive housekeeper determines who will work in the department, he or she needs to determine when each will work. Effective scheduling makes sure all the necessary tasks are accomplished.

## Creating Standing and Rotational Schedules

Using various management and forecasting tools, professional housekeepers generally make up a **standing schedule** that serves as a broad, long-term framework for scheduling. The standard schedule reflects the number of workers needed on average to do the work assigned to the department. Computers have eased the formerly labor-intensive task of scheduling.

In some properties, this standard schedule includes a rotation element. Previously, having weekends off was a perquisite of seniority. With **rotation scheduling,** all employees have regular opportunities to have weekends or at least one weekend day off. For example, if an employee works Sunday through Thursday one week, he or she may work Monday through Friday the next and so on. Rotation scheduling works equally well for individuals or teams (see Figure 3.6)

## Creating Daily Schedules

The executive housekeeper or an assistant housekeeper prepares the daily work schedule for the housekeeping department. He or she must determine how much work there will be in order to schedule the optimum amount of staff to get the work done. Generally, the actual schedule is posted one to two weeks in advance, then modified if necessary. Data needed to determine this includes:

- **Advance reservations,** which are reservations made prior to the day of check-in
- **Night auditor's report,** which indicates how many rooms will be **due outs** or check-outs, which means the guest's stay is ending, how many rooms are occupied, notes any last-minute reservation calls
- **Occupancy** or **rooms forecast,** an educated guess of how many rooms or functions will be booked for that day; initial forecasts are made months in advance, then recalculated several weeks in advance, one week in advance and finally, in detail, the night before
- Historic occupancy trends, actual rooms sales for the period tracked over a number of years
- Special events, such as conventions or trade shows and holidays

Typically, a next-day rooms forecast is sent to housekeeping daily between noon and 2 P.M. This information is the basis for the following day's

| | Sunday | Monday | Tuesday | Wednesday | Thursday | Friday | Saturday |
|---|---|---|---|---|---|---|---|
| Week 1 | On | On | | | On | On | On |
| Week 2 | On | On | On | | | On | On |
| Week 3 | On | On | On | On | | | On |
| Week 4 | On | On | On | On | On | | |
| Week 5 | On | On | On | On | On | On | |
| Week 6 | | On | On | On | On | On | On |
| Week 7 | | | On | On | On | On | On |

**Figure 3.6** *Rotational schedules give employees the benefit of two consecutive days off, and provide managers with a useful scheduling tool.*

schedule. If check-outs will be heavy, extra staff may have to be scheduled. Check-out rooms must be thoroughly cleaned before the next guest occupies them. Employees should check schedules at the beginning and end of their shifts because scheduling refinements are ongoing.

Technology plays a useful role in making sure the housekeeping department has the latest occupancy and reservation information. Computer links from the front office can update the information in the housekeeping department instantaneously, and the staff member doing the scheduling can respond accordingly (see Tricks of the Trade 3.6).

## Tricks of the Trade 3.6
## Overstaffing vs. Understaffing

*The Problem:* Occupancy varies and attendance can fluctuate, leaving professional housekeepers to weigh the benefits of overstaffing and understaffing.

*The Solution:* Manor Care's Schade recommends that professional housekeepers with a stable work force schedule strictly according to the rooms forecast. "At large hotels, the work force is usually fairly stable and there is enough staff to cover for someone who **calls off** (calls in to say he or she will not be at work just before the shift begins). At a smaller property, where the housekeeping staff may total 10 people, there's not enough people to take up the slack. In these cases, overscheduling may make sense." Extra people, called simply **extras,** should also be

scheduled if there is a pattern of heavy call-offs or no-shows after pay days or on holidays.

Understaffing is most useful during periods of low occupancy. If occupancy jumps unexpectedly, employees can be assigned more rooms or more hours. Cross-training helps support an understaffing approach. Trained staff can be moved over from laundry or other departments to respond to a staffing crunch. Supervisors and even the department's top management can clean rooms when necessary.

## Scheduling Part-Timers and Swing Staff

Most schedules assume that full-time workers will make up the bulk of core staff. However, as labor markets tighten, housekeeping departments are making room for more part-timers. Scheduling part-timers is more complex, but works well once it is organized.

Ideally, the hours and days assigned to part-timers would help fill the most obvious gaps in the schedules: perhaps a 4 A.M. to 8 A.M. shift during which thorough public space cleaning is done, a weekends-only schedule (assuming no wage premium is required for weekend work) or a 3 P.M. to 7 P.M. schedule during which late check-out rooms are cleaned and many guest request items are delivered.

In very tight labor markets, schedules may have to be adjusted to times when part-timers are willing to work. If the primary pool of part-timers consists of people looking for second jobs, the very early or very late shifts will give them the needed flexibility.

If parents of school-age children make up the primary part-time labor market, the start of their shifts may have to be staggered around school hours.

Larger housekeeping departments schedule swing staff. These "troubleshooters" work where needed on any given day. They may fill in on employees' days off or help room attendants faced with heavy early check-ins or late check-outs. Swing staff is made up of full-time employees whose assignments may differ from day to day. Some properties may require a swing shift. Employees who work the swing shift usually begin in the middle of one shift and work until the middle of the next.

Some hotels are developing nontraditional schedules to improve productivity and better accommodate employees' needs for more predictable working hours (see Tales of the Trade 3.2)

---

**Tales of the Trade 3.2**
**Scheduling for a Four-Day Week**

Kay Weirick, director of housekeeping services for the 2,832-room Bally's Casino Resort in Las Vegas, Nevada took advantage of a new union contract several years ago to offer employees a 10-hour shift, four days a week. Her goals at the outset of the program were:

1. To realize labor and benefit savings
2. To provide motivational advantages and expense cuts for employees
3. To cut down on absenteeism
4. To address the shortage of housekeeping personnel due to new hotel openings in the area

"We found that during peak hours our coverage was doubled. We also found that having two hours a day added to these departments enabled us to reduce personnel, especially on the swing and graveyard shifts. In our uniform and linen room, we consolidated the 8-hour graveyard shift by reducing coverage from 24 hours to 20. Very few employees need a uniform change between 2 A.M. and 5 A.M., and those who did could pick up their uniform at a later time. We began to hear positive feedback after the employees had their first three days off," Weirick says.

Working longer hours is particularly advantageous in Las Vegas where late check-outs are common. Roughly half of the hotel's 370 room attendants wanted to try the 10-hour shift. During the longer shift, their quota rose from 14 rooms cleaned in an 8-hour shift to 18 rooms in a 10-hour shift. "One of the problems we encountered was that some attendants were simply not able to do 18 rooms in a day. We have some of the largest rooms in Las Vegas, and it is really pushing it to clean 18, 400-sq. ft. to 500-sq. ft. rooms in a day," she adds.

Weirick points out that the system did save on labor costs and did significantly reduce call-offs. However, when the housekeeping department was downsized recently, the decision was made to return to traditional eight-hour shifts. "I believe the four-day work week has merit, but I think it would work better for a 400- to 500-room hotel," Weirick notes. "With 2,000 or 3,000 rooms, it takes longer to return the check-out rooms back to the front desk for resell."

---

## Handling Special Requests

Working weekends and holidays is standard practice for lodging employees. This leaves little time for scheduling doctor's appointments, dentist's appointments, car repairs, and so on. For this reason, executive housekeepers generally try to honor special requests for days off.

Requests for time off should be made in writing one week or more in advance. Requests are handled on a first-come, first-served basis. If there is a conflict, seniority is generally the deciding factor. When possible, as in the case of jury duty or a court appearance, the employee should accompany the written request with a copy of the official document.

Vacation requests should be made well in advance. Some properties require that all staff make vacation requests at the start of the year, with priority given to those with seniority. Staff, including supervisors and even the assistant and executive housekeepers, should be encouraged to plan vacations during periods of low occupancy.

## Handling Leave

Policies on sick leave, maternity leave, and bereavement leave are spelled out in the employee manual. The housekeeping department has adequate time to adapt the schedule for workers on maternity leave; swing employees or part-timers looking for more hours can cover the gaps created by sick leave or bereavement leave. Requests for sick leave should be accompanied by a note from a physician describing the medical reasons for the leave.

### Handling Call-Offs and No-Shows

Some call-offs may be justified: sudden illness, weather-related problems, a car accident. If possible, employees should contact a supervisor or other departmental manager at least two hours before his or her shift begins. Leaving a voice mail message is not acceptable, except in emergency situations. A physician's note is required for sicknesses that require several days off.

There should be zero tolerance for nonessential call-offs, call–offs for reasons that cannot be substantiated. However, in tight labor markets, this may not be realistic. The goal should be to keep call-offs to a minimum and begin disciplinary action promptly when an employee calls-off repeatedly.

No-shows—failure to report to work or even call—should not be tolerated, except in cases of emergency. Repeated no-shows are grounds for dismissal.

# SUMMARY

The labor-intensive nature of housekeeping makes recruiting, hiring, and training staff members an essential part of the executive housekeeper's job. Finding the right staff will increase productivity and reduce turnover. Each addition to the staff should understand the contribution he or she makes to the department and the entire hotel.

Staffing a department begins with savvy recruiting and interviewing. Executive housekeepers must develop ready sources of prospective employees to meet the challenge of high turnover. Working with the human resources department, he or she must learn to weed out applicants without the necessary skills and personality traits to perform well.

In addition to defining staff size and hiring capable staff, professional housekeepers must create schedules that take advantage of the staff's skills and help maximize their performance. Staffing and scheduling are core functions for professional housekeepers. In order to master these skills, professional housekeepers must:

- Determine the optimum size staff
- Develop clear definitions for job descriptions and job specifications
- Develop workable recruitment techniques
- Tailor recruiting and interviewing to the needs of a multicultural labor market
- Learn to ask the right questions during interviews
- Create a smooth hiring process
- Develop schedules aimed at maximizing performance
- Develop schedules that match the property's management structure and the makeup of the labor market

### Review Questions

1. What is the difference between a job specification and a job description?
2. What is a time and motion study?
3. What is a quota and how is it used in calculating labor needs?
4. What is an occupancy or rooms forecast and how is it used in the housekeeping department?
5. What is an employee handbook or manual? What is a procedures manual? What should each cover?
6. Give an example of some illegal interview questions. Why are they illegal?
7. How should an authorized alien's right to work be verified?
8. What is a rotational schedule?
9. What is historic occupancy?
10. What is orientation?

### Critical Thinking Questions

1. The executive housekeeper in a small luxury hotel in an area with only 4 percent unemployment needs to recruit entry-level employees. How could this recruitment search be handled?
2. Discuss the advantages and disadvantages of part-timers.
3. Call-offs increase to unacceptable levels after pay days and on holidays. How can this situation be rectified?

# 4

# Training, Motivating, and Evaluating Staff

## Chapter Objectives

To help staff achieve peak performance and make sure all staff members work effectively, the executive housekeeper must:

- Develop effective training programs for new hires
- Develop ongoing training programs for all staff
- Motivate employees through leadership
- Structure incentive programs that benefit the department's bottom line and satisfy staff needs
- Evaluate performance, reward good performance, and find ways to improve poor performance
- Handle disciplinary actions effectively
- Discharge staff without legal problems

Once staff members are hired, the focus of the executive housekeeper as a human resources manager shifts to performance-related issues. The professional housekeeper's goal is to use training, motivation, and evaluation to help all staff members optimize their job performance. Effective training helps employees develop the necessary skills to do the job well. Motivation instills pride in performance and encourages employees to continue to improve performance.

As a manager, the executive housekeeper must also find ways to measure performance. Performance measurement can be used in several ways to improve departmental results:

- To identify best practices and implement them throughout the department
- To reward staff members who perform well

- To identify areas in which retraining is needed or in which new training programs need to be instituted
- To identify cases of poor performance in an effort to rectify problems

All performance measurement must be as objective as possible. Use of objective criteria makes it easier to help employees understand both strengths and weaknesses. Objective criteria provide a good base of documentation for either promotion or disciplinary action.

## TRAINING FOR PEAK PERFORMANCE

Effective training programs are essential to a well-run department. Training shows each staff member which functions he or she is expected to perform and how to do them correctly. It is as valuable for the attendant who has never worked in the lodging industry as for an executive housekeeper with experience at a different property (see Figure 4.1).

The aim of training is to standardize the procedures that have been proven to work well without taking away the flexibility and motivation to find better procedures. Employees must have input into improving the processes and systems they use and be able to adapt them to changing guest demand.

Trainers within the department, trainers from hotel and motel chain corporate headquarters, trainers from professional associations, and other professional trainers all play a role in helping staff improve performance. The investment in training has a direct payoff in productivity and reduced per-

**Figure 4.1** *Training for supervisors must take into account not only the hours the employee will spend learning new skills, but also who will cover their cleaning assignments while they are in training.*

formance problems. Training should be an ongoing process. Providing regular training programs for staff not only helps improve performance, it also sends a clear message that management is willing to invest the time and effort to help staff members succeed.

## Teaching Employees How to Do Their Jobs

Training differs by property and job title. Training for an economy property in which all rooms are standardized and public spaces are limited is fairly straightforward. Teaching room attendants to clean rooms filled with antiques or resort villas that may include cooking facilities, a sleeping room, and living room requires more time and energy. Each job category also requires specific training. The basic job categories are:

- Entry level employees
- Supervisory employees
- Management trainees
- Managers

***Entry-level jobs.*** Typically, a new room attendant learns the basics of the job from a staff veteran. In a small property, the executive housekeeper is usually the trainer. In a larger property, a floor supervisor, team leader, or floor housekeeper shows the new hire what must be done. This system can be referred to as a "big sister" or "big brother" or a "one-for-one" (one old employee for one new employee). In many properties this takes the form of **on-the-job training.** Rather than attending formal training sessions or classes, the new hire trains on the job, usually following his or her trainer through a typical workday. Another approach is to have a training supervisor conduct classes for new hires in a room suitable for training, then follow up with on-the-job training.

Training for a room attendant would include:

- How to clean a check-out room
- How to clean an occupied room
- How to make a bed
- How to clean a bathroom
- How to care for and use housekeeping equipment
- How to fill out any necessary forms or work orders
- How to interact with guests and other staff

Similar training programs would be established for public area attendants and laundry attendants. Each attendant would be trained in how to do cleaning functions, use equipment, and fill out any necessary forms. Initial training for a room attendant can range from a day to a week, depending on the complexity of the property.

The next step is to assign the new hire a light workload, perhaps half the usual number of rooms or a small portion of public space. When the new hire demonstrates he or she is capable of doing this half-quota up to standard, the employee receives the full quota of rooms or public area assignments.

***Supervisory employees.*** Supervisory training programs reflect staff structure, including whether the supervisor is a manager who will supervise a crew or whether the staff structure is evolving toward **self-supervision,** which means that no inspector or supervisor checks the attendant's work. Supervisors should already have hands-on technical knowledge of cleaning. Training focuses on managing staff, identifying and correcting performance problems constructively, communicating with the front desk about how many rooms are needed and when, returning cleaned rooms to inventory, issuing and perhaps inventorying equipment and supplies and, in some properties, writing schedules for the attendants.

The self-supervised room attendant is responsible for cleaning the room properly, reporting any damage or need for repair, writing out work orders for damage or repairs, responding to guest requests, and returning the room to inventory. Nothing should be left undone in the hope the supervisor will deal with the oversight. Training should emphasize the room attendant's responsibility to see that the room is recleaned and ready to be resold. Training current staff to take on these new responsibilities could take as much as two months since it must be done within the regular workday.

In hotels that use a team cleaning structure, each team may have a **team leader.** This employee has a cleaning quota, but also conducts some overall checks of the room, such as making sure the room has all written collateral material such as guest services information or hotel stationery and reporting the need for repair. The team leader also may be responsible for checking with the front desk as to whether the floor has any VIP rooms or special requests. VIP rooms, reserved for guests the hotel's management or ownership deems worthy of special attention, must be serviced flawlessly. The team leader must learn enough managerial skills to motivate his or her team and maintain standards. Training should address time management if team leaders must split their time between cleaning and managing.

***Floor supervisor.*** Generally, it takes about one hour a week for 16 weeks to train a supervisor. If this is a promotion from within, another employee will have to be scheduled to fill the scheduling gap while the floor supervisor is in training. Executive housekeepers strongly suggest the supervisor trainee not be assigned to supervise attendants with whom he or she is working. The supervisory trainee should be assigned to a different floor or section of guest rooms.

The training for inspectors is similar. Inspectors should be shown how to use a checklist to inspect rooms as well as how to handle the managerial task of correcting performance problems without criticizing the individual.

***Management trainee.*** A management trainee is a student who has successfully completed a specified minimum requirement of coursework in hotel management and must put what has been learned in the classroom into practice at the property. Some are still undergraduates, but most are in graduate programs. Some who have undergraduate degrees are in management training programs run by the property's operator.

The length of time the management trainee spends in each post in the department is tailored to the individual's needs. Trainees with a college degree typically complete the program in one year; those with less than four years of college may take up to two years. Some training programs at the assistant managerial level are open only to graduate students.

During the first phase of the program, the trainee learns the basic, day-to-day functions and responsibilities of the housekeeping department. A good first assignment may be as the office assistant. Rather than using the trainee as a receptionist, he or she should be trained to enter cost analysis information and other data that familiarizes him or her with the financial responsibilities of managers. This work gives the trainee a broad overview of departmental activities.

During the second phase, the trainee acts as junior assistant housekeeper. This trains the person in operations management as well as in human resources management. The night shift is the best time to teach supervisory skills. During this slower shift, the trainee learns how to interact with guests' special requests as well as how to issue keys and supplies, fill out forms, and use the front office room report. The night shift supervisory position allows the trainee to supervise staff without the pressure of the fast pace of daytime positions.

*Managers.* Managers who set policy and make decisions for the entire department require the longest training period. The executive housekeeper and assistants need to learn not only about departmental operations and the property's technical requirements, but also its staff skills and management focus. It takes months for the department's top managers to fully master all the aspects of their job. Training may be done by the outgoing executive housekeeper or the rooms division manager, resident manager, or general manager, depending on the size and management structure of the property.

### Communicating with Staff and Guests

The executive housekeeper should outline the policies regarding staff interaction with guests and staff when a new hire begins work. Though different hotels have different styles and images, the general rule is that employees should be pleasant and helpful but professional and not overly familiar.

Staff members cannot avoid guest contact. This may present a challenge for staff employees who are reticent to talk with guests because they lack fluency in English or for some from cultures where service workers are viewed as subservient. Ed Conaway, executive housekeeper of the upscale U.S. Grant Hotel in San Diego, California uses this approach: "We train our staff members to think of guests as friendly employers. We encourage our staff to smile and say hello. Some of the room attendants who are not fluent in English are apprehensive about guest contact. But we remind them that guests are not interested in carrying on a long conservation. They just want to feel welcome or make sure that their requests are acted on."

Training staff to communicate with other departments is equally important. Staff should be trained to express needs clearly and concisely, explain by what time the task should be completed, and respond to requests from other departments. If the staff member cannot act on the request, he or she should know to whom it should be given.

Training also should encourage open communication within the housekeeping department. Teaching basic respect for all cultures is essential. Executive housekeepers whose staffs combine employees from cultures that historically have clashed or still may be at war face a difficult challenge. Using a team approach to special projects or regular cleaning can foster cooperation, especially if incentives are provided for the team with the best performance. If cultural clashes continue, the only solution may be assigning the various cultural groups to different floors.

## TEACHING THE BASICS AND BEYOND

Teaching the basic job function is only one aspect of training. Training can be used as a motivational tool. Cross-training, ongoing training programs, and continuing education help staff members broaden their skills, but also improve their performance.

*Cross-training.* A buzzword for modern managers, cross-training means that an employee is trained to do more than one job function. For example, if there is a need for an extra front desk clerk or a banquet server because an employee calls in sick, the general manager can shift a cross-trained worker from one department to another. Cross-training also benefits employees who can use their varied skills to earn a promotion and/or higher pay. Some union contracts allow for cross-training. Typically these contracts will permit cross-training within the department rather than from one department to another. However, other union contracts require very specific job functions. If the housekeeping department is unionized, the executive housekeeper must consult the contract carefully before launching a comprehensive cross-training program.

Cross-training most frequently begins with jobs within the housekeeping department. This approach minimizes training costs and training time. For example, room attendants already know something about how to treat various stains and how room linens are sorted and how and where they are restocked. This means less time is needed to cross-train a room attendant to work in the laundry.

Training also must include information on safety procedures. If the hotel requires extensive record keeping or reporting, a reliable employee with basic computer skills could be cross-trained to log in inventory reports or other nonconfidential information. Entry-level employees with good communications skills could be cross-trained to answer the departmental phone, handle guest requests and take messages. A few properties are experimenting with cross-training for certain aspects of room attendants' and house attendants' jobs (see Tricks of the Trade 4.1).

### Tricks of the Trade 4.1
### Boosting the Benefits of Cross-training

*The Problem:* Hotels may need six room attendants one day and eight the next.
*The Solution:* Charles Brown Smith, executive housekeeper of the historic La Playa hotel in Carmel, California uses cross-training to keep his department running smoothly in staffing emergencies. He trains new hires to do all the basic jobs in housekeeping, from cleaning a guest room to filling the mini-bars. House attendants are cross-trained in some basic duties of engineering, as well as the basics of how to clean a guest room. If a large group is waiting to check in, house attendants can strip sheets and empty trash while room attendants concentrate on cleaning the guest room and bathroom. Training generally takes one to two weeks. This system pays dual benefits for the department and staff: management does not have to wait for a specialist to get the job done and employees expand their skills. It also helps avoid having to call in extra help, which takes time and adds to payroll costs.

Because the need for room attendants can fluctuate unexpectedly as sudden bad weather closes an airport or a flight is canceled, the executive housekeeper should work with other department heads and the general manager to cross-train employees from other departments to do attendants' work. When cross-training, the focus should be on the basics of how to make a bed, clean the guest room and bathroom, and vacuum.

Housekeeping employees can cross-train in other departments. A housekeeping employee who learns how to book reservations and handle cancellations or interact with guests checking in and out at the front desk will gain a better understanding of how his or her job fits into the overall functioning of the hotel. Interdepartmental cross-training is particularly beneficial in properties with highly seasonal or cyclical business. Employees who would otherwise be laid off from housekeeping during periods of low occupancy or during slow seasons may be able to find work in another department.

**Team training.** Retraining housekeeping staff to team clean must address both job function and the psychology of working as a team (see Figure 4.2). During training, trainers should try out various combinations of staff members and job assignments. Two attendants can be assigned to a room—one to clean the guest room, the other the bathroom. In a three-member team, one attendant cleans and stocks the guest room, a second cleans the bathroom, and a third vacuums rooms and corridors. In some cases, two attendants are assigned to the sleeping area and one to the bathroom. Another attendant does all vacuuming on a floor or in a section. The teams can then be asked to assess their strengths and weaknesses, and to suggest ways to improve efficiency without making the job repetitive. Retraining room attendants to work efficiently in a team cleaning setting can take one to two months.

**Continuing education.** Training should be continuous to keep staff apprised of new housekeeping techniques and products, as well as the state of the industry. Most hotel chains and management com-

**Figure 4.2** *Public area team cleaning assignments can be based on task or area. However, rest rooms should always be assigned to staff members trained to do this specialized task.*

panies send out representatives from the corporate or regional office on a regular basis to update training. They may stay at the property for several days and inspect the operation as well as offering training tips. Most chains also conduct housekeeping seminars in various regions of the United States for executive housekeepers or assistants ready for promotion. The focus is on management skills. Chains and management companies also offer annual housekeepers' meetings with seminars and round table discussions. Some hotel companies have campuses for their own "universities" where general managers and department heads are trained.

Both the IEHA and AH&MA offer seminars, workshops, and continuing education training for professionals. Colleges and universities, including two-year institutions, have varied coursework for professionals. Trade magazines and books can also extend training. Manufacturers generally offer

training on how to use their products and equipment. Nearly all will conduct free training sessions at the property at the department's convenience. Most of these training sessions go beyond simple use of the product or equipment and will include tips on safety, monitoring usage, and general cleaning hints.

## Training the Trainer in One Day

Finding the right people to train staff is imperative. The executive housekeeper should select a candidate who has a positive attitude. The ideal person will be a good communicator in both oral and hands-on skills and should excel in all areas of housekeeping.

Following are steps that trainers should follow to create an effective in-house training program:

1. Develop training scripts for each area of work in the housekeeping department.
2. Practice these scripts under supervision, making any necessary adjustments or corrections.
3. Allow trainers to develop programs for new hires before taking on continuing education and refresher courses for existing staff.
4. Set aside time for demonstrating techniques to employee teams or groups.

## Training Methods

For success in training, it is important to keep training sessions interesting. There are a number of different methods that can be used. These include:

1. **A show-tell-do technique.** This works best for function-related jobs. Figure 4.3 illustrates how to teach this technique.
2. **Audio-visual aids,** from a simple flip chart to sophisticated computer graphics, can cover a lot of ground in a short time.
3. **Filmed videos.** Some properties film trainees on closed-circuit TV so that their performance can then be discussed with the supervisor. Videos also can be used to provide an overview of the property and all job functions. This is especially useful in cross-training because employees are able to see what kinds of skills they will be asked to learn.
4. **Training films,** produced by associations or independent producers of training films.
5. **The "fishbowl technique."** This concept opens up lines of communication. Managers sit in a circle on the floor with hourly employees surrounding them. The hourly employees are told only to observe, not comment. Then managers are asked what they think hourly employees want from their jobs. Managers offer their ideas. The two groups exchange places, and the hourly employees are asked if these are the things they really want. The group breaks out into discussion groups with one manager for every two to three workers. They discuss points made by both sides. The entire group reconvenes, with one worker from each group commenting on the similarities and differences between managers and workers. The final discussion can center on recognizing the objectives of both groups and how best to link them. The result is better communication and a better understanding of both groups' needs.

6. **Role playing.** Using this technique, employees and managers take on each other's roles in theoretical situations. This role playing enables managers and employees to see situations from a different perspective. For example, in some classic training modules, workers were told they were no longer room attendants but truck drivers. A new truck has been purchased and the group must decide which member will drive it. Will the choice be based on seniority? Or on who had the oldest truck previously? The question forces discussion, and the team setting helps increase cooperation and morale. This kind of decision making can be transferred to discussions regarding scheduling and layoffs.
7. **Benchmarking.** Measuring what other companies do and training staff in similar practices can improve performance. Says Ron Cribbet, of The Ron Cribbet Group, "Managers should find out how the best companies do what they do. That becomes the benchmark. From here, they can identify areas that need improvement. This also fosters innovation."

Training can be costly, but the investment has a payoff in terms of increased productivity. Improved morale and efficiency frequently reduce turnover while instilling confidence and job satisfaction. "The quality organization is constantly learning. Management encourages employees to constantly elevate their level of technical skill and professional expertise. People gain an ever greater mastery of their jobs and learn to broaden their capabilities," says Cribbet, a professional trainer and consultant.

If the property does not already have a training committee, management of the housekeeping department should work with other department heads to establish one. The volunteer members from the work force provide valuable input on what training is wanted most and what incentives or rewards would have the most impact. The constructive feedback channeled through such a committee also enhances communication and cooperation throughout the property.

## MOTIVATING STAFF

Motivation is an essential component of good performance. A motivated staff is more likely to be productive and to be loyal to the property. When

---

**HOW TO INSTRUCT**

There are four stages of job instruction. Each time you teach a man to do a job be sure the lesson has each of these four steps.

**Tell Stage**

- Put him at ease. Remember he can't think straight if you make him embarrassed or scared.
- State the job and find out what he already knows about it. Don't tell him things he already knows. Start in where his knowledge ends.
- Get him interested in learning the job. Relate his job or operation to the final production, so he knows his work is important.

**Show Stage**

- Show him, illustrate, one important step at a time. Be patient and go slowly. Get accuracy now, speed later.
- Stress the key points. Make them clear. These will make or break the operation—maybe make or break him.
- Instruct clearly, completely, and patiently—but no more than he can master. Put the instruction over in small doses.
- Place in correct position. Don't have him see the job backwards or from any other angle than that from which he will work.

**Do Stage**

- Have him do the job. Don't bawl him out. Right now is when he needs your patience.
- Have him do each key point for you. A lot of us find it easy to observe motions and not really understand what we are doing.
- Make sure he understands.
- Continue until you know he knows.

**Review Stage**

- Now is the time to give him extra help. Go back to the place where he is having problems. Have him rework these areas. The extra practice will really help now.
- When you're sure he has it let him go to work.

---

**Figure 4.3** *A simple, basic, tell-show-do review technique for instructing stresses the correct way to do the job, not merely how to please the instructor. Instructors should avoid saying, "I want you to . . ." and instead use phrases such as "It's best if you . . ." or "The easiest way to . . ."*

an employee is motivated, it reflects that he or she feels valuable to the establishment and that management is finding ways to make work more enjoyable and rewarding. Motivation leads to greater guest satisfaction and, often, productivity.

## Leading by Example

From grooming to attitude to a commitment to excellence, the executive housekeeper sets the tone for the entire staff. The executive housekeeper's work habits and work attitude can be a primary motivating tool for the department.

To break down barriers between management and staff, the executive housekeeper may assign himself or herself rooms or public spaces to clean periodically. Working alongside staff encourages communication and reinforces the concept of teamwork.

Regardless of the increasing load of paperwork that the executive housekeeper faces, there is no substitute for going onto the floors and observing staff. If the property has a night shift, the executive housekeeper periodically visits the property during the night shift not only to check on work, but to show second-shift workers they are not second-class staff.

## Supporting Staff

Being supportive of staff is one of the best motivators. Executive housekeepers frequently have to work hard to obtain higher salaries or better raises for valued employees. They must look for the best systems, supplies, and equipment to help staff members do their jobs better. They also will be expected to stand by an employee accused of theft during an interrogation. But the executive housekeeper also must be fair. Habitual misconduct or failure to perform up to standards cannot be tolerated, since they hurt the performance of the entire department. Firmness, fairness, and a willingness to listen to concerns are necessary qualities for the departmental leader.

## BUILDING THE RIGHT INCENTIVES

A system of attainable rewards is a tried and true motivator. To be effective, an incentive program must offer something the employee really wants. Incentive programs motivate workers to accomplish a certain task or reach a certain performance standard by offering some type of reward. Incentives can be monetary, such as cash bonuses, or nonmonetary, such as preferred duties, a free night's stay at other hotels within the chain, or free meals. Most properties offer both types to meet all employees' needs.

### Monetary Rewards

Incentives should be linked to staff's needs and departmental goals. If productivity is lagging, the incentives should be contingent on cleaning more rooms or public space. If quality is slipshod, a **point system** should be implemented. Using a point system, the executive housekeeper assigns a point value to each facet of job performance. Monetary incentives can be used to encourage staff referrals (see Chapter 3), input from staff for good ideas, or support for programs such as recycling. Incentives should be offered both for hourly employees and senior staff. Good incentives are ones that benefit both the property and employee.

***Point systems.*** Point systems frequently are used for quality-based rewards. Each staff member's performance is judged against a point system. For a room attendant, points are assigned to each component of a perfectly cleaned room, from dusting in places frequently overlooked to having towels hanging straight and collateral material correctly positioned in the guest room. Every omission or failure to meet standards results in a deduction of points. Some hotels pay a small amount, perhaps 25 cents, to each employee for each task performed correctly; others total up points and pay a larger amount, perhaps $50 to $100 or more, to the employee with the highest point total at the end of each month or each quarter. This program is contingent on daily inspections of all rooms. The same system would work for public area and house attendants and laundry attendants.

Point systems can be linked to specific problems. The executive housekeeper determines what functions need improvement, then designs a "champion bed maker" or "expert grout cleaner" award to recognize good performance in that area.

Point systems not only motivate; they also point out performance problems. If certain staff members consistently receive low scores, for example, they may need to be retrained or they may have other performance-related problems that need to be explored (see Tricks of the Trade 4.2).

---

**Tricks of the Trade 4.2**
**Boosting Productivity**

*The Problem:* Boost productivity.
*The Solution:* Anna Oh, executive housekeeper of the 495-room Crowne Plaza Ravinia, just a short walk across a landscaped garden from the headquarters of Holiday Inn Worldwide, developed a productivity incentive program for the housekeeping staff that does just that. Room attendants have a 17-room quota per 7.5-hour shift. However, any attendant who consistently cleans 18 rooms and still meets quality standards earns an extra 55 cents an hour. Those who clean two extra and meet standards earn an extra $1.10 an hour. Oh says this system has been a good motivator. Through their own productivity, employees have a say in determining how much they can earn. The departmental budget benefits because increased productivity reduces the need for overtime or calling in extra staff.

Oh says the dedicated housekeeping staff and careful inspections have helped maintain standards. Inspections are critical to the success of monetary programs aimed at increasing productivity. Oh also uses remarks on guest comment cards to gauge whether room attendants can clean more rooms without sacrificing quality controls.

Oh balances this program with quality-based rewards. Holiday Inn uses a guest satisfaction tracking system which monitors guests' reactions to their hotel stays through comment cards and other followup. If housekeeping can maintain a guest satisfaction rating of 90 percent or more for four months, the employees receive a bonus. Oh explains that bonus systems like this help staff members feel part of the success of the hotel.

**Team incentives.** To foster cooperation, the executive housekeeper would offer a cash bonus to the team or floor with the highest score each month. Bonuses of perhaps $25 per month are paid to all employees if the department as a whole averages over 90 percent in performance ratings. Additional bonuses could be paid to those with the highest point totals. This puts added peer pressure on all staff members to strive for peak performance.

**Lump-sum bonuses.** The executive housekeeper may offer a flat-rate bonus instead of an hourly increase. The bonus could be an extra $1–$4 per bed (including rollaways) at a family-oriented resort.

Managers can offer a cash bonus for the best idea of the month. Hotels concerned with the environment can offer cash incentives for suggestions on recycling or energy conservation. Some hotels pay out cash bonuses as incentives to improve cooperation and departmental, rather than individual, performance. A few hotel companies are beginning to offer bonuses based on overall quality performance within the housekeeping department.

**On-the-spot bonuses.** Another long-standing approach to drawing attention to neglected areas is to staple $5 or $10 to the executive housekeeper's business card. The card is then placed behind the armoire or on the top shelf of a closet. The room attendants who clean carefully will find the card and receive the bonus.

**Attendance bonuses.** Attendance bonuses can be beneficial if call-offs and no-shows threaten to undermine performance. Ideally, call-offs and no-shows should not be tolerated. But, in tight labor markets, more flexibility may be required. Incentives can be a positive motivator to increase employees' "want-to" factor in coming to work on time each day they are scheduled. The housekeeping department at the Inter-Continental Miami pays a $40 bonus every three months to employees who are on time every day.

**Property-wide bonuses.** Manor Care Hotels created its Gain Sharing program to boost productivity and encourage employees to work together for property-wide goals. Only hourly employees are eligible. The employees can earn a bonus of up to 10 percent of their earnings for the hours worked over a three-month period. The criterion is that the entire property must meet its financial goals. As with many hotel chains, executive housekeepers and other department heads share in the property's success in other ways, including bonuses based on departmental productivity.

Financial incentives should also be structured for senior staff. These incentives can attract potential hires and play a role in retaining staff. To compete with other businesses for talented employees, more and more lodging chains are offering mid-level managers and senior managers stock options at attractive rates. Profit sharing, salary investment plans, and investments for individual retirement accounts also are becoming more readily available for managers in the lodging industry. Most department managers are given bonuses based on departmental performance or attainment of property-wide goals. This bonus can be one-half to one percent of annual salary.

## Receiving Incentives from Guests

Tipping is a kind of guest recognition of the housekeeper's work. The property has little control over whether a tip is left for the room attendant. And, unfortunately, many guests feel no need to leave a tip for the housekeeping staff. Travelers are used to tipping the bellstaff who carry their bags, the door attendants who hail their cabs, and the restaurant waitstaff who bring their food. But in many cases they do not feel obligated to acknowledge the service-oriented housekeeping staff by tipping.

To bring more attention to the role of the room attendant, many properties have **room attendants' cards** in each guest room (see Figure 4.4). These cards may state the name of the room attendant and a brief welcoming message or may direct the guest to call this person if anything was overlooked.

**HELLO AND WELCOME!**

*I'm your Housekeeper.*

*I hope you enjoy your stay with us and your room meets your expectations. Please call our Front Desk by dialing 118 if anything is not to your complete satisfaction.*

*Come back and stay with us again soon. It's a pleasure to have you as a guest!*

*Thank You*

P.S. I have left a questionnaire for you to fill out. Your comments are important to us.

**Figure 4.4** *Comment cards are one tool for measuring whether guests find the housekeeping department's performance satisfactory. The St. James Hotel makes its "Welcome" card do double duty by not only introducing the housekeeper but encouraging the guest to fill out the in-room comment card. (Courtesy of the St. James Hotel, Red Wing, Minnesota)*

Room attendants' cards remain a controversial subject. Some hotel managers use them on the theory that a room attendant will take more pride in his or her work if the guest knows who cleaned the room. Some guests also may feel they are being attended to personally. However, other guests say they feel too pressured to leave a tip for a service they believe is covered by the room rate. One way around the problem is to use the room attendant's card as a point of information. Instead of simply telling the guest who the room attendant is, the card can add that this is the person to contact if the guest needs special request items such as extra pillows or an iron or if some cleaning function needs to be redone.

Because of the many variables involved in tipping, some hotel companies now offer monetary bonuses based on the in-room **comment cards** filled out by guests (see Figure 4.5). These guest comment cards should always include a question or questions regarding housekeeping. These questions should be worded in a way that would encourage the guest to mention the names of room attendants who provide outstanding service. Some hotels pay attendants a $5 bonus each time a guest mentions them favorably by name on a comment card.

If a "tip" is left in the form of a present, which may happen more frequently in clubs or casinos,

the room attendant must report it to the supervisor, assistant, or executive housekeeper. The room attendant must be issued a **package pass** before he or she leaves work. The package pass indicates the parcel has been inspected and what it contains. This is one way of controlling theft of hotel property or pilferage. Gifts of liquor must be turned over to the supervisor. Unopened bottles may be turned over to the food and beverage manager. If the bottle is usable, the room attendant will receive the price the hotel would have paid for such a brand. Opened bottles of liquor left by the guest in the guest room must be discarded.

The executive housekeeper cannot assume that tips will supplement regular wages or replace other monetary incentives. Tipping is strictly voluntary and beyond any manager's control.

## Nonmonetary Incentives

Additional money may be a good motivator, but it is not the only motivator. Knowing what staff members want increases the effectiveness of the incentive. There are a number of additional incentives used to motivate staff.

***Choice assignments.*** Some sprawling resort hotels reward good performance by assigning the room attendant contiguous rooms on easily accessible floors. Few room attendants would look forward to cleaning third-floor rooms with no elevator. Cleaning VIP rooms or suites is considered a prestigious assignment.

***Cross-training.*** Opportunities for cross-training can be used to motivate staff. During periods of low occupancy, the executive housekeeper may allow interested staff to learn basic computer skills by entering housekeeping data. Choosing skills that help the employee qualify for future promotions will increase the attractiveness of learning a new skill.

***Free stays.*** Nearly all major lodging chains reward seniority by offering employees the opportunity to earn free stays or pay rates that are only a fraction of rack rate, which is the published room charge for an overnight stay. For example, like many Holiday Inn properties, the Crowne Plaza in Chamblee gives employees and their families a free night's stay at the property after 90 days of service. After one year of service, some hotel chains offer employees a free three-day stay plus a 25 percent discount on meals at another hotel in the chain. After three years, the free stay may be extended to five days. Such incentive programs are based on avail-

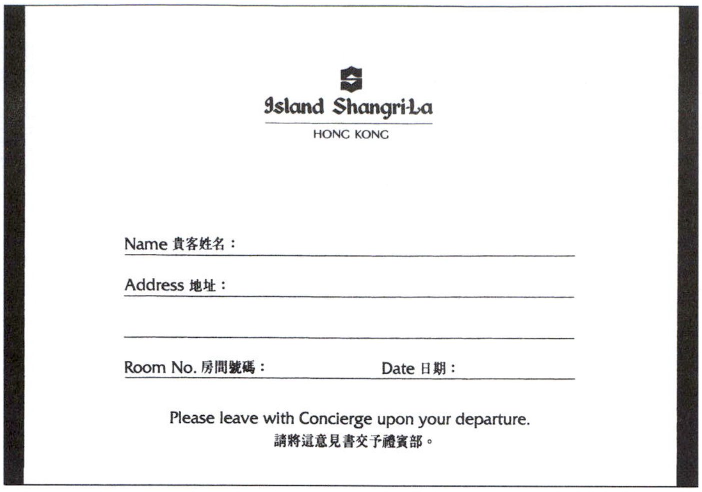
Island Shangri-La
HONG KONG

Name 貴客姓名：

Address 地址：

Room No. 房間號碼：　Date 日期：

Please leave with Concierge upon your departure.
請將這意見書交予禮賓部。

*Figure 4.5* *For comment cards to provide meaningful information, they should be as specific as possible—starting with the basics such as the date of stay and the room number. (Courtesy of the Shangri-La Hotels & Resorts, Hong Kong)*

ability and are not usually available during periods of peak occupancy. This system not only gives the employee a chance to show his or her family the work environment and take vacation; it also lets the employee experience what the guest experiences—to see the public spaces and guest rooms and interact with staff from the guest's perspective.

***Free meal tickets or vouchers.*** These usually work well as incentives because employees generally do not have time to leave the property for lunch.

***Early dismissal.*** Some hotels have implemented a system that allows room attendants and supervisors to leave after their daily assignments are completed. If the room attendant can clean 16 rooms *satisfactorily* in seven hours instead of 7.5, he or she can clock out or bid for extra rooms.

***Other incentives.*** Incentives can range from a free television to a free trip (most likely if the hotel chain is affiliated with an airline or cruise line). Generally, it is preferable to give a lot of inexpensive awards rather than a few expensive ones. Small incentives such as a recognition badge or even a special note from the executive housekeeper can be significant motivational tools. Chain affiliation may open up opportunities to participate in company-wide award programs with generous awards. However, motivation does not have to be expensive or elaborate. (See Tales of the Trade 4.1.)

### Tales of the Trade 4.1
### Pride As a Motivational Tool

Lyn Aoki, director of housekeeping for the 1,800-room Sheraton Waikiki Hotel, Honolulu, offers the following achievement awards to staff for each "perfect room." Inspection is done with the general manager, director of housekeeping and the housekeeping manager. Ten "HONU Dollars" (which equates to US$10) are awarded to each housekeeper for the outstanding work. Simultaneously, the "HONU Dollar" may be given to the attendant first, and each time a discrepancy is found, the attendant would then return one "HONU Dollar." The more mistakes that are found in the room, the fewer "HONU Dollars" or less money he or she will keep. This creates a lot of excitement and fun for the attendants, says Aoki.

While prizes and money are quickly recognized as being the "tricks of the trade," factors that go a long way to motivate staff are:

- Daily recognition of a job done well
- Positive "can do" attitude rather than a negative one

- Bringing out the best in everyone and making them smile
- Creating two-way communication and forming a Housekeeping Council to tackle new and improved ideas for guests, the department and employees. It enhances the housekeeping team to feel empowered and trusted and fosters good will.
- Letting everyone know that they are important and that they make a difference

Jackie Jones, veteran executive housekeeper now with the prestigious Windsor Court Hotel in New Orleans, uses pride as a motivator. The only reward of her customized point system, which she calls her "Star Report," is the knowledge that the employee has done well. Each room attendant's name is posted on a board in the housekeeping department. Performance is rated daily and scores are totaled each month. Anyone who receives close to 100 points for a perfect job receives a gold star; the next level is a silver star, then blue and red—an indicator of poor performance. "Employees work very hard to get the gold and silver stars. They are really angry with themselves if they receive a low grade. I don't use any extra monetary incentives. I want staff members to want to do their best," Jones says. But their accomplishments definitely are recognized. Jones is a firm believer in promoting from within.

Other motivators that work: giving "surprise" rewards such as free meal vouchers for employees with perfect attendance (this also motivates others to try to achieve this) or simply planning a departmental potluck luncheon which encourages socialization and a blending of the various cultures.

## Disincentives

In most cases, incentives are better motivators than **disincentives,** programs that penalize poor performance or low productivity. Used selectively, disincentives can be valuable. To demonstrate how much poor cleaning "costs" a hotel in terms of lowered guest satisfaction and, perhaps, prestige, some properties pay room attendants a flat-rate, up-front bonus at the beginning of each month, perhaps $10 to $20. For every error or oversight, the room attendant must return a certain amount of the advance. To give this program a positive twist, the executive housekeeper could offer a bonus for the most improved staff member each month. A staff member who returned 90 percent of the advance bonus one month but only 40 percent the next month deserves recognition for resolving certain performance problems.

Reversing improved status of employees is another type of disincentive. When dealing with self-supervised room attendants, make it clear that room attendants will lose that status if they fail to meet standards without an inspector. Taking away performance-related privileges is a realistic challenge for staff. The disincentive should be designed to correct a specific problem, not punish an employee. Offering retraining on a one-to-one basis or walking through a certain area and explaining exactly what must be improved to regain the previous status should correct the deficiency without demoralizing the employee.

## EVALUATING PERFORMANCE

Evaluation is a management tool. Handled constructively, it can help each employee maximize performance and contribute better to the department's overall success. Executive housekeepers must strive for professionalism in performance evaluations. Measuring according to objective standards is the best course. Evaluations should be private, fair, and constructive.

### Standards of Performance

For more than 28 years, **Standards of Performance** (SOP) have been part of modern management systems. SOP essentially define departmental tasks in terms of results in key areas. These areas represent the most important contribution the individual or team can make in helping the department accomplish its assigned objectives. The method and date by which a task is to be performed, plus all pertinent data, is incorporated into a standard of performance. At least in theory, the department head can use the SOP as a yardstick to measure the quality and quantity of every individual's performance. SOP also should (theoretically) enable the employee to measure and grade his or her own performance.

SOP provide an objective measure for performance. Objectivity is essential in creating measurement tools. It makes it less likely employees will be evaluated based on personality rather than performance. Each employee should be consulted before and during the development of his or her SOP. When completed, the employee's SOP should be reviewed with him or her as fully as necessary. The executive housekeeper should carefully weigh suggestions and/or objections. If the standards are unreachable or unworkable, morale may plummet or employees simply will begin leaving.

Involving employees in writing their own SOP also helps staff members understand their responsibilities and the work goals associated with them. Through meetings, posted reminders, or during evaluations, the executive housekeeper should encourage all staff members to refer to their own SOP periodically and use them to assess their strengths and weaknesses.

SOP cover both day-to-day tasks and tasks done periodically. Some important issues that need to be addressed include:

- What is the employee really doing on the job?
- Does the employee work well and quickly?
- Does the employee plan his or her work; if so, is he or she well-organized?
- Could the employee do a better job with help?
- Does the employee follow instructions?
- Should this employee be promoted?
- If this employee is promoted, what training would be necessary to prepare him or her for the next assignment?
- How does the employee handle responsibility: Is he or she looking for it or looking to avoid it?
- Does the employee profit from past mistakes?

The executive housekeeper should base his or her rating not only on his or her own observations of employees, but also on the observations of supervisory staff. Various levels of management should have the opportunity to present their views on how the employee performs. It is not uncommon for an employee to work better with one manager than another.

## Efficient Record Keeping

Modern technology has made it easier for executive housekeepers to monitor staff performance. Computerized time clocks track an employee's on-time performance and any tardiness or absenteeism. Computers make it much easier to track all aspects of departmental human resources management. In addition to personal information such as name, address, phone number, and social security number, the employee's file should contain a list of positions

held (including any the employee has been cross-trained to do), salary rate and salary history, performance awards, performance problems, and attendance/on-time history. Any general comments regarding the employee's performance, including recommendations for promotion, can also be logged into these files. Computer records help show the employee's pattern of performance. Privacy codes or passwords must be created to limit access to these files.

Technology supplies valuable objective data, but it is still the manager's responsibility to evaluate performance. Using objective criteria makes it easier to demonstrate why certain employees receive promotions and others do not, or why some are being demoted or disciplined. Objective, clear records are essential if employees should ever bring lawsuits citing unfair treatment.

*Inspection reports.* Daily inspection reports by inspectors or supervisors provide in-depth information on how well attendants perform cleaning tasks each day. The inspection sheet covers all basic cleaning functions. Employees should be given the chance to rectify small errors before any notation is made in their permanent record. Repeated problems should be brought to the attention of a supervisor, the assistant or executive housekeeper.

*Assignment sheets.* Tracking room assignments is one measure of productivity. An attendant or supervisor who consistently handles his or her workload well and still seems able and willing to take on more work should be considered for more challenging assignments or a promotion. If the employee is having trouble doing the assigned work, he or she may require retraining, a transfer to other duties (especially if this a good worker who has physical problems such as an injured back), or discharge.

*Awards and rewards.* Any awards or rewards earned by an individual should be weighed during an evaluation. Whether bonuses or consistently high ratings on guest comment cards, these examples of recognition can underscore the employee's dedication or willingness to put forth extra effort to achieve personal or departmental goals.

*Disciplinary records.* A written record of any disciplinary action should be shown to the employee and placed in his or her personnel file. Such records will be necessary if the employee is fired.

A standardized form as shown in Figures 4.6(a–b) outlines various performance categories,

**ST. JAMES HOTEL**
JOB PERFORMANCE EVALUATION

NAME OF EMPLOYEE: _____  JOB: _____

RATED BY: _____

REVIEWED & APPROVED BY: _____

REVIEWED BY
GENERAL MANAGER: _____

| | OUTSTANDING | ABOVE AVERAGE | SATISFACTORY | IMPROVEMENT NEEDED | UNSATISFACTORY |
|---|---|---|---|---|---|
| | O | AA | S | I | U |

| | O | AA | S | I | U |
|---|---|---|---|---|---|
| **1. QUANTITY OF WORK:** Amount of work done; speed of work: time required; consistancy of productive status. | | | | | |

Reasons for Rating (examples, etc.) _____

_____

_____

| | O | AA | S | I | U |
|---|---|---|---|---|---|
| **2. QUALITY OF WORK:** Accuracy of work; quality of performance (consider errors, etc.) observance of established policies, standards, procedures, methods, etc. | | | | | |

Reasons for Rating (examples, etc.) _____

_____

_____

| | O | AA | S | I | U |
|---|---|---|---|---|---|
| **3. ATTITUDE AND RELATIONSHIP WITH OTHERS:** Courtesy, cooperativeness with and acceptance of guests, supervisors, other employees. | | | | | |

Reasons for Rating (examples, etc.) _____

_____

_____

| | O | AA | S | I | U |
|---|---|---|---|---|---|
| **4. PERSONAL APPEARANCE:** Dress, grooming, personal hygiene, personal habits, conformity with policies and rules. | | | | | |

Reasons for Rating (examples, etc.) _____

_____

_____

*(a)*

**Figure 4.6** *(a–b) Performance Evaluation Form. Evaluation forms should assess key aspects of job performance: skill levels, the quality of performance, and communication. (Courtesy of the St. James Hotel, Red Wing, Minnesota)*

| | O | AA | S | I | U |
|---|---|---|---|---|---|
| **5. WORK HABITS:** Safety, sanitation, cleanliness, housekeeping, use of tools, equipment and materials, conformity with standards and procedures. | | | | | |

Reasons for Rating (examples, etc.) _____

_____

_____

| | O | AA | S | I | U |
|---|---|---|---|---|---|
| **6. DEPENDABILITY:** Attendance, loyalty, amount of supervision required, honesty, observance of standards and conduct. | | | | | |

Reasons for Rating (examples, etc.) _____

_____

_____

**OVERALL RATING:**

_____ OUTSTANDING        _____ ABOVE AVERAGE        _____ SATISFACTORY

_____ IMPROVEMENT NEEDED        _____ UNSATISFACTORY

RATER'S COMMENTS AND RECOMMENDATIONS REGARDING OUTSTANDING PERFORMANCE, IMPROVEMENTS, OR TRAINING NEEDED, PROMOTABILITY, ETC.

_____

_____

_____

COMMENTS OF EMPLOYEE:

_____

_____

_____

THIS RATING HAS BEEN DISCUSSED WITH ME
AND I HAVE RECEIVED A COPY OF THE SAME.

_____        _____
(Signature of Employee)                Date

9/94                              *(b)*

**Figure 4.6**   *(continued)*

making it easier to assess each employee's performance according to objective standards. When evaluating an employee's performance on a one-to-one basis, the executive housekeeper should focus on information obtained in objective measures such as SOP and departmental records. For example, the executive housekeeper could point out that the employee has consistently met the quota of cleaning 16 rooms a day, but inspections show he or she needs to pay more attention to cleaning the bathroom.

## Promotions and Raises

Promotions and raises are very real rewards for good performance. Like many hotels, the management of the Greenbrier Hotel, in White Sulphur Springs, West Virginia, tries to promote from within instead of hiring people from outside the company. All job openings are posted on a bulletin board and anyone who wishes to may apply for that position.

***Promotions.*** Promotions are the ultimate form of recognition for a job well done. With the current trend toward downsizing in mid-level management, the executive housekeeper must find creative ways to deal with promotions.

Good performance can earn a room attendant self-supervision status, which may or may not carry a salary increase. If no increase is given, the attendant may be given a special badge to wear indicating that he or she is self-supervised. A reliable laundry worker may be a good candidate for promotion to room attendant. Top-performing members of cleaning teams can be promoted to team leader status.

When considering an employee for promotion, some key skills to weigh include:

- Loyalty
- Communication skills, both oral and written
- Basic housekeeping skills
- Attendance record
- Desire to progress and assume responsibility
- Ability to delegate and correct constructively
- Ability to interact well with peers and supervisors
- Attitude
- Problem-solving skills
- Leadership abilities

***Raises.*** Pay increases are very basic motivational tools. But they are subject to many factors other than performance. If occupancy is slumping, there may be no money for raises until the next review period. Frequently, when new executive housekeepers take over a property, base salaries may cover a broad range, depending on when employees were hired and what competitive wages were at the time. Raises can be used to address some of these discrepancies—particularly if staff with seniority is working at a lower base rate than recent hires. Pay increases for room attendants are fairly small, perhaps only 25 cents an hour. For top management, annual salary increases are given on a percentage basis. Because base salaries are higher, even a small percentage raise can be a meaningful motivator. Good performance should be reinforced as often as possible with positive comments and documented performance information. Raises and promotions are the ultimate reward for doing a good job.

If the hotel is unionized, a base raise probably is covered in the contract. Raises should be fair and equitable. They should be based on objective criteria so that no employee can claim discrimination on this basis.

## Disciplinary Problems

Some performance problems are too serious to be addressed with a walk-through of a room. All employees should know and fully understand what constitutes a disciplinary problem and how it will be dealt with. The usual pattern for disciplinary action involves several verbal warnings, up to three written warnings and, if the problem remains unaddressed, dismissal. Although it may appear clear that an employee seems unwilling or unable to change his or her pattern of unacceptable performance or conduct, the supervisor must go into the disciplinary process with a positive attitude. Any disciplinary procedures must be completely confidential.

Disciplinary problems generally fall into two categories: misconduct and poor performance. **Misconduct** generally involves disregard for the property's rules and regulations. **Poor performance** refers to the failure to perform job functions.

### Misconduct

Misconduct occurs in many forms. Whether an employee is rude to a supervisor or guest or calls off too many times, misconduct should not be tolerated. Misconduct falls into several main categories.

- **Dishonesty.** Theft, pilferage, or illegal possession of the property of guests, other staff members, or the hotel are the obvious forms of dishonesty. Properties such as Mohonk Mountain House in New Paltz, New York, use a broader definition that also includes misrepresentation in obtaining employment, employee benefits, employee meals or privileges as well as "any action constituting a criminal offense." Any claim of dishonesty should be handled with the help of the security department and also in many (but not all) cases, the local police department.

- **Insubordination.** This is the refusal or failure to follow the instructions of or obey the orders of a supervisor, manager, or department head. Excessive chatting that interferes with the job performance of others, wasting time, abuse of privileges, or lack of cooperation also could be construed as insubordination. If the supervisor's instructions or orders are reasonable, there is no justification for not carrying them out. It should be noted, however, that refusal to perform duties that would violate a union contract is not insubordination.

- **Intoxication and drug use.** Employees should not come to work under the influence of alcohol or be under the influence of alcohol during working hours. Possession, sale, use, purchase, or storage of illegal drugs on property constitutes misconduct, as does working under the influence of illegal drugs. To prevent legal problems, claims of misconduct based on intoxication or drug use should be substantiated by a witness.

- **Discrimination or harassment.** Employees as well as managers should be aware of what constitutes discrimination and harassment.

- **Possession or use of any weapon.**

- **Excessive unexcused absences or tardiness.** Every case of unexcused absenteeism or tardiness must be documented and addressed. If not, it may be assumed that these practices are acceptable for this employee, and legal problems could ensue if the employee is fired on these grounds. The employee manual should state how much notice an employee needs to give before being absent or tardy.

- **Quarreling or fighting.** This would include any loud, abusive language or physical fighting.

- **Conduct contributing to moral delinquency on the job.** This can range from selling illegal drugs to prostitution.

- **Insolence.** In the family atmosphere of Mohonk Mountain House, insolence or "lack of courtesy" to staff members or guests is considered misconduct.

Misconduct also applies to violations of the property's stated rules: smoking in no smoking areas; sleeping on the job; discussing business matters with guests, media, or the general public; unauthorized or careless use of company property; or clocking in for another employee. A written record of each incidence of misconduct should be placed in the employee's file.

The property's definition of misconduct must be spelled out clearly, discussed with employees when they are hired, and included in an employee manual or handbook. The executive housekeeper also must make certain that all supervisory staff understands what does not constitute misconduct: simple negligence or an isolated, minor infraction of the rules.

Inefficiency or the inability to do the work assigned are not considered willful misconduct. These are performance problems. The executive housekeeper and supervisory staff must determine whether the employee can improve enough to perform up to expectations or whether the person will have to be discharged.

## Identifying Illness and Addiction

Performance problems caused by mental or physical illness or as a result of substance abuse (whether alcohol or illegal drugs) pose legal and ethical problems for the executive housekeeper.

The executive housekeeper should discuss the problem with the human resources department to find out what information can be obtained legally and how to substantiate it. If the illness is temporary in nature, perhaps recovery from surgery or a broken limb, the employee could be assigned to light duty. In cases of chronic illness that will affect performance, the executive housekeeper may be able to arrange for a transfer to another department with less physically demanding work and scheduling.

Problems with mental illness should be referred to experts. In cases involving substance abuse, the executive housekeeper should first discuss the correct procedures with the human resources department. Generally, substance abusers are given an opportunity to begin counseling programs unless their behavior justifies summary dismissal. A growing number of hotels have instituted zero-tolerance policies regarding illegal drug use.

## Finding Solutions

Not all employees with performance problems should be discharged. Supervisory staff and managers need to determine whether extra training or additional help could assist the employee in reaching performance goals. The following is a list of options that a supervisor could try before taking disciplinary action:

***On-the-spot retraining.*** If an employee makes a mistake repeatedly during a shift, the supervisor should point out the error and show the employee how to correct it. Then the supervisor should observe whether this mini-training session has done any good. If not, he or she should work one-on-one with the staff member over a few days or a week to make sure the problem is corrected.

***Counseling.*** If informal retraining steps do not correct the problem or if the employee does not respond after a verbal warning, he or she should be "counseled." This entails an official, confidential discussion of what specific things the employee needs to do to perform the job satisfactorily. This is done by the executive housekeeper. The executive housekeeper should be firm in pointing out where improvement is needed, but should also display a positive attitude indicating the employee has a chance to return to good standing. This should be filed in the employee's record. Some hotels allow employees to "erase" this incident from their permanent record if they can demonstrate for six to nine months that the problem has been corrected. This decision depends largely on the type of problem.

***Probation.*** A probationary period allows time for an employee to prove whether he or she can correct the disciplinary problem. It can be used to address either performance or productivity problems. Figure 4.7 is a typical probationary progress report and should be used to track the employee's performance while on probation.

## How to Discharge Employees

Firing an employee is always difficult. The executive housekeeper should work with the human resources department or, in a small property, the general manager, to make this process as professional and legally correct as possible.

Disciplinary action usually follows this course:

1. Minor violations result in verbal warnings or reprimands. The employee must be made to understand specifically what he or she has done incorrectly and what needs to be done to correct the situation. Verbal warnings should be documented, but this does not include suggestions made by supervisors for small matters overlooked during daily cleaning.

2. Major violations or repeated violations result in a written reprimand by the department head. Again, this must be specific and be spelled out clearly in terms of what steps need to be taken. This incident must be logged in the employee's record.

3. Three written reprimands result in grounds for immediate dismissal.

Copies of written reprimands, known as **warning slips,** should be filed with the human resources department and, if applicable, any union involved. A third copy is given to the employee who must sign it as evidence of having received it. If the employee refuses to sign, the supervisor must explain the seriousness of the incident. The employee's refusal to sign will be noted in his or her record, along with the name of the supervisor involved. Most hotels provide for a probationary period for employees who have been reprimanded in writing.

Executive housekeepers with unionized department members should check reprimand procedures with the union. The union may require that all three reprimands must be given for exactly the same infraction of the rules before an employee can be dismissed. In some areas, an arbitration board may determine whether the employee was discharged with cause or should be reinstated. All matters pertaining to disciplinary action must be handled by the executive housekeeper and documented carefully. The goal is to keep litigation to a minimum and to avoid any legal action that could undermine the basic rules and regulations of the property.

**Suspension** is another method of discipline. Like the written warning, the suspension should be made as soon as the infringement occurs. Suspending the employee from work for a certain number of days makes a strong point. The downside of this action is that suspending the employee during a very busy period could hurt the department overall.

**PROBATIONARY PROGRESS REPORT**

Date _____

Name _____

Department _____

Position _____

Hired on (date) _____

Attendance record _____

Skills _____

Experience _____

Training _____

Additional necessary data _____

_____

Performance quota met _____

Relations with peers _____

_____

Relations with supervisors _____

_____

Personality problems _____

_____

Settled satisfactorily? _____

_____

If no explain _____

_____

Does employee need longer periods of probation? (explain) _____

_____

_____

This report has been discussed with employer. (explain)

_____

_____

Employees goal _____

Additional remarks _____

Signed _____ Employee

_____ Supervisor

**Figure 4.7**  *Probationary Progress Report helps a department supervisor to keep track of employees who exhibit some sort of problem from a productivity or disciplinary standpoint.*

If all these steps fail or if an employee is convicted of a crime committed on property (or a serious infringement of house rules or regulations), the executive housekeeper has little choice but to discharge the employee—sometimes on the spot if the person is caught in the act of committing a crime. In most circumstances, the executive housekeeper works with the human resources department to make sure all documentation leading up to the discharge is in the employee's file and that all paperwork is completed correctly.

## SUMMARY

The goal of proper training, motivation, and evaluation is to build a staff that is productive, committed to quality performance, and motivated. Staff members who work under these conditions with equally dedicated co-workers are more likely to stay on staff. Staff retention not only aids in performance, it also helps to ensure the hotel will maintain a reputation for its standards of cleanliness and overall service.

Training must be continuous, thorough, and flexible. A good manager stimulates staff members to look forward to learning more about their jobs and improving their performance. As a departmental leader, the executive housekeeper should also capitalize on retraining programs.

In addition to keeping the department running smoothly, the executive housekeeper must learn to use motivational tools. Monetary and nonmonetary incentives can increase productivity and improve quality. These programs should be adapted according to the employees' needs.

An important part of the executive housekeeper's job is evaluating staff. Among the skills needed to maximize performance are:

- Finding which training methods work
- Creating monetary and nonmonetary incentives to improve performance and morale
- Evaluating staff constructively

- Keeping good records to substantiate that evaluation
- Learning how to turn around poor performance
- Instituting fair procedures for disciplinary actions
- Discharging employees who are unable or unwilling to perform up to standards

## Review Questions

1. Describe several different training methods and the value of each.
2. What is cross-training?
3. Name three incentives likely to increase productivity.
4. Describe some incentives for curbing absenteeism.
5. Define a point system and how it is used in motivating staff.
6. What are disincentives?
7. What are Standards of Performance and how are they used?
8. What records are used to evaluate performance?
9. Describe an instance of misconduct.
10. What is a warning slip and when is it issued?

## Critical Thinking Questions

1. Staff has become slipshod about cleaning bathrooms. How can training and motivation be used together to address this problem?
2. Low occupancy has limited money available for raises. What can the executive housekeeper do to help retain staff and keep morale high?
3. A talented, reliable employee begins underperforming and calling off frequently after being passed over for a promotion. His attitude verges on, but does not constitute, insubordination. How can this be handled?

# 5
# Cleaning Guest Rooms and Bathrooms

## Chapter Objectives

To manage guestroom cleaning operations effectively, the professional housekeeper must:

- Use forecasts and rooms reports to plan assignments
- Prioritize room assignments and create an even distribution of work
- Open the department quickly and efficiently
- Train staff as to how and when to enter guest rooms
- Set up proper cleaning procedures for sleeping areas
- Set up proper procedures for cleaning and sanitizing bathrooms
- Set up procedures for handling special cleaning problems, including bloodborne pathogens
- Conduct efficient inspections
- Communicate cleaning problems to room attendants constructively
- Schedule intensive cleaning work

Cleaning a guest room is not like cleaning one's own home. It is a vital business activity which enables a hotel, motel, or inn to attract guests and make a profit. As a business activity, it requires proper training, ongoing review, and quality control.

The executive housekeeper manages this cleaning operation. He or she is responsible for seeing to it that all guest rooms are cleaned to the property's standards, that they are ready when the front desk is ready to sell them, and that the needs of the guests who pay for the rooms are met. Cleaning procedures must be practical and flexible, and staff must be involved in working constantly to improve them. Only through cooperation and innovation can the staff meet the constant challenge of providing clean, attractive guest rooms.

## OPENING THE DEPARTMENT

Organization is essential to the smooth running of the department. Most executive housekeepers begin work an hour or more before their staffs in order to process paperwork and set the day's schedule before cleaning activities are in full swing.

The executive housekeeper typically starts work by:

- Reading through the night auditor's report
- Checking the occupancy forecast for the day
- Checking the **room status sheet** or floor vacancy report, a chart with the current count of how many rooms are occupied or vacant (see Figure 5.1)
- Conferring with the front desk staff; sales department, or general manager for any last-minute changes regarding check-ins or check-outs that day, special requests and special instructions regarding VIPs checking in that day

The executive housekeeper also reads through reports from the assistant housekeeper on the night shift or, if there is an assistant assigned to the graveyard shift, hears a verbal report as the assistant ends his or her shift. The executive house-

**ЯR**

**RIHGA ROYAL HOTEL**
**NEW YORK**

**FLOOR VACANCY REPORT**

DATE: _____

NAME: _____

FLOOR: _____

| SUITE # | STATUS | REMARKS |
|---------|--------|---------|
| 01 | | |
| 02 | | |
| 03 | | |
| 04 | | |
| 05 | | |
| 06 | | |
| 07 | | |
| 08 | | |
| 09 | | |
| 10 | | |
| 11 | | |
| 12 | | |
| 14 | | |

O = OCCUPIED
V = VACANT CLEAN
C/O = VACANT DIRTY

*Figure 5.1*  *Like most hotel departments, housekeeping has a language all its own. These are some typical abbreviations staff members need to know to understand room assignment sheets and report room status. Computerized room status reports, such as this section of the report used by RIHGA Royal Hotel, New York, give the executive housekeeper an up-to-the-minute overview of which rooms are occupied, which will be check-outs, and which need repairs.*

keeper also checks the year-long frequency schedule to see what special cleaning projects are planned for that day or week. (See Tales of the Trade 5.1)

---

**Tales of the Trade 5.1**
**The Executive Housekeeper's Day**

The challenge and reward of being a professional housekeeper is that no two work days are the same. Showcased here are sample work days for two executive housekeepers.

Rita Genslé, executive housekeeper, 644-room Inter-Continental Miami, Florida:

*6:15 to 6:30 a.m.:* Arrive at work. Check with lobby supervisor regarding performance of an outside contractor that does night cleaning; discuss next night's assignments; write day shift's work orders; read night clerk's report on checkouts; note any special requests or VIP check-ins on room assignments.

*8:00 a.m.:* Conduct staff briefing.

*9 a.m.:* (Thursday): attend executive committee meeting.

*Morning:* Complete necessary departmental paper work, from payroll to cost checks; inspect rooms on various floors. If the laundry manager is off, check laundry operations.

*Afternoon:* Check rooms and public space. Check any rooms not cleaned because of "do not disturb" status; check public areas; write work orders for night shift.

Lyn Aoki, director of housekeeping, 1,800-room Sheraton Waikiki, Honolulu, Hawaii.

*7 a.m.:* Arrive at work; review in-tray and e-mail.

*7:15 a.m.:* Do a quick inspection of the hotel.

*7:30 a.m.:* Brief room attendants; note VIP requests and room assignments; note rush rooms (ones that must be cleaned immediately); post any important departmental notices; attend any special meetings, such as project meetings on renovation.

*8:10 to 8:30 a.m.:* Meeting with housekeeping managers to go over the day's events.

*8:30 to 9 a.m.:* Operations meeting with the Executive Committee.

*Morning:* Handle departmental work. Key priority *now* is to prepare for renovation. Talk with interior design firm and architect. Items to be discussed vary from design and style to fabric and how items can be cleaned and best cared for. Return vendor calls and get product information. "Walk" (inspect) entire property at least twice.

*Afternoon:* Inspect guestroom floors and housekeepers at the same time. Work on budget and cost analyses; catch up on paperwork, check guest comment cards. Also meet with swing shift employees to ensure all work is properly assigned. Make sure everyone is happy.

*6:30 p.m.:* Leave work.

---

Knowing what the occupancy is expected to be, what special cleaning assignments need to be made, and whether any sudden problems need to be resolved is critical to setting up an effective assignment schedule for each day. By the time the supervisory staff arrives, the executive housekeeper should have available:

- A report on arrivals and special events scheduled for the day. Arrival reports indicate what rooms are reserved by room number.
- The room status report
- A set of assignment sheets broken down by section of the property
- A reservations forecast, which indicates what the total volume of check-ins is expected to be

All forms should be dated to eliminate any confusion in making the day's assignments. If supervisors prepare the day's assignments for their crews, they should be given copies of any special instructions pertaining to rooms on their floors or in their sections. Properties with housekeeping computers on each floor simply send these instructions via E-mail to all supervisors.

## ASSIGNING ROOMS

Despite every effort to plan ahead, there is no typical day in a housekeeping department. The housekeeping staff needs to be told each morning what will be the top-priority tasks. The first rule in assigning rooms is to make sure the rooms that will be sold first are cleaned first.

Advance reservations indicate how many early check-ins the property will have. The front desk or sales department usually sets aside a **block** of rooms, which refers to contiguous rooms on a floor, for groups. An individual may request a specific room when making the reservation. A **hard block** is placed on this room, which means the front desk cannot switch the individual to another room. Whoever makes the room assignment should strive to create a reasonable, evenly distributed workload for all employees.

## Starting the Housekeeping Day

Standard day shifts *generally* begin at 8 A.M. However, in Las Vegas, a 24-hour-a-day venue, shifts start later, usually at 9 A.M., because guests sleep later. In a hotel with a highly international client mix coming from many different time zones, the executive housekeeper may have to stagger shifts to accommodate checks-ins and check-outs throughout the day. Cleaning schedules on cruise ships concentrate stateroom and cabin cleaning during times when passengers are touring on-shore or during morning onboard activity programs.

Each department has its own routine, but a typical department opening includes:

1. **Roll call.** The **roll call** checks that everyone who is scheduled that day is present for work. Employees should have clocked in (see Figure 5.2) before roll call and be in uniform ready for work. Roll call, which usually is conducted as a **sign-in procedure** in which employees sign their names on an attendance log when arriving in the department each day, is held in the department headquarters. If staff is too large, room attendants generally sign in with and get room assignments directly from their floor supervisors.

2. **Staff meeting.** After roll call, the executive housekeeper, assistant housekeeper, or supervisor conducts a short staff meeting, perhaps only 5 to 10 minutes. Employees are given a brief overview of how many guest rooms must be **serviced** (cleaned). The staff member conducting the meeting points out which rooms have first priority, how many rooms are occupied, and whether there are any special requests, such as those for rollaways or special pillows. Instructions for any special events scheduled for that day, such as large meetings or conventions, are also pointed out. Assignments regarding **deep cleaning** or **general cleaning,** interchangeable terms for thorough cleaning beyond routine procedures, are also explained.

If particular procedural problems have surfaced, whoever conducts the meeting may point these out briefly and describe the correct procedure. More lengthy discussions are reserved for the weekly scheduled staff meeting usually conducted by the executive housekeeper. Anyone who is responsible for making room assignments must make sure employees understand what work they are ex-

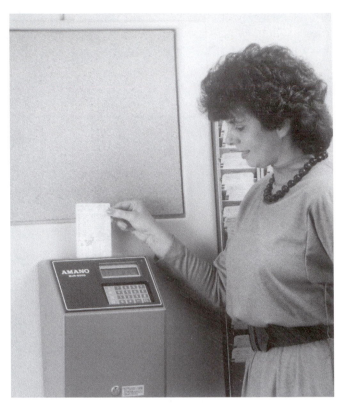

**Figure 5.2** *Computerized time clocks not only generate detailed information about attendance; they can also help the executive housekeeper identify trends in overtime and total labor hours. (Courtesy of Amano Cincinnati, Inc.)*

pected to do that day, even if language problems exist (see Tricks of the Trade 5.1).

## Tricks of the Trade 5.1
## Breaking Down Language Barriers

*The Problem:* Many staff members are not sufficiently fluent in English to understand all assignments, and performance problems arise.
*The Solution:* If the staff is made up of one predominant ethnic group and fluency is a problem, consider conducting bilingual morning staff meetings. Louis Fozman, executive housekeeper of the elegant, 426-room Adolphus Hotel in Dallas, Texas, has many Spanish-speaking employees in the housekeeping department. The assistant housekeeper is fluent in Spanish and translates during these meetings. "We conduct bilingual meetings by choice, not by mandate. We have found it actually saves time to explain everything in both English and Spanish, especially when detailed instructions are required.

By making all of the day's assignments and special instructions as clear as possible in both languages, we no longer have to deal with the issue of staff members not doing something correctly because they did not understand what they were supposed to do. We can also bring up situations we'd like to have addressed, without singling out anyone. And, management and staff can talk frankly in their own language about things they're having trouble with." The bilingual meetings have helped with performance problems as well as making all staff feel that departmental management was making an effort to listen to and understand their concerns.

Another option is to meet with trusted bilingual supervisors, discuss priorities and problems, then let them speak to the attendants. A long-term solution: Encourage staff to take English classes. Some hotels actually bring teachers in to instruct interested staff members after work; others offer tuition reimbursement.

3. **Room assignments.** Room assignments are then made to each room attendant or team. The assignment sheet includes the name of the attendant or team to whom the room is assigned, a list of the room numbers assigned to each attendant or team, and any special instructions pertaining to these rooms.

Room assignments take into consideration:

- **Occupied rooms vs. check-outs.** Occupied rooms, also called **make-up rooms,** take less time to clean than check-outs because they do not require certain steps such as changing the bed pad, bedspread, and bathroom rug, placing furniture back in its intended layout, and looking for lost-and-found items.
- **The timing of check-ins.** Extra staff may have to be called if there will be heavy early morning check-outs and check-ins.
- **Special requests.** Computerized reservations now include space to log in special requests on advance reservations. Satisfying requests for special amenities or supplies for a large number of rooms blocked for groups can add substantial time to the schedule (see Tales of the Trade 5.2).

## Tales of the Trade 5.2
## Handling Special Requests

The general manager and department heads of The Mansion on Turtle Creek in Dallas, a perennial choice on the list of the United States' top hotels, conduct a morning "new arrivals" meeting to review special requests made by their high-end, high-spend clients. Using computer printouts from files that store guest information/preferences noted when reservations are made, as well as detailed guest histories for returning guests, the staff can not only meet but often anticipate guests' demands.

For example, a rock star in the habit of sleeping late asks that all the windows of his suite be masked with blackout paper. Then, there are the more standard requests. A VIP traveling with his family will need to have a crib set up in the suite prior to arrival. A weekending couple asks not be disturbed by housekeeping until after 11 A.M.

Executive housekeepers must be prepared to handle all special requests, whether for special pillows or bedboards, bed extenders for taller clients, or the odd request from movie stars who want their suites painted a special color just for their stay. As one housekeeper puts it, "'No' is not a word in the housekeeping vocabulary. Housekeepers have to be creative and innovative if they are going to succeed."

- **VIPs.** Extra care must be taken with rooms reserved for VIPs. Typically, these rooms are assigned to veteran room attendants who pay close attention to every detail and have demonstrated top levels of performance. VIP rooms require extra cleaning time because they are intended to showcase the best of what the property offers. They usually have the most sophisticated design elements, a separate tub and shower, and extra amenities that frequently include in-room fax machines, second phone lines, wide screen televisions, and sometimes computers (see, for example, Figure 5.3).

## Setting Priorities for Room Assignments

Whenever possible, room attendants or teams should be assigned blocks of rooms on a single floor to minimize time spent walking from room to room. Unless special instructions indicate otherwise, rooms assignments should be done in the following order:

1. Occupied rooms requesting "first" service
2. Check-out rooms blocked for arrival
3. Check-out rooms
4. Occupied rooms

**Figure 5.3** *Attendants must understand that every guest is a Very Important Person. However, hotel managers put in extra effort to impress celebrities, key clients, and heads of state. Because rooms such as the Presidential Suite are meant to showcase the best the hotel has to offer, the attendant who cleans this space must turn in a flawless performance every time. The executive housekeeper would usually check the Presidential Suite personally before the guest checks in. (Courtesy of the Hotel Inter-Continental, New York)*

5. Rooms that are "due to depart" or due-outs but are still occupied. (These should be done only when no other guest rooms can be serviced.)

Special projects are also written on the room assignment sheet. If a room is scheduled for an unusually thorough cleaning, perhaps because a guest smoked in a no-smoking room or the room will be shown to a travel or meeting planner, it may take as much as twice as long to clean.

### Stocking Carts

Supplies and equipment should be waiting for the attendant at the beginning of the shift. The aim is to get the attendants to their assigned floors to be-

gin cleaning as quickly as possible. Each attendant should have enough supplies to cover the day's assignments to avoid losing time walking through the hotel to restock items or waiting for runners to deliver them.

Some properties require that room attendants stock their supplies on carts; others specify that supplies be stored in baskets. A few resorts have transformed electric golf-cart type vehicles or even station wagons into specially outfitted room attendants' carts for transporting supplies from a central housekeeping area to the various buildings that house the guest rooms. Whatever the medium of transport, the room attendants' supplies must be stocked in a standardized way that makes the various items easy to find, easy to reach, and easy to

## Island Shangri-La, Hong Kong

**ProHost Mobile Collector**                    **ProHost Mobile Supplier**
                                                     **(1 per butler)**

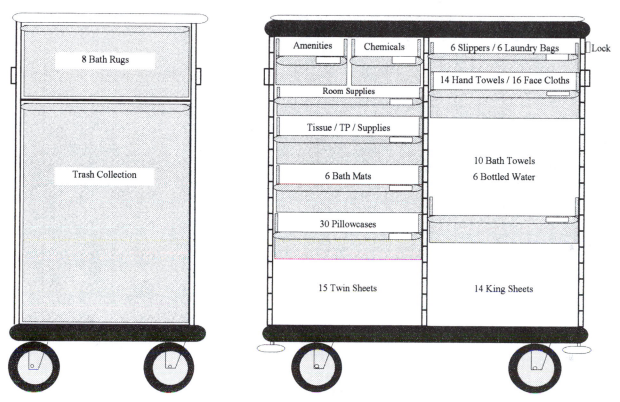

**Figure 5.4**  *To load a cart properly, linens are stored below where they can be stored neatly on shelves, while smaller items sit on top.*

replenish. The executive housekeeper should post a diagram of how the carts or baskets should be stocked in the linen room or wherever carts and baskets are stored and replenished (see Figure 5.4)

Guestroom supplies on room attendants' carts may be replenished by room attendants at the end of their shift. More typically, they are restocked by house attendants or other departmental staff during the night shift. Some items such as clean towels and sheets are standard supplies for the room attendants' carts. These items occupy most of the room under the carts. Towels and linens are stacked on the cart's shelves, along with pillowcases, wash cloths, and extra bath mats.

The top of the cart is reserved for cleaning fluids and guest supplies. Standard cleaners for the guest room include:

• Glass cleaner

• Wood polish

• Bathroom/tile cleaner

• All-purpose cleaner

• Germicide/disinfectant for the toilet

Room attendants' carts also may require special cleaners for surfaces such as marble or antique woods, depending on the type of hotel furnishings and finishes. **Johnny mops,** short-handled mops for cleaning the toilet bowl, and scrubbers may be placed in the portable caddy or carrier with other bathroom cleaning supplies. Guestroom literature usually is positioned on the top shelf of the cart. The sides of the cart are used for the vacuum, broom, and containers for dirty linen.

Supplies differ according to property type and cleaning requirements. Supplies for an economy hotel may include the standard soap/shampoo amenities package for the bathroom, plus guest literature, a bible, promotional materials, matches and, in many chain properties, an in-room coffee or tea maker. For a luxury hotel, the list of supplies could include a wide range of products, from bathrobes to an elaborate amenities package that could include extras such as suntan lotion and perfume or after-shave, paper for the in-room fax machine, and even a clothes brush or lint brush.

The room attendants' carts should be fully stocked, but not filled to overflowing. Room attendants' carts, often called **trolleys** outside of the United States, are highly visible because of their size and the fact that they must be positioned in the guest corridors all morning as guests are checking in and out. Carts with overflowing, dirty linen and untidy heaps of literature or disorganized cleaners do not convey the proper commitment to cleanliness. Supervisors should point out to attendants when their carts are not properly organized.

Some hotel companies or individual hotel owners have decided that room attendants' carts, even properly stocked ones, are simply too obtrusive. In these cases, room attendants carry baskets with cleaning supplies. This can work well, providing each floor has a linen supply closet for items that cannot easily be carried in baskets and must be replenished after each room is finished.

### Issuing Keys

Once room assignments are made and the room attendants take their carts, the executive housekeeper, assistant housekeeper or, in large hotels, the floor supervisor issues keys to the room attendants. Keys must be kept in a locked storage cabinet. Whoever issues the keys must sign them out at the beginning of the shift and sign them in at the end (see Figure 5.5). The room attendants also must sign out and in for the keys they receive that day. This helps protect the room attendant, as well as the hotel and the guest, in the event an item is discovered missing in a guest room.

More and more hotels use computerized locking systems for guestroom doors. Instead of actual metal keys, guestroom attendants and engineers insert specially coded plastic cards into the door locks. If the card has the proper access code encoded on it, the lock is released. If not, the door remains locked. The coding for each type of card— guest, room attendant, and engineer—registers differently so that management can track who was in the room, at what time or times, and how many people entered the room during a given period of time. At the end of that day, the codes are changed. Room attendants receive keys only for the rooms they will clean that day. There is no need to provide master keys or pass keys to room attendants.

## CLEANING THE GUEST ROOM

Systems and techniques differ from company to company, but the goal of housekeeping remains consistent: to provide clean guest rooms, with no trace of the previous occupant, as quickly as possible. Attendants must follow proper procedures and cleaning practices.

### How and When to Enter the Guest Room

Servicing guest rooms properly begins with the right approach to entering them. Every effort should be made not to disturb the guest, even when the guest has not had the foresight to put out a "Do Not Disturb" sign or double lock the door. Entering a room that is occupied may not only embarrass the guest; in some rare instances it also may put the employee at risk. For their own safety and the safety and privacy of the guests, room attendants should be trained in how and when to enter the guest room.

Some of the new locking systems are equipped with a small light on the exterior lock of the guest-room door that shows when the room is occupied. However, the guest must bolt the door from the inside to illuminate the light. A few deluxe hotels have installed special indicator lights outside the guest rooms. The guest can turn on the appropriate light to indicate whether the room should be serviced or whether the guest is in the room. In most cases the traditional door hanger, with its "Do Not Disturb" message, is the only indication that the guest is in the room and wants privacy.

### Entering the Room

Before entering a room, the attendant should check the room status report. Properties in which the rooms status is computerized can provide up-to-the-minute information on which rooms are occupied or vacant at the time the room attendant picks up the assignment sheet.

The attendant then:

1. Knocks three times
2. Announces "housekeeping"
3. Waits a moment for a reply

**Daily Sign In Sheet**

Date:_____

| Name of Room Attendant | Floor Keys | Time In | Time Out |
|---|---|---|---|
| | | | |
| | | | |
| | | | |
| | | | |
| | | | |
| | | | |
| | | | |
| | | | |
| | | | |
| | | | |
| | | | |
| | | | |
| | | | |
| | | | |
| | | | |
| | | | |
| | | | |

**Figure 5.5** *The U.S. Grant Hotel in San Diego, California, like most hotels, requires attendants to sign in for keys before starting work. Simple, computer-generated forms are all that is needed.*

4. If the door is bolted, notes on the assignment sheet that the room is occupied and marks it for later cleaning
5. If there is no reply and the door is not bolted, enters the guest room (see Tricks of the Trade 5.2).

**Tricks of the Trade 5.2**
**What to Do When the Unexpected Happens**

*The Problem:* Despite all of these precautions, the room attendant enters a room and, unexpectedly, finds the occupant inside.

*The Solution:* If the guest is sleeping or, as sometimes happens, in the shower, the attendant should simply leave. If the guest is awake, the attendant should apologize for the intrusion and leave the room as quickly as possible. As part of their training, attendants should be advised that they may encounter guests in various situations—just walking out of the shower or getting dressed. These circumstances are rare, but most attendants will face them at some time in their career. Executive housekeepers must prepare staff for these situations, stress the importance of remaining calm and poised, offer suggestions on how attendants should excuse themselves, and advise them to leave without further discussion.

Attendants should not begin cleaning while the room is occupied. This poses unnecessary safety and security risks for the attendant as well as the guest.

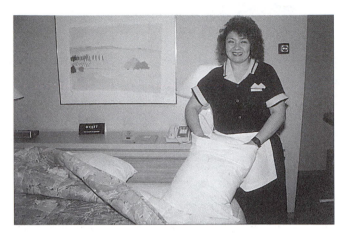

**Figure 5.6**　*Pillows, like bedspreads and blankets, should never be allowed to touch the floor for reasons of hygiene. Clean pillow cases or pillow slips should be put on as the last step in bed making, so that the clean pillow case does not touch a dirty sheet. (Courtesy of the Hyatt Regency, Chicago)*

## Do Not Disturb Rooms

Procedures should be set up for dealing with rooms that have "Do Not Disturb" signs after 2:30 P.M. to 3 P.M. Room attendants should point these out to their supervisors. The supervisors in turn usually will ask the rooms division to check these rooms by phone or in person. In most cases, room attendants should not knock on a door with a "Do Not Disturb" sign or enter the room. If the property's policy allows room attendants to knock on doors with "Do Not Disturb" signs after noon or 1 P.M., the room attendants should be instructed to follow the usual procedures for entering the guest room. If the guest is in the room, the room attendant should ask politely when the room could be serviced.

## Typical Approach to Cleaning

The most efficient way to clean a room will depend on both the type of room and type of cleaners being used. Based on constant evaluation, best practices should be developed and reviewed regularly to find further ways to improve cleaning procedures.

The focus of guestroom cleaning is on efficiency and quality. To reduce labor time in each room, the attendant should clean clockwise or counter-clockwise which eliminates criss-crossing the room and wasting both steps and time. Twenty minutes to clean a room is not much, so every movement has to count.

Typically, the attendant would follow these steps:

1. **Open up the room.** Open the black-out drapes and sheer curtains and turn on all the lights. In properties with windows that open, open the windows, weather permitting, to air out the room.

2. **Make the bed. Strip** (remove the sheets from) the bed and put on fresh, clean linens. Most beds are made from one side, which saves steps and speeds up the process. Posters showing the correct way to make a bed should be mounted in the linen room. An experienced room attendant using the proper technique should be able to make a stripped bed in less than three minutes.

Do not allow the bedspread, blankets, or pillows to touch the floor for reasons of hygiene (see Figure 5.6). Dirty linen is stored in specially designed areas on the sides of the room attendants' carts and should be emptied down the laundry chute on the floor when it is flush with the top of the cart, not when it is overflowing.

To prevent problems with bloodborne pathogens, such as the AIDS virus and hepatitis B, and contamination from bodily fluids, place any blood- or fluid-stained linen, including the bed pad, in a separate plastic bag, sealed and marked as a biohazard for the laundry. Gloves should always be worn in these cases. The supervisor is notified if there are stains on the mattress. It, too, is spot treated and disinfected or replaced.

3. **Collect and remove trash.** Collect all trash in the room and empty the ashtrays. (More information on trash removal and recycling will be covered in Chapter 14.) Ashtrays usually are emptied

into the toilet rather than into the trash to prevent any possible fire hazard. Dispose of or recycle used plastic drinking glasses; wash glass glasses and carafes for coffee or tea makers provided there is access to hot enough water to sterilize the glasses) or store them in the appropriate racks for transport to the kitchen to be washed. In properties with recycling programs, newspapers and cans are separated into different containers.

4. **Clean the bathroom.** The guest bathroom must be thoroughly cleaned and disinfected. Use of a germicide has become standard at a time when concern over pathogens borne in bodily fluids is paramount to both guests and housekeeping employees.

## CLEANING THE GUEST BATHROOM

The typical order for bathroom cleaning is to clean the tub first (or tub then shower stall if the tub and shower units are separate as they are in many modern luxury hotels), then the shower curtain or door, walls, basin, counter, toilet, and floor. Clean surfaces such as countertops with an all-purpose solution; marble should be cleaned with a special marble cleaner.

Many executive housekeepers are replacing all-purpose cleaners with cleaners that are also disinfectants. This new generation of bathroom disinfectants also works well on tile and surfaces other than marble.

Some environmentally friendly cleaners require a longer time to be activated and should be sprayed on the bathroom surfaces and poured into the toilet before cleaning the sleeping area. Though they need to be applied as the first step in room cleaning, they may actually save time because they require less scrubbing. Those that are activated on contact can be mixed in a bucket when bathroom cleaning begins. Then the bottom of the shower curtain is soaked in the bucket or sponged off to remove any soap scum or mildew (see Tales of the Trade 5.3).

speeches, he told his distinguished listeners, "Ladies and gentlemen, I have but one thing to say on this important occasion—please, please, please, put the shower curtain inside the tub before your shower."

Although told in humor, the comment points out how a small act, such as a guest or attendant leaving the shower curtain outside the tub, threatens to cause severe damage to a hotel. Even small amounts of water leakage, left unaddressed, can eventually cause deterioration of the flooring.

To clean shower doors, carefully climb inside the dry tub to clean the overlapping double doors. Whether sliding doors or hinged doors, the shower doors must be cleaned daily to prevent spotting or soap buildup. Applying appliance wax on the inside of the doors and rails make them less susceptible to buildup.

Clean bottom rails carefully to control mildew and soap buildup. Sponge off tub tiles and fixtures, then dry them to a shine. The new preformed fiberglass tub/shower combinations have reduced cleaning time because there is no need for a tile surround on the tub/shower.

Abrasive cleaners may be necessary to clean difficult stains on tubs or in sinks that can be treated with abrasives (many cannot). However, they should not be used on the metal sections of bathroom fixtures because they may remove the protective lacquer finish and cause the fixture to discolor.

In-room whirlpools are both challenging and time-consuming to clean. If reaching into the unit to clean it is impossible or impractical, make sure the unit is turned off, then climb inside and clean it (see Tricks of the Trade 5.3).

**Tales of the Trade 5.3**
**The Importance of Details**

The seemingly unimportant issue of whether shower curtains should be left inside or outside th tub has drawn concern from industry figures as renowned as Conrad Hilton. During several

**Tricks of the Trade 5.3**
**Cleaning Whirlpools**

*The Problem:* Hair clogs pose a tough challenge in cleaning whirlpools and keeping them running smoothly (see Figure 5.7).
*The Solution:* Lois Theis, executive housekeeper of the upscale 60-room, St. James Hotel in Red Wing, Minnesota, tried a long list of products before discovering a product designed to clean out

**Figure 5.7** *Whirlpool tubs, fast becoming a standard amenity in suites, pose a variety of cleaning challenges, ranging from how to dissolve hair clogs to how best to clean these deep tubs. (Courtesy of Kohler Co.)*

milking machines. It is gentle to the plumbing, says Theis, and effective.

Mildew is one of the most persistent cleaning problems the housekeeping department faces. The best way to control it is to prevent it. "We don't use bleach, so the only answer is to work at cleaning the mold and mildew constantly," says Peggy Andersen, general manager of the elegant 10-room Aveda spa/hotel in Osceola, Wisconsin, which is housed in a converted turn-of-the-century mansion. In some climates, room attendants may have to scrub the grout daily. Tile and especially tub grout should be wiped dry to prevent mildew. Grout cleaners and grout whiteners may be useful.

Disinfect the toilet bowl. Clean the toilet bowl itself with a Johnny mop or a **swab,** which is a nonabrasive scrubber with a long handle. Do not clean toilet bowls by hand using sponges. After cleaning the bowl, clean the seat, lid, tank, outside, back, and bottom of the toilet bowl and wipe them dry. Clean and dry pipes. Use disinfectant to clean overflow holes for drains. Supervisory staff should stringently enforce rules requiring that room attendants wear plastic gloves while cleaning the bathroom.

Once the toilet is cleaned, empty the trash basket. Used pieces of guest soap or partially used containers of liquid guest soap should be collected and stored on the room attendant's cart. Never throw bar soap into the toilet because it may cause clogs.

Clean vents with long-handled brushes and rags. Wipe off light fixtures with a rag or duster. Finally, wash the floor. The remainder of the all-purpose cleaner in the bucket should be sufficient.

5. **Restock in-room literature, supplies, and amenities.** If the room has a fax machine or copier, check and restock the paper supply on the units. Coffee and tea making supplies also should be restocked. If any paper from the in-room stationery packet has been used, replace the entire folder. This actually takes less time than reinserting additional paper. Some hotels are shifting away from restocking stationery in order to reduce paper waste.

6. **Dust.** Dust plastic laminate surfaces with a cloth dampened with all-purpose cleaner (see Figure 5.8a). Clean wood furniture with furniture polish or lemon oil. Pick up, dust, and put back anything except purses, wallets, jewelry, money, or medications. These items should not be touched. Never throw any guest belongings away. If surfaces are extremely cluttered, do not do any dusting that day. Note clearly on the assignment sheet why the room was not dusted and discuss this with the inspector or supervisor. Place room service trays in the corridor and notify the room service department the trays need to be picked up.

7. **Locate lost-and-found items.** If the room is a check-out, note any item the guest has left, indicating the room number where the item was found. Collect all such items and turn them in to Lost and Found. Note any item in the guest room that is in need of repair.

8. **Vacuum.** Before beginning the vacuuming, make sure there is no need to re-enter the room. Start vacuuming at the far corner of the room and work back toward the door. Turn off the light, close and lock the door, and move on to the next room (see Figure 5.8b).

## Occupied versus Check-out Rooms

Check-out rooms are cleaned more intensively than occupied rooms. As indicated earlier, all bed linen is changed, including the bed pad and sometimes the spread. Cleaning is more detailed in check-out rooms. In addition to the standard cleaning steps already described in this chapter, attendants cleaning check-out rooms should:

• Wipe out and/or dust closets and drawers
• Clean door sills, including sills leading to balconies

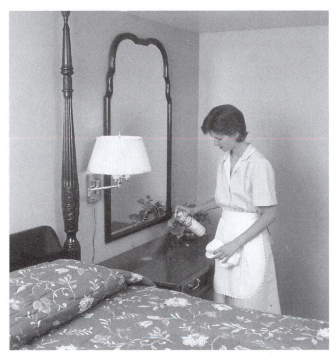

(b)

(a)

**Figure 5.8** *(a) Thorough dusting is an essential component in proper guestroom cleaning procedures. Room attendants should be trained to pay attention to often-overlooked areas such as mirrors and picture frames, as well as door frames and drawers. (Courtesy of Ecoloab) (b) Vacuuming is the last step in room cleaning. The attendant should begin at the back corner, work toward the door, turn off the light, and leave the room. (Courtesy of the Shangri-La Hotels & Resorts, Hong Kong)*

- Dust picture frames
- Remove marks or stains
- Disinfect surfaces such as the telephone mouthpiece that may harbor bacteria or bloodborne pathogens
- Set the thermostat back to the level established by the property's policy
- Check for any items left behind by the previous guest
- Replace furnishings to their original positions

## Rush Rooms and Brush-up Rooms

All rooms must be cleaned quickly, but there is a category of priority rooms in which time is of the essence. These are called **rush rooms.** They take priority over all other assignments because, in the case of the rush room, a guest is waiting to check in. The front desk alerts the supervisor via beeper or on a computer printer on the floor that the rush room is needed. As soon as an attendant is availa-

ble, the supervisor assigns him or her to the rush room. If possible, two attendants are assigned to the rush room. In the case of a VIP rush, an entire crew may be reassigned to work on the room. All cleaning procedures are the same as for any check-out room, and nothing should be overlooked.

A **brush-up room,** or **touch-up room,** does not require thorough cleaning. The most common brush-up rooms are those in which guests returned after check-out to use the bathroom or make a phone call or those in which guests were waiting while a hard-blocked room is cleaned. In a brush-up room, the bathrooms must be thoroughly cleaned and the linens changed. If the bed has been used, the attendant must change the linens.

## Specialty Cleaning

All-suites and resorts with kitchenettes require the extra step of kitchen cleaning. With more space and furniture, all-suite rooms require more time than traditional rooms (see Tales of the Trade 5.4). In all-suites, cleaning the "kitchen" may involve simply cleaning the microwave, the sink, countertops, the inside and outside of a mini-refrigerator and setting out dishes for the F&B department to collect and wash.

---

**Tales of the Trade 5.4**
**Meeting the Cleaning Challenges of an All-Suite Hotel**

The luxury, 500-suite RIHGA Royal Hotel in New York City poses the double housekeeping challenge of efficiently cleaning its spacious suites and maintaining its uncompromisingly deluxe standards. Miriam Albano, the executive housekeeper who joined the hotel's pre-opening team prior to its debut in 1990, designed innovative, flexible systems to meet this challenge.

She first laid out sections to reduce walk time and increase productivity. She and several staff members conducted time and motion studies before establishing a quota of 14 credits, which translates into seven standard suites. The hotel is segmented into three different types of suites, from the standard Royal Suites to the pampering Pinnacle Suites, which are worth more credits. Housekeeping staff are rotated so that all attendants have a rotation in each type of suite.

"Our staff members really get excited about this rotation. It keeps them motivated. It also means that the attendants become experienced in cleaning all three types of suites, so that the managers (who inspect and supervise) can expect the same service standards from one attendant to the next," explains Albano, who has worked at such prestigious hotels as the Waldorf-Astoria and The Plaza in New York and the Westin St. Francis in San Francisco, California. Equally important is the message the rotation sends: that every attendant is up to the challenge of cleaning the fine items in the best suites, which start at $500 a night, and that they are trusted.

Rotations last three months. This gives attendants enough time to learn to work efficiently in the setup of each suite. Attendants use the same system for all types of suites:

1. Beds are stripped and soiled linen is removed. "By removing soiled linens and towels first, the attendant knows exactly how much clean linen will be needed," Albano says. This is particularly important because the attendants do not use carts; they carry cleaning supplies in baskets and have special fabric bags for fresh linen.
2. Bathrooms are cleaned.
3. Sleeping area is cleaned.
4. Living room is cleaned.

Cross-training adds flexibility. When necessary, Albano assigns teams to clean suites. Not only has this system succeeded from an operational standpoint, it also works in terms of human resources. Turnover has been low, says Albano.

---

In extended-stay properties and other properties with full kitchens, cleaning is more involved. All appliances must be thoroughly cleaned, from the toaster to the oven and full-sized refrigerator. Both the interior and exterior must be cleaned and sometimes polished. Dishes must be washed. All supplies must be checked and restocked.

Fireplaces pose a time-consuming cleaning challenge. Not only do the fronts and grates have to be cleaned, but the windows in the room and, sometimes, fabrics, need more frequent cleaning. Charles Brown Smith, executive housekeeper for the elegant La Playa Hotel in Carmel, California, recommends cleaning the brick once a month with a scrub brush and detergent diluted in water. He also instructs attendants to use a nonfog cleaner on the windows daily when the fireplaces are in use in the property's villa-like "cottages." The special cleaner helps keep smoke from clouding the windows and makes them easier to clean.

## Team Cleaning

Cleaning procedures must be adapted for properties where attendants work in teams. The same work must be done, but it is assigned differently. As indicated in Chapter 4, one or two attendants clean the sleeping area while another attendant cleans the bathroom. If one attendant is assigned only to do vacuuming, he or she moves around the room in the same pattern as the attendant dusts (see Tales of the Trade 5.5).

# GENERAL CLEANING

Daily cleaning assignments cannot address all of the cleaning challenges of the guest room. **General cleaning,** also known as **deep cleaning** or simply **general clean,** refers to a thorough cleaning process that includes tasks such as cleaning under beds and heavy furniture and upholstery cleaning. General cleaning requires more time, equipment and, sometimes, personnel, than could be appro-priated on a daily basis when quick **turnaround** of the rooms from dirty to clean is critical.

## Scheduling General Cleaning

Although general cleaning functions are usually mapped out on annual basis, the exact scheduling must be rechecked against occupancy forecasts for the week the work is planned. Work that affects entire sections of the property, such as buffing and waxing wood floors, should be scheduled only during periods of low occupancy.

Some aspects of general cleaning, such as cleaning vents and high dusting, are usually added to regular room assignments without affecting the room attendants' quotas. By scheduling each room attendant an added task for one or two rooms a day, or several rooms for teams, each room will have been given this necessary special attention in a short period of time. Special general cleaning assignments should be added only when the room attendants will not be working under severe time constraints to accommodate a heavy volume of early arrivals.

General cleaning should not be scheduled for rooms or spaces in the midst of renovation or major repairs. For example, if bathroom tile is being regrouted or marble floors are being restored, general cleaning would be scheduled after this work is completed. All department heads are notified well in advance of the scheduling of extensive repair work.

The frequency of general cleaning depends on the work being done and the expectations of guests. Deluxe properties with light guestroom carpeting may have to schedule spot cleaning once a week. A mid-tier property with darker, patterned carpet would schedule spot cleaning less frequently. Mattresses are turned every three months. Some elements, such as scrubbing tile grout, may be done at least once a week.

## What Needs to Be Done

General cleaning involves a thorough cleaning of the guest room as well as some preventive maintenance. What it entails varies by the type of property and the furniture, fixtures, and equipment, but the basics should always be covered.

***Turning mattresses.*** Rotating mattresses regularly extends the life of the mattress and insures that they will wear more evenly. Generally, flipping and turning mattresses is done by the house attendants (see Figure 5.9a). The most efficient scheduling would be to have the house attendant working with two room attendants. The room attendants would strip the linens off the bed, the house attendant would rotate the mattress, and the room attendants could then make the bed. Rotating mattresses can be done by cleaning teams as well. It should be done every three months, and inspectors should check that mattresses have been rotated. An easy reminder is to have "January" and "April" written on tags on the opposite corners of one side, and "July" and "October" on opposite corners on the reverse side. Mattress manufacturers will add these tags on request (see Figure 5.9b). Blankets, spreads, and pillows should be exchanged for freshly cleaned items.

***Cleaning windows and draperies.*** Windows should be washed and window treatments, including draperies and sheers, should be cleaned (see Tricks of the Trade 5.4). Window sills, casings and ledges should be washed.

---

### Tricks of the Trade 5.4
### Cleaning Black-Out Drapes

Black-out drapes are difficult to clean because of care needed in the handling of the black-out lining. Margit Abendroth, executive housekeeper of the upscale Colombo Hilton in Colombo, advises that the black-out curtain be joined to the drape using Velcro™ tape. The two sections can be easily separated for cleaning purposes, and each can be cleaned in the most efficient way to maximize the life of the fabric.

---

***Washing finishes and fixtures.*** Baseboards with a washable finish should be washed and wiped dry; wooden baseboards should be wiped dry. Lamps and shades should be washed; glass covers on lights also should be washed. Glass tops on desks should be removed and the area underneath cleaned thoroughly. Everything that is washable in the room, from towel hampers to wastebaskets and closet shelves and poles, should be washed and dried.

***Stain removal.*** Whitener may be needed to brighten tile grout. Spots and stains on carpets and upholstery fabric should be treated, and repairs made where necessary. Toilet bowls should be scoured and checked for corrosion under the rim. Paint spots should be scraped off of surfaces. Marks should be removed or painted over.

***Vacuuming.*** All furniture should be moved and the carpet underneath should be vacuumed. Upholstery, too, should be vacuumed during a general cleaning. Cushions should be removed so that stains can be treated, lost objects can be removed, and dust or other particulate matter can be vacuumed.

House attendants should be scheduled to do tasks such as clean mirrors over chests of drawers, clean closet ceilings, clean room ceiling lights, and vacuum upholstery and box springs. In some hotels, the house attendant and room attendant work in two-person teams, with the house attendant doing heavy work such as vacuuming, turning the mattresses, and positioning the furniture and the room attendant cleaning the room.

## Night Service

Guestroom cleaning tasks generally conclude at the end of the day shift in economy and mid-tier hotels. If a problem arises after that time, a staff member may be called from another department to resolve it. However, in upscale properties and in casino hotels, the housekeeping department also may be responsible for night service. Pressures to downsize staff are making night service less common. Hotel companies must weigh how important it is to their guests. In some cases, the compromise is to provide night service to all **upgraded rooms,** such as those on executive or club floors, junior suites and full suites, and to make it available on a "request only" basis for standard rooms.

The most common feature of night service is **turndown.** This typically involves removing the bedspread, folding it and storing it, then pulling back the blanket and sheet to form a triangle. Generally, the room attendant turns down the side of the bed facing the nightstand. If the room has two beds and two occupants, both beds should be turned down. The standard amenity for turndown service is a "goodnight" mint left on the pillow, though give-aways range from cookies to packets of relaxing herbal tea and even teddy bears for children. Since many special requests are made during the night shift, as guests return to their room after their business or leisure day is over, the room attendant may leave a card with instructions for the

*(a)*

*(b)*

**Figure 5.9**  *(a) Rotating mattresses quarterly dramatically extends the life of the mattress. The mattress is flipped over and turned to ensure more even wear. (Courtesy of Leggett & Platt) (b) To help mattresses wear evenly and thus prolong their life, these two labels clearly define alternate rotations. A built-in calendar system shows when to rotate—quarterly. Completely self-contained, this tagging requires no record keeping. The labels, guaranteed effective for the life of the mattress, have directions in English and Spanish.*

# BALLY'S
## LAS VEGAS

*Dear Guest,*

*We are hesitant to remove articles from your bed.*

*Please touch Housekeeping on your telephone for service.*

*Thank you.*

**Figure 5.10** *A card like this makes it clear that housekeeping was unable to provide proper service because personal items were left on the bed.*

guest to call the housekeeping extension with any special requests.

Room attendants doing only turndown can be assigned up to 120 rooms per night. However, at some deluxe hotels the service is more demanding and a more realistic quota would be about 50 to 60 rooms. Usually, two attendants work together in each room for full night service. Full night service would include:

- Airing out the guest room, if the room has windows that open.
- Emptying the ashtrays and wastebaskets.
- Removing glasses if the guest had bar service.
- Checking the bathroom for cleanliness and replacing used towels and bathroom supplies.
- Closing the draperies.
- Turning down the bed.
- Turning on the nightstand lamp.
- On cold nights, placing an extra blanket at the foot of the bed.
- If the room is occupied by two people, making sure there is enough bathroom linen and soap for the second person.

A polite notice from the hotel's management should be posted in each room explaining that guests should clear their belongings off the bed if they want turndown service (see Figure 5.10).

## INSPECTION

The saying that "your last look at the room is the guest's first look" is still the working guideline for inspection. Self-inspection or staff inspection should monitor the general cleanliness of the guest rooms, as well as often overlooked details such as cleaning the receiver on the phone or vacuuming behind heavy furniture. The bottom line is that the guest should not be the one who discovers what was overlooked or done improperly.

### Inspection Checklists

In properties that have inspectors, inspection begins with the rooms report. Using the rooms reports handed in by the room attendants, the inspectors begin checking the room attendants' progress. The inspector first looks at the room attendants' carts to see whether they are properly equipped and supplied. If the cart is not stocked properly or is messy or dirty, the problem should be brought to the room attendant's attention and be rectified promptly.

An inspection checklist is a valuable tool. Inspection procedures differ for rooms with different status, as outlined in the following.

1. Inspect check-out rooms that have been cleaned. A check-out room should not be out of inventory for more than an hour after the guest departs. Pick up an updated list of check-out rooms at least once every hour from a printer on the floor or have it relayed from housekeeping. Some key areas to inspect are:

- Bathrooms. Lights or lamp shades should be clean and dust-free. Bulbs should be the correct wattage. Shower walls should be clean. Drains should be free of hair and soap scum. All amenities should be stocked. Floors and pipes should be clean and free of dust and hair.
- Beds. Lifting spreads and blankets will insure the linen has been changed. Pillows, spreads and dust ruffles (if applicable) should be straight and properly positioned, not off to one side. If the bed frame does not extend to the floor, the area beneath the box spring should be checked to make sure it has been vacuumed and that nothing has been left in the area.
- Carpets. Carpets should have been vacuumed well. Corners and areas around furniture should be checked for dust.
- Lamps. All lamps should be dust free and in working order, with bulbs of the correct wattage.

- Night stand or night table. The proper guest supplies, such as note pads, should be stocked and properly positioned—both on top of the night stand and in the drawer. The radio and/or clock should be checked to insure they are working properly. The inspector should pick up the phone to make sure the mouthpiece has been cleaned, checking for dirt or unpleasant odors.

- Closets. Walls should not show any marks from baggage. The shelf and clothes pole should be dust free. Hangers should be properly positioned; bent hangers should be replaced. Laundry bags should be restocked. Any mirrors or louvers should be clean and free of dust. Doors should open and close properly.

- Vents. All vents should be clean and in working order.

- Mini-bars. The entire unit should be clean, stocked, and checked to make sure it works properly. Clean glasses should be stocked inside. Ice buckets should be free of water spots inside and out.

- Walls. Walls in the bathrooms should be cleaned daily. Guestroom walls should be checked to determine whether they require washing, painting, papering, or other repairs. Pictures or paintings should be free of dust and should be hanging straight.

- Windows. In addition to having clean tracks and sills, windows should be smudge free. Sheers should be closed; draperies should be opened to the ends of the windows.

- Guestroom supplies. All items in the guest room should be stocked and in good condition. This includes the rate card which is in the holder on the back of the door and the diagram showing how to exit the room in case of fire. Paper items such as phone books should be replaced if they are torn or dog-eared.

- Waste baskets and ashtrays. These should be empty and clean.

- Metal fixtures. All metal fixtures, including door knobs and faucets, should be free of dust, smudges, and fingerprints. Badly scratched fixtures or those in need of repair should be reported.

- Lost items. Inspection of any check-out room should include checking for any item the guest may have left behind.

 2. Inspect occupied rooms. Focus on whether the bathroom has been thoroughly cleaned, whether the bed linen and towels have been changed, whether the main components of the guest room are in working order, whether amenities and guest supplies have been restocked, whether the trash baskets and ashtrays have been cleaned and emptied, and whether the room has been vacuumed. Guests' belongings should never be disturbed during an inspection.

*Suites.* In addition to checking the sleeping area and bathroom, inspect the living room or parlor and kitchen area. Check under any loose cushions and between the sides of cushions and chairs to make sure they are clean and that no small articles have slipped into this area. If the living room or parlor has a sofa/sleeper, make sure the linen has been changed. Microwaves, countertops, and sinks should be clean.

 In all rooms, inspectors should look for any damage or any items in need of repair. Inspectors and floor supervisors also should monitor wear, especially on fabrics, linens, and carpet. Part of the inspection process should be to make sure no hotel property is missing from the room. If hotel property is missing, the loss should be reported to the security department. A final rooms report should be compiled, showing which rooms could not be serviced. This report is turned in to the executive housekeeper. A copy is provided for the night shift as well. Inspectors also may collect keys from the room attendants on their floors at the end of the shift and inspect room attendants' carts and closets.

## Commonly Overlooked Areas

With experience, inspectors can check the points mentioned earlier in this chapter quickly and accurately. During slow seasons or before planning a general clean, the inspectors should take time to check some areas that may have been overlooked.

- **Cords.** Dust on electrical cords not only detracts from the overall cleanliness of the room; it is also a fire hazard.

- **High spaces,** which includes the tops of furniture and picture frames

- **Hard to reach floor areas,** such as mopboards and corners.

- **Hair dryers.** If the bathroom is equipped with a hair dryer, the lint screen should be checked for dust or hair.

- **Ceiling fixtures,** which should be checked for cleanliness and bulbs of the proper wattage.

- **Neatness.** Furniture, linens, and guest amenities and supplies must be properly positioned. Towels must hang evenly, as well.
- **Odors.** Inspectors should check for foul odors upon entering the room. Checking for smoke odors in nonsmoking rooms is a priority because the rooms cannot be resold until all of the smoke odor has been removed.

## Communicating Problems

Finding out what has been done incorrectly or overlooked is only half of the supervisor's job. The other half is to bring the error or oversight to the attention of the room attendant and make sure it is corrected. Discussions between inspectors and room attendants should be objective, constructive, and tactful.

The best approach in communicating oversights to room attendants is to use inspection procedures that are as objective as possible. Use of a pre-printed form such as the one shown in Figure 5.11 allows objective feedback by listing the components of cleaning a guest room. This enables the inspector to simply circle or check what was done incorrectly or write down a short note of explanation. The time the report was completed as well as the time by which the problem should be corrected should appear on the inspector's report.

Most inspector's or supervisor's reports are self-explanatory. However, if the inspector sees a certain aspect of cleaning overlooked repeatedly, he or she should point this out to the room attendant and discuss how to resolve the problem. In most instances, simply pointing out that there is a problem will remind the room attendant of the correct procedure and no follow-up action will be necessary. However, if the problem continues, the room attendant may require retraining. (See Chapter 4.)

Supervisors also should watch for patterns of problems that involve several staff members. Perhaps room attendants are forgetting to wear gloves or carts are not being stocked properly. These kinds of problems should be discussed with the executive housekeeper. He or she will point out these broad problems during staff meetings and suggest ways in which to correct them.

## Returning Rooms to Inventory

Guest rooms should be returned to inventory as soon as possible after they are cleaned and inspected. A supervisor, inspector, team leader, or

### ROOM INSPECTION CHECKLIST

Room Attendant _____

Supervisor _____

Room Number _____

Date _____

| Yes | No | Bathroom |
|---|---|---|
| | | 1. Front, side, back tile of tub |
| | | 2. Shower head & nozzle |
| | | 3. Drain & inside of tub |
| | | 4. Grab bar/soap dish/hook |
| | | 5. Water spout & drain opener |
| | | 6. Vent & ceiling |
| | | 7. Shower curtain rod & curtain |
| | | 8. Appropriate linen |
| | | 9. Extra t.p. & kleenex w/ VIP fold |
| | | 10. Vanity/shelves/razor box clean |
| | | 11. Wash basin & sink drain clean |
| | | 12. Sink chrome clean |
| | | 13. Glasses/ice bucket/mat clean |
| | | 14. Soap/shoe mitt/ashtray/matches |
| | | 15. Soap dish clean |
| | | 16. Wastebasket clean inside & out |
| | | 17. Under sink & sink pipes clean |
| | | 18. Toilet chrome clean |
| | | 19. Toilet seat & lid clean |
| | | 20. Toilet bowl & outside clean |
| | | 21. T.P. holder clean w/ VIP fold |
| | | 22. Mirror clean |
| | | 23. Light clean |
| | | 24. Walls clean |
| | | 25. Floor/outside tub/threshold clean |
| | | 26. Light switch |
| | | 27. Back of door & hook |
| | | 28. Front of door & frame |
| | | 29. Heat lamp dusted & metal clean |

***Figure 5.11*** *This straightforward inspection checklist provides an easy but thorough basis for room inspections.*

room attendant who has earned self-supervision privileges is allowed to report on room status. Rooms should never be returned to inventory if repairs are needed or oversights in cleaning need to be addressed. Rooms in need of repair are designated as **out of order** until the necessary repair is completed.

Technology is speeding up the process of reporting room status. In most properties, employees authorized to return rooms to inventory simply touch a certain number on the phone. One four-digit code may indicate a vacant/clean/inspected room; another may indicate a room that is occupied/clean/inspected. This system transmits the room status information directly to the front desk. Front desk staff has an instant record of which rooms are available.

Some properties have interactive programs which enable guests to check their **folio,** or bill, on the television screen. These programs can be adapted to include room status reporting. The housekeeping staff members authorized to use the program access the correct menu with the television's remote control, then click on the correct status for the room. This information, too, is transmitted instantly to the front desk.

Even with the most reliable technology, it is still advisable to have the room attendant or inspector write in the room status on the inspection sheet. This provides a necessary backup document if a room's status is questioned or an error has been made.

## REPORTING PROCEDURES

The room assignment sheet or the inspection should have space for remarks on each room as it is cleaned. Reporting for each room includes such broad areas as: items that require repair; guest damage to the room; necessary pest control; lost and found items; and guest illness.

### Repairs

Room attendants and inspectors should be trained to notice small problems before they become too serious or expensive to repair. For example, if a drain is running slowly, it may indicate a large clog is developing. Left unattended, the clog could cause a major backup that could damage the entire bathroom. The sooner these problems are reported, the sooner they can be resolved and the sooner the room can be sold again. Frequent repairs on the same item may signal the need for replacement.

### Damage

Petulant celebrities and disgruntled gamblers are not the only guests who leave guest rooms in a shambles—though their antics are most likely to make headlines. Whether by accident or intent, guests do damage guest rooms. Since most general managers adhere to the policy that the guest is always right, dealing with damage caused by guests is a delicate issue.

When the room attendant or supervisor notices damage to the room, he or she should bring this information directly to the attention of the executive housekeeper. The executive housekeeper documents the date, room number, damage done, and cost to repair or replace what was damaged. Bedding or linen that has been burned, torn, or stained is removed and sent to the linen room for repair or discard. If the damage is extensive, the executive housekeeper may ask that the assistant manager or general manager also view the damage. Depending on who damaged the room, whether a loyal client who broke an item in a hospitality suite or a reckless VIP, the sales manager, assistant manager, or general manager will have to determine who pays for it: the property, the insurance company, or the client (see Tales of the Trade 5.6).

---

**Tales of the Trade 5.6**
**Assessing Damage**

A political party that took over the suites of a newly opened California hotel for hospitality sessions during a convention left an aftermath of minor damage and major stains. The executive housekeeper asked the sales manager to help assess the damage. She saw the challenge of how much work it would take to return the spaces to the pristine condition of opening day. The sales manager had another view. "If these suites look like they did on opening day, it means we haven't done any business. It's better to have a few spots and some wear and know the hotel is busy and people enjoyed themselves." This advice should be conveyed to the attendants who clean these spaces. Do not stress what a mess it is, but how much the guests must have enjoyed themselves.

---

Room attendants or inspectors also should note any items missing from the guest room. Again, the property probably will absorb the cost of small items such as an ashtray or washcloth. More aggressive attempts at cost recovery may be made for large items, ranging from video cassette recorders to televisions.

With more and more hotels allocating rooms as nonsmoking, the definition of "damage" is being expanded. Smoking in a nonsmoking room should be reported because the room will have to be deep cleaned and all smoking odor removed. Some hotels now fine guests as much as $100 for smoking in nonsmoking rooms.

## Pest Control

No matter how well cleaned and maintained a property is, pests can be a problem. Roaches can be attracted by substances as innocuous as the glue on boxes in storage areas. Pests can multiply in drawers, in vents, in door sills, and window sills, and even in the electrical wiring system. Room attendants and supervisors should constantly check for any signs of pests. Because most pests multiply rapidly, the room attendant or inspector who notices the problem should discuss this directly with the assistant housekeeper or executive housekeeper.

## Lost and Found

The record of the lost item should include the date the item was found, the room number in which it was found, and a description of the item. The front desk will supply the name and address of the guest. (More detailed information on Lost and Found will be covered in Chapter 8.)

## Guest Illness and Injury

Dealing with guest illness or injury is one of the most challenging aspects of housekeeping. Though room attendants and inspectors may understand the theory of dealing with the aftermath of an illness or accident, some may not be prepared for the reality. "I never ask my staff to do anything I won't do. If they come upon a situation they can't handle, I tell them to call me," says Robin Diaz, executive housekeeper of the historic Mohonk Mountain House Resort in New Paltz, New York.

In cases where room attendants or inspectors discover that a guest is seriously injured or ill, they should call the emergency number at the front desk and ask that paramedics be called, then call the assistant housekeeper or executive housekeeper. If any staff has paramedic training or other appropriate life-saving training, that staff member should be dispatched to the room as soon as possible (see Tales of the Trade 5.7).

---

**Tales of the Trade 5.7**
**Saving a Life**

Attendants as well as supervisors must be trained to respond to emergencies. A supervisor recalls checking a Do Not Disturb room at the end of a shift, only to find the guest in a diabetic coma. She responded quickly and most likely saved the guest's life. An executive housekeeper at a mountain resort was conducting room checks and found an elderly man unconscious on the bathroom floor. In this case, too, her prompt call for emergency help probably saved his life. Later, he thanked her and told her he had become disoriented after a strenuous hike and apparently fainted.

Training for attendants and supervisors must prepare them to face the challenges of dealing with a sick or injured guest, or, very occasionally, a guest who has died. The executive housekeeper must establish programs to cover both the professional and psychological difficulties of handling this situation.

---

Once the guest has been treated and transported to a hospital, the housekeeping department goes to work immediately to remove any stains. Stains related to illness and injury are difficult to remove after they set. Most stains can be removed with deep cleaning. Blood stains are more difficult. Club soda is effective in removing fresh stains. Some new products are specifically designed to work on blood stains. A staff member wearing rubber gloves, and other protective clothing if necessary, should place any blood-stained linens or towels in special bags and tag them as containing hazardous waste. The executive housekeeper and head of engineering will have to decide whether blood stains on carpeting can be removed or whether that section of carpeting will have to be repaired or replaced.

If a crime is suspected, the attendant should use the front desk emergency number to ask that paramedics and police be called. Even after the guest is treated, nothing should be disturbed or cleaned until the police have investigated thoroughly.

## Writing Work Orders

**Trouble reports** are written reports to note what needs to be fixed. In a large hotel, a separate report would be written for each craft: carpenters, electricians, engineering, seamstresses. In other hotels, they are combined with the attendant's daily report and list all items needed to be repaired by each group of craftspeople.

Trouble reports and/or **work orders** (if the hotel uses these in addition to trouble reports), which assigns the repair to a certain department and indicates when the repair is completed, should be written in triplicate, with one copy sent to the department that will correct the trouble, the second to the executive housekeeper, and the third to be placed on file until the job is done.

In most hotels this is still done in writing. However, new computer software is on the market which links housekeeping and engineering. Work orders are sent via computer. Some hotels use e-mail systems on the computer to transmit work orders from housekeeping to engineering. Using the comment area on the screen, the housekeeping manager can point out which jobs have priority. It is also easier to track information on when work orders were made and whether that particular repair has been requested more than once.

If supervisors find that a defect or damage reported previously has not been attended to, they should phone the department to which the report or work was sent; make sure it was received; and inquire about how soon the situation will be rectified. If work orders or trouble reports are not being handled promptly as a rule, the executive housekeeper contacts the head of engineering to discuss the problem. Failure to make repairs promptly takes too many rooms out of inventory.

## SUMMARY

Cleaning and maintaining guest rooms to standards that will satisfy guests is not a simple matter. How to clean, when to clean, and, in some instances even what to clean all must be taken into consideration by the executive housekeeper. And, all of these factors must be weighed against what levels of service guests demand and how to meet these demands while staying on budget and keeping employees satisfied.

Organization and planning are helpful tools in accomplishing these goals. The executive housekeeper must work closely with the rooms division, sales division, and engineering to make sure rooms are not only clean, but in good repair, ready in time for new arrivals, and stocked with the amenities and any special request items guests will expect.

Managing this aspect of the housekeeping department properly requires the diverse skills discussed in this chapter, such as:

- Making room assignments
- Training staff in how to enter guest rooms
- Standardizing daily cleaning tasks
- Stocking carts correctly
- Reporting malfunctions, damage, or needed repairs
- Making productive inspections
- Planning night service
- Scheduling general cleaning

## Review Questions

1. What types of reports and other information are needed to make room assignments?
2. What general categories of items should be stocked on an attendant's cart?
3. What is the proper order for servicing guest rooms?
4. Describe the proper procedure for entering the guest room.
5. What are the proper procedures for cleaning blood stains or other substances that may pose a hazard?
6. Explain the purpose of inspecting the guest rooms and some typical items that may be covered on an inspector's checklist.
7. How and when are rooms returned to inventory? When should rooms not be returned to inventory?
8. Define the responsibilities of those who provide night service.
9. What is general cleaning and how is it scheduled?
10. Describe how cleaning differs in departments that use individual room attendants versus cleaning teams.

## Critical Thinking Questions

1. Management has decided to offer free coffee service along with the complimentary morning newspaper. The general manager decides room attendants will take the coffee to the room on a tray, leave it outside the guest room, and knock. This will be done soon after the start of the day shift. How would the executive housekeeper respond to this directive, and how would it affect daily room assignments?
2. What are the advantages and disadvantages of individual room attendants versus team cleaning in guest rooms?
3. The new long-haul travel market for a resort means guests are sleeping later and a growing percentage of Do Not Disturb rooms are being reported as of 2 P.M. What can be done to address this problem?

# 6

# Cleaning Public Areas and the Back of the House

## Chapter Objectives

To manage cleaning operations for the front and back of the house, the executive housekeeper must:

- Create workable schedules and reasonable workloads
- Calculate labor needs
- Define cleaning procedures for each area
- Develop systems for the special challenges of F&B outlets and function space
- Define how and when to clean public rest rooms
- Define how and when to clean the back of the house
- Create proper inspection procedures
- Set the schedule for general cleaning procedures
- Work effectively with contract cleaners

City center properties of more than 500 rooms may cover nearly an entire city block. Resorts, especially the low-rise, eco-friendly designs now being built, sprawl over acres. Whatever the property's size and complexity, guests, visitors, and employees expect every inch of the property to be clean (see Figure 6.1).

It is the housekeeping department's responsibility to make sure these expectations are met in the rooms as well as the front of the house and the back of the house. The **front of the house,** also known as the public space, includes the lobby, restaurants, corridors, meeting rooms, function rooms, and business centers that are used by visitors and guests alike. For the many people who

dine in the hotel's restaurants or attend social functions in the ballroom, the public spaces will provide the only basis on which to judge the hotel's appearance.

The **back of the house,** which includes service corridors, kitchens, and areas used only by employees such as employee cafeterias and lockers, offices, service elevators, and internal stairwells, must also be spotlessly clean. The standard the executive housekeeper sets for these areas will influence the standards employees use for the public areas and guest rooms. By enforcing cleaning standards as strictly in the back of the house as in the front of the house, the executive housekeeper reinforces the message that employees' needs must be respected, not just the guests'.

## CLEANING THE FRONT OF THE HOUSE

Guests may spend more time in the guest room than in any other part of the property, but most guests start forming their opinion of the hotel long before they unpack. Guests' initial impressions are based largely on the condition of the property's public areas, especially the entry, lobby, and restaurants.

Public spaces are under constant scrutiny and must look their best at all times. Guests leaving a gala party in the hotel's ballroom at midnight expect the same standards of cleanliness in the lobby, corridors, and public rest rooms as new arrivals checking in during the busy day shift. The housekeeping department has round-the-clock responsi-

**Figure 6.1**   *Large banquets or social functions will serve as many people's introduction to the hotel. Failure to adhere to strict housekeeping standards in banquet rooms and other front-of-the-house space could take away sales opportunities. (Courtesy of The Plaza Hotel, New York)*

bility for keeping the public spaces spotlessly clean and in good repair.

The demands of cleaning the front of the house differ from the challenges involved in cleaning guest rooms. Unlike guest rooms, where design and layout are fairly standardized to control costs, public spaces feature dramatic design intended to impress. The executive housekeeper may need to find ways to clean priceless chandeliers, keep 40-foot artificial palm trees dust free, or erase the constant smudging of fingerprints from brass handrails that define the public spaces. Heavy foot traffic and the size and scope of the public spaces generally require heavier equipment to meet cleaning needs, as well as the physical ability to clean high, hard-to-reach places (see Figures 6.2a and 6.2b).

Creating workable schedules, conducting regular inspections, and providing staff with the right tools are essential for managing public space cleaning. Maximizing the performance of contract clean-

(a)                                                                          (b)

**Figure 6.2**  *(a) The guest's eye sees only the drama and grandeur of the Palace Hotel's rotunda-capped lobby. However, the executive housekeeper of this South African resort sees the interesting cleaning challenges posed by the variety of materials and surfaces that must be cleaned, as well as the various high details—from the artwork to the palm trees and the rotunda itself. (Courtesy of Sun International, Sandton, South Africa) (b) Glass walls, slices of color from the flowers, and a soaring ceiling make the lobby of the Kempinski Hotel at Munich Airport a favorite spot for high-end travelers and film crews. The innovative housekeeping staff had to create proper schedules and find the right equipment to keep this hanger-like space sparkling. (Courtesy of Kempinski Hotels)*

ing services also plays an important role in maintaining and extending the design life of the property's public spaces.

## SCHEDULING PUBLIC AREA CLEANING

Scheduling cleaning for the front of the house is different than scheduling room attendants. Typically, the day shift concentrates on keeping public areas neat in appearance. More thorough cleaning of the front of the house is done during an early morning shift that starts at 4 A.M. or 5 A.M., depending on the category of hotel and areas to be cleaned, or during the night shift and/or graveyard shift.

Scheduling generally is based on a **labor analysis,** which shows an average of how many labor hours it takes to complete a task. Figure 6.3 shows a labor analysis for the upscale, 233-room Radisson SAS Scandinavia Hotel in Aarhus, Denmark. After

**Radisson SAS**
H O T E L S   W O R L D W I D E

Amager Boulevard 70, DK-2300 Copenhagen S, Denmark
Telephone: +45 3396 5710  Fax: +45 3396 5550

(C) AmKa 1995

# Radisson SAS Scandinavia

Date:_____

| Night Attendants Section | Estimated time | Assigned to | Signature |
|---|---|---|---|
| **Section 1** | | | |
| Lobby / Busstop | 3,50 Hrs. | | |
| Business Service Center | 0,15 Hrs. | | |
| SAS Check In | 0,10 Hrs. | | |
| Mana's & Papa's    (Cleaning / Set up) | 2,00 Hrs. | | |
| Casino Office | 0,30 Hrs. | | |
| | | | |
| **Section 2** | | | |
| Banquet Foyer | 2,00 Hrs. | | |
| Banquet Rooms | 0,15 Hrs. | | |
| Banquet Toilets | 1,50 Hrs. | | |
| Stairs to Lobby | 0,10 Hrs. | | |
| Team Scandinavia Office | 0,30 Hrs. | | |
| | | | |
| **Section 3** | | | |
| Canteen | 0,30 Hrs. | | |
| Personel Toilets | 0,30 Hrs. | | |
| Blue Corridor | 0,10 Hrs. | | |
| Basement Toilets | 1,50 Hrs. | | |
| Basement Offices | 1,00 Hrs. | | |
| Guest Elevators | 0,30 Hrs. | | |
| Executive / Sales Office | 1,00 Hrs. | | |
| Blue Elephant Corridor | 0,30 Hrs. | | |
| | | | |
| **Diverse Section** | | | |
| Stone Staircase | | | |
| Staff Elevators | | | |
| Spiral Staircase | | | |
| Room Service Corridor | | | |
| Brown Staircase | | | |

**Figure 6.3**  *This labor analysis conducted by the Radisson SAS Scandinavia shows on average how long it takes to clean each area of the public space. Using this analysis, the executive housekeeper can calculate how many employees will need to be assigned to each area.*

averaging cleaning time for the lobby, the hotel's executive housekeeper, Cornelia Erhardt, calculated that 3.5 hours should be allotted for lobby cleaning—whether by one person working the entire 3.5 hours or a team working a total of 3.5 hours.

The design of the front of the house must be factored in to the labor analysis; it also may affect how the area is cleaned most effectively. A team concept, with each person assigned a certain task, may work best in a large open space. One person dusts, a second empties wastebaskets, and a crew of two to three vacuum. A lobby divided into **bays**—sections defined by architectural elements such as sunken or raised floor areas, partial walls or columns—is more easily cleaned by one person assigned to all duties within each bay. Rest rooms should be permanently assigned to one attendant who will become expert in using the special chemicals and equipment required for rest rooms.

## Making Assignments

Because of the variety of work that must be done, most executive housekeepers create a yearlong frequency schedule, which lists what tasks need to be done daily, weekly, monthly, and periodically during the year (see Figure 6.4). These schedules serve as a framework for staffing and budgeting throughout the year. However, they must remain flexible and accommodate the last-minute changes that are inevitable in lodging operations.

Most executive housekeepers have computerized these schedules. They create the yearlong frequency chart, then list which tasks should be done during various weeks or months. In some cases, it is possible to merge this year-long schedule with the file that holds daily assignments.

## Lobbies

The appearance of the lobby can play a key role in favorably impressing a new arrival or a meeting planner weighing the decision to bring a lucrative event to the hotel. Yet, it is also the space subject to the most wear and tear. Lobby floors and floor coverings must withstand a steady stream of foot traffic and the effects of snow, rain, sand, or mud. Suitcases and bell carts roll through during much of the day. Guests and visitors leave behind a trail of rumpled newspapers, paper waste, and even cups from complimentary morning coffee. Not only must executive housekeepers find ways to meet these cleaning challenges, they must also make

sure the necessary cleaning procedures do not unduly disturb guests or visitors in the public spaces or interfere with efficient guest and staff traffic patterns.

***Day cleaning.*** Day shift assignments are fairly standard (see Tricks of the Trade 6.1). Primary daily duties for public areas include:

- Clean out ash urns or ash trays. Remove debris. A lightweight basket makes a workable, attractive receptacle for debris and is unobtrusive. This light cleaning should be done frequently throughout the day.
- Clean the entryway throughout the day. **Runners,** long, narrow strips of carpeting, or vinyl matting have to be put down during wet weather to protect the flooring or carpeting. The runners or mats should be mopped frequently or changed if they become saturated.
- Straighten up the lobby and reposition furniture moved by guests. This should be done as needed.
- Clean public rest rooms and replenish supplies. (This is covered in detail later in this chapter.)

---

**Tricks of the Trade 6.1
Experts' Cleaning Tips**

*The Problem:* Public spaces suffer heavy wear.
*The Solution:* Seal and protect surfaces whenever possible. Louis Fozman, executive housekeeper for the elegant Adolphus Hotel in Dallas, Texas, suggests sealing carpet as soon as it is installed, and after each cleaning. Jackie Jones, executive housekeeper for the luxurious Windsor Court hotel in New Orleans, has all upholstery fabrics sprayed with fabric protector before they are put in place. Some housekeepers also recommend sealing some brass surfaces. To protect wood tables, consider having glass tops made to cover delicate surfaces.

---

***Overnight cleaning.*** The bulk of lobby cleaning must be done at times when traffic is low. Traditionally, that has meant the night shift or the graveyard shift. Many executive housekeepers still use this schedule. However, problems with finding and retaining good workers for these shifts and the inconsistent performance of some contract services

H O T E L S   W O R L D W I D E

Amager Boulevard 70, DK-2300 Copenhagen S, Denmark
Telephone: +45 3396 5710  Fax: +45 3396 5550

# Radisson SAS Scandinavia

(C) AmKa 1995

| Area | Cleaning method | Cleaning Material | Comments | Daily | Weekly | Monthly |
|---|---|---|---|---|---|---|
| **Buisness Service Center** | | | | | | |
| Carpet | Vacuum | | | ✓ | | |
| Tables / Desk | Dusted | Spraycleaner | | ✓ | | |
| Chair | Vacuum | | | | ✓ | |
| Ashtrays | Emptied / Clean | Spraycleaner | | ✓ | | |
| Waste / Bin | Emptied | Plastic Bag | | ✓ | | |
| Telephone | Clean / Disinfected | Spraycleaner | | ✓ | | |
| Walls | Vacuum | | | | | ✓ |
| | | | | | | |
| **SAS Check-In** | | | | | | |
| Desk | Wiped / Dusted | | | ✓ | | |
| Floor | Vacuum | | | ✓ | | |
| Telephones | Dusted | | | ✓ | | |
| Computer | Dusted | Dry Cloth | | ✓ | | |
| | | | | | | |
| **Service Desk** | | | | | | |
| Desk | Dusted | | | ✓ | | |
| Bins | Emptied | Plastic bag | | ✓ | | |
| Computer | Dusted | Dry Cloth | | ✓ | | |
| Telephone | Disinfected | Spraycleaner | | ✓ | | |
| Carpet | Vacuum | | | ✓ | | |
| | | | | | | |
| **Mamas & Papas** | | | | | | |
| Carpet | Vacuum | Vacuum Cleaner | | ✓ | | |
| Carpet | Spotclean | Spotcleaner Brush | Upon Demand | ⇐ | ⇐ | ⇐ |
| Tables | Washed | Damp Cloth | | ✓ | | |
| Base of table | Vacuum | Vacuum Cleaner | | ✓ | | |
| Chairs | Vacuum | | Upon Demand | ⇐ | ⇐ | ⇐ |
| Chair legs | Dusted | | | | ✓ | |
| | | | | | | |
| **Bar - M&P** | | | | | | |
| Floor | Vacuum / Wash | Vacuum / Mop | | ✓ | | |
| Counter | Dusted | Damp Cloth | | ✓ | | |
| Glass shelve | Dusted | Spraycleaner | | | ✓ | |
| Bar Stools | Spotclean / Vacuum | | | ✓ | | |
| | | | | | | |
| **Marble Floor** | | | | | | |
| Marble Floor | Wash | Machine | | ✓ | | |
| Marble Floor | Polish | Polish Machine | | | ✓ | |
| Buffet | Clean | Damp Cloth | | ✓ | | |
| Window Shelve | Vacuum | Soft Brush | | | ✓ | |
| | | | | | | |
| **Waiter Area** | | | | | | |
| Floor | Vacuum / Wash | Damp Cloth | | ✓ | | |

**Figure 6.4**   *A frequency chart, such as this one used by the Radisson SAS Scandinavia, simplifies the scheduling of daily and general cleaning assignments. Since the form is computerized, last-minute adjustments can be made easily.*

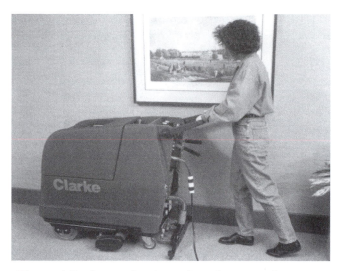

*Figure 6.5  Carpet cleaning is best done at night to minimize inconvenience to guests. It should be scheduled early enough, depending on the method, to ensure adequate drying time. (Courtesy of Clarke Industries Inc.)*

have encouraged some executive housekeepers to shift lobby cleaning to an early morning schedule. Attendants typically begin work at 4 A.M. to 5 A.M. For a 500-room hotel, four to five employees would be scheduled on this shift. Dusting, vacuuming, and cleaning elevators or escalators can be done before the morning business rush begins. If the lobby takes roughly three hours, they would be assigned to clean the offices, which may take about an hour, before the majority of staff comes to work. Some hotels cross-train these employees to clean guestroom floors on the latter part of the shift; others assign them day-shift public space duties. This early morning shift has a financial benefit as well. In some areas, no night pay premium is required for employees starting at 5 A.M., as it would be for those starting at 11 P.M. or midnight.

Certain projects, such as spot cleaning carpet, still must be done on the graveyard shift to allow for adequate drying time. Some deep cleaning procedures also are reserved for the night shift or graveyard shift because of the time required or the size of or noise generated by the equipment.

Standard night shift assignments at the popular JW Marriott in Hong Kong are typical for upscale and deluxe hotels:

- Dust all furniture and the lobby reception counter
- Empty and clean all ash urns
- Polish all guest elevators (called **lifts** in Europe and Asia) and clean elevator floors and walls
- Clean mirrors

- Vacuum all carpeted areas
- Remove fine marks and spots from walls and woodwork
- Polish metal handles, rails, and doorknobs

The night supervisor or night assistant executive housekeeper assigns these kinds of basic tasks, then consults the frequency chart to determine which general cleaning projects must be completed during the week. He or she would also communicate with the executive housekeeper, either verbally or through memos, to decide which tasks have priority and whether there are any special instructions for that night.

At an economy hotel, night cleaning may be as simple as cleaning the reception counter, vacuuming or cleaning the public area floors, emptying ash trays, and generally straightening up the lobby. This may be done by a maintenance person or, sometimes, the front desk clerk.

Color coded maps of the public spaces can be helpful in making assignments for day or night staff. For example, one employee may be responsible for cleaning all the areas colored in pink. The attendant also receives a smaller map with detailed illustrations of all items to be cleaned in the pink shaded area. Although preparation of these maps takes time, even with computers, it can help clarify assignments for staff members who are not fluent in English. After employees receive their assignments, they should sign out keys for locked areas such as the janitor's closet and storage areas. They sign them back in at the end of their shift.

## Cleaning Public Rest Rooms

Public rest rooms must be cleaned and sanitized throughout the day. How often this work needs to be done depends on the traffic flow in the hotel. Public area attendants should be assigned to check the public rest rooms at least once an hour. A sheet should be provided so that work must be signed off on.

Before entering the rest rooms at any time, the attendant should:

- Knock on the entrance door
- Announce "housekeeping"
- If there is no reply, the attendant may enter. If someone is using the rest room, the attendant waits outside until the rest room is not occupied
- Place a **traffic control device,** whether a sign explaining the rest room is being cleaned, a tape or

a plastic cone, at the entrance door when the rest room is being cleaned

• Begin cleaning

During the day, the lobby attendant should replenish the rest room supplies, including toilet paper, tissue, and towels—whether paper towels or the fabric towels used in luxury properties. Luxury properties also provide hampers for dirty towels. These should be checked regularly and emptied when full. Ashtrays should be emptied at regular intervals during the day. Supplies for rest rooms should be stored in an adjacent closet so that attendants do not have to carry stacks of supplies through the lobby. If no closet is available, a lockable storage box should be installed in the rest room.

Regular checks of the public rest rooms are also scheduled during the shift that ends at 11 P.M. or midnight. At this time, particular attention should be paid to the rest rooms near function space if events are under way and also the rest rooms near the lounges and restaurants that are open in the evening.

## Essential Supplies

All cleaning products required for cleaning public rest rooms are stocked in easily portable caddies. Basic supplies include:

• A sterile disinfectant that is pre-mixed or marked with the proper formula for dilution

• Cleanser

• Glass cleaner

• Special cleaners for marble or tiles

• Mops or toilet brushes

• A long-handled, lighted mirror which is used to inspect the underside of the toilet rim

Attendants in deluxe hotels where a small make-up or lounge area may be provided in the ladies' rest room also will need to carry cleaners for the seating in this area. Equipment and supplies for the caddies is stored in the janitor's closet adjacent, or as near as possible, to the rest room. The closet should have a ready supply of rags for cleaning everything except toilets and urinals and disposable rags specifically for washing toilets and urinals. Rags to be used for drying should be soft and clean. Lint-free rags or paper towels are needed for mirrors.

Also stored in this closet should be supplies for rest rooms, including paper towels or fabric towels,

liquid hand soap for refilling dispensers, toilet paper, and keys for the dispensers and waste containers. In deluxe hotels, standard supplies in rest rooms may include a moisturizing skin lotion and even hair spray. Buckets needed for diluting the disinfectant also should be stored in this closet. The executive housekeeper will need to test water hardness before determining which chemicals work best and whether extra chemicals are required to remove lime scale or rust stains.

## Cleaning Public Rest Rooms

Typical procedures for cleaning public rest rooms are:

• Refill all the soap, seat cover, tissue and towel dispensers

• Empty all trash containers

• Using a cloth dipped in diluted disinfectant solution, damp wipe all the fixtures including the mirror, pipes, faucets, and dispensers. Spot clean cubicle partitions and entrance door handles as needed

• Rinse the cleaned surfaces, wringing out the cloth under the tap as needed

• Using the same diluted disinfectant, clean the tops and bottoms of toilet seats and all exterior surfaces, including the pipes. Wipe dry all exterior surfaces with a soft cloth. Clean and dry the exterior surfaces of urinals, including the pipes, in the same way

• Using cleansers, clean the wash basins. Abrasives should not be used on other areas including the toilets

• Clean toilet bowls and the inside of urinals with an applicator, being careful not to drip on the floors or chrome. (Some manufacturers sell a quart-sized bottle of disinfectant with a hose attachment so the attendant need not touch the disinfectant or the bowl.) The solution must remain on the fixture for several minutes. Flushing rinses off the chemical. Never clean toilet bowls by hand—with or without gloves. The risk of disease, and of skin rashes from harsh chemicals, is too great

• Clean the floors. Begin by **de-gumming** if necessary, using a putty knife to scrape off sticky substances. Use a *very wet* mop to apply detergent/disinfectant solution. Do not wring the mop; allow excess solution to drip back into the bucket. Allow the floor to remain wet for several minutes to maximize the effectiveness of the disinfectant. Using a squeegee, push excess solution toward the floor drain. Rinse the floor with a mop set aside for rinsing, using clean water stored in a bucket with a wringer. The mop should be slightly damp, not wet. Once a week, dump a bucket of disinfectant/detergent into the floor drain to prevent odor buildup. Some drains may require a diluted enzyme drain treatment to keep them free of clogs

A growing number of hotels recommend or require that attendants wear protective eyewear when cleaning toilets and urinals. Gloves must be worn by any attendant who cleans rest rooms.

## Scheduling Special Cleaning Projects

General cleaning assignments are added on a rotating basis to each night's work. Special cleaning projects could be scheduled as follows:

**Monday.** After polishing the mirrors, polish all chrome with a creme cleanser and soft cloth

**Tuesday.** Thoroughly wash cubicle doors and partitions. Dry with a soft cloth so as not to leave streaks

**Wednesday.** Scour and polish the sinks, including the underside

**Thursday.** Wipe and dry entrance doors. If the doors are wood, polish them

**Friday.** Wash all tile walls

## Elevators and Escalators

Like lobbies, elevators and escalators are used almost continuously. They generally require thorough cleaning each night.

Elevator floor carpets are among the most difficult of all areas to keep clean. They sustain concentrated wear, with people pivoting on the carpet throughout the day. Many hotels now are shifting to elevator floor carpets that can be removed and washed, rather than shampooed in place. Thorough washing cleans out both grit and dirt. Having several sets of elevator floor carpets insures the carpet will have adequate time to dry thoroughly before it is returned to the elevator (see Figure 6.6). Some hotels have turned this replacement system into a guest service by using floor carpets with the day of the week printed on them.

Glass or mirrors must be serviced regularly during the day and night. All metal surfaces, es-

**Figure 6.6** *Carpeting that can be removed and washed rather than shampooed in place is a money-saving, convenient alternative for high-traffic areas such as elevators and other public spaces. (Courtesy of TacFast Carpet System, marketed by 3M)*

pecially the Braille plate on the elevator panel, should be cleaned.

Elevator walls present another problem. Those with carpet on the sides and ceiling are somewhat easier to maintain. Fingerprints are less obvious, and the material is less vulnerable to vandalism such as graffiti. However, hard surfaces such as laminates or stainless steel are durable. Some executive housekeepers recommend applying baby oil with cotton wool to keep stainless steel elevators gleaming and spot free.

Escalators in a busy convention hotel also require nightly cleaning. Tar and gum must be removed from the step-off plates. Metal grids must be cleaned; the railings must be dusted, and the glass shields must be polished (see Figure 6.7).

## Restaurants

Housekeeping and the F&B department work together to keep restaurants clean and neat on the day shift. Housekeeping is responsible for the front of the house restaurant spaces, while the F&B department staff cleans the kitchens. Contract cleaning services may also be hired to do night cleaning of both the restaurant and kitchen.

Some hotel restaurants are run on a **concession basis,** which means the owner/operator of the restaurant sets up and operates the outlet within the hotel building. Usually, the restaurant operator pays the hotel a fee consisting of a certain percentage of sales and, perhaps, some fee for use of the space. In these cases, the restaurant's management is also responsible for cleaning and maintaining the restaurant and kitchen space (see Figure 6.8).

## Cleaning and Maintaining Restaurants

The executive housekeeper and F&B director must clearly define the responsibilities of their staffs. **Waitstaff,** F&B employees directly involved with taking orders for and serving food, and buspersons are responsible for everything that has to do with ordering and serving food and drinks, setting up the tables, and cleaning the tables after meals. In economy hotels, the waitstaff may be assigned all of these functions. In mid-tier, upscale, and deluxe hotels, waitstaff takes orders for meals and serves them, while the buspersons clean off tables, replace tablecloths and napkins, and reset the table for the next seating.

In some hotels, buspersons also make the rounds of the carpeted restaurants with a small broom and dustpan or small Japanese carpet sweepers to pick up debris. If not, the primary assignment for the day shift and night shift (not graveyard) will be to keep the floors of food-service outlets as neat as possible. These assignments are based on the square footage an attendant can monitor and sweep.

The first priority is dealing with spills. Liquid spills, spills of oil-based foods such as sauces or salad dressings, wine spills, especially red wine and coffee—particularly decaffeinated, must be attended to immediately. The stains must be diluted or spot treated before they set. Spotting kits should be stored in janitors' closets near the entrance to the food-service outlet for these emergencies. Spot treating the carpet close to the time the stain occurs may help prevent a permanent stain or the need for replacement of that section of carpet. Decaffeinated coffee and red wine are particularly difficult to remove. Stewards should be advised to report these spills immediately to housekeeping. Spilled bits of food should be swept up before they

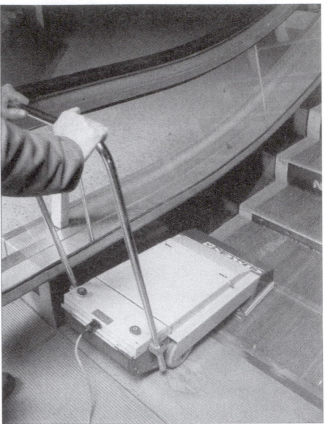

Courtesy Cimex International

***Figure 6.7*** *Cleaning escalators nightly reduces maintenance costs by preventing hard-to-clean buildup of tar, gum, and other foot-borne soil. A clean escalator runs more smoothly and reduces operating costs. (Courtesy of Cimex International)*

are stepped on and ground into the carpet pile. This makes vacuuming and shampooing easier and more effective. Complete stain removal should be scheduled during a slow period in the late afternoon, if necessary, or, preferably, after the outlet closes.

## Night Cleaning Assignments for Restaurants

As with lobby cleaning, the bulk of front of the house food-service cleaning must be done after the outlets close. This can be from 10 P.M., when a family restaurant or coffee shop closes, to 1 P.M. or 2 P.M. when the lounge ends its business day. Most upscale hotels in major cities have 24-hour casual

**Figure 6.8** *Whether mini food courts or traditional restaurants, hotel dining facilities and the kitchens that service them must not only be neat but hygienic. This requires specialty equipment as well as specially trained staff. (Courtesy of Holiday Inn SunSpree Resort, Lake Buena Vista, Florida)*

dining outlets, in which cleaning must be scheduled during the slowest period—usually from 2 A.M. to 5 A.M.—and done with as little disruption as possible.

Housekeeping attendants assigned to thoroughly clean restaurants generally use a cart. These carts should be stocked with a trash bag, a vacuum, cleaning chemicals in dispensers, spray cans and squirt bottles of cleaners, gloves, a feather duster, and a treated dust mop for small tiled areas or for woodwork. The tasks involved in restaurant cleanup are done most efficiently by two people working together. For example, one person can be moving tables or chairs while the other sweeps up food debris.

Standard assignments for late night/early morning cleaning of food-service outlets are:

1. Pull out tables and chairs; remove all crumbs on the seats and closed backs of chairs. A whiskbroom will do the job quickly and effectively on areas where the fabric is smooth. A **piggy-back vacuum**—a lightweight vacuum worn like a backpack—with a **crevice tool**—a vacuum attachment that narrows to a slit-like opening—is more effective on **tufted** upholstery—upholstery in which buttons or seams are sewn in such a way as to create high areas and recessed areas, and fabric booth backs. (See Figure 6.9.)

2. Wash vinyl booths or seats, bar stools, and bar fronts with the appropriate cleaner. Leather must be cleaned carefully and conditioned periodically.

3. Pick up large pieces of debris around each table before vacuuming to save wear and tear on vacuums.

4. Vacuum around each table.

5. Wipe window ledges or other horizontal surfaces, table posts, legs, and metal floor vents with a cloth dampened with all-purpose cleaner.

6. Wipe the hostess' or maître d'hotel's desk.

7. Wash phones.

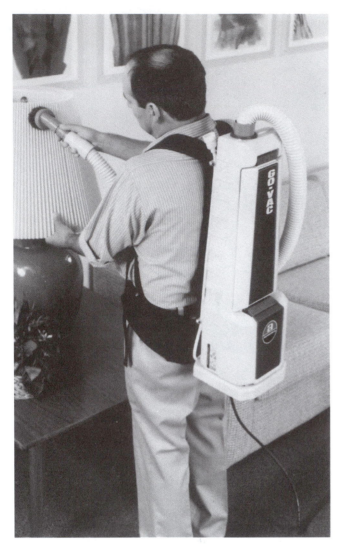

**Figure 6.9** *Lightweight, piggy-back vacuums are convenient tools for delicate tasks such as cleaning lamp shades, as well as tasks in which attendants must have their hands free for safety reasons, such as work that must be done on a ladder. (Courtesy of the Advance Machine Company)*

8. Dust and polish metal chairs, paying special attention to chrome, which shows fingerprints easily.

9. Polish foot rails and metal trim on the bar.

10. Dust wood on chairs using a chemically treated cloth.

11. Spot clean walls. If there is a counter, clean the front of it. Countertops should be cleaned by waitstaff.

12. Clean the foot plate or treadle that opens the restaurant door.

The same piggy-back vacuum can be used to clean any stairs within the dining area, as well as accessories, decorations, or light fixtures. Some of these vacuums are battery-operated and must be recharged; all have retractable cords so that they can be carried up ladders. Lights on the tables should be washed or dusted, depending on the type of fixture. Many candle lamps are designed with glass chimneys that can be washed in an automatic dishwasher. Fine dining restaurants may include antique sideboards used to enhance the decor or one-of-a-kind designer accents (see Figure 6.10). These must be dusted, as should any art elements in the room.

Cleaning bar and lounge areas includes many of these same procedures. Bar stools upholstered with vinyl or vinyl-like material should be dusted nightly and damp-wiped weekly. Fabric bar stools and chairs should be vacuumed nightly and spot treated as necessary. Bar tables require nightly cleaning. Dance floors with hard surfaces should be washed and wiped dry each night; carpeted dance floors should be vacuumed nightly, with spot treatment as required.

## Cleaning Meeting and Banquet Areas

Meetings and functions held at hotels and conference centers are meticulously planned. The executive housekeeper will know weeks, even months in advance, exactly when the function will begin, how many people will attend, and about when it will conclude. This information is doubly beneficial because cleaning up after large functions requires the largest, latest night cleanup crew scheduled by the housekeeping department.

In most hotels, banquet cleanup is a joint effort between the banqueting or F&B department and the housekeeping department. Generally, the job of the banquet stewards is to remove all dishes and linens from the tables. Banquet house attendants, who are employees of the F&B department, then sweep up large pieces of debris and **break down** the room, that is, reversing the setup process by stacking or folding the chairs and tables and storing them. Folding doors, partitions, or dividers also may have to be removed or repositioned if the room requires a different configuration for the next day's events or meetings.

Housekeeping generally is responsible for cleaning the shell of the room—the walls, including windows, floors, and ceilings. Typical duties for the housekeeping department would include the tasks listed in Figure 6.11. If the room has windows, it is important to keep them sparkling. Chemicals used for cleaning these areas of the banquet space fit into a caddie. Because the banquet spaces are so

***Figure 6.10*** *Despite their signature wall treatments and designer furnishings, fine dining restaurants must be able to stand up to cleaning fluids and heavy equipment required to keep the area hygienically clean and stain-free. (Courtesy of the Waldorf-Astoria Hotel, New York)*

large and work needs to be done in a concentrated period, teams of cleaners are usually assigned to the area. Four to five people may be assigned if the room needs to be cleaned quickly between functions and set up again.

Cleaning work does not end at the function room door. The pre-function area or **banquet foyer** must be cleaned with the same attention to detail. Frequently, cocktails or hors d'oeuvres are served in this space before functions begin and this will be the guests' introduction to the banquet area.

After the room is cleared and dusted, house attendants from the housekeeping department would use a **space vac,** a large vacuum with an extra-wide, 30-inch head, to clean the carpet. Specialized equipment, such as large riding vacuums that look and operate like riding lawn mowers, reduce cleaning time substantially for large function space. Vacuuming alone rarely suffices to clean the carpet. Spots and stains must be treated. A damp foam shampoo frequently is scheduled. This may be followed by use of a **pile lifter,** which raises the pile back to its original height (or as closely as possible) to keep the carpet from looking dull and matted.

Some hotel managers also make the housekeeping department responsible for setting up meeting and function rooms. In order to create the most efficient setup, the executive housekeeper must obtain the following information from the sales, F&B or banquet department:

- How many seats will be needed.
- What style of seating is required: a **schoolroom setup,** with evenly spaced rows of long tables; a semicircular or **auditorium style setup;** a **banquet setup,** which allows for tables to be set up throughout a large room with only walk space between, or angled seating (see Figure 6.12).
- Whether tables are needed. If tables are required, the housekeeping department must know what supplies will be provided—notepads, pencils, pens, even cups or glasses and pitchers of water.
- Whether a stage will be needed and, if so, where it should be set up. Also, whether a podium will be needed.
- How long the event will take.

House attendants generally will begin by setting up a stage if one is required. A diagram showing how to set up the stage should be stored with the equipment. The house attendants then attach pleated skirting to the edge of the stage. The assignment for the setup work should include any special instructions, such as whether carpeting or special supports will be needed.

Tables are then put in place. For meetings, many folding tables on the market now have scratch- and mark-resistant services and are well-designed enough to use with no covering. Banquet tables always have tablecloths or some type of table

Amager Boulevard 70, DK-2300 Copenhagen S, Denmark
Telephone: +45 3396 5710  Fax: +45 3396 5550

# Radisson SAS Scandinavia

(C) AmKa 1995

| Area | Cleaning method | Cleaning Material | Comments | Daily | Weekly | Monthly |
|---|---|---|---|---|---|---|
| **Personel Canteen** | | | | | | |
| Table | Tops / legs | Damp Cloth | | ✓ | | |
| Chairs | Dusted | Damp Cloth | | ✓ | | |
| Floor | Washed | Machine | | ✓ | | |
| Pictures | Dusted | | | | ✓ | |
| Hanging lamps | Dusted | Damp Cloth | | ✓ | ✓ | |
| Coffee Machine | Cleaned | Spraycleaner | | ✓ | | |
| Food Counter | Cleaned | Damp Cloth | | ✓ | | |
| Food shelves | Cleaned | Spraycleaner | | ✓ | | |
| Lamps above shelves | Dusted | Damp Cloth | | ✓ | | |
| Wall towards kitchen | Washed | Sponge | | ✓ | | |
| | | | | | | |
| **Canteen Corridor** | | | | | | |
| Floor | Washed / Vacuumed | Machine | | ✓ | | |
| Walls | Spotclean | | | | ✓ | |
| Doors | Spotclean | Spraycleaner | | ✓ | | |
| Doors | Washed throughly | Washed throughly | | | ✓ | |
| | | | | | | |
| **Personel Toilets** | | | | | | |
| Marble Floor | Mopped | Marble Clean | | ✓ | | |
| Marble Floor | Polished | Polish Machine | | | | ✓ |
| Marble Floor | Corners | Sponged | | | | ✓ |
| Urinals | Washed | Toilet Brush | | ✓ | | |
| Toilets | Cleaned / Dechalked | Klorin / Kalcinol | | ✓ | ✓ | |
| Doors | Spotcleaned | Spraycleaner | | ✓ | | |
| Tiles | Spotcleaned | | | ✓ | | |
| Tiles | Washed | | | | | ✓ |
| Mirrors | Cleaned | Spraycleaner | | ✓ | | |
| Sinks | Washed / Dried | Ecoline | | ✓ | | |
| Ceiling | Washed | Spraycleaner | 3 x Yearly | ⇐ | ⇐ | ⇐ |
| | | | | | | |
| | | | | | | |
| | | | | | | |
| | | | | | | |
| | | | | | | |
| | | | | | | |

**Figure 6.11**  *Function room cleaning follows much the same schedule as other public spaces. One major difference is the increased frequency of carpet cleaning.*

covering. Skirting is required for speakers' tables and display or buffet tables.

During setup and break down, the house attendants or supervisor assigned to the public spaces should check function chairs for wear or damage. Fire regulations in some states require that chairs set up theater-style to accommodate 300 or more must be bonded together in groups of three. This is so that, in case of fire, people scrambling to leave a crowded meeting room will not knock over the chairs, causing tripping and obstruction. Properties in states with this regulation usually purchase chairs with a **ganging device** along the side of the chair that interlocks with the device on the next chair. Supervisors and attendants should check that these devices fit properly and hold the chairs correctly.

Chairs must be set up with enough space between the rows to allow for easy passage. A good rule of thumb is to allow 33 inches from one chair

 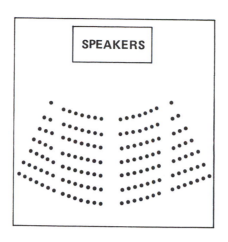 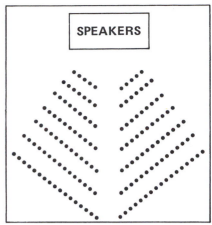

**Figure 6.12** *Seating arrangements: (1) In a long, rectangular room, starting with the center aisle at the front, arrange the chairs in eight rows with eight chairs per row, for a total of 128 seats. (2) In a square room, an auditorium layout is best: start with a center aisle and set up seven rows with seven chairs on each side; the outside section gets one seat at the front and one additional set in each succeeding, for a total of 154 seats. This arrangement can also be used in a rectangular room. (3) To achieve this effect, starting at the center aisle at the front, angle the chairs, beginning with five and adding two chairs on each succeeding row as far as necessary.*

to the next back. The aisles that lead to and from a stage should be 44 inches wide, increased by 1.5 inches for every 5 feet of travel to the farthest exit. Sections of local fire department regulations regarding setup should be posted for the house attendants

## GENERAL CLEANING

Not all public space elements require daily or even weekly cleaning. Some tasks are done only once a month, some only once or twice a year (see Tricks of the Trade 6.2). Certain assignments can be added to regular daily assignments without creating an unreasonable workload. Others, such as carpet cleaning or floor buffing, will take up an entire shift, perhaps for days.

**Tricks of the Trade 6.2**
**Cleaning Specialty Hotels**

*The Problem:* Older hotels, inns, and other specially designed facilities require special efforts.
*The Solution:* The 10-room Aveda Spa hotel in Osceola, Wisconsin, is housed in a mansion that dates from the turn of the century. It has long, open stairways connecting the floors. Since attendants could not carry vacuum cleaners up and down the stairs, management purchased lightweight shoulder vacuums for routine fabric cleaning. In January, the property shuts down for a deep cleaning. All upholstered items are sent out for deep cleaning. Because the property is small and storage space is limited, this has proven more cost effective than purchasing upholstery cleaning equipment, says Peggy Anderson, general manager..

Anderson suspects her biggest cleaning challenge is yet to come. The spa is adding natural hide tipis as part of its expansion. "We're still looking at how we'll clean them," she says.

Charles Brown Smith, executive housekeeper for the 75-room La Playa hotel, Carmel, California (built in 1904), says daily dusting of walls is a simple but effective method of maintaining this historic property. Attendants use a fabric duster that works by using a static field to attract dust, which does not harm the wood. "Daily cleaning really extends the life of the surfaces," says Brown.

### Assigning Monthly Tasks

Among the tasks to be assigned to public space crews once a month are:

1. Vacuum upholstered furniture and draperies. If dust is building up, this must be done more frequently.

2. Wax lamp bases and any decorative items to prevent dust buildup.

3. Wash and polish all the sides and drawers of nonwood furnishings. Polish wood furniture and cabinetry. This task should be assigned on a **skip-clean** basis, which means that a few items are cleaned each day. By month's end, all elements will have been cleaned.

4. Wash and polish all the clear glass except the windows, which should be spot cleaned daily. Window exteriors are cleaned by specialty firms.

5. Wash or spot clean walls, depending on the wall covering. Carpeted walls should be vacuumed and spot cleaned.

6. Polish marble floors.

7. Scrub grout and wash wall tiles in public rest rooms. This may have to be done more frequently.

## Assigning On-Demand Tasks

A select few tasks are done on demand. One that requires an inordinate amount of planning for the executive housekeeper is **relamping** all of the chandeliers and light fixtures in the property. Relamping means replacing all of the light bulbs in a fixture. Changing bulbs in ceiling fixtures is not simple, even if they are on pulleys, as is the case in most modern hotels. The house attendant still must find time to lower the fixture, change the bulb, and raise it. In historic properties, the task is complicated by the fact that special scaffolds or rigs often are required to reach chandeliers and ceiling fixtures. Rather than losing this much time each time a bulb burns out, fixtures are relamped periodically as preventive maintenance. Used bulbs that are not burned out can be sold at low cost to employees or donated.

Washing and cleaning these large fixtures also requires detailed advance planning (see Figure 6.13). Cleaning a large crystal chandelier in the conventional manner using ammonia and soft rags will take a house attendant seven to eight hours. Whoever does the scheduling must plan for this and allocate the attendant's workload to other or several other workers or schedule an extra employee. Another approach developed at the Century Plaza Hotel in Los Angeles is to put ammonia into an upholstery machine with a fine spray adjust-

ment. A house attendant or maintenance person sitting atop a scaffold sprays the ammonia onto the chandelier. The drippings are caught in a huge plastic structure much like an inverted umbrella suspended beneath the chandelier.

Floor care, including carpet cleaning and waxing and polishing wood floors, is scheduled as needed. These tasks should be done at least twice a year. However, a thorough cleaning will have to be scheduled more frequently if the property has light carpeting in its public spaces or during times of year when wet weather causes extensive stains. The cleaning schedule for wood, marble, or other hard-surface floors usually is more predictable because these surfaces do not absorb stains in the same way as carpet fiber (see Chapter 7).

Schedules for periodic work should be re-evaluated on a regular basis. Budgetary constraints may mean that some general cleaning jobs, such as oiling furniture, that should be done monthly may have to be done every six weeks. Monthly window cleaning may be unnecessary during certain seasons. Essential tasks, such as cleaning rest rooms and maintaining basic cleanliness standards, should never be postponed.

## CLEANING THE BACK OF THE HOUSE

Though back-of-the-house space is being reduced as properties seek to maximize the amount of revenue-generating space, the back of the house still may be nearly as large as the public space. As with public spaces, schedules for cleaning the back of the house are based on the amount of square footage each employee is expected to clean or the time a task takes on average. Daily assignments will be much like those for the front of the house, with necessary daily cleaning tasks assigned along with one or two general cleaning projects.

### Employee Areas

Cleaning employee areas is a necessary part of maintaining the back of the house. It should be budgeted for and inspected just as the front of the house is. Unless the employee "cafeteria" is simply a few tables and a vending machine, in which case it is cleaned by one housekeeping employee, cleaning cafeterias is usually the responsibility of the F&B department. In the rare cases in which it is not, housekeeping staff should follow the same procedures as for restaurants. Employee rest rooms

***Figure 6.13*** *Cleaning a large crystal chandelier can take a house attendant seven or eight hours. Relamping should be done at the same time, particularly if the chandeliers are hard to reach. (Courtesy of The New York Palace)*

should be cleaned on the same schedule and with the same procedures as public space rest rooms. The rest rooms, too, should be checked once an hour for cleanliness and the need to restock supplies. In some hotels, the attendant who cleans the public area rest rooms also cleans employee rest rooms and locker rooms. Only the exterior of lockers is cleaned; only the general manager or security staff can enter an employee locker. Rest rooms are cleaned first, then showers. Floors are cleaned last. Tile and grout should be cleaned once a month. The executive housekeeper or assistant should inspect these areas on a monthly basis.

## Service Corridors and Stairways

Service corridors and stairways provide vital links for hotel operations. Carts and racks can reach their destinations quickly without disturbing guests. These corridors also link the back-of-the-house offices where all the administrative work of the property is done.

Cleaning and maintaining service corridors usually is scheduled at the start of the 3 P.M. to 11 P.M. shift. Most of the room service traffic ended in the mid-morning. This also is a lull for the banquet department. Many areas of the back of the house, from offices to kitchens, cannot be cleaned until

later when shifts end or F&B outlets close. Assignments are much the same as those for the front of the house and are scheduled on the same frequency. Interior stairways are often overlooked; they should be swept daily and mopped as needed. Walls and vents should also be cleaned regularly.

## Offices and Business Centers

The housekeeping department has limited responsibility for cleaning and maintaining employee offices. Offices should be cleaned on the 3 P.M. to 11 P.M. shift and usually are scheduled to be done after 5 P.M. OR 6 P.M., when the majority of the administrative employees leave. Attendants who do night service or turndown may be scheduled to clean offices as well.

The only tasks usually assigned on a daily basis are emptying waste baskets and vacuuming. Employees are expected to keep their desks or offices neat. To save time, some hotels now ask that employees set all trash outside their offices when they leave work each day. At times, some hotels may ask that employees clean their own offices periodically.

Supplies for offices and business centers include a cart into which trash is emptied and, sometimes, glass cleaner for windows. Periodically, perhaps once a year, the executive housekeeper may schedule a general cleaning of office space that would include polishing or wiping down the exterior surfaces of desks, book cases, and filing cabinets, depending on the surface material; vacuuming fabric or carpet-covered partitions; vacuuming and spot cleaning chairs; and washing the draperies. Draperies should be washed or dry cleaned only on an "as needed" basis because this type of cleaning increases wear.

Well before general cleaning is scheduled, the executive housekeeper sends a memo to all employees explaining on what date the cleaning will take place and requesting that all items be removed from the tops of surfaces and partitions. Cluttered surfaces are not cleaned and are mentioned as not serviceable in the attendant's report.

The one exception to this schedule is the general manager's office. This is particularly true in upscale properties where the general manager must conduct business in his or her office, often on short notice. Dusting, cleaning tables with glass, wood, or marble tops, and vacuuming should be scheduled daily during the 3 P.M. to 11 P.M. shift since the general manager usually leaves work from 6 P.M. to 7 P.M. The attendant should not dust the desktop if any papers are on it. These are considered confidential. Upholstery, carpet, and window treatments should be spot cleaned and vacuumed on the same schedule as the public space.

Many hotels now feature **business centers,** which provide essential business services for guests ranging from copying and faxing to the use of computers and translation services. The supervisor should check with the business center assistant or concierge for any reservations after the standard closing time, since some centers are available round-the-clock by reservation. Wood surfaces should be dusted, glass partitions cleaned, phone receivers disinfected, and carpets vacuumed nightly. Attendants who clean this area must take extra care cleaning around the equipment. Cleaning and maintaining the equipment itself is the responsibility of the audiovisual department.

### Buildings, Grounds, and Fitness Areas

The responsibilities of the housekeeping department may not be confined to the properties' interiors. In small properties of 100 rooms or less or in some resorts, housekeeping's role may extend to the buildings and grounds.

Assignment sheets should have ample room for special instructions, since this aspect of cleaning covers tasks from removing litter from walkways to cleaning pool decks, the tiled or paved areas immediately surrounding the swimming pool. The following are typical assignments, which may have to be repeated at regular intervals throughout the day and night shifts, especially if outdoor events are planned:

- **Dry-picking,** or removing trash and debris from walkways, outdoor stairways, planters, and landscaped areas
- Sweeping walkways, or using outdoor vacuums on wide areas
- Sweeping garages and parking areas
- Cleaning pool decks, including mopping, sweeping, or vacuuming and rearranging the furniture
- Cleaning rest rooms near pool areas
- Cleaning storage closets and custodians' closets
- Dusting handrails along sidewalks

The maintenance or engineering department cleans the pool itself. But in hotels with spas or exercise facilities, housekeeping may have to clean the pool deck, carpets, locker rooms, and exercise facilities. Exercise machines are wiped down according to manufacturers' instructions. Massage areas must be cleaned each night with disinfectant. Since guests or clients of the spa probably will not tolerate strong cleaning odors, the disinfectant used in this area should not leave a strong odor. If a product cleans well but does leave an odor, the attendant can apply another chemical which removes odors, like those used to remove cigarette or cigar smoke odors from guest rooms.

### Kitchens

In cases in which the housekeeping department cleans the kitchen, which is becoming more and more rare, the most important assignments are to degrease and sanitize the exterior surfaces of the equipment, filters, and floors. F&B stewards clean the insides of the equipment, interiors of storage areas, and surfaces where food containers are left or stored.

*Cleaning equipment.* Improved equipment has made this time-consuming job easier. Most attendants cleaning kitchens now use steam cleaners and power spray machines with nozzles. Retractable hose reels with sprayers enable one employee to wash down kitchen equipment and the floor. The spray valve has a dish guard to protect racks of dishes and glasses. An insulated handle remains cool. High-pressure hoses are particularly important for cleaning the nonskid mats, runners, or floor coverings that have been installed in kitchens to reduce accidents. Cleaning this material would be extremely time-consuming and ineffective if done by hand. This equipment uses pressurized hot water at 193°F, which can even dissolve grease (see Figure 6.14).

Grease is a particular problem in cleaning kitchens because of the threat of fire and hygiene problems. Grease must be removed from all surfaces each night. Attendants should be trained to pay particular attention to exhaust flues and the hoods above the main bank of equipment. These are the critical danger areas for fires. Grates and filters are cleaned as needed. **Lifting forks,** long-handled tools with heads designed to lift off grates and filters, enable employees to remove some of the greasiest filters and grates without touching them. Some equipment has disposable filters which are changed regularly. Reusable filters are removed and cleaned in the kitchen's dishwasher.

*Lamps and light fixtures.* Electric heat lamps should be cleaned daily. After being unplugged and allowed to cool, these lamps, which are used to

***Figure 6.14*** *Power spray equipment enables one employee to wash down both kitchen equipment and the kitchen floor. Pressurized hot water from these machines can even dissolve grease. (Courtesy of Advance Machine Co.)*

keep food warm, are cleaned with a degreasing cleaner diluted in water. They should be wiped off with this dilution, rinsed with clear water and allowed to dry well before they are turned on again.

The cleaning of light fixtures should be assigned far more frequently than for fixtures in other areas. Grease and dust combine to form a buildup of soil; steam further aggravates this problem and causes streaking. Failure to remove this buildup will necessitate using stronger cleaners which may dull the metal surface and allow even more buildup to collect.

*Walls and ceilings.* Kitchen walls and ceilings are cleaned on an as-needed basis, but at least once a month. Walls and ceilings in bakery areas may need to be cleaned only every other month. Tiled walls can be washed down easily. If the grout has been sealed properly, there is little problem with permanent stains. Stainless steel does not stain permanently, but it can become discolored from constant spillage and shows every fingerprint. This makes frequent cleaning with special cleaners designed for stainless steel and frequent inspections essential. Mild acidic cleaners can renew the finish.

The attendant who does the application should be well trained in this procedure since these products can etch, that is mark or scratch, or discolor surfaces if used improperly.

The challenges of cleaning the kitchen are heightened by the fact that some very effective cleaners cannot be used on surfaces on which food will be prepared. Manufacturers are introducing more environmentally friendly cleaning liquids and compounds that will clean kitchens with less food safety-related side effects. The executive housekeeper must weigh these factors when deciding which chemicals to use.

## INSPECTIONS

Public space inspectors or supervisors cover a lot of ground, both literally and figuratively. Even in large hotels, there may be only one public space inspector per shift. The inspector or supervisor must see that all assigned tasks were completed during the shift and that the work was done correctly. Any errors or oversights should be pointed out to the attendants and rectified before the end of the shift.

Checklists used by public area supervisors should leave ample room for comments on items that require repair, general cleaning, or replacement. Work orders should be written up for maintenance or engineering indicating on what date the damage or repair was noted, what needs to be done, and by what date the repair should be completed. The inspector or supervisor writing up work orders for public areas should indicate which work, if any, has priority. This is important because some repair jobs in public areas can be done only during the night shift or graveyard shift when cumbersome or noisy equipment can be used with minimum disturbance to guests. The time required to do these types of difficult repairs, such as repairing damage to a chandelier that is not on a pulley, may preclude doing numerous repairs on one shift.

Most inspections in public areas focus on neatness and cleanliness. It is not enough for all furniture to have been dusted; it also must be positioned correctly in the space. Inspections of public rest rooms require more time and expertise. The day shift inspector or supervisor should check that the toilets and sink basins are clean, that supplies have been replenished, that waste baskets have been emptied and that the floor is clear of debris. The night shift or graveyard shift inspector or supervisor must make sure that the entire rest room has been thoroughly cleaned, including vents and

push plates on the doors. Supervisors also are trained to focus on overlooked areas, from the tops of picture frames and mirrors to electrical, planters and the Braille plates in elevators.

Because these public areas are so critical in forming first impressions for guests and visitors, the executive housekeeper should check them personally. "I try to walk all public areas before 8 A.M.," says Lyn Aoki, director of housekeeping for the Sheraton Waikiki in Honolulu. Ed Conaway, executive housekeeper for the U.S. Grant Hotel in San Diego, California, checks the lobby several times a day and the balance of the public space "as often as possible." Using follow-up forms along with assignment sheets, such as that shown in Figure 6.8 reminds employees that they, too, are responsible for making sure all work is done properly (see Tales of the Trade 6.1).

**Tales of the Trade 6.1**
**Surprise Inspections**
Jackie Jones, executive housekeeper of the Windsor Court, says there is no substitute for regular checks by the executive housekeeper. "I occasionally show up at midnight. When staff members ask me what I'm doing at the hotel at that hour, I say, 'I came to see what you're doing.' We have a good contract company and good workers. But not all night cleaners are dependable. The executive housekeeper should check up on them," says Jones. Showing up at night also gives the executive housekeeper the opportunity to talk with night staff and make sure they are made to feel as valued as their day-shift colleagues.

Checking for pest problems should be part of the regular assignments for inspectors. Kitchens and storage areas are the most likely spaces to have pest problems. However, pests are not restricted to areas where food is prepared and stored. Both interior and exterior areas should be checked regularly.

## WORKING WITH CONTRACT CLEANERS

To control labor and equipment costs, some executive housekeepers **outsource,** or hire commercial cleaning companies or contract cleaning services, for some or all tasks assigned during the night and graveyard shifts. This decision is made in conjunction with the general manager and, usually, the F&B department. Before hiring a company, the executive housekeeper must determine what needs to be done, obtain bids, and check references.

## Assessing What Needs to Be Done

Contract cleaning services most frequently are hired to do tasks that would require a disproportionate amount of training or specialized equipment. The most likely tasks to contract out include cleaning kitchens and, in more and more cases, restaurants and lounges, thoroughly cleaning carpeting, washing exterior windows, and cleaning and maintaining outdoor fitness facilities such as tennis courts.

## Advantages and Disadvantages of Contract Cleaners

Most executive housekeepers acknowledge that this approach has advantages and disadvantages.

*Advantages.* Using a contract service reduces labor costs and the cost of training, and provides a solution for staffing problems. It also reduces equipment costs, particularly for specialty equipment such as heavy-duty carpet cleaners. Plus, there is the value of their expertise.

*Disadvantages.* The biggest problem is inconsistent performance. Since the contract service is looking for workers in the same tough labor market as the hotel, it, too, may have a difficult time finding qualified workers for all of its accounts. Correcting poor performance is often harder because the crews are not employees of the property. The hotel supervisor can point out instances of unsatisfactory work, but has no authority to carry out disciplinary procedures. The only recourse ultimately is to look for another service when the contract runs out, or—if work is completely unsatisfactory—break the contract.

Another concern is that it is difficult for the hotel's management to investigate another company's employees in cases of suspected theft or pilferage. As a practical matter, hiring outside services may also mean that the housekeeping department is not able to buy some of the equipment it needs for general cleaning. The department must hire an outside contractor whenever hard-surface floors need buffing, for example, because this kind of equipment is not often used in guest rooms. The pros and cons must be weighed carefully before deciding whether to do night cleaning in-house or on a contract basis.

## Finding a Reliable Company

Some hotel chains have a list of preferred vendors and service providers. These companies probably would offer the lowest prices and would work hard to please chain members. If not, the search for a contract cleaning service frequently begins with a check of commercial listings in a phone book. Ads in the commercial listings will give an overview of what services the company offers and whether it specifies lodging as one of its areas of expertise.

**Networking,** which is obtaining information from professional colleagues, may be more time-consuming initially but may help narrow the field faster. Executive housekeepers can consult with colleagues at other hotels, university residence halls, senior living centers, or hospitals to find out which firms have done satisfactory work. For specific tasks such as carpet cleaning, the manufacturer of the carpet may be able to recommend a company that has participated in special training programs in how the carpet should be cleaned and maintained.

Any recommendation, from however valuable or trusted a source, should be checked carefully. The executive housekeeper should ask for and call several current references. For specific tasks such as carpet cleaning or marble floor care, the executive housekeeper may request a demonstration to measure the company's performance and capabilities. At least three written bids should be obtained before awarding the contract.

The executive housekeeper must make clear exactly what is to be done and make sure the company has the labor supply and equipment to do the job. Both parties must agree on what the contract will cover before the bidding process begins. Before evaluating bids, the executive housekeeper must find out whether there are surcharges for any tasks or use of certain equipment. Value for money, not price alone, should be the deciding factor.

## Monitoring Performance

The inspector or night supervisor should check the contract cleaning service's performance against the same standards that would be used for staff. Each task performed unsatisfactorily or any oversights should be listed on the inspection sheet and reported to the person in charge of the crew on that shift, or for the specific task, and the night assistant housekeeper. A copy also should be left for the executive housekeeper.

If the hotel is using a contract cleaning service for all night cleaning, occasional problems may arise (see Tricks of the Trade 6.3). The crew may be short-staffed on a particular night or equipment may fail. The assistant night housekeeper or supervisor on the graveyard shift should discuss these problems with the executive housekeeper, who would point out these problems to the service and discuss solutions.

---

**Tricks of the Trade 6.3**
**Communicating Better with Contract Services**

Miriam Albano, executive housekeeper of the deluxe, 500-suite RIHGA Royal Hotel in New York City, works regularly with a variety of contract services. She uses careful monitoring to ensure that quality standards are met.

"We keep communication books, which record any problems with the work or oversights. These are turned in by the night manager responsible for housekeeping at the end of the shift. Every Tuesday, I walk through the hotel with the contract service's supervisor and discuss any special needs for the upcoming work and point out any problems," Albano notes.

However, if the problems are serious, such as suspected theft or refusal to perform assigned duties covered in the contract, the executive housekeeper should cancel the contract. Contracts have clauses which allow for cancellation based on failure to perform the duties outlined.

---

## SUMMARY

Creating a year-long schedule of what needs to be done in the front and back of the house daily, weekly, monthly, and periodically during the year will enable the executive housekeeper to better organize assignments and scheduling. This kind of organization also makes it possible to obtain bids for and check references on any contract cleaning service required well in advance of the time the work must be scheduled. Advance planning and organization makes all public space and back-of-the-house cleaning more efficient and effective.

Though the number of housekeeping employees assigned to clean public spaces is not as large as that assigned to clean rooms, staff management is a concern. The workload must be reasonable and assignments must be explained in detail, especially on night shifts when the executive housekeeper is not usually on the premises. Employees, supervisors, and top department management must constantly check on the cleanliness and neatness of these spaces, as well as the need for repair or replacement.

To achieve these goals, the executive housekeeper must be familiar with:

- Assessing workload requirements in public areas and prioritizing assignments
- Creating the 24-hour-a-day schedule that is typical for public areas
- Creating frequency charts for general cleaning projects
- Solving the challenges of hard-to-reach and hard-to-clean areas
- Working with the F&B department to make sure areas of shared responsibility are fair to each department
- Creating effective inspection techniques
- Working with contract cleaners, and assessing when to use these services

## Review Questions

1. What is the front of the house?
2. What is a labor analysis and how is it used in assignments for public areas?
3. Describe some typical tasks that must be done on a daily and weekly basis in the lobby.
4. How do the duties of day-shift and night-shift attendants differ for public spaces?
5. Describe how public rest room cleaning differs from guest bathroom cleaning.
6. What is banquet setup and for which tasks would housekeeping typically be responsible?
7. Describe several key assignments that could be done only on the night or graveyard shift and explain why.
8. What is outsourcing?
9. What are typical tasks done by contract cleaners rather than housekeeping staff?
10. Describe the equipment usually used in cleaning kitchens. What cleaning problems have priority and why?

## Critical Thinking Questions

1. The hotel's management is considering hiring a contract cleaner to do the nightly public area cleaning. How will this impact housekeeping costs and standards? Discuss the pros and cons.

2. Several room attendants have asked for a regular rotation in the public areas. What are the benefits and drawbacks of rotating rooms staff to front- and back-of-the-house assignments?

3. During a renovation, the designer has replaced the hotel's signature dark patterned wool carpet with one featuring a cream-colored background and floral accents. How will this impact scheduling and cleaning costs?

## Assignment

Sit in a hotel lobby. Take on the role of the inspector. What areas have been missed or cleaned unsatisfactorily? What elements need repair or replacement?

# 7
# Maintaining Floors

## Chapter Objectives

To master the massive challenge of floor care in the lodging industry, the professional housekeeper must:

- Develop an understanding of how carpets and floors are constructed or made
- Establish procedures for routine maintenance
- Establish procedures for spot and stain removal
- Establish deep-cleaning procedures
- Determine which types of equipment and supplies are most effective
- Determine which products should be used to seal and finish different types of floors
- Determine which products and floor surfaces should be avoided
- Assess wear and damage
- Schedule repairs and maintenance

More than 20,000 people walk through the lobby of Bally's hotel and casino in Las Vegas *each day*. Though few hotels can equal this kind of foot traffic, the carpets and floors in every hotel must be able to withstand constant use and still look good. Keeping carpets and floors clean and in good in repair is one of the toughest challenges facing the housekeeping department; it is also one of the most important. Dirty floors or heavily stained carpet are noticeable indicators of slipshod housekeeping practices. If guests notice the floors are dirty, it will be hard to convince them that any area of the hotel is properly cleaned.

Nearly 70 percent of the cleaning time and budget is spent on floors. It is the housekeeping department's responsibility to find ways to protect this investment (see Tales of the Trade 7.1).

> ### Tales of the Trade 7.1
> ### Maintaining the Floors in Bally's
>
> On average, 40,000 feet and an endless variety of carts and other wheeled vehicles traverse the floors of Bally's hotel and casino in Las Vegas, Nevada each day. Neil Hackworth is the housekeeping department's public area supervisor who has responsibility for keeping the hotel's floors clean and fresh looking around the clock. "The biggest challenge is maintaining the marble in the public area. We have so much foot traffic it really is hard to keep it polished," Hackworth says.
>
> Diamond pads have been a boon, he adds. The buffers work with five different diamond pads, which range from quite coarse to fine. The $3,200 cost of the machines is well worth it, says Hackworth. "If you polish the marble floors with powder, you have to do it regularly. But the diamond pads resurface the marble, and that lasts for a full year," he notes. Less expensive than outside contractors, the machines protect the far greater investment in the signature marble flooring.

## SELECTING AND CARING FOR CARPETING

Affordable pricing and overall ease of maintenance make carpeting the most popular choice of floor covering for areas other than the lobby and some back-of-the-house space where heavy cart traffic makes it impractical. Knowing the basics of carpet construction and how to care for carpet are essential to effective housekeeping. Carpets are subject to a full range of abuse, from the mud or wetness tracked in on shoes to the inevitable spills of food and drink in the restaurants and function rooms. Maintaining and protecting carpets properly is essential to extending their life.

## Carpet Construction

All professional housekeepers will need to know how carpet is constructed in order to find ways to maintain it properly. The key factors in assessing carpet include:

- **Construction**
- **Pile density,** which refers to the number of yarns, and weight
- **Pile height,** which refers to the height of the yarns, and style
- **Fibers**
- **Resilience,** which refers to how quickly the yarn springs back after being compressed
- **Backing,** which refers to the material to which the yarns are attached

Appearance is a consideration as well, because the large amount of floor space covered by carpeting makes a strong visual statement about the property's image and marketing positioning. But appearance alone is not the determining factor in carpet selection. Durability and ease of maintenance should take precedence. With all of the carpets on the market, properties no longer have to give up aesthetics to find a carpet that will perform well.

## Construction

Carpet construction refers to: (1) the type of surface, usually called the **pile** or **face** yarns; (2) how these yarns are anchored to the backing; and (3) the type of backing.

Although the professional housekeeper should be familiar with all the basic types of carpet construction, more than 90 percent of the commercial carpet used in the lodging industry is tufted. To make tufted carpet, thousands of needles threaded with yarn are forced through backing to produce loops or tufts (see Figure 7.1). A latex adhesive is applied to the primary backing to hold the tufts in place.

The loops can be level, so that all are the same height which produces a fairly uniform surface that can withstand heavy traffic, or multi-level. For plush carpet, the loops are cut. A recent modification mixes straight tufts with slightly curled tufts

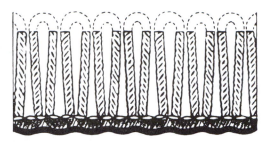

**Figure 7.1** *This drawing shows tufted construction. Tufted construction is used for more than 90 percent of all of the carpeting used in the lodging industry.*

for a plush that minimizes the show of footprints and vacuum tracks.

*Woven carpet.* A loom interlocks face and the backing. The three mains types of woven carpet are: **Velvets,** usually a uniform pile height; **Wiltons,** known for their intricate pattern capabilities and named for the loom on which they are made; and **Axminsters,** which have most of the pile yarn on the surface (see Figures 7.2a, 7.2b and 7.2c.) Wovens are found most often in upscale or deluxe hotels.

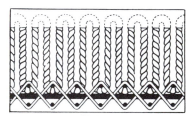

*Velvet*

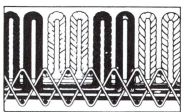

*Wilton*

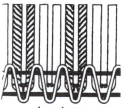

*Axminster*

**Figure 7.2** *Velvet; Wilton; Axminster. These are the three types of woven carpet, usually reserved for upscale or deluxe hotels.*

**Knitted carpet.** The pile yarns and backing are interlaced in a series of connected loops. An additional backing may be added to produce a more stable carpet. Most are produced in solid colors or tweedy effects, though a variety of patterns and textures are possible.

**Needle-punch carpet.** Compacting and interlocking the fibers into a structural backing forms a felt-like surface. Normally latex is added to the backing. This carpet is usually used for outdoor or indoor/outdoor areas.

**Flocked carpet.** Synthetic fibers are deposited on soft adhesive that is applied to a woven back. The adhesive is hardened after the fibers are firmly embedded. The surface is a single-height, level-cut pile.

Carpets are available as:

- *Broadlooms,* rolls 12 feet wide or 15 feet wide
- *Narrow carpets,* 26 to 36 inches wide, usually for corridors
- *Squares or tiles,* usually 18-inch, but also 24-inch, squares with a semi-rigid backing for easy replacement
- *Area rugs,* in standard or custom sizes, from 3 feet by 5 feet to 10 feet by 12 feet or larger. In the lodging industry, area rugs typically are used as decorative elements in lobbies. Depending on their construction, they should receive the same care as carpeting. Only fringe or other borders would require special care to prevent equipment from snagging these edges.

## Pile Density and Weight

How well any carpet performs is a matter of the density of the pile. If the pile yarns are sufficient, the carpet will resist compression from traffic of both feet and carts, withstand repeated vacuuming and cleaning longer without showing wear, and suffer less abrasion despite ground-in soil. How **dense** the carpet is, or how thick it feels, depends on the gauge (the number of needles of tufts per inch of width), pile height, stitches per inch, **face weight** (which refers to yarn weight), yarn size and more.

Although many factors can be used to judge density, the following formula is simple and effective:

Density = 36 × Face weight ÷ Pile height

The 36 indicates the number of inches, that is, one yard; the face weight is the number of tufts. So,

**Figure 7.3** *The pitch indicates the number of warp yarns in a 27-inch width of carpet.*

1/8 gauge means that there are eight tufts across the inch.

**Pitch** is a density indicator for woven carpet. It refers to the number of **warp** or lengthwise yarns in a 27-inch width of carpet (see Figure 7.3). The standard pitch for Velvet is 216; for Wilton, 256; and for Axminster, 189. Yarn weight, also known as face weight, is the number of ounces of yarn per square yard. Contract carpet generally ranges from 20 to 48 ounces. Minimum weights per yard for heavy- and medium-traffic areas are given in Table 7.1.

## Pile Height and Style

Table 7.1 contains a reference to average pile height. The differences, measured in tenths or even hundredths of an inch, may seem slight, but they are not. These seemingly nominal variations can have substantial effect when magnified over the width or length of the entire carpet. Generally, the heavier the carpet, the better it will withstand heavy traffic.

**Polyester.** *Advantages:* It is fairly stain resistant, durable, and easy to maintain. *Disadvantages:* It has low resilience, which may lead to matting in heavy traffic areas. Some carpet experts claim polyester is not suitable for contract carpet.

**Polypropylene,** also called Olefin. *Advantages:* It is durable, nonabsorbent, and stain resistant, especially since spilled liquids, other than oil-based spills, do not penetrate the fibers; it resists static buildup, and will not fade. *Disadvantages:* It is less comfortable under foot, and it is susceptible to heat or friction damage.

These fibers are compared in Table 7.2. Other natural fabrics such as **sisal,** a product made from the hemp plant, or even cotton may be used for large area rugs. Their most likely use is in hot or humid resort settings. Other synthetics, ranging

**TABLE 7.1**  *Minimum Specification Requirements Based on Pile Density for Wool Carpets*

| | Average heavy traffic | | Average medium traffic | |
|---|---|---|---|---|
| | Minimum weight per sq. yd. (ounces) | Average pile height (inches) | Minimum weight per sq. yd. (ounces) | Average pile height (inches) |
| Axminster carpet | 36 | 0.200–0.310 | 28 | 0.200–0.310 |
| Knitted carpet | 42 | 0.250–0.300 | 36 | 0.200–0.250 |
| Tufted carpet | 42 | 0.250–0.300 | 36 | 0.200–0.250 |
| Velvet carpet: | | | | |
|   Woven through the back | 42 | 0.200–0.250 | 32 | 0.175–0.230 |
|   Not woven through the back | 36 | 0.200–0.250 | 28 | 0.175–0.230 |
|     Twist | — | — | 42 | — |
| Wilton carpet | 42 | 0.200–0.250 | 34 | 0.200–0.250 |

**Source:** Bernard Berkeley, "The Selection and Maintenance of Commercial Carpet." *Cornell Hotel & Restaurant Administration Quarterly,* Ithaca, New York, 1970.

from acetate to rayon, are also used in carpet. For the lodging industry, the most common choices are wool, nylon, a blend of wool and nylon, or Olefin.

### Resilience

The professional housekeeper must use different criteria for weighing resilience in public areas and guest rooms. In public spaces, corridors, and high-volume restaurants and function rooms, the carpet must be resilient enough to bounce back after heavy foot traffic as well as a steady stream of cart traffic. If it is not resilient enough, it will become permanently crushed in certain areas and show a fast-wearing walk pattern. In the guest room, however, where traffic is less, comfort under the guests' bare or slippered feet is more important. For some back-of-the-house areas where tile floors would be

too slippery, indoor/outdoor carpeting, with its nonresilient surface, is best.

### Backings and Padding

What is under a carpet is as important as its surface. Carpet has a **primary backing,** which is the actual underside of the carpeting, and, usually, a **secondary backing,** which is bonded on for additional strength. The secondary backing also helps the carpet resist stretching. A foam back may also be added to the primary backing to eliminate the need for a separate pad.

In low traffic areas, such as guest rooms, padding can extend wear by softening the intensity of abrasion, and add comfort, insulation, and a layer of sound absorption. A thicker pad in low traffic areas also adds to a more luxurious feeling. Pad-

**TABLE 7.2**  *Minimum Specification Requirements Based on Pile Density for Nylon or Polypropylene Carpets*

| | Average heavy traffic | | Average medium traffic | |
|---|---|---|---|---|
| | Minimum weight per sq. yd. (ounces) | Average pile height (inches) | Minimum weight per sq. yd. (ounces) | Average pile height (inches) |
| Tufted carpet | 28 | 0.190–0.290 | 22 | 0.190–0.290 |
| Velvet carpet Woven through the back | 28 | 0.210–0.290 | 22 | 0.210–0.290 |

**Source:** Bernard Berkeley, "The Selection and Maintenance of Commercial Carpet." *Cornell Hotel & Restaurant Administration Quarterly,* Ithaca, New York, 1970.

ding should not be too soft in areas such as corridors where heavy carts can cause rippling and buckling.

In high traffic areas, carpets are usually glued to the floor and have no pad. Some experts contend this method extends the life of the carpet 25 percent in heavy traffic areas because friction and air pockets that could otherwise form between the carpet and the subflooring—the hard floor beneath it—are eliminated. New adhesives can be easily scraped up when the carpet is removed. A newer option still is carpet that is essentially "taped" down, making it easy to move, repair, or replace.

## Aesthetics

Color and pattern selection do not affect the durability of fiber, but they can make a significant difference in how long the carpet looks good. Imprecise, fairly heavy patterns work best for restaurants and function rooms where spills and stains are part of everyday operations. Lobby carpets are expected to set the design standard for the hotel, but still must withstand heavy foot traffic. To accommodate these needs, irregular patterns also work well. Guestroom carpets can be more subtle, but these, also frequently have some sort of understated pattern to disguise soils and wear.

The scale of the pattern is linked to the scale of the space; in other words the bigger the room, the bigger the scale of the pattern can be (see Figure 7.4). Solid carpet is rarely used because it does not mask stains. Carpets that are too light show stains; carpets that are too dark show lint and debris. However, carpets that use lights and darks as accents to other tones still provide ease of maintenance and expand the design possibilities.

## Purchase and Installation

Whether the executive housekeeper writes the purchase order or works with the purchasing agent, the goal in purchasing carpet is to get a product that will be durable and easy to maintain and will look appropriate in the property.

After-sales service is important. Most carpets carry a warranty: typically 5 to 10 years on the carpet and 10 years on the fiber. Many warranties also include **color fastness,** which means the color will not run or bleed when cleaned. This information should be kept on file. The carpet company also should have some type of guarantee covering **re-**

**stretching**—stretching the carpet tighter and trimming off the excess.

The vendor generally takes responsibility for installation. Carpets should be installed by a certified floor covering installation contractor. There should be a written agreement as to when the installation is to be done and what the cost will be. Since carpet is hard to store, installation should be scheduled to begin the same day the carpet is delivered. The contract should include a clause on restretching after six months, in case wrinkles or bubbles develop.

## Regular and Preventive Maintenance

Carpeting in public areas has an average life expectancy of three to five years in a busy, upscale hotel. Good quality guestroom carpeting with a good pad can last up to 10 years. The goal of the housekeeping department is to extend the useful life of the carpet as much as possible through proper daily cleaning procedures, preventive maintenance, and regular spot cleaning and shampooing.

Von Schrader, a manufacturer of carpet cleaning equipment products based in Racine, Wisconsin, developed its Textile Appearance Protection Plan™ which recommends a five-step approach to carpet maintenance:

1. Soil prevention
2. Routine vacuuming
3. Spot removal
4. Traffic lane maintenance
5. Overall cleaning

## Preventive Maintenance

It is far easier to prevent soiling than to deal with it once it happens. In terms of carpeting, *soiling* means a buildup of soil particles and oily materials that cling to, and dull, carpet fibers. Research indicates that 80 percent of carpet soiling in the lodging industry is footborne. "It is the primary reason carpet must be cleaned," according to Durkan, a carpet manufacturer based in Dalton, Georgia. "Therefore, soil prevention is a major factor in carpet maintenance."

To help prevent soiling, place walk-off and soil trap maps—which use rough surfaces to scrape mud off shoes—outside and inside the entrances to collect the worst of the wetness, grime, and grit

**Figure 7.4** *The patterned carpet in the function room of the Regal River Front Hotel, St. Louis, Missouri, humanizes the proportions of this large space with the blocks in the pattern while masking stains with interesting patterns and colors. (Courtesy of Durkan Patterned Carpet, Dalton, Georgia)*

carried in by foot traffic (see Figure 7.5). A large piece of carpet that matches the lobby or foyer carpet should be used in conjunction with the mats immediately inside the entrances to pick up soil or moisture not caught by the mats. The type of mat chosen will depend on the weather and main soil problems.

- Vinyl link mats are able to withstand heavy foot traffic, but are not recommended where mobile equipment is used often, because the wheels can get caught.

- Rubber link and corrugated link mats provide excellent traction and perform well in wet or dry conditions, but also are impractical for areas where mobile equipment is used often.
- Vinyl runners protect the floor, absorb noise, and have good underfoot comfort.
- Vinyl-backed cocoa mats feature a brush action that removes sand, snow, and moisture.
- Steel mesh mats, along with flexible wood or synthetic duckboards, maximize drainage and so are suitable for kitchens or back bars.

**Figure 7.5** *Runner outside the main entrance remove the worst of dirt from shoes before guests enter the lobby. (Courtesy of The Plaza Hotel, New York; from Lawrence D. Harvey, A Plaza Wedding)*

- Cut nylon pile mats are suitable for elevators, doorways, pro shops, locker rooms, and entry from kitchen to dining room where people can clean grease off shoes.

Durkan maintains that, "Approximately 80 percent of all soil is removing by vacuuming." Carpet cleaning in public spaces should be continual. During busy hours, a carpet sweeper or brush and pan can be used in the lobby to sweep up debris (see Chapter 6). Thorough vacuuming should be done at least once a day, or as needed. Restaurants should be vacuumed after each meal or at least tidied with a carpet sweeper. Function space should be vacuumed before setup and after knockdown. Guest rooms are vacuumed daily, or as needed, with a lighter weight upright vacuum. The house attendant may do a thorough vacuum with a heavier machine once a week.

Attendants should not try to vacuum too fast, since allowing the full push-pull motion of vacuuming maximizes the machine's capacity to pick up dirt and debris and decompress the carpet fiber. The best vacuum will depend on the type of carpet.

Different vacuums accommodate different types of carpets. Finding the right match is important:

- A vacuum with a brush and a beater (see Figure 7.6) bar is preferable for carpets installed over padding because it agitates the carpet fibers and can remove embedded soil.
- Vacuums with a brush only are best for carpet tiles and carpets glued directly to the floor.
- Upright vacuums with strong suction are preferred for general cleaning over canister models.
- Canister models can be used for specific cleaning jobs that upright vacuums cannot reach.
- Piggy-back vacuums are used for situations in which the attendant must take the vacuum up stairs or up a ladder. A crevice tool is the most important attachment; a pile lifter is also beneficial.

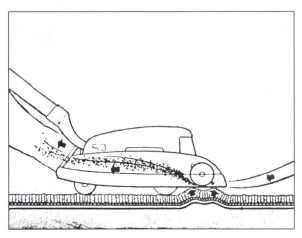

**Figure 7.6** *This beater-bar vacuum effectively removes loose soil that is buried in the pile. (Courtesy of the American Hotel & Motel Association)*

- Space vacuums, with a wider, 30-inch head, can save significant labor hours in corridors and function space.
- Ride-on vacuums may be required for huge, pillarless banquet space.

Vacuums should be scheduled for regular maintenance. Belts and brushes should be checked for wear. Vacuum bags should be emptied before they are half-full. A vacuum can lose 50 percent efficiency when the bag is half-full, according to Von Schrader.

## Spot Removal

When it comes to spot removal, the goal is to treat the spot as soon as possible so that it does not become a permanent stain. Restaurant waitstaff and banquet stewards should be trained to deal with spills when they happen or call the housekeeping department (see Tricks of the Trade 7.1).

---

**Tricks of the Trade 7.1**
**Spot Removal Tips**

*The Problem:* Hotel carpet gets spotted almost every day.
*The Solution:* Von Schrader and Durkan recommend these spot removal procedures:

1. Blot liquid spills with a clean, white absorbent towel. For dry spots or spills, scrape up the excess with a dull knife.
2. Test the cleaner on a small, inconspicuous area of the carpet to check for colorfastness. If it is colorfast, place a small amount of spot remover on an absorbent towel. Blot the spot gently; do not rub (which is too abrasive), working from the outside edge toward the center to avoid spreading.
3. After the spot is removed, rinse the area with water.
4. Blot the area again with a white absorbent towel to remove excess water and residue.

---

The type of spot removers stocked by the housekeeping department will depend on the most typical types of spots. While white vinegar or ammonia work on some types of stains, there are also highly specific products available for removing difficult stains such as dye, rust, and coffee. Though all staff should be trained to begin dealing with spills by blotting up excess liquid or scraping dry material, one or two departmental employees should be given special training in assessing and treating spots.

A common problem in spot removal is caused by **wicking,** a process in which wetness or stains are drawn up from the backing through the pile yarns to the surface. It may not be enough to spot treat the surface. If the spot wicks up, the backing and the padding may also have to be cleaned.

## Better Communications with Contract Cleaners

Properties that use contract cleaning services should take extra care to make sure room attendants and public area attendants note where spot treatment is needed. Larger properties that use contract cleaners should discuss provisions for emergency cleaning as part of the bid process. Some stains cannot be left to soak into the carpet for several days until the contract cleaners show up. Even with a cleaning service, attendants should be trained to blot spills as soon as they happen.

To maximize the performance of the cleaning service, it is important to give detailed instructions on what must be done. Anna Oh, executive housekeeper of the 495-room Crowne Plaza Ravinia, in suburban Atlanta, gives a representative from the carpeting cleaning service a detailed list of guest rooms and other areas to be shampooed and spot treated when she meets with him each Monday. She also goes over guest comment cards. If there are comments about the carpet maintenance, she discusses these as well.

### Cleaning Heavy Traffic Areas

Simple vacuuming cannot remove the oil-based spills in restaurants nor the ground-in grit in the entry area. Nightly shampooing is usually done in these areas and high traffic lanes with a dry foam shampoo, sometimes in conjunction with a degreasing pre-spray. It is crucial that the foam be thoroughly removed from the carpet. The detergent residue from the foam can be as big a villain as the dirt itself. If this sticky residue remains in the pile yarn, it actually attracts more soil.

There are several options for dealing with this problem. The simplest is to make sure the area is thoroughly vacuumed with a vacuum that has sufficient suction power to remove the dry foam. The second is to invest in a **dry foam extractor,** a machine that uses a dry foam cleaner and low moisture, usually less than 10 percent, so the carpet dries quickly and the threats of mildew, browning, or dry rot are minimized. If the buildup is a serious problem, the only solution may be to call in a professional company that will flush the pile yarns of this residue (see Figure 7.7).

Since most footborne carpet soil is acidic, it is best to choose carpet detergents that are moderately alkaline in order to neutralize and remove the embedded soil. Von Schrader, which also runs tuition-free seminars and training schools, also recommends that professional housekeepers test carpet detergents for their anti-resoil ability to minimize buildup.

Some properties opt for a **dry powder cleaning system.** One machine applies a powder or crystals on the carpet to bind with the dirt. A second brushes this powder into the carpet. The powder or crystals are then removed by thorough vacuuming. Using this dry cleaning system, down time is negligible. This means a high-traffic restaurant or public area carpet can be cleaned during regular hours since the carpet can be walked on immediately. Also, in winter, buildings do not have to be heated to higher average temperatures to help carpet dry. This system works best if it is the only system used on the carpet—that is, if the carpet has not been foam cleaned previously. Some residue may still remain with the dry powder system (see Figure 7.8).

### Deep Cleaning

Regular vacuuming, spot treatment, and traffic lane management will contribute significantly to keeping carpeting looking clean and performing well. But periodic deep cleaning is also necessary. Some properties schedule this quarterly, some biannually or even annually. How often this is done is determined exclusively by need.

Nightly cleaning or weekly cleaning may be limited exclusively to heavy traffic lanes or restaurant carpets. In most cases, heavy furniture is not moved. For deep cleaning, the furniture should be moved and the entire carpet should be cleaned. It should be completely dry before the area or guest room is back in use.

# CARPET CARE EQUIPMENT AND SUPPLIES

Carpet care equipment ranges from the basic sweeper or vacuum to ride-on space vacs. The equipment list should be tailored to the needs of the hotel. The following is a list of the types of machines used for carpet cleaning and maintenance.

### Lightweight Cleaners

These are most suitable for guest rooms, light traffic areas, and areas in which heavier, noisier equipment would be too disruptive.

**Carpet sweepers.** Working on an electrostatic principle, these sweepers attract dust and debris to their underside. They are suitable for level carpet with a low pile.

**All-purpose sweepers.** These tiny, modular tools are used for quick cleanups on restaurant carpet. They can pick up sand, dirt, broken glass, and cigarettes.

**Electric brooms.** Weighing in at only 6 pounds, these machines can get into small places and under beds.

**Lightweight upright vacuums.** Usually weighing 8.5 to 11 pounds, these vacuums are suitable for guestroom cleaning and may also handle corridors on a daily basis.

| METHOD | EQUIPMENT/PREP | | | CLEANING PROCESS | | | | | | POST CLEANING AFFECTS | | | | | |
|---|---|---|---|---|---|---|---|---|---|---|---|---|---|---|---|
| | EQUIPMENT | MANPOWER | REQUIRED OPERATOR SKILL | AVERAGE HOURLY COVERAGE | TRAFFIC DOWNTIME | EARLIEST APPRAISAL TIME | ANNUAL CLEANING FREQUENCY | BLENDING ABILITY | CHANCE OF COLOR BLEEDING | AMOUNT OF RESIDUE | RESOIL RATE | SHRINKAGE/ SEAM SPLITTING | MILDEW | SPOT WICK BACK | BROWNING |
| ROTARY WET | | | MOST SKILLED | 719 SQ. FT. | 6-24 HRS. | 6 HRS. | 4 TIMES | GOOD | POSSIBLE | HEAVY | RAPID | LIKELY | LIKELY | VERY LIKELY | POSSIBLE |
| ROTARY SPIN PAD | | | LESS SKILLED | 1600 SQ. FT. | 1 HR. | 1 HR. | 6-8 TIMES | GOOD | POSSIBLE | LIGHT TO MEDIUM | VERY RAPID | UNLIKELY | UNLIKELY | LIKELY | POSSIBLE |
| MIST/PAD | | | LESS SKILLED | 1200 SQ. FT. | 1 HR. | 1 HR. | 3 TIMES | GOOD | POSSIBLE | LIGHT | SLOW | UNLIKELY | UNLIKELY | LIKELY | POSSIBLE |
| FOAM | | | MORE SKILLED | 1000 SQ. FT. | 1-4 HR. | 1 HR. | 5-7 TIMES | FAIR | POSSIBLE | HEAVIEST | MOST RAPID | UNLIKELY | UNLIKELY | LIKELY | POSSIBLE |
| HOT WATER EXTRACTION | | | MORE SKILLED | 638 SQ. FT. | 6-24 HRS | 6 HRS | 2-3 TIMES | POOR | POSSIBLE | LEAST | SLOW | VERY LIKELY | VERY LIKELY | UNLIKELY | POSSIBLE |
| DRY SOIL EXTRACTION | | | LEAST SKILLED | 750 SQ. FT. | NONE | IMMEDIATE | 1-2 TIMES | EXCELLENT | NONE | DRY RESIDUE | VERY SLOW | NONE | NONE | NONE | NONE |

**Figure 7.7** *The amount of residue that remains on the carpet after each type of cleaning depends on the type of chemical used. The back of the carpet should never be wetted through during cleaning.*

**Lightweight tank vacuums.** These typically are used for upholstery, draperies, lampshades, and vents, and have special attachments for these purposes.

**Piggy-back vacuums.** As discussed in Chapter 6, these are strapped onto the back and easily carried up ladders or stairs or into other hard-to-reach areas.

### Heavyweight Vacuums

These vacuums are usually used for a thorough cleaning of corridors, restaurants, and public areas.

**Heavyweight upright vacuums.** These vacuums usually have two motors: one to drive the brush and one to furnish suction. Some have such powerful suction that they can inhale crumpled paper and cigarette packages. The giant upright space vacs, which may carry a five-bushel bag, can clean most corridors in just two passes. Wet-dry models are also available.

**Commercial tank vacuums.** These are used more often for wet-dry pick-up because they can accommodate more water than the uprights. Some use a top unit that fits over a bucket or drum, making these units a workable backup for larger, more specialized wet vacuums. These units may

| Steam-Extraction<br>The steam-extraction system is based on injection of a jet of hot water containing detergents at a prescribed rate and subsequent extraction by a vacuum system. | | Does not cause pile distortion or flaring.<br>Built-in vacuum removes soil.<br>There is no residue of shampoo to collect more dirt.<br>Slower, more expensive. |
| --- | --- | --- |
| Cylindrical Brush-Dry Foam<br>This system has a cylindrical brush which scrubs and picks up in one pass the foam generated by the machine. | | Causes severe pile distortion and flaring of tufts in high plush or shags.<br>Has built-in vacuum which removes shampoo and dirt. |
| Rotary Brush-Wet Shampoo<br>A rotary brush cleaner using wet shampoo. A complete line of accessories including vacuum and drying equipment is also employed. | | Causes severe pile distortion and flaring of tufts in high plush or shags.<br>Does uniform cleaning.<br>Does not remove shampoo and soil. |
| Small Rotary Brushes-Wet Shampoo<br>This is also a rotary brush cleaner but employs two brushes instead of one and is somewhat smaller than the rotary brush-wet shampoo machine. | | Causes severe pile distortion and flaring.<br>Does very little cleaning.<br>Does not remove shampoo or soil. |

**Figure 7.8**  *Although comments in the right column would imply that steam extraction is the only effective method of carpet shampooing, skilled operators can obtain good results with a rotary wet shampoo, a dry particle, or a dry foam technique—if the proper detergents are used and if the vacuum that picks up the foam and soil is powerful enough. Certain types of brushes, carpet mops, and yarn pads will help lessen pile distortions.*

be all that a small property with limited food service needs.

## Deep-Cleaning Machines

Vacuums pick up dirt, but purpose-built equipment is needed for deep cleaning. Dry foam and dry powder cleaning machines were discussed earlier in this chapter. Some other equipment used for deep cleaning includes the following:

*Hot water extraction.* In hot water extraction systems, incoming water from a hose connected to a faucet is shot into the carpet by high-pressure spray nozzles. Dirt is flushed to the surface, picked up by the vacuum, and carried to a sink drain through a discharge hose (combined with the supply hose). Although this leaves minimal residue, it does leave the carpet far damper than dry foam methods and takes the area out of service for several hours until the carpeting is dry and has been vacuumed. A defoamer may be needed if the carpet

has been dry foam shampooed repeatedly. This will help the detergent penetrate better.

If hot water extraction is used in guest rooms, the preferred equipment is a machine that carries a tank for hot water and another for soiled water. Then guest bathroom sinks do not have to be used for water supply and discharge. A **tank extractor,** a machine which looks like a tank vacuum on wheels, has a hose with a spray head 14 inches wide. It sprays hot or cold water into the pile, then squeegees the nap and recovers the foam and deep soil. This step is followed by vacuuming with a powerful wet-dry vacuum.

*Bonnet cleaning.* This rotary machine has special bonnet pads that agitate the carpet as they clean. After the carpet and bonnet are sprayed with shampoo, the operator passes the machine fitted with the bonnet over the area to allow the bonnet pad to absorb dirt and soil as it spins. The bonnets must be rinsed and wrung dry after using, and the carpet should be vacuumed after it is thoroughly dry.

*Rotary brush wet shampooing.* A rotary brush cleaner using wet shampoo cleans the carpet by agitating the pile as the shampoo is dispensed. A tank is used for the detergent solution which is driven into the pile with a flat revolving brush combined with the weight of the machine. Some procedures call for wet vacuuming to remove dirt and water; others require the carpet to dry, after which the powdered detergent is vacuumed away (see Tricks of the Trade 7.2). To protect the investment in equipment and the carpeting itself, it is best to specially train any employee who will operate this equipment. These employees also must be carefully trained in working with chemicals used in spot treatment, detergents, and other cleaning agents or compounds (see Chapter 8).

---

**Tricks of the Trade 7.2**
**Benefits of Dry Powder Systems**

*The Problem:* Steady, day-long function business means long drying times rob the hotel of revenues.

*The Solution:* Setup time and drying time are key considerations in selecting equipment, points out Charles Brown Smith, executive housekeeper of the 75-unit La Playa Hotel, Carmel, California. "We bought a dry powder system that cut our labor costs by half. The setup time is short and the area is ready for use immediately afterward. The cleaning process in some areas takes only 40 minutes," says Brown Smith.

---

When it comes to heavy machinery, bigger is usually better. Although some of these top-end, oversized units can cost $6,000 to $7,000, they save labor and help protect the investment in the flooring. These machines generally are built to last. Repairs can be expensive, as new motors can cost several hundred dollars, but the machines should easily outlast the carpet. **Pile shavers,** which remove pills, are labor-intensive but may be necessary. It is important to lay down runners to protect the areas not being cleaned. Any attendant touching the solutions should wear gloves. Goggles will be needed to protect eyes if fluids are being mixed or diluted. Some executive housekeepers recommend using carpet rakes to help raise pile and prevent traffic lane wear.

## Repair and Replacement

However vigilant the care, carpet does show wear. In times when budgets are tight, there are several options for coaxing one or two more years from tired carpeting.

1. A thorough deep cleaning followed by pile lifting may rejuvenate carpet that is matted and dirty.
2. In a lobby, dyeing may mask sun damage. Some nylon carpeting may be dyeable to mask fading or stains, but this must be done by a professional. Several patch tests should be done in inconspicuous areas to make sure the dye will take evenly. Also, the area should be cleaned to test colorfastness.
3. Carpets without an obvious pattern can be picked up and turned. This can move worn areas out of the central traffic lane. If the property has carpet tiles, the worn tiles can be moved to inconspicuous edges of the room while the unworn edge tiles can be placed in the center.

When the carpet is worn out, the executive housekeeper should be asked for some input, even if an interior design firm will specify the new carpet. The executive housekeeper should have the opportunity to test a sample for ease of cleaning and colorfastness.

## SELECTING AND CARING FOR HARD FLOORS

It is important that the professional housekeeper understand the different types of hard floors in order to decide how best to care for them.

Generally, hard flooring can be divided into two types: **nonresilient flooring,** which resists denting because of its hardness, and **resilient flooring,** which is made from materials with a certain amount of give. Impact will dent resilient flooring, but the impressions will more or less fade away as the material springs back to its natural shape. Marble and other types of stone, terrazzo, and ceramic tile are all examples of nonresilient flooring. Resilient flooring includes wood, cork, rubber, vinyl tile, and other composite tiles.

**Sealers** are designed to fill the pores in a flooring material and to provide a protective coat against moisture and chemicals. The goal is to do this without compromising the flooring material itself. **Finishes** are devoted to protection from wear and the enhancement of the flooring's surface. It is important to know which types of floors require sealing and/or finishing, and how this affects the wear and maintenance of the floors once it is applied.

## Caring for Nonresilient Floors

Nonresilient flooring is found most often in high traffic areas and areas where excessive dampness or water would damage carpeting. The following section looks at some of the most common types of nonresilient floors and how best to care for them.

## Stone

Marble is the best known of the natural stones, but **travertine** (a type of marble), granite, slate, terrazzo—a marble aggregate mixed with Portland cement—and other types of stone are also used in commercial flooring. Surfaces range from polished to honed mat, which is dull, and from satiny smooth to roughly textured.

Stone flooring adds a look of elegance to the property, and is also durable and relatively easy to maintain. But disadvantages of stone include susceptibility to damage by humidity and acids, which can cause cracking, powdering, or surface chipping. When stone floors are laid, surfaces should be coated with a pregrouting film to protect them from staining during the grouting process. Nonacid cleaners should be used to remove any trace of grout. Then, the stone should be sealed.

A **curing agent,** a temporary finish that controls the loss of moisture, may be necessary on floors with a lot of new concrete. Urethane-based or enhanced products that block the pores of the stone should be avoided.

**Slate,** which is naturally resistant to staining and wear, will not allow most finishes to adhere. If finishing is desired, two thin coats of terrazzo sealer can be applied, followed by two thin coats of a soft, buffable finish. However, any finish on slate will have a tendency to track off.

**Terrazzo,** which has a natural sheen and is resistant to wear, is advertised as needing no artificial or applied finish, but still must be protected from chemicals and humidity. Sealers made specifically for terrazzo should be used. They usually require no separate finish and can be stripped easily.

***Maintaining stone floors.*** Dust removal is the most basic aspect of stone floor care. Dust, especially that from sandy soil, can literally grind off the surface of the floor. Daily sweeping and dust mopping with a nonoily dusting compound is essential. Water-based compounds should be used, since oil-based products will produce permanent stains. A no-rinse stone soap is effective. Attendants should be trained to damp mop the floors, taking care not to saturate the stone.

The buffing compounds and **finish restorers** used on these floors should not interfere with the permeability of the sealer or finishes. Thin coats of an easily removable product that will not block the pores of the stone can be used on a weekly basis. Some surfaces can be **spray buffed,** a procedure in which the floor is sprayed with a buffing spray solution, then buffed with a floor machine equipped with pads or brushes. Other surfaces will react better to **dry buffing** or **burnishing,** which polishes through the friction created by high-speed buffing.

Buffers and burnishers can produce dramatic results, but only if done correctly. The first step is to make sure pads are centered on the machine. If not, they could fly off at high speed and hit someone in the area, ruin the floor or, at the very least, damage the pad (see Figure 7.9). Pad retainers can be purchased for almost any brand of high-speed buffer. Attendants should be trained to keep the buffer well away from the baseboards. The edge of the pad or pad holder could damage them. Also, mounted metal door stops or latch insets should be picked up or removed before buffing. They can tear up the pads.

Attendants using electric models should begin buffing at the farthest reach of the cord and buff in a straight line to the opposite point. The machine can be turned around by taking off the machine off the floor and rotating it on its back wheels. It is best to overlap the first pass by one-third of the width of the pad.

A brush rather than a pad should be used when polishing slate or other highly textured surfaces, since the rough texture could tear the pad. Slate also is susceptible to pitting. These pits can then turn black due to the chemical action of salt and alkali. Various commercial products can draw out these stains. A sealer can be applied to refill the pits.

## Concrete

All concrete floors require sealing. Otherwise, they continually powder, and that powder is tracked through the property. Sealing should be done when

**Figure 7.9** *Attendants should check that buffer pads are centered before beginning to clean floors to prevent buffer pads from flying off at high speeds. The attendants should be trained to use buffers properly, keeping them well away for baseboards. (Courtesy of Ecolab)*

**Figure 7.10** *Current standards require that tiled floors, whether marble or ceramic, generally be polished to a high-gloss shine. Vigilant care keeps the floors of The Greenbrier polished to a mirror finish. (Courtesy of The Greenbrier, While Sulphur Springs, West Virginia)*

the concrete is new because stains set easily in this porous material. Because this sealer controls the drying process to achieve maximum hardness, curing takes up to one year. Concrete floors should be swept, then thoroughly mopped and vacuumed with a wet pick-up prior to sealing. Ground-in soils must be scrubbed. The surface of interior concrete floors may also be finished with a floor finish, but this is necessary only in extremely heavy traffic areas.

### Ceramic Flooring

**Ceramic flooring** or **vitreous flooring** refers to flooring materials that have been made of some clay product and fired in a specialized, very hot oven called a kiln to produce a hard, stonelike quality. Common types include quarry tiles, brick, glazed tiles and paving stone (see Figure 7.10).

The *advantages* of ceramic tile are that they are impervious to water and soils, resistant to abrasion and wear, and they are relatively easy to maintain.

The *disadvantages* of this type of flooring are that it can crack, and it requires grouting, which is vulnerable to staining and mildew buildup.

***Sealing and finishing.*** Ceramic floors can be **glazed** or **unglazed.** Glazed tiles are coated with an impervious glossy or matt layer which bonds to the tile and makes it totally nonabsorbent and nonresilient. Glazed tiles require no finish. Unglazed tiles, such as terra cotta, are naturally impervious to water. They are often used in kitchens and entryways. One type that has sharp bits of sand protruding from the surface helps increase skid resistance on greasy floors.

***Grouting.*** All ceramic floors require grout. Grout must be sealed with the appropriate sealer to reduce staining, and cleaned with special grout cleaners. Periodically, it may have to be whitened with a grout whitener.

***Maintaining ceramic floors.*** Sweeping and mopping with a tile cleaner should keep glazed tile floors looking shiny and clean. It should be dusted often, because dust will scratch and abrade the shine.

Unglazed floors such as terra cotta, brick, and paving stones, should be swept. A brush and wet vac work best to thoroughly clean interior floors or sidewalks that lead to the entryway or outdoor pre-function space.

Some older properties may have a variety of hard flooring that may also include poured floors such as epoxy, magnesite, or oxychloride. These usually can be cared for like concrete, with sweeping, damp mopping, or scrubbing. As with any floors, the surface should not be saturated. Standing water can damage many types of floors.

## Resilient Flooring

Resilient flooring such as wood can be showcased in the public spaces, while other types of resilient flooring have increased safety and ease of maintenance in the back of the house. Care procedures are very different for wood, especially old wood, than for the new generation of vinyl tiles.

## Wood

The type of wood determines how much resilience the floor will have. New wood floor products often are combined with impregnated resins that also determine their resiliency (see Figure 7.11).

The *advantages* of wood floors are that they provide a warm, elegant look, comfort under foot, and they are durable if properly finished and maintained.

The *disadvantages* of wood floors include their porosity, absorbency, and their susceptibility to water damage. If unfinished, wood floors may dry out, splinter, or lose finish under heavy abrasion of foot traffic.

***Sealing and finishing wood floors.*** For commercial purposes, wood floors must be sealed and finished. Most new floors benefit from a finish applied at the factory. Various techniques are used, ranging from applications of tung oil and wax to polyurethane and liquid acrylics. Some vinyl finishes are also being used. Epoxy resins provide good resistance to sun fading and good adhesion and bonding. Prefinished floors, either plank flooring or parquet tile, and wood floors cured in plastic provide the beauty of natural wood without the headaches. Varnish- or shellac-type chemicals should be avoided, since they can yellow and peel.

***Caring for and maintaining wood floors.*** Daily maintenance consists of frequent sweeping and dusting. Wood floors sealed with polyurethane also

**Figure 7.11** *Daily dusting or sweeping is all that is needed to keep most wood floors clean. Older floors require periodic conditioning, applying paste wax with a buffer. Even some newer floors benefit from buffing, but the manufacturer should be consulted first. (Courtesy of Marriott International, Washington, D.C.)*

require periodic damp mopping. Some wood floors will benefit from buffing. Older wood floors may need a biannual or annual treatment with paste wax and a buffer. For new floors, it is best to follow the manufacturer's recommendations on floor care. Spills should be removed as soon as possible, either with a wood cleaner or slightly damp mop. Wood floors should never be cleaned with a wet mop or have standing water on them.

The only way to clean deeply stained wood or damaged wood is to have the floor **sanded,** that is, made smooth with sandpaper (usually with a sanding machine). It will then need to be sealed again. Sanding should be a last resort, since it definitely limits the life of the floor. For some wood floors, three sandings is the maximum they can withstand before the surface becomes too thin.

## Vinyl Flooring

Vinyl flooring has many back-of-the-house uses in the lodging industry, as well as some creative front-of-the-house applications in hospitals, residence halls, and senior living centers. The two main types of vinyl flooring used in the lodging industry are homogenous vinyl and composition vinyl. **Homog-**

**enous vinyl,** the most popular type, is all vinyl with no fillers or laminates. **Vinyl composition** flooring is composed of vinyl resins, plasticizers, coloring pigments, and mineral fillers. It usually is sold as 12 inch by 12 inch tiles. Its main uses are as flooring over concrete at or below grade and over plywood suspended floors.

The *advantages* of this type of flooring are that it is easy to maintain, it is generally resistant to alkali chemicals (a few types are susceptible), and it is indention- and impact-resistant.

The *disadvantages* of vinyl flooring are that it is susceptible to damage by particulate matter, may closely follow uneven contours of subflooring (making it hard to clean evenly), and some may have film coatings that can be worn off or buffed through.

***Sealing and finishing vinyl floors.*** Most so-called "no-wax" vinyls have their glossy finishes applied at the factory. Most have, or should have, a scratch-resistant finish as well. Vinyls generally do not require sealing.

***Maintenance of vinyl floors.*** Daily dusting with a treated mop, treated sparingly, is essential to avoid damage from abrasion. Use of a neutral cleaner will prevent the damaging buildup of alkalines on the floor. Seams, corners, edges, and baseboards should be cleaned regularly, as they are the weakest points of a tile floor. Mopping with special **restoration coatings,** chemicals that in most cases can restore the factory shine on some types of vinyl floors, often will bring back the appearance of the floor. This can be intensified with the use of a high-speed buffer.

## Rubber Flooring

Rubber flooring is usually made from synthetic rubber. Its main use is as matting or in damp or greasy areas in which a nonskid surface is important. Studded rubber flooring, characterized by its continuous pattern of raised, circular dots, helps control wet spills. Moisture runs off the circles and into the depressions between them.

The *advantages* of this type of flooring are that it maintains a good luster without finishing, it is resistant to most chemicals and surface moisture, it is resistant to cigarette burns, and it affords good traction.

The *disadvantages* of rubber flooring are that it is difficult to scrub, it may become brittle due to environmental effects, and it cannot be used in areas of extreme wetness.

***Sealing and finishing.*** Most finishes do not adhere well because of the nonporous surface and flexibility. These floors buff to a high shine without the use of a finish or high-speed buffer. High-speed buffing may cause **pad burn,** which occurs when pads on the buffer go through the finish and mark the floor.

***Maintenance of rubber floors.*** Mild alkalines can be used to clean rubber floors; harsh alkalines will damage them. None should be left on for more than 5 minutes because they can cause leaching of the synthetic rubber and damage the floor. As with all floors, daily dusting and periodic damp mopping constitute the basics of cleaning.

Studded flooring should be thoroughly cleaned immediately after installation. The molds used to make it are sprayed with a silicone that stays on the surface of the tile and combines with the paraffin in the tile that migrates to the surface. The result is a sticky surface that looks dull and attracts dirt. Low-alkaline strippers should be used to remove this film. After this, all that is needed is buffing with a soft brush. The paraffin migrates to the surface and, when buffed, attains a soft luster.

## Repair and Replacement

Repair procedures for hard flooring can be as simple as picking up and replacing a vinyl tile or two or as complicated as sanding, refinishing, and restaining an aged wood floor. The useful life-spans of these various types of hard floors also vary. Proper preventive and daily maintenance will insure the property gets the longest life possible out of each type.

Both attendants and supervisors should be trained to assess wear. Making spot repairs is less costly and time-consuming than refinishing an entire floor. However, floors in heavy traffic lanes will need to be refinished periodically. The decision as to whether to do this with departmental staff or hire a contract company will depend on how often the procedure needs to be done, how much expertise is necessary, whether funds are available for the necessary labor and equipment, and just how much of the floor surface is involved.

## EQUIPMENT AND SUPPLIES FOR HARD FLOORS

For an economy property with little hard floor surface and a small budget, it may be hard to justify any major floor equipment purchases. Mops, brooms, dust pans, and wet floor signs are essentials for all properties. But, if the budget allows for just one purchase, it should be some kind of single-disc floor machine, capable of scrubbing, buffing, sanding, and polishing. Many models also will shampoo carpets. Mega-hotels with a lot of hard floors and a heavy volume of foot traffic may require a long equipment list that begins with high-speed buffers and separate scrubbers and may go on to include specialty equipment for the miles of each different floor surface. The deciding factor is to buy only what the property needs and what can be fiscally justified.

## Equipment

The following is a description of the major types of equipment for hard floor care.

*Scrubbers.* The single-disc scrubber's most basic function is to apply the appropriate solution, then scrub or strip the floor. It vacuums up the dirty solution, leaving an almost dry floor behind. Most are lightweight and easily portable. Some newer models have hydraulic or pneumatic controls. These higher tech models require extensive operator training.

Although they are called scrubbers, these machines are among the most versatile in the housekeeping department and can handle any task from scrubbing to buffing and stripping floors. Different pads and brushes are used for different jobs.

For smaller properties, the all-in-one scrubber may be the only machine needed for hard floor care. Larger properties require separate scrubbers and buffers.

*High-speed buffers.* Unlike the single-disc scrubber which operates at 175 revolutions per minute (rpm), high-speed buffers and burnishers operate from 350 rpm to 2,500 rpm. To put this into perspective, a pad traveling at 1,200 rpm is going about 60 miles per hour.

Buffers are available in electric models, battery-powered mode, and gas-powered. The main problem with the electric models is the cord. Stopping to find outlets and working around the cord both cut productivity.

For these reasons, the battery-powered units are usually preferred for large spaces and hallways. They typically can buff from 4 to 6 hours on one charge and run at 2,000 rpm (revolutions per minute). The savings in labor costs and increase in productivity mean quicker payback times for these battery-operated buffers. However, an expensive battery charger must be purchased and the batteries themselves must be serviced. A well-ventilated area must be set aside for charging because acid fumes are given off during the process.

Gas-powered burnishers, with their own internal combustion engines, are the most heavy-duty machines. They provide more weight and a faster pad speed, which produces an extremely high shine. These machines also can complete more square footage per hour than the electric models. Although extremely efficient, these machines are also extremely complex mechanically and require a lot of maintenance. Some other problems are that they are noisier than electric machines and give off noxious fumes during operation. With gas or propane as fuel, they also may present a fire hazard. Indoor use may be restricted to times when guests are not around or when the area being cleaned is closed off. Before purchasing these units, it is best to check municipal regulations. In some cities, they are illegal.

*Floor pads and brushes.* Most pads used on scrubbers are now made of plastic. Pads are made from fiber, some type of grit, and a binder that holds the pad together. Traditionally, pads were made of nylon and were color coded according to their purpose—red for spray buffing, white or off-white for drying buffing, black for stripping and so on. Pads for high-speed buffers are not dyed to prevent the risk of color transfer onto the floor. Nylon has been replaced by polyester for high-speed pads. Only pads specially designed for high-speed buffers should be used with these machines. Attendants should be trained not to buff too long without turning over the pads. If used too long on one side, the heat and friction will fill the pores of the pad with the hardened finish, which will then scratch the floor.

The latest innovation is a **crystallization process** which involves special pads for renewing marble floors. Benefiting from the strength of industrial diamonds as the grit, or sanding substance, these diamond pads come in varying levels of coarseness that can resurface and restore marble floors subjected to heavy traffic. "Crystallization and diamond pads are the best technology in handling all kinds of floors, rather than stripping and waxing which consume a lot of time. With the old system of handling floors, you needed a lot of machinery and manpower. It costs more without the best results," says Napoleon Laono, executive housekeeper of the JW Marriott Hong Kong.

Brushes also come in various grades for stripping, scrubbing, polishing, and carpet cleaning.

Most now are made from sophisticated polyester fibers imbedded with abrasives. Brushes do not load up as quickly as pads, so they can be used longer. They also are easier to clean. However, they are not as effective for stripping and may not produce as high a shine during buffing.

While still moist, pads can be cleaned with a high-pressure stream of water. If they dry, cleaning is much harder. They can be soaked overnight in a strong solution of stripper, then rinsed thoroughly in the morning. There are also emulsifiers designed especially for pads. Spray buffing pads and dry buffing pads accumulate the worst buildup. If necessary, these pads can be sent to special laundering services that clean and recondition pads. Most pads can be reconditioned 40 to 50 times without losing their usefulness.

***Sealers and finishes.*** Sealers fall into two categories: primary sealers, which are used as the only coating on the floor, and those that are designed to be used in conjunction with a sealer. Sealers are more permanent than finishes. Finishes absorb the wear on the floor and protect it, but are used up in the process.

The trend now is to choose products that will result in a shiny, still-wet look. A side benefit of the finishes and equipment used to achieve this highly polished look is that burnished floors usually are harder and more resistant to wear than those with conventional finishes.

It is important that sealing and finishing products be compatible, both with the type of flooring and with each other. Most vendors sell complete lines of compatible strippers, sealers, finishes, and buffing or restoring compounds.

## SUMMARY

Dirty, dull floors or soiled carpeting send the wrong message to guests. Guests expect that despite rainy, muddy weather or crowded banquet rooms, the property's floors will be spotless and neat. Selecting flooring with ease of maintenance and durability in mind is key. Although the executive housekeeper rarely chooses the flooring, except in small properties, he or she should have input. It is the housekeeping department that must maintain what the interior designer selects.

In order to offer an educated opinion on flooring and create maintenance procedures, the executive housekeeper must have an understanding of:

- Carpet construction, and how various constructions and fibers will react to cleaning, spot treatment, and wear by foot traffic and carts

- The proper procedures to be used for various carpets and flooring
- What equipment and supplies to use for maintaining and protecting carpets
- The differences between resilient and nonresilient flooring, and what chemicals should be used or avoided
- What daily maintenance will entail
- What weekly maintenance will entail
- What equipment and cleaning supplies will be necessary for daily and preventive maintenance
- Incorrect practices that will wear or damage flooring
- How to repair and when to replace flooring

## Review Questions

1. For carpets, what are pile and density and how do they affect wear?
2. Describe several key considerations in selecting carpeting.
3. How does padding affect carpet wear?
4. What are the primary and secondary backings of carpeting?
5. Describe the steps in a preventive carpet maintenance program.
6. Define the differences between nonresilient and resilient flooring, giving several examples of each.
7. Describe daily maintenance procedures for most resilient and nonresilient floors.
8. Why should alkali cleaners be avoided?
9. What are the differences between a scrubber and a burnisher and how do their operations differ?
10. Explain the importance of matting.

## Critical Thinking Questions

1. Discuss the advantages of wool versus nylon carpeting.
2. As part of a renovation, in the lobby a signature light blue rug is being replaced by a dark patterned rug. How will this affect the frequency of cleaning and the budget?
3. A buffer's motor has burned out. Repairs will cost $500. A new unit, costing several thousand dollars, would be more effective and less labor intensive. Discuss the merits of repair and replacement.

# 8

# Managing the Care of Interior Design Elements

## Chapter Objectives

To keep a property's interiors looking their best and to maximize their useful life, the professional housekeeper should:

- Understand the basic construction of interior design elements in order to assess their durability and ease of maintenance
- Understand the basics of interior design
- Establish best practices for caring for various types of wall coverings and wall finishes
- Establish best practices for routine maintenance and deep cleaning
- Determine which equipment and supplies will be needed for various types of fabrics, furnishings, and wall coverings or wall surfaces
- Establish best practices for delicate items and hard-to-reach ceiling areas
- Assess what impact design will have on the housekeeping department's bottom line

An essential part of the professional housekeeper's job is to protect the property owner's investment in physical assets such as the FF&E. The professional housekeeper must be familiar with the design process, as well as the FF&E, wall coverings and wall finishes, and flooring materials (discussed in Chapter 7). This information is necessary to set up the proper procedures for cleaning and maintaining all interior design elements.

## THE HOUSEKEEPER'S ROLE IN INTERIOR DESIGN

Decades ago, many professional housekeepers did double duty as interior designers. Working with the owner or general manager, they contacted vendors or manufacturers, reviewed samples, and selected which FF&E would be purchased for the property. As mentioned in chapters 5 and 6, this work is now is done by interior design firms for most upscale and deluxe hotels. For some mid-tier or economy properties affiliated with large lodging chains, the corporate office of the chain may provide samples of room designs and a precise list of **specifications**—a detailed description of an item which might include height, width, and information on its construction—for the design elements. The owner, as a franchisee, receives ample information on suggested room designs created by professional designers to fit the exact size of the chain's standard rooms. The franchise company also provides lists of approved suppliers, some of whom have national sales contracts with the chain (see Chapters 10 and 11). In these cases, executive housekeepers provide input and advice rather than making the purchasing decision.

Professional housekeepers will be expected to know how design elements perform. They should be prepared to offer an educated opinion regarding:

- Durability
- Ease of maintenance
- How long the item can be expected to look like new
- How often the item is likely to need repair or replacement

The goal for professional housekeepers is to give the owner, operator, and designer a practical assessment of whether the design and design elements will work. For example, an all white guest room will require more frequent deep cleaning than one designed with stain-masking colors and patterns. That will affect the housekeeping budget and, perhaps, the longevity of some design items. The owner and operator must understand this before approving labor-intensive design.

Executive housekeepers should be actively involved in assessing both fabrics and furnishings. They should request **fabric swatches,** small fabric samples, and participate in the review of the **model room.** Before a hotel is opened or renovated, the interior designer usually obtains samples of the FF&E that will be installed and sets them up in a model room. The purpose of the model room is to give the owner, operator, some department heads and, more and more frequently, key prospective clients a chance to try out the new design and evaluate it. Depending on the comments, adjustments can be made to tailor the room to the needs of the marketplace and make them more practical for the operator.

Before a new opening or renovation, the executive housekeeper should test-clean the fabrics, finishes, and floor coverings that will be used. Not only will this determine how easily the FF&E can be maintained, it also will indicate how long it will take, on average, to clean the room.

### Talking the Designer's Language

Design, like housekeeping, has a language all its own. Although professional housekeepers do not have to be fluent in the language of design, they must be familiar with the basic terms.

Professional housekeepers need to understand how to read a **floor plan** (see Figure 8.1). Less detailed than the highly technical drawings called **blueprints,** a floor plan functions more as an outline for a particular space, showing where walls and windows will be and where larger FF&E items will be placed.

The ability to read floor plans is important for two reasons. First, the executive housekeeper should be able to point out any areas in which the planned furniture layout would interfere with efficient staff traffic patterns or where the layout would make routine or deep cleaning difficult. Second, since public area furnishings are moved and rearranged by guests and staff, the housekeeper needs a record of where the furniture should be placed.

### Design Trends

Styles in interior design, like styles in fashion, change frequently. Professional housekeepers are not expected to keep pace with the shifting whims of style. It is more important for housekeepers to know whether a chair will hold up to heavy usage than to recognize whether it is Chippendale or Art Deco. Professional housekeepers should know how many different styles of furnishings will be used for the property. This affects factors ranging from labor scheduling to the selection of supplies and equipment and the calculation of inventory levels.

The general trend in the lodging industry over the last two decades is to provide a home-away-from-home residential look, rather than a standardized institutional look. Patterns are used more throughout hotels, and patterns tend to complement each other. Even plumbing fixtures are taking on a more residential look, with more highly styled faucets and water saver toilets. Although some very chic hotels use design to surprise or even challenge the guest aesthetically, most properties aim for a classic look of comfort.

## WALLS, CEILINGS, AND WINDOWS

Walls and ceilings are not subject to the variety of soils and stains that make floors difficult to maintain. They present a different kind of cleaning challenge. Wall finishes and wall coverings must be able to withstand frequent abuse from suitcases, carts, and even rolling shelves. Partitions used to subdivide banquet and function space must hold up under regular handling without showing permanent stains from dirty or oily hands or wear marks. While ceilings are exempt from this type of abuse, they must be easily washable.

### Evaluating Wall Coverings

Key questions to ask about painted and papered surfaces include:

- Will the surface be washable? In the case of wallpaper, is it scrubbable?
- How porous is the paint? With wallpaper, how heavy is it and what kind of backing does it have?
- How well can the paint or paper withstand spot treatment? Can standard spot removal practices and supplies be used?

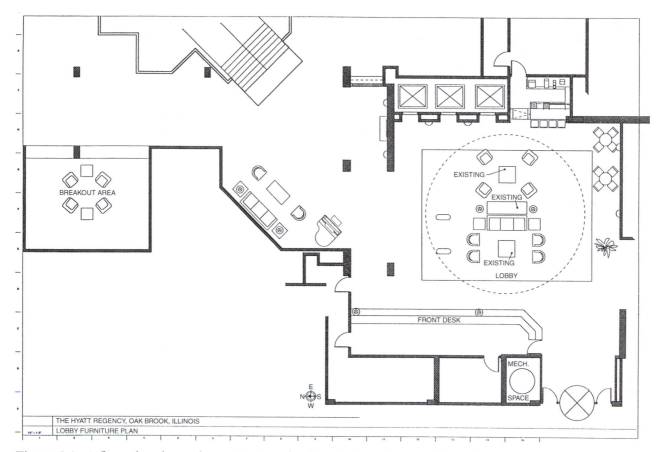

*Figure 8.1* *A floor plan shows the positioning of walls, windows, doors and furnishings.*

- How well will the color or pattern hide marks and stains?
- Can the surface be cleaned with existing equipment and supplies?
- How many different types of wall finishes or wall coverings will be required?

## Materials Selection

The key areas to consider when giving input on wall coverings and finishes include:

- Durability
- Ease of maintenance
- Flammability
- Suitability based on the function of the space and the category and image of the hotel

## Durability

Durability must be weighed differently for wall coverings and wall finishes than it is for hard flooring.

Although long-wearing marble and ceramic tiles are still the standards for walls in guest bathrooms, public rest rooms, pool and spa areas, and kitchens, other areas are more likely to be painted or wallpapered. Painted or papered walls are susceptible to wear and damage; they also have a finite life expectancy in design terms. Vinyl wall coverings installed in guest rooms may last more than the standard five-to-seven-year renovation for **soft goods,** the fabrics and bed coverings, but they have to be replaced in any case before they are out of style.

Hard-surface durability is particularly important for wall surfaces in wet, humid areas. Also, wall surfaces in bathrooms and rest rooms will have to withstand fairly harsh chemical cleaners and/or disinfectants. Materials selected for these areas also should be both chip- and stain-resistant.

Durability has a slightly different meaning for papered and painted surfaces. For these surfaces, durability means that the finish or wall covering will look like new as long as possible. The best choices are products that can stand up to spot treatment and cleaning without apparent damage. A good warranty also boosts the product's appeal. Unusual colors and patterns should be avoided. Not only do they become outdated; they are also hard to match when doing touch-ups or repairs.

Clear plastic corner guards add to the durability of any wall treatment. Hotels use them on any corner that is vulnerable to mars and scrapes from suitcases and carts. They protect both painted and papered surfaces.

## Ease of Maintenance

Elements from color and pattern to weight and construction can affect ease of maintenance for wall finishes and wall coverings. As mentioned in Chapter 7, hard surfaces such as marble or tile must be finished or sealed so that they can be cleaned regularly without wearing. Special cleaners will be required for marble; tile is cleaned with a general-purpose cleaner or tile cleaner (see Chapter 5). Both tile and marble are currently the standard choices for any wall subject to wetness, humidity, and grease. The only drawback, in terms of maintenance, is the challenge of keeping the grout clean and stain-free.

## Flammability

Wall coverings, like bedding, must comply with flammability regulations (see Chapter 11). The **specifier** of the wall coverings, that is, the person who writes the detailed descriptions of the items, must check local codes on flammability and toxicity, which vary by city and state. An increasingly popular choice for guest rooms are wall coverings that emit an odorless, colorless vapor when heated to a certain temperature. This vapor in turn sets off the smoke detectors. Polycotton backing is preferable to cotton backing because it is less flammable.

## Suitability

Like floors, walls have a major impact on the overall design of a room. Distracting wallpaper or a shoddy paint job can detract from the image of the property. The category of the property, its location, climate, and even the standards and specifications of the operator all influence the selection of wall finishes and wall coverings.

Wall finishes and coverings must complement the look of the space and reflect its function. Banquet rooms and meeting rooms usually require some type of acoustical wall and ceiling materials to help absorb sound and keep them from becoming too noisy. Lobbies require more dramatic wall treatments than guest rooms. Back-of-the-house walls should be attractive, but easy to maintain.

## Caring for Walls and Ceilings

Each type of wall finish or wall covering requires different cleaning procedures. Most walls do not require daily maintenance; weekly cleaning is sufficient. Only walls in guest bathrooms, public rest rooms, employee locker rooms, locker rooms adjacent to pools and spas/fitness facilities require daily washing. Some of the new generation of properties that aggressively target the family market have created special play areas for children. The walls in these areas, too, must be washed and disinfected daily.

Ceilings are cleaned on a quarterly basis or, at least, twice a year. The exceptions are ceilings that serve as decorative elements, such as the fabric or glass ceilings sometimes used to make a design statement in restaurants, lounges, or bars. These must be cleaned regularly to remove stains and dust (see Figure 8.2).

## Painted Surfaces

Paint remains one of the least expensive (at least initially) wall finishes. It can easily and quickly change the look of an area and does not require a long down-time for repairs. Nearly anyone can touch up paint, and it is easy to maintain. However, some experts say it may take as much as four paint jobs to last as long as one vinyl wallpaper job, and some marks or stains can be difficult to remove.

## Routine Maintenance of Painted Surfaces

As discussed earlier, routine maintenance consists of weekly dusting. During this weekly cleaning, attendants and supervisors should check for marks, chips, and scrapes. One painting expert recommends a mildly abrasive soap for removing black marks from walls without damaging paints.

Bad soils can be removed by saturating the area of the stain or soil with the cleaning solution and allowing it to penetrate for a few minutes. Where dust and smoke have accumulated, it may be necessary to apply a little abrasive powder on a wet sponge or pad. Any abrasive must be used sparingly, since it may dull the finish on the wall. The soiled area must be thoroughly rinsed and dried.

**Figure 8.2** *Unlike hard-surface ceilings which may require only semi-annual cleaning, fabric ceiling treatments must be scrupulously cleaned on a regular basis. Problems can range from mildew to infestations of pests. (Courtesy of Le Madri Restaurant Toscorp.)*

## Deep Cleaning Painted Surfaces

Wall washing is usually done twice a year (see Tales of the Trade 8.1). Before wall washing, the walls should be dry dusted, preferably with a very soft hair or lamb's wool brush on an extension handle. This can be done only on a dry day. Dry dusting may cause streaks if the walls are at all damp. Pipes, high moldings, and door tops should be dusted with a treated rag.

### Tales of the Trade 8.1
### Wall Washing Builds Team Spirit

General Manager Don Hartley has turned the chore of wall washing into an annual event for his staff at the 248-room Holiday Inn Brentwood near Nashville, Tennessee. Since the hotel enjoys high average occupancy, general cleaning work such as wall washing must be done quickly. "We pick a slow day in December and involve the entire staff. All employees, including me, are assigned to four-member teams. Each team is assigned a hand-held vacuum cleaner; some even bring their vacuums from home. Each member does a different job: vacuuming, cleaning, rinsing, or drying. It takes only one, eight-hour shift to wash all the walls in the hotel. It's hard work, but this way it becomes a team building event. Then, sometime before the end of the year, we have a banquet to celebrate," says Hartley.

Hand washing can be done with a sponge or a mop. Mops are frequently used for rush jobs in unconfined spaces.

For hand washing with a sponge:

1. Begin from the bottom up to avoid streaks. Clean the lower half of the wall from one corner to the other.

2. Rinse the lower half of the wall before beginning the upper half. Wipe the wall dry after rinsing.

3. Clean, rinse, and dry the upper half in the same manner.

4. Change the solution and the rinse water frequently to insure good results.

For washing with a mop:

1. Work from the top down. Swing the mop from side to side in rhythmic strokes as far as possible without stepping ahead. Do not use excess pressure, which could rub soil into the wall.

2. At the point where side-to-side cleaning is impossible, swing the mop in long, vertical arcs from the cleaned upper surface down to the baseboard. Use a scrub brush for stubborn spots.

3. Before the cleaning solution dries on the cleaned areas, use the rinse mop with the same swinging motion.

4. Dry the cleaned and rinsed area with a dry mop.

For wall-washing machines:

1. With an applicator in each hand (some manufacturers call these pads **trowels** or **gliders,** begin cleaning from the top down. The applicator fed by the solution tank is used first; then the applicator with the rinse.

2. Work in left-to-right arcs as far as possible without stepping ahead.

3. Change the solution pad when it becomes too soiled. Another option is to shift the rinse applicator to the detergent applicator, and the dry pad can be used for rinsing.

4. After rinsing, dry the cleaned section of wall with the drying pad.

## Equipment and Supplies for Cleaning Painted Walls

Sponges or mops and pails are all that is necessary for hand washing. The best sponges are cellulose and about the size of a brick. Cleaning with mops requires two, 10-inch cotton dust mops with non-swivel heads or two sponge mops with hand wringers to control excess moisture. A telescoping mop handle makes it easier to reach high places on the wall. For either method, attendants also require two, three-gallon pails—one for the cleaning solution, the other for the rinsing solution.

Wall-washing machines are available with a single tank. However, the more commonly used type has two tanks—one for the cleaner, the other for the rinse water. These containers should be filled before use, allowing enough space for air pressure to build up. Plastic or rubber tubes from each tank connect to the metal trowels that hold the pads. Terry cloth pads are needed for smooth walls; special brushes or synthetic pads are used for rough walls. The operator uses a trigger on each trowel to control the flow of liquid into each pad. This eliminates trickles that form streaks. Manufacturers claim that even an inexpensive wall-washing machine washes walls and ceilings four times faster than by hand. Hand methods may take about four hours to thoroughly clean 1,000 square feet of painted wall.

A strong alkaline cleaner such as trisodium phosphate removes dirt but may also remove some paint. A weak solution should be patch tested on an inconspicuous area first. Additional tests should be made until the detergent is at full strength. Synthetic detergents made of sulfonated hydrocarbons are usually preferable to soap, which may leave residue and hasten future soiling.

Chamois cloths are expensive but ideal for drying walls. Absorbent rags are affordable and acceptable substitutes.

## Routine Maintenance of Vinyl Wallpaper

Durability, ease of maintenance, and the variety of textures and colors have made vinyl wallpaper a popular wall surface for the hospitality industry. However, it does have some drawbacks. The biggest problem, especially in humid areas, is that mildew can build up behind the wallpaper. Also, there is the ongoing risk of tears and edges lifting up.

The first rule for any kind of wallpaper maintenance is to check the manufacturer's instructions. Most vinyl wallpapers need only once-a-week dusting. Vinyl wallpaper used in hotels and motels should be not only washable but scrubbable. Various cleaners can be used, but it is best to consult the manufacturer with specific questions. For non-washable wallpapers, veteran housekeepers recommend using a thick paste of **fuller's earth** (a claylike, earthy substance) and benzine or a non-flammable dry cleaning fluid to remove oil and grease stains. If the fuller's earth/benzine paste is used, it should be removed when dry. For smaller grease marks, the attendant should press a small piece of white blotting paper against the spot with a warm iron. The iron should be held against the paper and spot for a few minutes.

## Deep Cleaning Vinyl Wall Coverings

Again, the manufacturer's instructions are the starting point for deep cleaning. The general rule of thumb is to start at the bottom of the wall and work up. Each area should be rinsed thoroughly and dried before moving to the next section.

Attendants and supervisors should watch for seams that are opening up or curling. These seams should be reglued with wallpaper adhesive.

## Equipment and Supplies for Cleaning Vinyl Wallpaper

A hard-bristle brush for scrubbing and a low-sudsing detergent diluted in warm water should suffice for most cleaning needs. Abrasive cleaners, acetone, and strong solvents should not be used because they may discolor the vinyl. The only exception is wallpaper treated with a polyvinyl film. This can stand up to solvents without any adverse effect. Attendants will also need two buckets—one for the washing solvent and one for clean rinse water. A soft, lint-free cloth or towel will be needed for drying.

## Fabric Partitions and Acoustical Walls

Fabric covering is used on partitions that subdivide function space into smaller, more intimate areas or on cubicle walls in back-of-the-house offices. The fabrics used for these walls are a heavier weave than the delicate fabrics discussed earlier and far more durable.

Acoustical walls or ceilings are made of sound-absorbent material. Most frequently, they are used in function space or other areas in which deadening sound is a priority. Some acoustical walls are painted; others are fabric covered.

## Routine Maintenance of Fabric Partitions and Acoustical Walls

Fabric partitions, whether acoustical or not, should be vacuumed regularly. Edges should be inspected closely. Since the setup crews generally handle partitions along their edges, these are the first areas to show dirt, grease, and smudge marks. Painted acoustical walls should be cleaned with the same

procedures as any other painted surface. A brush can be used to keep the bases and edges clean.

Spots should be treated as soon as possible. A piece of art gum will remove small spots from unpainted acoustical walls. Larger spots on acoustical walls may require dry steel wool or a synthetic abrasive pad. A putty-type wallpaper cleaner also will remove spots from unpainted acoustical walls.

Colored chalks are ideal for touching up nicks in acoustical walls. Spray paint can be used on painted acoustical walls, taking care not to fill in the holes, as this lessens sound absorbency.

## Deep Cleaning Fabric Partitions and Acoustical Walls

With these, too, cleaning should follow the manufacturer's instructions. The best approach is to begin deep cleaning on a small inconspicuous piece of the partition or wall. The area should be allowed to dry thoroughly before assessing whether there has been discoloration, shrinkage, sagging, or other damage.

## Equipment and Supplies for Fabric Partitions and Acoustical Walls

All that is needed for routine cleaning is a vacuum with a soft nozzle brush. Some fabric cleaners are sold with their own soft-brush attachment. If no attachment is included, a small sponge or soft brush will be needed for deep cleaning. Only cleaning products designed for use on fabric should be used.

## Tile Walls

As discussed earlier, tile can be used in any area of a property that must withstand frequent cleaning and/or disinfection. Ceramic tile is the most popular choice because of its durability and flexibility as a design element, but terra cotta tiles are also used—most frequently as accents in restaurants or in the lobby.

## Routine Maintenance for Tile Walls

Tile walls are cared for in much the same way as tiled floors (see Chapter 7). As discussed earlier, walls in public rest rooms, guest bathrooms, locker rooms, and pool and spa areas must be washed daily with a tile cleaner or all-purpose cleaner. A disinfectant that is compatible with tile should be used regularly to make sure these areas are free from germs and bacteria. Walls separating shower stalls in pool/spa areas and employee showers must be cleaned daily with a disinfectant. As a general rule, all employee areas and back-of-the-house office space should be cleaned with the same frequency as front-of-the-house space.

Kitchen walls should be cleaned each night. In most cases, a mild alkali or synthetic detergent works well. A mild abrasive may be needed for stubborn stains.

## Deep Cleaning of Tile Walls

Periodically, the grout between the tile must be deep cleaned. How often this is done will depend on the soil accumulation, discoloration, and problems with mildew and/or mold. If mildew is a constant problem, the grout may have to be scrubbed daily or every other day. "Training has to stress the importance of drying the grout in order to prevent mildew. The attendants also should be trained to put the shower curtain in the center or to one side, not pulled across, in order to let air circulate. If mildew takes hold, we've found that bleach is the only solution. Use of bleach is restricted to supervisors," says David Green, director of housekeeping for the 491-room Renaissance Hotel, Cleveland, Ohio.

A whitewash mixture of an abrasive cleanser and hot water should eliminate discoloration. The mixture is applied after the wall is washed and still damp. A thin paintbrush makes an effective applicator. After 24 hours, the grout is scoured, using a stiff brush and the whitewash solution. Attendants should try to avoid the edges of the tiles as much possible. Commercial grout cleaners are also available.

## Equipment and Supplies for Tile Walls

Sponges work well on ceramic tile walls. Brushes are preferable on terra cotta. Wall-washing machines usually have brush attachments available for rougher surfaces.

As stated above, mild detergents, abrasives, grout cleaners, and whiteners make up the basic cleaning supply list. Number 1 steel wool pads are useful for removing tough stains such as lipstick or coffee from grout. Disinfectants and degreasers should also be supplied.

## Other Wall Materials

Deluxe hotels may occasionally have fabric-covered walls in special areas to convey a look of unstinting elegance. However, the high cost and extreme delicacy of these coverings make them impractical.

Linen once was the traditional choice for fabric wall coverings. Today, cotton, wool, silk or some combination may be installed. Great care is required in cleaning. Some may shrink if cleaned with water. Others may mildew. Still others may require treatment with fire retardant chemicals after each cleaning. Delicate fabrics can be vacuumed with a soft brush nozzle so as not to pull threads or cause the fabric to sag or pucker.

Professional housekeepers may also encounter wall coverings and finishes ranging from marble to cork and from wood veneers to brick and stainless steel. The same procedures used on marble, wood, or brick floors work equally well on walls. All that needs to be adjusted is the frequency.

Modern technology may hold some solutions for wall-cleaning problems. A new process that is applied somewhat like plaster produces a durable, easy-to-clean wall surface. Since the pigment is mixed into the wall material during manufacturing, the color permeates the entire surface. The surface does not discolor, even when scraped with metal. This material may have a smooth or textured look. It can be cleaned with an all-purpose cleaner. Currently, it is being tested in several different hotel products.

## Strategies for Cleaning High Areas

Whatever the finish, ceilings are a challenging task. In public spaces or for very high guestroom ceilings, **high dusters** are a must. These long-handled dusters are safe and efficient. Regular dusting of ceilings extends the time before deep cleaning is required.

Deep cleaning can be done by hand or by machine. A scaffold is required for cleaning ceilings by hand. For safety reasons, two people must be assigned to any task that requires a scaffold or ladders: one will work on the scaffold or ladder, the other will secure the base. If machines are being used, it is best to select models with telescoping poles that are balanced so as not to fatigue the operator.

Deep cleaning ceilings involves the following steps:

1. Move or cover all FF&E. Use ropes or signs to close off the area under the ceiling scheduled for cleaning.
2. Vacuum any loose dirt, soot, cobwebs, or other debris. Clean vents and ceiling fixtures.

3. Clean the ceiling by hand or machine and rinse it. Ceiling accents, such as special moldings around light fixtures, or embossed patterns, may require special cleaners if the glue that holds them is susceptible to water damage.

## Cleaning Windows and Window Coverings

The housekeeping department generally is responsible for cleaning interior glass doors and windows. Some unions have regulations that will not permit room attendants to clean windows. In hotels of more than 500 rooms, one employee may be assigned almost exclusively to the task of cleaning glass doors and interior windows. Cleaning exterior windows is usually done by contract window cleaners with the necessary specialty equipment. All contract cleaners, whether for windows, walls, or ceilings, should be required to provide their own equipment and supplies.

## Caring for Glass Windows and Doors

Glass doors or dividers in the public area require the most attention. Heavy usage frequently leaves them smudged with fingerprints and even splashed with the residue of mud and snow.

***Routine cleaning.*** The outside of the entry doors should be cleaned twice for each time the interior is done. Entry doors leading into the lobby should be cleaned several times each day. All other glass doors should be cleaned once or twice during the day and night shifts, or as needed. The supervisor who inspects the area should note when additional cleaning is required and assign the task accordingly.

Some hotels schedule weekly cleaning of the guestroom windows with a glass cleaner. Others do this less frequently. Sliding glass doors, which are fairly common in resort properties, usually are cleaned on check-out to remove any fingerprints.

***Deep cleaning.*** Windows and glass doors are deep cleaned twice a year or more. The deep cleaning process usually follows these steps (see Figure 8.3):

1. Remove all window dressings, including shades and blinds. Vacuum and wash screens. Some blinds can be cleaned by dipping them in a gentle, all-purpose detergent. Wash or dry clean draperies, as indicated by the manufacturer's instructions, before rehanging them.

**Figure 8.3** *The attendant should begin washing glass door panels from right to left (left to right for a left-handed) person, then back again, working in a downward pattern to the bottom of the panel. (Courtesy of the Shangri-La Hotels & Resorts, Hong Kong)*

2. Clean sills inside and out, and dust or wash frames to prevent edge streaks on the glass. Metal-framed windows should be kept rust-free and clean by rubbing them lightly with fine steel wool. Wooden frames should be sealed if possible. A crevice tool can be used as a vacuum attachment to clean out the metal rails under sliding glass doors.

3. Sponge or wash the window in continuous strokes from left to right (right to left for a left-handed person), then back again, in a downward pattern until the bottom is reached. Begin at the lower left corner and wash with up-and-down strokes working toward the right side of the pane.

4. After the window is cleaned, use a squeegee to remove excess water and dirt. It does not matter whether the squeegee is used side to side or up

and down. Wipe excess water off the squeegee after each stroke. Excess water tends to collect along the rail or sill and, if it seeps under either, can cause damage to the room.

***Equipment and supplies.*** Window cleaning essentials include a squeegee, a sponge for putting on liquids, two buckets—one for cleaning and one for rinsing—and a lint-free cloth for wiping the squeegee. Gloves and goggles also may be required, depending on the cleaner being used. Safety ladders are required for higher windows. Some type of drop cloth or other covering may be needed to protect the sills.

Although glass cleaners may be appropriate for routine cleaning, many housekeepers prefer the tried-and-true formula of a mild liquid detergent and water for deep cleaning. Adding a little ammonia will soften the water and increase the shine. Alcohol helps loosen dirt, particularly in cold weather when grime tends to congeal and adhere to window panes. Scouring agents should be avoided because they could mar the glass.

## Window Treatments

Draperies and sheers are still a popular window treatment for city hotels, but shutters, shades, and a variety of fabric treatments are also used.

***Selection.*** A fabric's life expectancy depends on the amount of sun exposure it will have. All fibers, whether man-made or natural, will bear indirect sunlight fairly well. Silk is the only exception; it is too fragile. The most durable of all fabrics are tweeds, tapestries, damask, friezes, and pile weaves, especially those constructed of chemical fibers.

Some of the essentials in long-wearing draperies include:

- Heavy denier yam
- Black-out lining to minimize sun damage
- Color-fastness, to resist ultraviolet rays and the effects of dry cleaning, water spotting and **crocking,** or rubbing off
- Solution-dyed fibers, which means the yam is dyed before being spun into fibers, rather than just coating the fibers after spinning
- Low susceptibility to yellowing
- A good warranty covering color-fastness and wear

An extensive warranty is one indicator that the manufacturer not only has faith in its product, but will stand behind it if anything does go wrong. But nothing replaces on-site testing. The executive housekeeper should require that a sample be provided before the purchase order is written. The sample should be tested for color-fastness by washing it or dry cleaning, whichever is recommended. It should be vacuumed to determine how much this affects the threads. And, with the guest in mind, the sample should be hung at a sunny window to find out just how much light leaks in and how the draperies look and hang.

**Sheers,** the delicate, see-through panels usually hung between the draperies and the window are less durable. They deteriorate fairly quickly, unless the window is completely shaded. Frequent replacement is simply planned into the budget. Some housekeepers recommend using several single panels rather than one wide one. The initial cost may be more, but they can be rotated so the most damaged ones can be moved to the sides and the fresher ones to the middle. Ricky Watts, executive housekeeper of the Ramada Plaza in sun-drenched Ft. Walton Beach, Florida, advises executive housekeepers to tint windows and schedule daily cleaning to reduce sun damage.

Some properties have shifted to fabric shades instead of sheers. The preferred shades, usually constructed as pleated shades, have an ultra-thin layer of aluminum bonded onto the fabric to reflect heat back out of the window. Blinds and shutters also may be used. Wooden shutters, which are finished with polyurethane, do require more effort to clean, but are effective in protecting other fibers in the interiors and can hold up to both sun and storms.

Delicate decorations should be avoided. Balled fringe, called **poms,** may add a note of Victorian elegance but the fringe attracts dust and is not washable. A rod-type pull is far preferable to the old-fashioned drawstring cord, which tends to stick and break.

***Routine cleaning.*** Attendants should open and close draperies every morning to prevent dust from settling on them. Regular vacuuming, using an attachment designed for draperies and upholstery, will keep draperies looking fresh between deep cleanings. The drapery rod also should be dusted. Attendants and supervisor should check for any signs of yellowing, stains, or tears. They also should check that draperies are hanging correctly. Draperies and sheers should not touch the frame or sill; this prevents undue wear on the bottom. Blinds should be dusted regularly. Shutters, too, must be dusted at least once a month to prevent buildup and sticking.

***Deep cleaning.*** Dry-clean-only draperies should be dry-cleaned at least once a year. Draperies with sewn-in linings or backing must be dry-cleaned, regardless of the fabric content, to prevent shrinking or stretching of the lining and backing.

Blinds and shutters are usually cleaned with a sponge using warm suds. Attendants should use overlapping strokes, then rinse the blinds or shades with a damp cloth. Blinds and shutters must be dried thoroughly before rehanging them.

## FURNISHINGS, FIXTURES, AND EQUIPMENT

FF&E is a broad category that covers everything from the grand piano used in the ballroom and the finest furnishings in the presidential suite to the ceiling and plumbing fixtures and the ash urns. Furniture usually is broken down into these categories: **casegoods,** which is anything with a top and sides, such as dressers, armoires and desks; softgoods, such as fabrics and bed covers; seating, such as sofas, chairs, bar stools and decorative benches; tables, from accent or occasional tables to restaurant and function tables; and lighting and accessories, including artwork and plants.

### Selecting FF&E

Furnishings and fixtures help define the image of the hotel. Key factors to consider in furniture selection include:

- Appearance
- Availability
- Comfort
- Cost
- Function
- Guarantees and/or the integrity of the manufacturer or vendor
- Durability

### Appearance

The most subjective of all criteria, appearance is still important. Though styles vary, there are certain rules for choosing design elements:

1. Large patterns belong in large rooms; small patterns in small areas. Complementary patterns can be mixed, as long as they harmonize in terms of style and color.
2. Light colors make a room look bigger; dark colors make a space look smaller. Sometimes this rule is broken for effect, often to make a small restaurant look even more elegant and secluded.
3. Avoid colors that clash.

Appearance must be weighed against the look of the property's architecture, the size of its space, and its geographic setting. Furnishings should blend with the wall coverings, floor coverings, and architectural elements rather than drawing attention to themselves—unless they are meant to make a strong statement (see, for example, Figure 8.4).

### Availability

Availability is an important concern, especially when opening a hotel. The interior designer notifies department heads on the pre-opening team when the FF&E will be delivered. Availability for every item, no matter how small, must be checked. Late arrival could postpone the opening and hurt the hotel's image.

Replacement is another consideration. Although properties generally stock a certain number of replacement pieces for furnishings, they cannot afford to carry replacement for the entire inventory of furnishings. The executive housekeeper should determine how long it will take to get replacement pieces; how long replacement pieces will be available to the company (many styles eventually go out of stock); and what provisions will be made for matching dye lots or wood tones.

### Comfort

Comfort is paramount for guestroom chairs, chairs used in auditoriums and meeting rooms, and chairs in fine dining restaurants where it is desirable to have patrons linger. **Ergonomic chairs,** which provide both full back support and, frequently, a height adjustment, are becoming standard as desk chairs in business-oriented properties, from the deluxe range down to economy hotels. However, in outlets where a high customer turnover is the goal, seating is usually less comfortable. Stackable chairs used for banquets and large conventions fall somewhere between the two extremes.

Climate also influences comfort. Breathable fabrics, such as cotton or cotton blends, are better

**Figure 8.4** *Behind the strong design statement made in the guest rooms of the SoHo Grand Hotel are common-sense touches appreciated by guests and the housekeeping department alike: an emphasis on quality, from the long-lived, imported bed linens to the comfortable, stain-hiding carpet; an uncluttered furniture layout; and a predominance of hard surfaces that are easy to clean. (Courtesy of the SoHo Grant Hotel, New York)*

choices than vinyl or molded plastic for warmer climates. Also, fabrics should be soft. At times, in the search for durability, the fabrics selected are durable but too stiff or rough to be comfortable.

## Cost

Contract seating may range from under $30 for a utility dining chair or folding chair, to several hundred dollars for custom chairs upholstered with premium fabrics. Cost means more than the initial capital outlay. To figure the true cost, other factors must be considered:

- The average life expectancy of the piece
- The cost and projected frequency of repairs
- The cost of regular maintenance

- The cost of deep cleaning

Cost also will be influenced by how much repair can be done on the property. Another consideration is how often the piece can be refinished, reworked, or reupholstered.

## Function

The function for which a space is intended definitely influences the choice of FF&E. The primary considerations when making the determination include whether the furniture is appropriate for the function of the room, and whether it will wear well under these conditions.

Other factors also affect function. For example, a chair with **wall-saver legs**—legs that splay out to the back so that the chair hits the baseboard before hitting the wall—take up extra space but save on maintenance and repair costs for the walls. Coasters or rollers may be desirable on chairs in a dining room with deep pile carpet. Ease of maintenance is another aspect of function.

## Guarantees and/or the Integrity of the Source

This consideration is particularly important to the executive housekeeper, who will have to invoke the guarantee of any design element that fails to live up to the manufacturer's claims. Well-made furniture carries a guarantee or warranty. If any piece doesn't live up, the dealer or vendor usually will pick it up, replace it and then settle the matter with the manufacturer. Because of the volume of furniture purchased by a hotel, finding a defective item is common.

Fabrics are usually warranted by their manufacturer rather than the furniture manufacturer. Each item should be checked for its warranty or guarantee, and this paperwork should be kept on file. A date of delivery should be noted on each item's record.

## Repairability

The easier an item is to repair, the longer it will last and the more cost effective it will be. Wood is among the easiest materials to repair. Often, a stain stick to touch up dents and scratches will delay complete refinishing. Even complete refinishing is not an overwhelming task.

## Durability

Deluxe hotels may have solid wood furniture. Most hotels have furniture that combines wood with plastic or laminate. In fact, laminates made to look like wood are far more durable because they can withstand wetness and stains and simply be wiped clean. For the future, most mid-tier and economy hotel chains will be moving more and more toward nonwood furnishings.

It is not only the material but the construction that affects longevity. Hardwood chairs should have joints that are both glued and screwed together. Connecting rods, called **stretchers,** should join all legs together except at the front of the chair. Rear legs of wood chairs should be steam-bent with the wood grain, rather than cut from cross-grain pieces that can split easily.

Generally, softgoods—the bedspreads, sheers, and pillow shams—are replaced every three to five years. Casegoods are expected to last 10 to 20 years. Upscale hotels renovate more frequently than mid-tier or economy hotels. Upscale rooms may be renovated every five to seven years; a fullscale, property-wide renovation may be undertaken every 10 to 15 years.

## Care and Maintenance of Furnishings

Proper care and maintenance extend the life of furnishings and fixtures. Routine procedures for cleaning FF&E items were discussed in chapters 5 and 6. As with other surfaces, the first step in care should be to read and follow the manufacturer's instructions. This applies to the front and the back of the house.

## Deep Cleaning of Fabrics

In terms of FF&E, cleaning upholstery is probably the most challenging aspect of deep cleaning. While shampooing vinyls and plastics is relatively fast and easy, cleaning woven fabrics requires expertise. One or more staff members should be specially trained for this task. Deep cleaning of upholstery fabrics should be done as needed, or at least twice a year. Fabric-covered lampshades should also be cleaned on this schedule.

The steps to follow in deep cleaning upholstery include (see Figures 8.5a, b, and c):

1. **Ventilation.** Make sure the area is well ventilated.

2. **Vacuuming.** Vacuum the upholstery thoroughly. Pile fabrics should be brushed with a stiff nylon brush, which will bring up the nap and soil from the bottom of the nap.

3. **Spot treat.** Any heavily stained areas that require it should be spot treated with solvents that will remove oily soil before shampooing. Other spots should be identified if possible and removed with the recommended solutions listed on the spotting charts furnished by the manufacturer of the chemical cleaners. Most spots should be blotted rather than scrubbed. Hard or prolonged scrubbing can cause wear and permanently mar the fabric.

4. **Test for color-fastness** according to the steps described earlier in this chapter. If the color is not fast, it should be tested again with a slightly acid cleaning solution. If the color still bleeds,

*(a)*

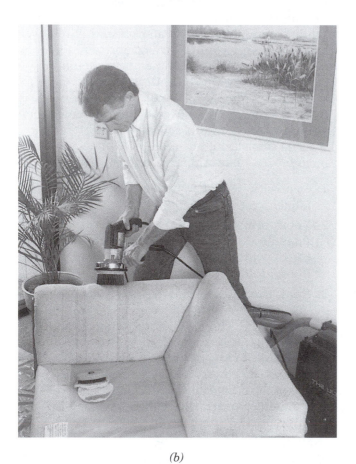

*(b)*

*(c)*

**Figure 8.5** *(a) Vacuuming generally should be the first step in deep cleaning upholstery. However, pile fabrics should be brushed with a stiff nylon brush to bring up the nap and soil. (Courtesy of the Association of Specialists in Cleaning and Restoration) (b) Fabric shampooing should be done from the bottom up to avoid staining and water marking. All fabric should be tested for color-fastness prior to shampooing. (Courtesy of U.S. Products, Inc.) (c) Vacuuming can keep draperies looking fresher and dust-free between dry cleanings. Because drapery fabrics can be delicate, staff should be trained to check the manufacturer's instructions before attempting either spot treatment or deep cleaning. (Courtesy of U.S. Products, Inc.)*

the only safe cleaner is a dry solvent. Padding should also be tested for color-fastness. Some padding is dyed and may bleed. Some types of padding must be dry cleaned.

5. **Test for shrinkage.** A section of the back or pillow side should be cleaned and allowed to dry thoroughly. Only then can it be tested accurately for shrinkage.

6. **Shampoo.** If the fabric passes the two previous tests, it can be shampooed. (If not, a dry solvent is used.) Furniture should be shampooed from the bottom up to prevent stains and water marks. Delicate fabrics, like those on some lampshades, should not be saturated.

7. **Dry.** The item should be dried in a warm, well-ventilated area. Some executive housekeepers suggest having a fan blowing on the cleaned items to speed up drying time. Some fabrics require occasional brushing during drying time.

8. **Hand brush or vacuum.** After the item is clean and thoroughly dried, hand-brushing or vacuuming restores the nap.

If the fabric is not inherently flame retardant, it may have to be retreated with a flame-retardant chemical after each cleaning. The manufacturer's instructions should be followed or the manufacturer should be contacted with any questions.

***Equipment and supplies for fabric cleaning.*** The type of cleaning solution must be matched to the fabric. The standards include dry solvents or dry foam for finer fabrics, and foam shampoos for more durable woven fabrics.

Dry solvent is usually applied with terry cloth and wiped dry with another terry item. Dry foam is applied gently with a sponge on fragile fabrics, since a brush would spoil silky surfaces. Foam shampoos with neutral synthetic detergents can be applied with a rotary brush machine.

Upholstery cleaning can be done by hand, with a rotary brush machine or with an **upholstery extraction system.** This system, which works much like a carpet extraction system (see Chapter 7), first vacuums the dirt, applies the foam, then vacuums up the dirt-laden foam and collects it in a recovery tank. Manufacturers claim these systems will work equally well on fine fabrics, such as velvets, and on soiled, carpeted stairs and risers.

***Deep cleaning hard surfaces.*** Wood and unsealed brass need to be deep cleaned on an as-needed basis, or at least twice a year (see Chapter 6).

***Equipment and supplies.*** Cleaning products are matched to the surface to be cleaned, ranging from wood cleaners to all-purpose cleaners for plastics. Equipment usually includes soft, lint-free rags.

Some executive housekeepers who deal with antiques or who are looking for more natural cleaning products are going back to time-honored cleaning products (see Chapter 14). For example, instead of using a spray, some still prefer wood oil. The housekeeping department can make its own by using 1 gallon of good oil such as mineral oil and 2 ounces of lemon extract. This is cost effective and also effective for cleaning purposes.

## SUMMARY

Whether the professional housekeeper is actively involved in the design process or steps in after the design is completed, he or she must deal with the bottom line of design. Executive housekeepers must understand which cleaning and maintenance procedures combined with what cleaning frequency will coax the longest useful life from each design element.

The executive housekeeper is a working partner in design. He or she must be expert in:

- Evaluating the operational practicality of FF&E, wall coverings, and wall finishes
- Creating routine maintenance and deep-cleaning procedures for all design elements
- Caring for a variety of surfaces and finishes, from delicate silks and antiques to sturdy laminates
- Assessing the need for repair and replacement
- Determining which equipment and supplies will be most useful in maintenance programs
- Understanding the language of design in order to preserve the integrity of the design
- When necessary, replacing individual items

### Review Questions

1. Give some examples of FF&E.
2. What is a model room?
3. Give examples of which wall coverings or surfaces would be appropriate for a guest bathroom and which for the guest room's sleeping area.
4. What is the best backing for vinyl wall covering and why?

5. What is the typical frequency for deep cleaning walls and ceilings?

6. What is the typical frequency for deep cleaning upholstery fabric?

7. What is the typical cycle for renovation of soft-goods and casegoods?

8. What tests should be conducted on fabric before cleaning begins?

9. How do procedures for wall-washing machines differ from those for hand washing walls?

10. What is a floor plan? Why is it important?

## Critical Thinking Questions

1. The interior designer says some delicate fabrics, such as silk, and very light colors should be used in the dining room. How would the executive housekeeper respond to this proposal and balance the need to create an image for the outlet with the operational concerns and costs of maintaining it?

2. As part of a renovation, the designer has proposed introducing four different guestroom schemes. How will this affect the housekeeping department's budget and labor hours?

3. Discuss the merits and disadvantages of painted walls versus vinyl wall coverings.

# 9

# Managing Equipment and Supplies

## Chapter Objectives

To properly manage supplies and equipment, the professional housekeeper should develop the following skills:

- Determine which supplies and equipment are needed by staff for efficient day-to-day operations
- Determine what capital equipment will be needed to clean and maintain the hotel
- Determine what furnishings will be needed for renovation and replacement
- Use forecasts to determine minimum and maximum supply levels
- Determine which guest supplies will satisfy guests' expectations yet still fit budgetary guidelines
- Develop proper procedures for planning and tracking consumable inventory
- Assess new products and replacement costs for existing products
- Work with the purchasing department to get the right product at the right price
- Set up an effective bidding process
- Weigh the real costs of purchasing, rental, and contract service

The basic process of equipping and supplying the housekeeping department involves determining what is needed, how much is needed, and how much it will cost. The executive housekeeper uses past experience, knowledge of staff skills, occu-pancy forecasts, and other projections to make these determinations effectively.

While all of this information is essential to projecting inventory needs, the day-to-day fluctuations in occupancy inherent in the lodging industry make the reality of planning and purchasing supplies challenging indeed. Dips or upswings in business can leave the department with a costly oversupply or a dangerously low stock level unless realistic minimums and maximums are established. The executive housekeeper must find products that meet the property's cleaning needs, while developing inventory control programs that will fit within the department's budget (see Chapter 12).

## SUPPLIES AND SMALL EQUIPMENT

Employees require the proper "tools" to do their jobs efficiently and effectively. In housekeeping terms, **supplies** are generally consumable goods, while **equipment** refers to durable goods. Housekeeping department employees need cleaning supplies, small equipment for day-to-day cleaning needs, uniforms, protective gear, and the **capital equipment** items—generally equipment that will last a year or more to do their jobs. But this is only part of the executive housekeeper's responsibility for supplies. He or she must also monitor and anticipate guests' needs and buy what is needed to satisfy guest demands without going over the budget.

Both cleaning supplies and guest supplies are referred to as **operating supplies** because they are depleted in less than one year. Consumable supplies are sometimes broken down into two categories: **recycled inventory**—items that can be used again, such as uniforms, linens, machinery and equipment; and **nonrecycled inventory**—items that are consumed or used up, such as cleaning supplies and guest supplies. Small equipment also falls into the nonrecycled inventory category.

Some inventory items are necessary for all housekeeping departments, regardless of the size or category of the property. They include:

- Linens and towels (for details on linens and towels, see Chapter 11)
- Bedding and pillows
- Cleaning supplies
- Guest supplies
- Safety supplies

Other types of equipment and supplies vary with the property's guest market, the property's category and setting, directives from the hotel management company or chain, historical data regarding consumption and pricing, and employee preference. Any purchasing decisions for equipment and supply must focus on what works, what will produce a value-for-money return, and what will satisfy both staff and guests.

## Determining Supply and Small Equipment Needs

In order to decide exactly what supplies are needed, the executive housekeeper must look first at the property's **physical plant,** which refers to the building itself and the structural elements and materials used within it. The design elements, including the choice of flooring and floor coverings, upholstery fabrics, finishes, and fixtures, also dictate the range of products needed to accomplish housekeeping's varied cleaning tasks.

The category and age of the property also influence the list of supplies. An historic property filled with antiques and aged wood requires a far different list of both cleaning and guest supplies than a newly built economy hotel with many surfaces that can simply be wiped clean. Though both require the same standard of cleanliness, the work and products required to achieve these standards may be vastly different (see Chapters 5 and 6).

The property's category and segment also affect supply and equipment needs. All-suite hotels have a microwave, which must be cleaned daily, more furnishings, extra sinks, and more counter space. Deluxe hotels provide bathrobes and a full amenities package that may include moisturizers, co-

logne, or after-shave and even slippers. Extended-stay properties require cooking and eating utensils.

## Cleaning Supplies and Small Equipment

Selecting cleaning supplies and small equipment begins with finding the products that work best for the property and those that reflect the best value. For example, a multi-purpose product may have a higher initial cost, but its usefulness for various cleaning tasks may make it less costly in the long run than buying and stocking various specialty products. Product needs differ from property to property, but a basic list of nonrecyclable cleaning supplies and small equipment for most properties would include items listed in Tables 9.1 and 9.2.

The list of necessary supplies expands or contracts with guest demand and the needs of the individual property (see Tricks of the Trade 9.1). For example, some executive housekeepers are experimenting with multi-purpose products that combine all-purpose cleaning features and disinfecting agents to address the threat of bacterial or viral contamination. The advantages are clear: not only is the risk of contamination reduced or eliminated but the housekeeping department can simplify its cleaning product inventory. The problem is that some multi-use products may be too harsh for certain surfaces such as wood but not strong enough to be effective on bathroom surfaces. They do work well on laminates and can clean both metal and fiberglass.

---

### Tricks of the Trade 9.1
### Inventive Cleaning Solutions

*The Problem:* No housekeeping department can stock all of the specialty products needed to meet the many and varied cleaning challenges of a hotel.

*The Solution:* Innovation. An attendant at one historic Tennessee hotel accidentally sprayed graffiti remover on a marble vanity top. The graffiti remover did an excellent job of cleaning the marble and protecting its shine. Peggy Andersen, manager of the Aveda spa/hotel in Osceola, Wisconsin, found that the same plant-based, aromatherapy hair salon product that parent company Aveda uses as a Detoxifier to remove build-up on hair also removes nearly any stain from fabric, including ink and blood. Aveda's Active Oil, which keeps skin supple, is an excellent

**TABLE 9.1** *Basic Non-Recyclable Cleaning Supplies*

| Cleaning Supplies | Purpose |
|---|---|
| All-purpose liquid cleaner | Cleans most surfaces |
| Glass cleaner | Cleans windows, glass, and mirrors |
| Furniture oil or polish | Cleans wood |
| Disinfectant cleaner and/or germicide; some are multi-purpose/disinfectant combinations | Cleans and sanitizes/sterilizes bathrooms, rest rooms, food-service areas, and other areas where contamination is a threat |
| Cleansers (1); paste cleaners (2) | (1) Fine-ground abrasives for cleaning surfaces such as porcelain sinks; (2) Nonabrasive cleaners, which require more effort but will not scratch |
| Drain cleaners | Clean drains (see Chapter 10 for details on enzyme cleaners) |
| Metal cleaners | Clean, polish metal surfaces |
| Toilet bowl cleaners | Clean, disinfect ceramic toilet bowls |
| Tile and grout cleaners | Clean ceramic tile or grout; different cleaners required for marble |
| Carpet cleaning chemicals; other floor care products | Clean carpets and floors |
| Deodorizers; ionizers | Mask unwanted odors; specialty products remove smoke odors |
| Protective clothing and biohazard gear | Protects from hazardous materials and body fluids |
| Pesticides | Dry or wet chemicals to control pests |

Some new products coming on the market combine some of these functions, but the basic work of cleaning a property requires a variety of supplies.

cleaner for metal and stainless steel. Half a lemon dipped in salt cleans copper, as well as iron rust. Worcestershire sauce can be rubbed on and washed off to clean brass. A paste of dry mustard and oil will remove dried rings from crystal or glass vases.

## Public Space Supplies

The housekeeping department is responsible for supplying chemicals and small equipment to keep public spaces clean, as well as guest rooms. Items such as sand for ash urns and the carriers or baskets into which the littered sand will be emptied (see Chapter 6) must be purchased, as must items such as soap dispensers and sanitary supply dispensers for public rest rooms. In deluxe hotels, the housekeeping department supplies the fabric, finger-tip towels used in public rest rooms and paper towels, as well as the hampers provided for the fabric towels and the waste baskets for the paper towels.

"Wet floor" signs are needed throughout the property and are particularly important in the front of the house where guest traffic is the heaviest. If the property's guests and visitors speak a variety of languages, the executive housekeeper should choose signs illustrated with universally recognized picture symbols or ask the manufacturer to print all cautionary wording in a second or even a third language (see Figure 9.1).

Public areas such as spas, health and fitness centers, and business centers may require specific cleaning fluids and equipment. Most manufacturers of the fixtures and equipment used in these areas have detailed instructions on what cleaning fluids may be used.

## Protective Gear

Whether as a regulatory mandate in some cities or states or as a realistic precaution, protective clothing is now a necessary cleaning supply. Gloves are the most basic piece of protective gear. Some executive housekeepers require attendants to wear them for all cleaning functions; others require the use of gloves only when dealing with harsh chemicals or biohazards. In either case, disposable gloves must be readily available to attendants. Generally, tight-fitting, disposable plastic gloves, such as surgical gloves, are used for cleaning. Because of their tight fit, they are less clumsy and less apt to cause the attendant to mishandle cleaning fluids

**TABLE 9.2** *Small Equipment*

| Types of Small Equipment | Purpose | Advantages; Disadvantages |
|---|---|---|
| Washable dust mops (1); floor mops and wet mops | Clean areas such as floors and walls | +Treated to collect dust (1); efficient; easy to use; −Types are not interchangeable |
| Synthetic brooms | Sweeping | +Rinseable; clean well; durable −Must be washed carefully |
| Compartmentalized buckets | Carry supplies | +Lightweight; convenient |
| Buckets with built-in wringer | Take excess water from mop | +More stable than set-ons; −Cannot be used as multipurpose buckets |
| High dusters | Clean high, hard-to-reach areas | +Fairly lightweight; effective in cleaning high areas |
| Carriers, baskets, caddies | Carry cleaning supplies | +Lightweight −Different types required for various tasks |
| Steel wool | Cleans by sanding the surface lightly | +Effective, low-cost −Can be too abrasive for many surfaces |
| Scrubbing pads | Less-abrasive surface cleaner than steel wool | +Less scratch potential than steel wool; can be used on more surfaces |
| Spray bottles | Hold fluids dispensed from bulk containers | |
| Whisk brooms | Sweep loose dirt | |
| Toilet swabs, johnny mops | Long-handled equipment for cleaning toilet bowl | +Eliminates risks of cleaning toilet bowls with sponges |

All small equipment should be durable and lightweight.

or other tools. However, there is debate as to whether this kind of glove affords sufficient protection against biohazards. Some emergency medical technicians advise using a sturdier type of glove for biohazard removal. The increased weight is not a hindrance in picking up and removing soiled items, as it could be in routine cleaning.

Protective eyewear such as goggles is also essential. These are disposable supplies that should be required for certain tasks such as cleaning toilets and mixing chemicals. Biohazard kits, complete with protective clothing, gloves, eyewear and, in some packs, tape to cover any places where gloves, shoe covers, or helmets attach to the basic suit should also be supplied.

## Uniforms

Uniforms are part of the visual identity of a property, but they are also workwear for staff members.

The typical uniform list for a larger property would include:

- Room attendant's and public area attendants' uniforms
- Waitstaff's uniforms
- Janitors', engineers', and parking attendants' uniforms
- F&B stewards' uniforms
- Front desk staff's uniforms

These are broad categories, and there may be numerous subcategories depending on the type of hotel and the number of departments. A hotel with a fine dining restaurant would require special uniforms for the maître d'. The concierge staff would have different uniforms. Banquet waitstaff may have different uniforms, or at least a different color scheme than restaurant waitstaff. A themed, ethnic restaurant may require culturally correct "cos-

**Figure 9.1**  *Wet floor signs are essential "equipment" for floor cleaning. Cordoning off the area with two signs helps bring attention to the wet area and prevent slips and falls. (Courtesy of Rubbermaid Commercial Products)*

**Figure 9.2**  *Uniforms must reflect the requirements of the job title. A room attendant's uniform, such as the one at left, must be long enough to accommodate both bending and reaching and allow freedom of movement for deep cleaning. (Courtesy of Superior Surgical Manufacturing Co., Inc.)*

tumes" rather than uniforms. The key consideration is that the uniforms are well made, comfortable to work in, and appropriate for the overall image of the property (see Figure 9.2 and Chapter 11).

## Environmentally Friendly Cleaning Supplies

The shift toward environmentally friendly cleaning products also influences the choice and variety of cleaning supplies. In most cases, executive housekeepers choose items that are biodegradable and phosphate-free. Some of these products are less harsh on skin. Many are more easily disposed of after use because they do not pose the same threat to storm sewers as harsher chemicals. As with any cleaning products, some are more effective than others (see Chapter 14).

## Portion Size

Packaging is a significant issue. Should the executive housekeeper buy cleaners in large, 55-gallon drums and mix and dispense them at the property or buy pre-mixed cleaning chemicals?

The majority of executive housekeepers recommend buying pre-mixed cleaning chemicals. This reduces the risk of an accident, controls the

dilution ratio and, in most cases, saves money because the proper amount of chemicals is being used rather than over-used. Many manufacturers now sell systems in which the pre-mixed solutions can be dispensed directly into spray bottles without any contact with skin. Since aerosol cans pose environmental hazards and waste removal problems, spray-top pump bottles are preferable. Spray bottles require active pumping, so they also help control how much cleaning fluid is used.

Another option is to use **portion-control** cleaners, that is, cleaners which are pre-packaged to hold just enough of the cleaning substance to clean one specific area or a certain amount of square footage. Some executive housekeepers say that, although the initial cash outlay is somewhat higher, portion packs are easier to monitor and can lead to savings of up to 40 percent on the overall product costs. With portion control, the supervisor issues only as many prepacks as needed. If floor cleaning requires four changes of water daily, the supervisor needs issue only four packages of pre-measured cleaning solution. "We buy pre-measured cleaners in bulk. This has two advantages. Buying pre-measured cleaners helps eliminate over-filling or over-mixing and wasting product. Buying in bulk saves money," says Greg Parsons, general manager of the 200-room Radisson Arrowwood Resort in Alexandria, Minnesota.

If the housekeeping department still finds it economical to mix solutions on property, this duty should be assigned to a specific employee. This staff member must be adequately trained in mixing these sometimes volatile chemicals—some of which can trigger explosions if mixed improperly.

The only way to find out which of these packaging solutions is most effective for the property is to test each one and cost it out. Tests should be conducted during periods of varying occupancy before a decision is made.

## SELECTING GUEST SUPPLIES AND AMENITIES

The housekeeping department is responsible for supplying both **guest supplies** and **guest amenities.** Guest supplies refer to the items the guest *requires* as part of the hotel stay. Guest amenities refer to nonessentials that enhance the guest's stay (see Table 9.3). Both amenities and supplies must be stocked.

When evaluating these products, the executive housekeeper must understand and anticipate the tastes and preferences of the hotel's guests. New hotels should have adequate market research available. Existing hotels may be able to provide preference information based on computerized guest information files. Executive housekeepers working in senior living centers also should actively seek the residents' input on the items supplied, whether through a board or committee representing their interests or through direct contact with management. Whatever the type of property, residents' or guests' wishes must be considered when choosing supply items. Rough sheets, stiff facial tissues, or watery liquid soap can lead to vocal guest dissatisfaction.

### Amenities

There was a time when soap and, perhaps, stationery were all the "guest amenities" most hotels offered. Today, hotels seek to pamper their guests with personal care products, pens, laundry bags, matches, stationery, shoe shine cloths or sponges, and even bathrobes (see Figure 9.3). Even the most basic amenity—soap—has evolved from necessity to marketing tool, as upscale hotels supply imported, hand-milled varieties, soothing, herbal cleansing bars, or creamy, moisturizing soaps.

What kinds of amenities are considered to be supplies is determined by four key considerations:

- Budget
- Guest expectations
- What the competitors offer
- Hotel category

**Budget.** Building an amenities package starts with the budget. If the budget is tight, it is better to scale back amenities than the quality of supplies. Amenities packages may range from less than $1.50 for a single bar of soap and few extras such as a shower cap to up to more than $50 in a new, deluxe resort that includes bathrobes, slippers, coffee makers, and a wide range of personal care products. In many properties, the amenities budget is defined as a certain percentage of room rate, typically from 1.5 percent to 3.5 percent. However, the trend is definitely moving away from luxury for its own sake and toward providing an amenities package that meets the needs of guests without a lot of wasted investment or unnecessary items.

**Guest expectations.** A guest paying $250 or more a night for an upgraded room or suite in a deluxe property would neither expect nor be satisfied by a single, .75-ounce bar of deodorant soap as the sole amenity. Any property that markets to frequent travelers, whether high-spend corporate executives or budget-conscious salespeople who literally spend half their work week on the road, should supply an amenities package that includes shampoo, two to three bars of soap—including one facial bar near the sink and a bath soap, a shoe mitt, a shower cap, stationery, pens, and a sewing kit. For chain hotels, these items usually are bought through the **central purchasing department,** the department that makes the major buying decisions for the entire chain. If not, the property's sales department or management company should have ample guest profile information to help make this decision.

**Studying the competition.** If the competition offers bathrobes, the property that does not could be at a disadvantage. In many cases, the actual amenities do not matter as much as the perception they

***TABLE 9.3*** *Guestroom Supplies and Amenities*

| Guestroom Supplies | Guestroom Amenities | Bathroom Supplies | Bathroom Amenities |
|---|---|---|---|
| Pillows | Stationery | Wash cloths | Facial soap |
| Pillow cases | Postcards | Hand towels | Bath soap or shower gel |
| Sheets | Pens | Bath towels | Shampoo |
| Blankets | Laundry bags | Bath mats | Moisturizer |
| Water pitcher | Utility bags | Shower curtains and liners | Shower cap |
| Clock | Packets of coffee or tea, sugar, and powdered creamer, stir sticks | Toilet tissue | Shoe mitt or shoeshine kit |
| Radio | | Facial tissue | Shoe horn |
| Glasses | Chocolates or mints provided with turndown service* | Sanitary bags | Sewing kit |
| Plastic Drinking cups | | Waste baskets | Bubble bath* |
| Coffee or tea maker | | Toilet seat band | Hair conditioner* |
| Trays | | Hair dryer | Cologne or after-shave* |
| Ice buckets | | Makeup mirror* | Razor* |
| Hangers | | Bathrobe* | Amenities container |
| Ashtrays | | Disposable slippers* | |
| Waste baskets | | Scale* | |
| Telephone directories | | | |
| Stationery folders | | | |
| Ironing board/iron | | | |
| (Mattress pad covers) | | | |
| Television program guide | | | |
| Bibles | | | |
| Do Not Disturb signs | | | |
| Table tent cards | | | |
| Fire safety | | | |

*Denotes upscale or luxury hotel.
The above list indicates the range of supplies and amenities typically provided for guests. Some properties provide only the most basic items; others pamper guests with amenities that include fresh fruit and flowers.

create: that the hotelier is giving something extra to the guest.

***Hotel category.*** Chains that have brands in several segments have blurred the boundaries of which amenities are offered by which category of hotel. In-room coffee makers appear in mid-tier Courtyard by Marriott brand hotels, just as they do in the upscale core brand Marriott hotels and the chain's all-suite properties. Modems and computer hookups are becoming standard amenities in all but the most streamlined budget hotels. Generally, though, the array and quality of amenities is linked to the category of hotel.

Deluxe resorts are the most pampering, with many offering luxurious treatments and personal care items developed exclusively for them as sig-

nature products. To stretch the payback potential of these items, the executive housekeeper should work with the marketing department to determine which amenities would best showcase the property's spa services and stimulate further sales of these services or, at least, sales of the personal care products.

## Guest Loan Items

In addition to guest supplies and amenities, the executive housekeeper must also stock **guest loan items.** This category includes everyday items the guest may have forgotten to pack or items such as irons and ironing boards (if they are not routinely provided in the guest rooms) and personal care items. In small hotels, these items will be stocked

| **What Guests Want in Guestrooms** (Features "most appreciated" by frequent travelers) | |
| --- | --- |
| **% of guests naming as one of top three** | |
| Bathroom amenities | 19.5 % |
| Coffeemaker | 15.5 |
| Large work desk | 13.7 |
| Refrigerator/minibar | 11.4 |
| Extra blanket/pillow | 9.2 |
| In-room movies | 8.8 |
| Windows that open | 6.3 |
| Others named | 15.6 |
| *Source: Lodging Hospitality research* | |

**Figure 9.3** *Market research on what guests expect is an important factor in selecting guest supplies and amenities. (Courtesy of Lodging Hospitality)*

at the front desk during the evening when the housekeeping department is closed. In a larger hotel, they are the 24-hour responsibility of the housekeeping department.

This list of guest loan items typically would include:

- An ironing board and iron, if not a standard supply
- A hair dryer, which now is usually a standard supply
- Foam or nonallergenic pillows, or pillows that are harder or softer than those that are standard supplies
- Heating pads
- Hot water bottles
- Ice packs
- First aid kits
- Extension cords
- Sewing kits, if not provided as a guest amenity
- Razors or electric shavers

- Voltage adapters, which are especially important if the hotel attracts a large volume of international visitors from countries where appliances such as hair dryers and electric shavers work on a different current

Guest loan items are attractive amenities and may incur high losses. To control this, the guest should be asked to sign a form detailing what was loaned and when (see Figure 9.4). This form should be stored in the housekeeping department until the guest returns the item. The return date also would be noted. Monitoring what is loaned and how often may also influence purchasing decisions (see Tales of the Trade 9.1).

**Tales of the Trade 9.1
Figuring the Bottom Line on Loan Items**

Calculating which loan items guests request most often may lead to better purchasing deci-

| RIHGA ROYAL HOTEL, NEW YORK | | | | | | | | | | | | | | | | |
|---|---|---|---|---|---|---|---|---|---|---|---|---|---|---|---|---|
| HOUSEKEEPING DEPARTMENT | | | | | | | | | | | | | | | | |
| USAGE FROM 6/96 - 5/97 | | | | | | | | | | | | | | | | |
| ITEM | | | | | | | | | | | | | Ave.Month | Unit | Value per | Usage per |
| Room Nights | 6/96 | 7/96 | 8/96 | 9/96 | 10/96 | 11/96 | 12/96 | 1/97 | 2/97 | 3/97 | 4/97 | 5/96 | Usage | Price | Occ. Room | Occ. Room |
| | | | | | | | | | | | | | | | | |
| Bathrobe Card | | | | | | | | | | | | | | | | |
| Bumper, Crib | | | | | | | | | | | | | | | | |
| Clock Radio | | | | | | | | | | | | | | | | |
| Cots | | | | | | | | | | | | | | | | |
| Crib | | | | | | | | | | | | | | | | |
| DND - Attempt to Clean | | | | | | | | | | | | | | | | |
| Do Not Disturb | | | | | | | | | | | | | | | | |
| Folder, Plastic for Stationery | | | | | | | | | | | | | | | | |
| Heating Pad | | | | | | | | | | | | | | | | |
| Housekeeping Attendant Sign | | | | | | | | | | | | | | | | |
| Ironing Board Cover | | | | | | | | | | | | | | | | |
| Luggage Rack | | | | | | | | | | | | | | | | |
| Soap Dish Liner | | | | | | | | | | | | | | | | |
| Telephone Book Cover | | | | | | | | | | | | | | | | |
| Vase for Plants, (foyer)square | | | | | | | | | | | | | | | | |
| Vase for Plants, LR round | | | | | | | | | | | | | | | | |
| VIP Soap Box | | | | | | | | | | | | | | | | |
| VIP Vase | | | | | | | | | | | | | | | | |
| Weather Cards | | | | | | | | | | | | | | | | |
| Adapter | | | | | | | | | | | | | | | | |
| Amenity Holder - tortoise | | | | | | | | | | | | | | | | |
| Bed Board, Double | | | | | | | | | | | | | | | | |
| Bed Board, King | | | | | | | | | | | | | | | | |
| Bed Board, Twin | | | | | | | | | | | | | | | | |
| Facial Tissue Holder - beige | | | | | | | | | | | | | | | | |
| Facial Tissue Holder - Tortoise | | | | | | | | | | | | | | | | |
| Folder, Guest Directory | | | | | | | | | | | | | | | | |
| Hairdryer | | | | | | | | | | | | | | | | |
| Hanger, Pants | | | | | | | | | | | | | | | | |
| Hanger, Satin | | | | | | | | | | | | | | | | |
| Hanger, Skirt (Clip) | | | | | | | | | | | | | | | | |
| Ice Bucket | | | | | | | | | | | | | | | | |
| Iron, Steam/Dry | | | | | | | | | | | | | | | | |
| Ironing Board | | | | | | | | | | | | | | | | |
| Pillows, Foam | | | | | | | | | | | | | | | | |
| Scale | | | | | | | | | | | | | | | | |
| Soap Dish | | | | | | | | | | | | | | | | |
| Wastebasket, Bathroom | | | | | | | | | | | | | | | | |
| Wastebasket, Living Room | | | | | | | | | | | | | | | | |
| QTips/Cottonball Holder | | | | | | | | | | | | | | | | |
| | | | | | | | | | | | | | | | | |
| | | | | | | | | | | | | | | | | |
| GA ROYAL HOTEL, NEW YORK | | | | | | | | | | | | | | | | |
| OUSEKEEPING DEPARTMENT | | | | | | | | | | | | | | | | |

**Figure 9.4** *Any guest loan form should allow room for all the necessary tracking information on the item, including a signature. Some forms add a column for comments or a return date. (Courtesy of the U.S. Grand Hotel, San Diego, California)*

sions for guestroom supplies. Laura Mengel, director of housekeeping for the Hilton at Walt Disney World Village, Lake Buena Vista, Florida, found that the department had averaged nearly 400 requests for hair dryers each month. Only 20 percent of the hotel's 814 rooms were equipped with hair dryers. "I calculated the labor time spent logging these requests and delivering the hair dryers. Based on the time saved and the resulting increases in productivity, the return on investment would be about 18 months," notes Mengel. After seeing the figures, the general manager agreed that hair dryers should be a standard guest supply for the hotel.

Most hotel companies also make available personal care items that guests may have forgotten, such as a toothbrush, toothpaste, or comb. In most larger chain hotels, these items are provided free of charge. However, at some properties, they are not categorized along with "loan" items but are sold in vending machines.

Some guest loan items technically are capital equipment. These would include:

- Cribs
- Rollaway beds
- Crutches
- Wheelchairs
- Canes

• **Bed boards,** which are stiff boards inserted between the mattress and boxspring to give the bed a firmer feel, and extensions to be placed at the foot of the bed to add comfort for very tall guests. Some of these items must be coordinated with other departments.

For example, if the property has a large number of wheelchairs, they would more likely be stocked by and stored in the security department. High chairs are a common guest loan item. In most properties, the request for a high chair would be made to the housekeeping department, but the item would be supplied by the F&B department. If the property has no F&B department or if there is high demand for high chairs in the restaurant outlets, the executive housekeeper may order one or two high chairs and store them in the housekeeping department for the convenience of families with small children who want to eat in their guest room.

## FINDING THE RIGHT PRODUCTS

The sources of hotel supply continue to expand. The executive housekeeper must be familiar with what products are available and what they claim to do. Working alone or in conjunction with the purchasing department, the executive housekeeper must first determine which of these products are worth considering and testing. Factors that should be weighed in making this decision include:

• Quality versus price
• Effectiveness
• Ease of use
• Durability

### Sources of Supply

Domestic and international manufacturers have broadened the range of supplies and equipment. In some cases, executive housekeepers in chain-affiliated hotels will have the list of suppliers predetermined by the hotel chain's central purchasing department. Central purchasing may negotiate a **national supply contract** with various manufacturers. The national supply contract achieves substantial discounts because it covers orders for the entire chain. Not only does this ensure massive discounts based on volume, especially for the larger chains, but it also reinforces cleaning and guest supply standards by making sure each property has the same supplies and equipment.

The drawback to central supply contracts comes when the products included in the contract do not meet the needs of the individual property, though this is rare. In this case, the executive housekeeper should discuss the matter first with the property's director of purchasing or the general manager. If the property has no purchasing department and the general manager agrees, the executive housekeeper may contact the local representative of the nationally approved supplier. He or she would explain the problem and try to find alternatives within the product line. Another option is to contact the central purchasing office directly and find out whether other companies hungry for the account may have a new product that would work well for the property. If so, the executive housekeeper may arrange to test the product and report the results to central purchasing.

Some chains, hotel associations, and marketing/reservation services may have a list of **preferred suppliers.** Though not bound contractually, these suppliers offer the properties a substantial discount in return for what is essentially an endorsement from the lodging company or association. Properties in marketing/reservation services independent properties that belong to associations may be far more diverse than their counterparts in highly standardized chains. The added flexibility of a preferred suppliers list rather than a contractual agreement may give the executive housekeepers more leeway in finding products to meet the property's needs.

An increasingly small group of hotels do not benefit from any of these arrangements. The executive housekeeper, perhaps with the director of purchasing, must negotiate each deal individually. Janitorial supply houses in large cities have goods in every category that housekeeping might want, ranging from heavy equipment to cleaning supplies and guest supplies. Distributors carry the manufacturers' product lines to hotels and motels both within and outside major urban areas. Trade shows and trade publications showcase innovative new products alongside already established brand names.

### Obtaining Bids: Quality versus Price

As a department manager, the executive housekeeper alone or in conjunction with the purchasing department must make sure the department is getting a value-for-money return on its investment in supplies and equipment. Obtaining competitive bids is essential. The general rule of thumb is that three bids should be obtained if possible. Bids may not be required for small expenditures totaling $500.

The executive housekeeper should provide each bidder with as much detail as possible on:

- The specific type of supply or equipment and what it is expected to do
- Delivery requirements, including provisions for emergency supply
- Training, and how much the vendor will provide at no charge
- After-sales service expectations

Price is a factor that needs to be weighed carefully. Since products differ, the executive housekeeper must find a way to adjust for these differences in order to make a fair cost comparison. One factor that is sometimes overlooked in pricing products is how concentrated each substance is. For example, a scrubbing solution mixed at a ratio of 30 parts of water to one part of concentrate, with a cost of $3 a gallon for the concentrate, would cost 10 cents per gallon, or $3.00 divided by 30, which equals 10 cents. This could then be compared with a pre-measured product. If the pre-measured product cost 32 cents per package and each package makes four gallons of solution, the comparable cost would be 8 cents per gallon, or 32 divided by four, which equals eight. Purchasing agents generally use this system of comparables in making buying determinations. They make their decisions based on the cost per usable gallon of solution.

Executive housekeepers who do their own purchasing must become expert negotiators. They can stretch their budget without sacrificing quality by looking for ways to increase the order volume in order to obtain better pricing or reduce unnecessary overage. Some properties within the same chain may work together to bid out jobs to local service providers, such as recycling pickup, in order to generate volume discounts and become a more important customer.

Quality also counts. In terms of guest amenities and supplies, guests will not accept items that are harsh or have an unpleasant, chemical smell. Some executive housekeepers prefer to use recognizable, name-brand products with a long history of high quality. To reduce the possibility of adverse reactions, many hotel companies now supply guest amenities that are designed for sensitive skin. Low-quality guest supplies are not a bargain, since they

frequently will result in a high volume of guest complaints. It is preferable to use a less costly presentation item, perhaps a standard plastic tray instead of a decorative wicker basket, than to stint on the quality of the amenities themselves.

All these factors must be weighed when making the purchasing decision. It is the bid that combines the best product, price, and service that should win the contract, not necessarily the bid with the lowest price.

## Effectiveness

A product that does not consistently perform well is no bargain, whatever the price. Having the opportunity to test the products should be a required part of the bidding process. Even if the hotel has a purchasing department, the executive housekeeper and departmental staff should test the effectiveness of products on the job.

Some key tests include:

1. Does the product work effectively under the conditions of the individual property? If so, does it work on the most difficult cleaning challenges or will a specialty product have to be supplied for these tasks?

2. How easy is the product to use? Will extra training be required, or more day-to-day supervision?

3. Is the product hazardous and, if so, will special protective gear be required to use it? Is a less harsh alternative available?

4. Does the product clean as large an area as it claims?

5. Does the product require any special equipment for proper usage that then would have to be purchased?

6. Does this product have multi-use capabilities?

7. Will the product require a special storage area to reduce the risk of fire or explosion?

8. How does the product perform after several uses? Is there a buildup of the product, residual, unpleasant odor, or inconsistent results after several days of usage?

New products should be tested by staff at the property before the purchasing decision is made. Staff input is an important factor in weighing effectiveness. The only exception stems from safety or security issues. For example, staff may prefer vacuum cleaners with cloth bags, but the risk of bacterial contamination is too great to follow staff preference. Executive housekeepers should let local health codes and regulations be the guide for these decisions.

If possible, products should be tested under different conditions to determine whether they will meet the toughest cleaning challenges the property offers. Oswell Melton, assistant rooms division manager of the upscale, 218-room Radisson Mikayo Hotel in San Francisco, California, points out that line employees should be involved in evaluating new products and be asked for their input on how the products work. "After all, they are the people who will have to use them every day. Too often the people who will be most involved with the product are the least involved in the decision making process," says Melton, who also directly oversees the hotel's housekeeping department.

Having line employees test products also may help determine how much training time will be necessary to use the products correctly. Most companies that sell products and equipment will train staff in proper usage free of charge.

### Ease of Use

Cleaning supplies, laundry supplies, and all operating equipment should be easy to use. If the product is too complicated to use or requires a great deal of specialty equipment, employees will be less likely to use it and less likely to use it correctly.

It is also important that the skill level, cultural backgrounds, and physical capabilities of staff be taken into consideration when selecting products. One Central American hotel was losing many labor hours each week because no one consulted the staff or executive housekeeper before determining the proper height for countertops and shelving. All were specified to standard heights used in U.S. hotels. However, the housekeeping staff of this hotel was substantially shorter than the average U.S. staff and some required step stools to reach items needed each day. Stature may vary widely in many staffs, and the executive housekeeper must take this into consideration when assessing whether handles are long enough and comfortable to hold, how large and heavy caddies and buckets can be, and even what size gloves to order.

### Durability

Durability and quality are often synonymous when it comes to small equipment. Buckets, mops, spray bottles, and other small equipment used by the housekeeping department must be dependable day after day.

Plastic buckets must be thick enough to hold an appropriate amount of water and floor cleaning without buckling or tearing. Mop handles have to be sturdy enough to withstand constant pressure. The heads of mops and brooms should hold together and clean effectively. All small equipment wears out; the point is to find products that do not wear out prematurely.

On-property tests for durability should be conducted by new hires as well as veteran employees. This helps determine the wear and tear the equipment must withstand. It also points out any inherent problems in the way the equipment is made or functions—even in the hands of an inexperienced employee.

### Determining How Much Is Needed

After selecting which supplies and small equipment to use, the executive housekeeper must determine how much will be needed. Par levels must be set for each category of supplies and small equipment. This is necessary to insure the department carries the proper amount of inventory. Too much inventory means the department is overspending and must find storage space for the excess stock. Too little inventory means attendants will not have the necessary supplies to do their jobs.

### Using Forecasts

The executive housekeeper uses the profile of business developed by the rooms division and/or sales and marketing department to determine what the cleaning needs will be for the next year. Projected occupancy figures dictate how many guest supplies, guest amenities, and guestroom cleaning supplies must be ordered for the year to come. The number of attendants needed to service this level of occupancy influences how much small equipment must be purchased.

These projections should be checked against historical performance to establish realistic minimum and maximum levels of inventory. The **minimum inventory level** is the lowest level stock should reach before reordering. The minimum should cover the property's needs until the next scheduled delivery. A **maximum inventory level** also should be set. When supplies reach this maximum, no more should be ordered until some is used up. By tracking purchase orders and inventory reports for the last year or two, the executive housekeeper can see which months have the highest average occupancy and therefore require the most supplies, and which months are less busy. These reports also indicate which inventory levels were too low, forcing too many reorders, and which were too high, resulting in overstock or excess stock.

For public areas, inventory levels of cleaning supplies are calculated on the basis of how much will be needed to clean certain areas. Floor and carpet cleaners cover a certain amount of square footage. This coverage, multiplied by the number of times this task must be done, will determine how much of these products will be needed. Tracking previous purchase orders may be the best means for calculating how much furniture oil or polish, glass cleaner, and bathroom cleaners will be required for public areas. Inventories of laundry detergents and water softening chemicals are based on projected occupancies.

Robin Diaz, executive housekeeper of the 266-room Mohonk Mountain House resort in New Paltz, New York, uses a three-year usage history to set inventory levels. Then she reforecasts for each month based on near-term occupancy projections. Reforecasting is important because it allows the executive housekeeper time to adjust inventory levels to accommodate unexpected upswings or downturns in occupancy.

## Tracking Inventory

Forecasts are important in estimating overall need for the coming year. But, actual consumption must be tracked on a regular basis and the inventories adjusted accordingly. Taking inventory of supplies is essential in calculating how much has been used, how much remains, and how much must be reordered to meet par levels.

Executive housekeepers differ on the frequency of physical inventories, depending on the delivery schedule of suppliers, location of the hotel, and even the category of hotel. Some require that physical inventories be taken twice a week, some as infrequently as every other month or quarterly. Monthly inventories are typical for operating supplies; capital equipment is usually inventoried quarterly. Whatever the schedule, the inventory should be regular and workable for the individual property.

Physical inventories should be taken in floor linen rooms and the main linen room. The employees assigned to take the physical inventory count up the supplies, both those on hand and ready for use and those still in storage. This number is then subtracted from the total ordered. The

resulting difference shows how much of the supply was used up since the last inventory. Inventories taken for capital items are used to make sure all items are accounted for. Whoever takes the inventory of capital items should also make sure they are in good condition.

Supervisors who take physical inventories should be trained to recognize both minimum and maximum inventory levels. They should alert the executive housekeeper when levels reach either extreme, but especially when it is time to reorder.

Careful records of inventory should be maintained. A useful form, usually called an **inventory record** or **inventory report,** would list each supply item, show current levels of stock, indicate minimum and maximum stock levels and show some cost data (see Figure 9.5). Inventory information on all supplies and equipment should be kept in a computer file or, if done manually, in a log book. It will be useful in budgeting, purchasing, and controlling loss and pilferage. Computerized inventory control forms are most helpful because they can be designed to show current inventories and compare them with previous years. They also can show where expenditures stand on a year-to-date basis.

Any dramatic increase in consumption should be checked against occupancy figures. The executive housekeeper needs to determine whether the increase is justifiable, or whether pilferage and loss are more likely causes. Checks should also be made against repair orders and equipment performance. If too many sheets are being discarded, thereby depleting the linen supply, it may be possible that they are being torn on rough edges of the laundry chutes or that the laundry compounds require some adjustment. The executive housekeeper needs to find out why consumption increased during a certain period rather than automatically adjusting the next purchase order based on inventory levels alone.

## Establishing Inventory Controls

Some smaller operations and family-run bed and breakfast properties still operate on an inventory system in which attendants replenish their supplies as needed directly from central storage. More commonly, the supervisor issues supplies and equipment to each attendant. There are two main approaches to supply control. In one, the attendant essentially signs out a certain number of linens and supplies each day and must account for them at the end of the shift. In the other, the attendant is issued pre-counted supplies sufficient for his or her quota.

| HOUSEKEEPING DEPARTMENT | | | | | | | | | | | |
|---|---|---|---|---|---|---|---|---|---|---|---|
| GUEST AMENITIES INVENTORY - MARCH, 1997 | | | | | | | | | | | |
| Occupied Room Nights - | | | | | | | | | | | |
| ITEM | Inventory on Hand | Purchases | Total | Inventory on Hand | Amount Used | Room Nights | Usage Per Room Night | Unit Cost | Cost Plus Tax | Value Per Room Night | Total Inventory Value | Monthly Expense |
| Ashtray | | | | | | | | | | | |
| Coaster, Glass | | | | | | | | | | | |
| Facial Tissue (Klnx Boutique) | | | | | | | | | | | |
| Glass Tumber | | | | | | | | | | | |
| Laundry/Dry Cleaning Bag | | | | | | | | | | | |
| Lint Rollers | | | | | | | | | | | |
| Matchbook | | | | | | | | | | | |
| Memo Pad | | | | | | | | | | | |
| Pen | | | | | | | | | | | |
| Postcard | | | | | | | | | | | |
| Sewing Kit | | | | | | | | | | | |
| Shoe Bag (plastic) | | | | | | | | | | | |
| Shoe Horn | | | | | | | | | | | |
| Toilet Tissue | | | | | | | | | | | |
| Body Lotion | | | | | | | | | | | |
| Bath Gel | | | | | | | | | | | |
| Shampoo | | | | | | | | | | | |
| Glycerine Soap | | | | | | | | | | | |
| French Milled Soap | | | | | | | | | | | |
| Bath Soap | | | | | | | | | | | |
| Shoe Mittts | | | | | | | | | | | |
| Shower Cap | | | | | | | | | | | |
| Slippers | | | | | | | | | | | |
| Guest Comment Cards | | | | | | | | | | | |
| Umbrellas | | | | | | | | | | | |

**Figure 9.5** *Using this type of form, supervisors should be trained to recognize minimum and maximum inventory levels for all guest supplies and amenities. (Courtesy of The RIHGA Royal Hotel, New York)*

If this is insufficient, the attendant requests additional supplies on an as-needed basis.

Locks are a useful tool in terms of inventory control. Although people still are required to issue supplies and equipment, locking up storage areas heightens security (see Chapter 13).

## SELECTING AND CARING FOR CAPITAL EQUIPMENT

Housekeeping operations require a wide variety of large, expensive machinery. The basic categories include machines, materials handling equipment, various tools and, mechanical and electrical supplies (see Table 9.4). Key factors in selecting capital equipment include determining the average life expectancy of the machine, whether it can be repaired in-house, the cost of replacement parts, and the length of the **warranty.** The warranty is issued by the manufacturer and insures the buyer that the item will be replaced or repaired at no cost during the period covered by the warranty.

In addition to machinery, the capital budget also includes FF&E items. Although the initial purchase of these items would have been provided for in the property's pre-opening budget, pieces re-

quired for regular renovation or replacement will be part of the housekeeping department's budget and inventory. Though the role of the executive housekeeper in selecting or critiquing design items will be detailed in Chapter 13, it is important for inventory purposes that the departmental manager understand how much will be needed.

### Determining What Is Needed

The capital equipment list must be tailored to the hotel. Not every hotel needs equipment for polishing marble floors or even laundry equipment. However, basic items such as vacuums will be required by all categories of properties. Before the executive housekeeper can determine the property's capital equipment needs, he or she will need to discuss with the general manager or rooms division manager what will be cleaned by the department and what cleaning tasks will be contracted out.

FF&E inventories depend on the number of rooms and amount of front-of-the-house space. The executive housekeeper must also allow for **storage stock,** sometimes called **attic stock,** which refers to furnishings kept in storage to replace items that become damaged or worn. Although the executive housekeeper cannot guess exactly how much dam-

*TABLE 9.4*  *A Capital Equipment Roster*

| Machines | Materials Handling Equipment | Furniture, Fixtures, Equipment | Tools, Electrical, Mechanical Supplies |
|---|---|---|---|
| Attendants' vacuums | Room attendants' carts | Chairs | Ladders |
| Wet/dry vacs | Linen carts for clean linen | Tables | Scaffolds |
| All-purpose vacs for furniture, draperies, and vents | Pick-up carts for soiled linen | Mattresses | Casters |
| Back-pack vacs | House attendants' carts | Boxsprings | Chair glides |
| Space vacs | Dollies | Bed frames | Extension cords |
| Extraction machines | Hand trucks | Headboards | |
| Buffers | Mobile shelving | Night tables | |
| Scrubbers | | Guestroom desks | |
| Burnishers | | Armoires | |
| Steam cleaning machines | | Sleeper sofas | |
| High-pressure sprayers | | Televisions | |
| Dry-foam shampoo machines | | Radios | |
| Pile lifters | | Lamps | |
| Electric brooms | | Mirrors | |
| Carpet sweepers | | Paintings | |
| Wall washers | | Decorative accessories | |
| Glass washers | | Telephones | |
| Fogging machines and/or insecticide sprayers | | Wall-mounted light fixtures | |
| Sewing machines | | Draperies | |
| Trash-handling equipment | | Blinds | |
| Laundry washer/extractors | | Towel bars | |
| Dryers | | Toilet tissue holders | |
| Spreader/folder | | Make-up mirrors | |

This list is merely an overview of what capital equipment may be required. A hotel with its own furniture repair facilities would require many specialty tools. Dry cleaning plants also have their own requisite equipment. In some properties, house attendants would be issued hand tools and required to do some minor repairs. In others, this task would be assigned exclusively to maintenance.

age will occur, he or she can use historical performance as an average to forecast how much storage stock will be needed. Generally, this would not equal more than 1 percent of total FF&E inventory except in the case of cruiseships. Planned renovations will affect both the rooms and storage.

## Finding the Right Capital Equipment

Machines selected for the property must be both effective and durable. Because there are so many models of each machine, the executive house-keeper must match the machinery with the staff's skills and the physical requirements of the property.

Room attendants' carts must be sturdy enough to carry not only heavy bed and bath linen, but also heavy-duty laundry bags and trash bags that are quickly filled with additional weight. These carts also must hold cleaning supplies, certain guest supplies, guest amenities and, usually, a vacuum cleaner. They should be lightweight but with wheels large enough for easy maneuvering, even in tight corridors. Shelves should be able to accommodate the attendants' supplies. Some executive housekeepers prefer open carts with covers because they are lighter weight; others prefer those with closed backs for greater security and a neater appearance. Some carts even have built-in, high-powered vacuum units. All should have bumpers or guards to protect corridor walls. Large casters with brakes are advisable on heavy carts. They can be stopped and locked by use of the foot. Fiberglass carts, which do not chip or fade, may be preferable for collecting soiled linen or trash. They also are easier to sanitize.

Machinery should not only be durable but safe. Laundry equipment and other machines that can pose a risk of injury should have the lockout features discussed in Chapter 13.

FF&E items must be chosen on the basis of appearance as well as durability (see Chapter 8). They must fit into the color scheme of the space, and their proportions must suit the surroundings. It may be possible to find a classic chair that will work with all the schemes, thereby reducing the amount of storage stock and investment.

## Preventive Maintenance

Training employees in proper equipment usage and care is the first step in preventive maintenance. Most manufacturers will provide at least basic training on-site. For larger equipment, such as carpet and floor cleaning machines, manufacturers may offer special training classes at a regional plant. All training and maintenance manuals should be provided in English (or the mother tongue of the country) and, if necessary, in the language spoken by most of the house attendants who will use and maintain the equipment.

Working with the maintenance department, the executive housekeeper must create a schedule for regular maintenance, such as greasing these machines, replacing parts, or doing whatever is necessary to maintain them. Routine maintenance procedures such as winding up cords, drying off the exteriors of the machines, or emptying the machines should be checked daily by supervisors or inspectors. Some executive housekeepers also post reminders near the area where the equipment is stored. It is helpful to post a checklist outlining the necessary procedures to be completed before putting the unit into storage.

## Setting a Replacement Schedule

Replacing capital equipment and FF&E is an expensive proposition. Unless new equipment can demonstrate remarkable cost savings, repair may be the more cost-effective option. "You may have to pay $400 or $500 to fix a motor on a major piece of equipment, but that is a lot less expensive than the $7,000 it would take to replace the equipment," notes Laura Mengel, director of housekeeping for the 814-room Hilton at Walt Disney World Village. The executive housekeeper should train employees in preventive maintenance and work with the maintenance or engineering department to keep capital equipment in good working order as long as possible.

An **equipment inventory,** a detailed list of each piece of equipment, should be kept in the departmental files. This inventory lists the purchase dates, source of supply, purchase price, warranty and other pertinent information for each piece of equipment. Copies of subsequent repair orders, including how long the repair took and what work was needed, would be attached to the data sheet on each piece of equipment along with the cost of the repair, if applicable. It is also advisable to stencil or mark in permanent ink the purchase date on each piece of equipment in an inconspicuous place. If possible, it is helpful to add the number of units purchased. So, if the machine were marked with 97-2-6, it would mean that six units were purchased on the sixth day of February (the second month) of 1997.

As was mentioned in Chapter 5, room attendants and house attendants should note any FF&E item with damage or wear marks on their daily report or assignment sheet. They also should be trained to report any faulty equipment, from frayed cords on vacuum cleaners to equipment that is malfunctioning. These records also will prove useful when considering replacement.

FF&E items have a fairly standard replacement schedule. In a luxury hotel, public area carpet is replaced every three to five years. Guestroom carpet may last seven or more. Softgoods generally are replaced every five years to keep the styling current. Casegoods may last 10 years or more, again depending on how important styling is to positioning the hotel. As competition increases, property owners feel more and more pressure to keep their properties looking fresh. This means current standards for replacement may get shorter and shorter as time goes on.

## PURCHASING, RENTING, AND CONTRACTING

After the executive housekeeper has decided what the department needs, he or she decides whether to rent or buy the item or whether to hire a contract company to do the necessary work. The department purchases most consumable supplies, although linens may be purchased or rented. While the property purchases FF&E items and materials handling equipment, other machinery may be owned or rented or brought in by a contract cleaning service. Each of these decisions must be evaluated in terms of cost benefit and productivity.

## Purchasing

In some properties, the executive housekeeper makes the purchasing decision, negotiates the purchase with vendors, and awards the contracts for supplies to the vendors. In properties with purchasing departments, the executive housekeeper must write up a specification or "spec" sheet, which is a detailed description of a product, including the size, color, material, standard of quality, price, and function. Spec sheets for equipment may also include what after-sales service is expected, shipping directions, and what training will be expected from the vendor. If the executive housekeeper has a clear preference for one company's product, it is customary to write on the spec sheet "A.J. Smith Co. or equal" or "A.J. Smith Co. or comparable."

When working with a purchasing department, the executive housekeeper would write a **purchase requisition order,** a formal written request for a certain item or category of items. The purchasing department uses this as the basis for issuing the **purchase order,** which is essentially an offer to buy something. When the vendor accepts the purchase order, it becomes a contract and must be considered as such. The purchase order should contain all the pertinent information needed by the vendor to perform the delivery and the invoice in accordance with the buyer's wishes. Purchase orders should be written in multiple copies so that at least one company can remain in the purchasing department and another retained by housekeeping.

## Rentals and Contract Services

The decision to buy, rent, or contract out certain cleaning tasks must be weighed carefully. The executive housekeeper must consider the costs, the quality of the work being done, the frequency with which the task needs to be done, and how quickly the task must be done.

## Cost

The executive housekeeper must weigh all the expenses involved with in-house, rental, and contract options before deciding which is most cost effective.

The cost of buying the equipment involves not only the purchase price, but the cost of the labor needed to operate it and any costs necessary to maintain and repair it. Training cost and time must also be computed. Some of this cost may be offset by the fact that the employee who operates this equipment would perform other tasks. In addition, the equipment may be flexible enough to use for several tasks.

Rental costs are pure expenses. Purchased equipment is a **capital asset,** an item with real, long-term value. Rented equipment adds no value. However, for a specialty task which is done only twice a year, the cost of the equipment may not be justifiable. Rental is a viable option for small properties unable to make the cash outlay for equipment or those with few areas that would require the use of large equipment to clean.

Contract cleaning services provide both labor and equipment. Although the property will not have the asset, neither will the executive housekeeper have to allocate thousands of dollars for equipment purchases. The benefit of a reputable contract cleaner is that the company can provide a broader range of specialty equipment than the property could afford and experienced workers to operate it. Also, with contract services, there are no repair or replacement costs to consider.

## Quality of Work

In addition to weighing the cost, the executive housekeeper also must analyze the important issue of quality control. Purchasing equipment gives the executive housekeeper the most control. Departmental employees operate the equipment, and the equipment is available as soon as it is needed. This makes it less likely that soils will become permanent stains or that small emergencies, such as water leakage, will result in major replacement costs. It also means any performance problems or quality issues can be addressed promptly and remedied.

Departmental staff also operate rental equipment, so that aspect of quality control is maintained. Problems could arise if the staff is not adequately trained. An inexperienced employee may not be able to make the equipment work to its capacity or do the task correctly. In some cases, it may actually worsen the cleaning problem and experts would have to be called in. Also, equipment rental must be planned for a certain period. If occupancy or function business suddenly jumps, the equipment would have to be returned and re-

rented. The advantage is that some equipment is used rarely, and renting it gets the job done without a heavy front-end investment or storage problems.

Contract services have the advantage of providing trained staff to do the task. "We contract with two major outside contract services, one for window cleaning and one for carpet cleaning. We just don't have the expertise. It is more economical to use these services with trained staff than to risk someone hurting themselves by breaking a window or having an inexperienced employee ruin a costly carpet," says Louis Fozman, executive housekeeper of The Adolphus Hotel, Dallas, Texas.

To maximize quality control for contract services, many housekeepers recommend visiting the hotel periodically while the company is working to monitor the performance of the contract service. The departmental supervisor on the shift should evaluate the service's work. The executive housekeeper should discuss any problems or special instructions with the service's supervisor during weekly walk-throughs. Failure to perform properly will result in termination of the contract (see Chapter 6).

## SUMMARY

Supplying and equipping the hotel is both an operational and administrative task. The executive housekeeper must be able to assess the effectiveness, durability, quality, and price of products, as well as their effect on the bottom line. He or she also must determine which products and equipment best fit with the skills of the staff and the property's overall requirements.

As with other aspects of departmental management, these decisions require a lot of input. Coworkers must be involved to arrive at the best choice. Wise choices regarding supplies and equipment make for a more productive department. The executive housekeeper must also develop plans for keeping the department well-supplied and equipped, whatever the variance in occupancy is.

The skills that are important to master include:

- Weighing quality versus price
- Tracking inventory
- Assessing new supplies and equipment
- Specifying what will work best for the property, staff, and guests

- Using records, forecasts, and input from staff and other departments to calculate minimum and maximum inventory levels
- Assessing capital equipment needs and setting replacement schedules
- Writing a detailed spec sheet for a purchasing department
- Working with vendors
- Weighing the pros and cons of purchase versus rental
- Evaluating what is best left to experts and outside contractors

## Review Questions

1. Describe some differences between operating supplies and capital equipment.
2. What are guest supplies? What are guest amenities?
3. How are forecasts used in determining supply needs?
4. What are minimum and maximum inventory levels?
5. What forms are helpful in controlling inventory?
6. Explain what information is needed to obtain bids.
7. List several key factors that affect the selection of supplies and amenities.
8. What is central purchasing?
9. What information should be recorded for capital equipment items?
10. What factors should be taken into account when deciding whether to purchase, rent, or contract out equipment or services?

## Critical Thinking Questions

1. The property has extensive public spaces with a variety of cleaning needs, and the capital equipment has not been replaced for more than seven years. Some would need expensive repairs to be more dependable. What are the advantages of repair or replacement versus hiring a contract cleaning service?
2. The performance of a regular supplier has become slipshod, but the product supplied is effective. How can this situation be rectified?
3. Consumption of cleaning supplies is far beyond expectation and cost per occupied room is rising as a result. How could this be handled?

# 10

# Managing the On-Premise Laundry and Working with Contract Laundry Operations

## Chapter Objectives

To establish effective laundry management practices, the executive housekeeper must be able to:

- Determine staff size for the on-premises laundry
- Assess equipment needs for the on-premise laundry
- Establish proper procedures for the on-premise laundry
- Communicate clearly with staff and other departments
- Understand the environmental impact of on-premise laundering and dry cleaning
- Restock linens efficiently
- Reduce waste and loss
- Set up procedures for controlling costs for laundry cleaned by contract services
- Set up quality control programs for on-premise or contract services

Well-managed laundry operations are essential to the successful housekeeping department. Any employee who requires a freshly laundered uniform, any F&B employee who sets a table, and any attendant who changes guestroom linen, depends on efficient laundry management to start their workday. In many ways, the laundry is the hub of the housekeeping department.

The executive housekeeper sees to it that the property has a ready supply of uniforms, linen and **napery,** which refers to the table linens, when they are needed. If the laundry is on-premise, the executive housekeeper and laundry manager work together to find the equipment, train staff, write schedules, and create systems to insure that linen and uniform demand is met. For contract laundry services, the executive housekeeper must find the right firm, coordinate deliveries, monitor quality, and review costs.

## MANAGING THE ON-PREMISE LAUNDRY

Most executive housekeepers prefer to have an on-premises laundry facility (see Figures 10.1a and 10.1b. Having the laundry within the hotel gives the executive housekeeper more control over cleaning procedures and availability of linens, and a lower cost of operation. On-premise laundries are perhaps as low as 11 cents to 16 cents per pound as opposed to 35 cents to 50 cents per pound for laundry done by a contract service. Having an on-premise laundry operation also lowers the property's linen **par.** Par means the number of sets of towels and linens that are in use, in the linen room and **in soil,** which means linen waiting to be laundered and returned to inventory. Par for a hotel with an on-premise laundry is three. Par for a hotel using a contract laundry service would be five. In

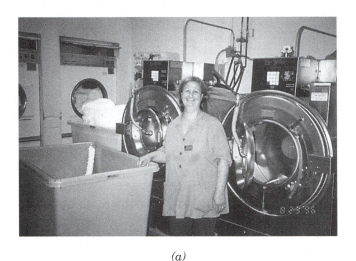

(a)                                        (b)

**Figure 10.1**  *Whether compact (a) or nearly commercial size (b), on-premise laundries reduce costs and maximize control.*

addition to the linen in use, in storage and in soil, allowances need to be made for the linen on the truck going to the laundry plant and the linen in the truck scheduled to make a delivery to the hotel. Managing on-premise laundry operations involves analyzing equipment and supply needs, determining the correct number of laundry staff, and regulating operational costs.

## EQUIPPING THE ON-PREMISE LAUNDRY

Equipping the on-premise laundry begins with analyzing just how much work must be done in the laundry. Key factors to consider in equipment selection include:

- Property size and category
- The space available for the laundry
- Budget
- Occupancy forecasts
- The profile of business
- The forecast for function business

The focus should be on automated equipment. Although the initial cost may be higher for more highly automated equipment, the cost can be recouped in the first two to four years of operation

because these machines frequently reduce labor needs by as much as one-half. Equipment that saves energy and/or water or reduces chemical usage also speeds up the payback time. These benefits will continue to be felt over the 10- to 20-year life of this equipment.

### Tales of the Trade 10.1
### Overhauling the Outmoded Laundry

When George H. Martens (R.L.L.O.) took over as the director of laundry and dry cleaning for the 1,206-room Fontainebleau Hilton Resort & Spa in Miami Beach in the early 1980s, the laundry was running three full shifts a day staffed by 68 employees, and had some outdated equipment, including an ironer that dated back to 1918.

When Martens began work on his plans, the laundry had only four small washers, two small dryers, and "one even smaller dryer." Martens laid out a long-term plan to modernize the equipment and create a more efficient staff structure. "Too many properties build laundries based on estimated occupancy. If occupancy averages 50 percent, they build a laundry based on that. If occupancy later rises to 100 percent, the hotel is caught short and has to run two or three shifts to meet demand," notes Martens, who also does laundry consulting.

Following a long-range plan and making changes as budget allowed, Martens eventually grouped laundry operations into three rooms: the main laundry, the drying and folding room, and the linen room. Martens concentrated on purchasing equipment that had a large enough capacity to handle the demand and looked for features that would reduce labor and handling.

Through his progressive automation of the laundry, Martens was able to cut staff levels by two-thirds, and now runs only one shift. Martens revamped scheduling for the laundry staff. Most staff now starts after 3 P.M. "When we started early in the morning, the staff had little or nothing to do for hours while waiting for room attendants to strip linens. Guests don't check out or leave their rooms until 10 A.M. Also, energy costs are far cheaper at night," Martens points out. One employee starts work at 7 A.M. and does all guest laundry.

Innovation is continuous. When he discovered eight computer memory chips were not being used on the towel folders, he worked with the manufacturer to use the chips to create computerized memory settings for small, medium, and large towels. Attendants simply press the appropriate button and let the machine take over. Martens says this eliminates human error and has reduced jamming significantly. He also has begun using enzymes to clean sewer pipes exiting the laundry. These colonies of soil- and grease-eating bacteria eventually coat the inner lining of the pipes. The waste that flows through the city sewers is easier to deal with and clogs are lessened. Martens also prefers using hydrogen peroxide as a bleaching and disinfecting agent because it is not as harsh as bleach nor does it have the same fumes or the same capacity to cause chemical burns.

With automated and innovative equipment and a dedicated staff of 22, the Fontainebleau's laundry each year washes:

12 million pounds of laundry
2 million pillowcases
2.4 million sheets
250,000 tablecloths
2.8 million napkins
4.8 million towels
196,000 uniforms

Efficient laundry layouts help save steps and reduce labor costs. Professional laundry facilities designers can create a floor plan that maximizes space usage in the laundry and can specify an equipment list best matched to the property's needs (see Figure 10.2). Hotel management companies and franchisors have **technical services departments,** corporate departments with expertise in areas such as hotel design, facilities design, and architecture, that work with the property staff to provide model layouts and develop equipment lists. In properties with a **mini-laundry,** a laundry with only a few machines that clean a small volume of laundry, the executive housekeeper may have to be both designer and equipment specifier.

## Equipment

The equipment list for an on-premise laundry starts with a washer and dryer. However, most properties' needs are far more sophisticated. The following is an overview of the equipment used in hotel laundries.

## Washers

Washers are the most basic items of equipment. Most properties require **washer/extractors.** The wash cycle launders the load. Then, during extraction, the items in the load are spun at very high speeds to remove as much moisture as possible. This extraction process saves energy and substantially reduces drying time. For laundries with washers that do not have extraction capabilities, separate extractors can be installed. Key factors to consider in washer selection include:

- Capacity
- Automation
- Computerized controls
- Water systems

Sufficient **capacity** is a major factor to weigh when assessing washers and washer/extractors. On-premise laundries generally require washers with a capacity of 50 pounds or more to handle linen requirements. Some giant commercial laundries use machines with 1,200-pound capacities (see Table 10.1). Overloading machines puts an unnecessary pressure on the washer's motor that may cause breakdowns. It also usually results in poor cleaning, because the items in the laundry cannot flow freely through the laundry chemicals and rinse water.

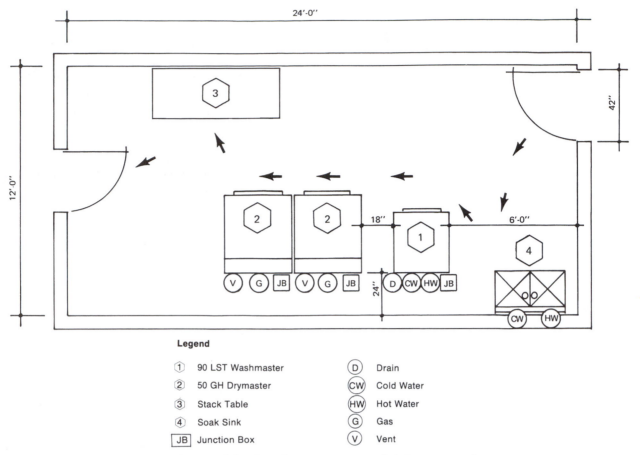

**Legend**

| | | | |
|---|---|---|---|
| ① | 90 LST Washmaster | Ⓓ | Drain |
| ② | 50 GH Drymaster | Ⓒ̶Ⓦ | Cold Water |
| ③ | Stack Table | Ⓗ̶Ⓦ | Hot Water |
| ④ | Soak Sink | Ⓖ | Gas |
| JB | Junction Box | Ⓥ | Vent |

**Figure 10.2** *The step-saving layout of this laundry in a 175-room hotel requires only three employees.*

**Automation** is another essential feature for commercial washers. Washers with automatic detergent and dispensing cycles are preferable. The attendant can add the detergent and washing solutions at the beginning of the cycle, and then move on to other tasks. In addition, the detergents and solutions are properly mixed and flow onto the load at the correct point in the cycle. This helps eliminate chemical damage that could result if improperly diluted chemical solutions were poured onto the load.

**Computerization** and technology also play a role in washer selection. Washers with microprocessors offer several advantages (see Figures 10.3a and 10.3b). Electronic sensors or microprocessors automatically dispense liquid detergents at the proper time in the machine's cycle, reducing labor and handling. Machines with microprocessors can be preprogrammed to preset laundry settings for particular fabrics or soils. The operator simply presses a button on the washer/extractor marked "towels," "uniforms," "sheets," or other major categories of loads, and the programmed washing begins.

Some washers have **water recycling systems** controlled by microprocessors which recycle water that would otherwise be drained out. The hot water that would have been drained is stored for the next flush or suds cycle. These systems can reduce energy costs, too. Some can save up to 40 percent on gas, for example. Energy-efficient extractors with a venting system preheat air coming into the machine. This system captures heat from the air being exhausted without recirculating the hot, lint-laden air.

Washers with self-monitoring water systems are equipped with a bell ringer that sounds if the water becomes too acid or alkali, or if water quality sinks below a certain standard. Though expensive, these machines can pay for themselves. Attendants do not have to be assigned to check water quality regularly. Since water quality must be determined before laundry chemicals are chosen and mixed, it is important that the water quality remain the same

***TABLE 10.1*** *Washer-extrator Capacities*

| | MILNOR 35 lb. models | MILNOR 55 lb. models | MILNOR 75 lb. models | MILNOR 95 lb. models |
|---|---|---|---|---|
| King size sheets | 15 | 24 | 32 | 40 |
| Queen size sheets | 17 | 27 | 36 | 46 |
| Double bed sheets | 23 | 36 | 50 | 62 |
| Twin bed sheets | 28 | 44 | 60 | 76 |
| Pillow covers | 116 | 182 | 250 | 315 |
| Bed spreads (84×118) | 7 | 11 | 15 | 19 |
| Blankets | 8 | 13 | 18 | 22 |
| Bed pads | 12 | 19 | 25 | 33 |
| Pillows | 6 | 9 | 14 | 16 |
| Bath towels | 61 | 96 | 132 | 165 |
| Hand towels | 195 | 306 | 418 | 529 |
| Wash cloths | 875 | 1375 | 1875 | 2375 |
| Bath mats | 26 | 41 | 57 | 70 |
| Table cloths (54×54) | 37 | 59 | 81 | 100 |
| Napkins (20×20) | 206 | 324 | 442 | 559 |
| Dress (uniforms) | 38 | 60 | 82 | 103 |
| Jackets (attendants) | 25 | 39 | 54 | 68 |
| Aprons (bib) | 83 | 129 | 178 | 225 |
| Aprons (tea) | 175 | 275 | 375 | 475 |
| Pants | 29 | 46 | 62 | 79 |
| Shirts | 74 | 116 | 159 | 200 |
| Draperies (84×96) | 6 | 9 | 13 | 16 |
| Entry mats (36×60) | 2 | 3 | 4 | 5 |
| Furniture covers | 17 | 26 | 36 | 46 |
| Cleaning rags | 79 | 124 | 170 | 214 |
| Mop heads | 23 | 36 | 50 | 62 |

These figures are based on sample items. Weights and sizes of some brands differ, and therefore the figures should be used only as guidelines.
***Source:*** Pellerin Milnor Corporation, P.O. Box 400, Kenner, LA 70063-0400.

to keep chemicals working at peak efficiency. If water with a high iron content is allowed to flow into the laundry untreated or under-treated, several loads of linen could be stained from the rusty water. Monitoring water quality is particularly important for laundries aboard cruise ships.

Rusty water stains sometimes can be removed with special cleaners or a bleaching agent, but they cannot be returned to supply until they are treated and relaundered. Self-monitoring systems are designed to prevent this time-consuming mishap.

## Dryers

Dryers finish the process of moisture removal. The general rule is that two dryers are required for every one washer; some properties stretch this to three dryers for every two washers. Since drying time is longer than washing time, often more than twice as long, more dryers are needed for efficient operation. As with washers, it is important to have sufficient capacity and automatic controls.

## Ironers, Rollers, and Folders

**Ironers,** or **pressing machines,** remove wrinkles from clean laundry. Ironers roll over the item; pressers flatten the item. Laundry must be free of soils, well rinsed, and have a slight amount of moisture when it is fed into an ironer or placed on a presser. Soil and chemical residues can adhere to

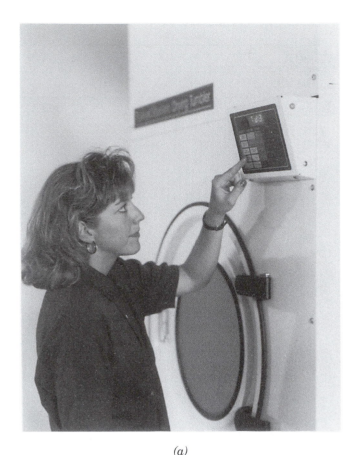

(a)                                                    (b)

*Figure 10.3* (a) *Computerized washing machines reduce labor costs and prevent waste of laundry chemical. (Courtesy of Raytheon Commercial Laundry) (b) The computerized MicroMaster panel on this 120-lb Speed Queen tumbler allows the laundry attendant to pre-program the machine for a particular fabric type. It also shows at-a-glance the status of the load. (Courtesy of Raytheon Commercial Laundry)*

the equipment's surface and result in stains on the fabric or cause items to roll.

Some ironers also have a folder. **Separate folders** and **roller/folders** are also available. The simplest folder anchors one end of the item so that it can be folded by one employee. Highly automated roller/folders actually complete the drying process and iron the item during the rolling function, then fold the item and even stack it. Some also have a spreader function that actually spreads out the item as it is fed into the machine. Tumble drying usually is not necessary if roller/folders are in use.

Roller/folders with special counters free up attendants from the tedious job of having to count out how many napkins, sheets, or tablecloths are run through before adjusting the machine to a different width and/or length. Computerized units are self-adjusting. A master count of work can be set each day. Units without these features require the

attendant to preset the quantity to be folded, then reset it once adjustments are made for producing a different length or width. Small properties that do not have a large or varied volume of laundry do not need such fully automated machinery. However, in larger properties, speed and accuracy increase productivity markedly.

## Other Equipment

In addition to the washing, drying, ironing, and folding equipment, the laundry must have space and equipment in which to sort soiled linen, soak it, stack clean linen, and distribute it. City center hotels with laundries in the basement usually have **laundry chutes.** Room and public space attendants put all soiled linen down the chutes. Some newly built properties with first-floor laundry operations use a **blow tunnel,** in which a column of continuous heavy air actually blows linen from the floors to the laundry room.

In most low-rise resorts with separate buildings housing guest rooms or long guestroom wings, laundry equipment must include an adequate number of linen carts to transport soiled linen to the laundry. A dozen carts may suffice for a mid-sized (300 to 500 rooms) property; a property of more than 650 rooms may require 20 or more.

In larger properties, linen is sorted into bins. Computerized lifts are necessary for large properties because they can handle larger, heavier loads than employees could lift safely. Use of these lifts reduces labor hours and the risk of injuries.

An adequate **soaking sink** is essential for treating heavy stains. More than one may be required even for a mid-sized hotel because of the concern over biohazards and bloodborne pathogens. The laundry also must have a **stack table,** where folded linen is stacked when ready for distribution, and **rolling shelves,** shelves on a wheeled base. Stack tables are essential equipment for every hotel laundry. In a small property, the clean linen may be distributed on carts rather than on special rolling shelves.

## Special Considerations

Technology is making laundry operations more efficient and cost effective. One manufacturer has developed a computerized laundry system that links the microprocessor controls to all of its equipment and relays this information into a central work station. Using this terminal, the attendant, supervisor, and laundry manager not only program the equipment but also track information and retrieve production data. At any given time, a staff member can call up information on a specific machine to determine what the contents of the load are and at what point in the cycle it is. He or she can also determine what water temperature and what amount of chemical were used. Through information tracking, the system can compile data on chemical, water, and energy usage. Its modem link into the manufacturer's central office offers on-line help in diagnosing problems.

Ozone washing systems, which made their debut in the 1980s, are back on the scene (see Tricks of the Trade 10.1). In these systems, ozone is injected into the load through the cold water lines. Because of its oxidizing qualities, ozone facilitates the breakdown of insoluble soils. This reduces detergent and water use, cuts the amount of hot water

needed for proper laundering, and reduces output into the sewage system.

> **Tricks of the Trade 10.1**
> **Ozone Washing Systems**
>
> **The Problem:** Finding an efficient, cost-effective laundry system.
>
> **The Solution:** The 176-room Ramada Inn in Fairfield, New Jersey, invested $20,000 in an ozone washing system in 1995. Less than a year later, a property spokesperson says that ozone washing generated a savings of $12,000—a 40 percent reduction in laundry operating costs. The largest savings realized were: a 40 percent reduction in water and sewage costs, a 52 percent reduction in natural gas costs, and a 54 percent reduction in energy costs.

Automation has its cost, but most executive housekeepers say that the savings in labor, quality of the work done, and added controls it provides produce a quick return on investment (ROI). Pre-programmable settings eliminate guesswork and overuse of laundry chemicals. They also reduce the amount of time an attendant is assigned simply to monitor the equipment and wait to add chemicals at the proper time.

Safety features are not extras but essentials. Laundry equipment should have built-in safety features, such as roll-bars that prevent the operator's arm from being caught between rollers. Washers and dryers should have ample insulation to keep the front of the units from heating up sufficiently to cause burns.

## Calculating Equipment Needs

The amount of laundry that must be done is the key determining factor in assessing how much equipment is needed. The budget for the laundry, available floor space, and staff size must also be considered.

Jonathan Schade, vice president of operations for Manor Care Hotels, Silver Spring, Maryland, offers these general guidelines on laundry planning (see Table 10.2):

Larger properties may require heavier capacity equipment if the laundry volume is particularly

*TABLE 10.2* *Equipment Needs*

| Size of property | Equipment list | Special requirements |
|---|---|---|
| 120 rooms | 2 50-lb. or 55-lb. washers<br>3 75-lb. dryers | Percale sheets which do not have to be ironed |
| 250–400 rooms | 2–3 90-lb. washers<br>3–5 110-lb. dryers<br>Roller/folder<br>Ironer | Percale sheets will be needed if there is no budget for the folder and ironer |
| 1,000 rooms or more | 1–2 90-lb. washers<br>5 225-lb. washers<br>Extractors<br>7–10 110-lb. dryers<br>Computerized lifts<br>Roller/folder<br>Small-piece folder<br>Ironer | A good grade of no-iron muslin may be used, but this fabric still needs light ironing to be free of wrinkles |

Laundry equipment must be closely matched to each property's needs

heavy. Spreader/roller/folders that also stack linens can save two to three staff positions. Small equipment, such as machines that sanitize down pillows, may also benefit certain categories of hotels.

## EQUIPPING THE MINI-LAUNDRY

Larger properties may have the room and budget for full-size laundries. However, with space and investment dollars at a premium, the trend in smaller properties is toward mini-laundries, laundries with as little as two three pieces of customized equipment (see Figure 10.4). The availability of good quality, no-iron sheets has reduced equipment needs. New liquid detergents make mini-laundries easier to operate. The equipment for a mini-laundry may include two washer/extractors, a large-capacity dryer and, for some properties, a simple folder.

Some motor hotels, residence halls and high-rise hotels have installed a mini-laundry on each floor. Each of these laundries can handle the linen needs for up to 100 rooms.

### Laundry Supplies

Typically, laundry supplies include laundry compounds, detergents with bactericidal properties, a bleaching agent—either bleach, a bleach-based agent, or hydrogen peroxide, water softening chemicals, and fabric softener. Special disinfectants also may be required for laundry and chute areas. Pes-

ticides, specifically roach killers, should be stocked in the laundry. If F&B linens come through the chute with food debris, they can attract roaches and other pests. Executive housekeepers generally recommend stocking some all-purpose cleaners in the laundry area to wipe down folding tables.

When it comes to fabric softeners, less is usually the best. This is particularly true for towels. Guest comment cards indicate guests prefer some roughness on towels because they dry better. Towels also are easier to rinse without excess softener.

Water quality and the type of equipment often affect the selection of laundry chemicals. As part of the bidding process, the executive housekeeper should ask that each vendor assess the water quality and tailor the list of laundry products to the result. Many newer laundry machines use pre-mixed chemicals, which reduces the risk of attendants using too much or too little of a laundry chemical. It also extends the life of the washables because they are being laundered with the correct amount of the chemical, not an overly harsh dosage.

The chemical makeup of laundry agents may also help determine which product or products to buy. For example, **antichlors** remove chlorine, at least excessive chlorine, from fabrics. **Alkali,** an abrasive, can pump up the detergent's cleaning power and is especially useful for removing grease or oil stains. However, since alkali is harsh, it has to be neutralized by an acid. **Sours** are mild acids that can neutralize the alkalinity of detergents and bleach. This can reduce the yellowing and fading that can result from an alkali residue. Some sours

**Figure 10.4** *With properly selected equipment and a space-saving layout, one employee can operate a hotel's mini-laundry. (Courtesy of Pellerin Milnor Corp.)*

boost this effect by integrating bluers or whiteners in the product. Many detergents contain **optical brighteners,** chemicals that help retain the original color, even after many washings. If mildew is a problem, **mildewcides** may be required to prevent mildew buildup.

Dry cleaning operations require the proper fluids or dry cleaning solvents. The type of machine determines what chemicals will be needed. Traditional machines use the solvent Perc. Several new machines on the market use less harsh solvents.

## STAFFING THE ON-PREMISE LAUNDRY

A property of 500 or more rooms may require five to six laundry attendants if the laundry operation is highly mechanized; 12 to 15 if it is not. Factors such as linen demand (see Chapter 11) and the labor intensity of the equipment both affect how large the staff must be. Purchasing labor-efficient equipment is one of the few ways to limit the size of laundry staff. Cross-training also increases productivity, though it rarely eliminates the need for an entire position. This is not a staff that can be downsized easily. A certain volume of work must be done each day and adequate staff must be assigned to do it.

The essential tasks consist of sorting, washing, drying, folding, and stacking the linen for distribution. The large laundry operation will require sorters, who wait at the chute exits or wait for carts, then sort the laundry; washpersons, who may mix chemicals if necessary; and laundry attendants, who operate the balance of the equipment and ready the linen, terry, and uniforms for distribution. A **laundry manager** or supervisor makes daily assignments and is responsible for the daily laundry operation. Some operations may have a need for two shifts; one starting at 7 A.M. or 8 A.M., the other starting at 3 P.M. or 4 P.M.

All laundry employees should be cross-trained to do every job in the laundry. "You cannot tell a guest, 'I'm sorry, you'll have to wait for a napkin because the laundry is running behind'," notes Ed Conaway, executive housekeeper for the upscale U.S. Grant Hotel, San Diego, California. Conaway prepared a *Housekeeping Manual* for the department, which provides an overview of all key operations and job descriptions. In the section on laundry, he advises that every employee in the laundry should be trained in the following skills:

- Knowing how each machine works
- Knowing how long each cycle runs
- Knowing how long different types of fabric or weights of fabric take to dry
- Knowing how much time it takes to fold items that are needed
- Knowing at what temperature to run the ironer so that the product is not damaged by too much heat or running too slowly
- Knowing how to use chemicals properly so as not to endanger staff or damage the product

Laundry work is physically demanding. Employees assigned to work in the laundry will need both the stamina to be on their feet most of the day and the ability to lift heavy loads at times. The laundry area usually is warm, though efforts are made to control an excessive heat buildup. Laundry employees must be able to work productively in this environment.

In large or upscale hotels, the laundry department may also include a dry cleaning operation. For a hotel with 600 or more rooms, the dry cleaning operation would require two to three employees. One would operate the dry cleaning equipment; the other one or two would press the dry cleaned items. A thorough knowledge of fabrics and stain treatment procedures is required, as well as an expertise in dealing with dry cleaning chemicals. The dry cleaning operation does not lend itself well to cross-training. Expertise is essential.

### Making Daily Assignments

Laundry attendants clock in and should be in uniform at their appointed starting time. The laundry manager or a supervisor starts work 15 minutes before the shift to turn on the machines and make sure they are working properly. Laundry managers or supervisors may use different approaches to scheduling, depending on the type of property and linen demand. Some prefer a staggered schedule. Two or three employees may be scheduled to begin work at 7 A.M. and would do the sorting and begin the wash cycle. Two more employees may start at 8 A.M., when these loads are ready to go through extractors and dryers. Two more may not start until 9 A.M., when the bulk of the rolling and folding work begins. While each employee works an eight-hour shift, this staggered schedule reduces nonproductive time while employees wait for machines to complete cycles.

A schedule in which all employees start at the same time can be workable and productive, particularly if the shift begins in the afternoon and the bulk of the work is done at night. By this point in the day, most of the soiled linen would have been gathered and is ready for cleaning. After sorting the soiled linen and other items and beginning the wash cycle, the attendants would begin folding towels that were washed and dried at the end of the previous day's shift or during the night shift.

The laundry supervisor or manager makes the daily assignments, as well as handling any special instructions from the executive housekeeper or F&B department. Each employee is told with what task or at what equipment he or she should start.

## THE LAUNDRY PROCESS

Sorting is the first step in laundering. Concern over bloodborne pathogens and biohazards has made sorting a responsibility for room attendants as well. Any biohazard must be bagged and properly labeled before being sent to the laundry. This alerts the laundry attendants to wear gloves and any other protective gear required by the property or local regulations in handling hazardous material.

Sorters should be trained to sort soiled linens, terry, and uniforms according to fabric content, weight, and the type of soil. Efficient sorting reduces washing and drying time, as well as preventing chemical and heat damage to product.

### Biohazards

Linens marked as biohazards should be dealt with immediately. They should not be allowed to sit, allowing bacteria to grow. If the attendant is not certain how to wash them or whether to discard them,

**LINEN DISCARD RECORD**

HOUSEKEEPER'S INITIALS: _MKB_　　　GENERAL MANAGER'S INITIALS: _CSD_　　　PERIOD ENDING: _7/3/88_

| Date | Bath Towels | Hand Towels | Wash Cloths | Bath Mats | Shower Curtains | Double Sheets | King Sheets | Double Pillow Case | King Pillow Case | Double Pillow | King Pillow | Double Blanket | King Blanket | Double Mattress Pad | King Mattress Pad | Double Bed Spread | King Bed Spread | Crib Sheet | | |
|---|---|---|---|---|---|---|---|---|---|---|---|---|---|---|---|---|---|---|---|---|
| 6/3 | 2 | 0 | 6 | 0 | 0 | 0 | 1 | 0 | 0 | 2 | 1 | 0 | 0 | 1 | 0 | 0 | 1 | 0 | | |
| 6/5 | 0 | 4 | 1 | 0 | 0 | 1 | 0 | 1 | 0 | 0 | 0 | 0 | 0 | 0 | 0 | 0 | 0 | 0 | | |
| 6/8 | 3 | 1 | 0 | 1 | 0 | 1 | 1 | 0 | 2 | 0 | 0 | 0 | 0 | 0 | 0 | 0 | 0 | 0 | | |
| 6/9 | 1 | 0 | 2 | 0 | 1 | 0 | 2 | 0 | 0 | 0 | 0 | 1 | 1 | 0 | 1 | 0 | 0 | 0 | | |
| 6/12 | 0 | 2 | 2 | 0 | 0 | 1 | 0 | 0 | 0 | 0 | 0 | 0 | 0 | 0 | 0 | 0 | 0 | 1 | | |
| 6/18 | 2 | 3 | 3 | 1 | 0 | 2 | 0 | 0 | 0 | 0 | 0 | 0 | 0 | 0 | 0 | 0 | 0 | 0 | | |
| 6/20 | 1 | 1 | 0 | 0 | 0 | 2 | 1 | 0 | 1 | 0 | 0 | 0 | 0 | 0 | 0 | 1 | 0 | 0 | | |
| 6/25 | 2 | 1 | 2 | 1 | 1 | 0 | 0 | 0 | 0 | 0 | 0 | 0 | 0 | 1 | 0 | 0 | 0 | 0 | | |
| 6/28 | 1 | 2 | 2 | 0 | 0 | 2 | 0 | 1 | 0 | 0 | 1 | 0 | 0 | 0 | 1 | 0 | 0 | 0 | | |
| | | | | | | | | | | | | | | | | | | | | |
| | | | | | | | | | | | | | | | | | | | | |
| | | | | | | | | | | | | | | | | | | | | |
| | | | | | | | | | | | | | | | | | | | | |
| **TOTAL DISCARDED** | 12 | 14 | 18 | 3 | 2 | 9 | 5 | 2 | 3 | 2 | 2 | 1 | 1 | 2 | 2 | 1 | 1 | 1 | | |

**Figure 10.5** *The front side of a linen discard record shows exactly how many linens were discarded on what dates.*

the laundry manager should be called. Those stained with blood or other bodily fluids should be washed as a separate load with a disinfecting detergent or a disinfectant/bleach detergent and the hottest water that can be used on the fabric. Essentially, they are steamed and boiled. Fabric heavily stained with blood may have to be burned. Stains caused by hazardous chemicals should be washed according to instructions provided by the manufacturer of the chemical.

**Stained/discard linen.** Special bins or barrels should be set aside for stained or discarded linens. These containers should be color-coded so that this system can be understood by anyone, regardless of fluency in English. Twice per day, these bins or barrels are emptied into a large cart and inspected by the laundry inspector or an experienced attendant to make sure no unstained linen is mixed in. Frequently, the laundry manager will use a certain item as a flag, which indicates the last load of stained items requiring special laundry chemicals. Any linen that does not come clean after one washing or any linen with holes is then discarded. Discards should be tracked on a **linen discard record** to monitor usage, wear, and loss (see Figure 10.5).

**Torn linen.** Some items are relegated to **rag out,** which means they are too frayed or torn to be reused in guest areas. Room attendants generally are trained to tie a knot in larger items that are torn before putting them down the laundry chute or into the laundry carts. If sorters find a lot of torn linen that has not been singled out by room attendants, the problem may be the laundry chute. A loose or rough piece of metal in the chute may be tearing linen on the way down. This should be reported and repaired as soon as possible. Laundry should be transported in carts, if possible, until the repair is done.

## Spot Treating Laundry Items

Spot treatment can remove some stains before the wash process begins. Removing stains prior to laundering means the items can be placed in regular loads instead of using extra laundry detergent, energy, and labor to launder them in a separate load. A deep double sink, a table, chemical supplies, and a stain removal chart will be needed for effective spot treatment. A few linen rooms make space for this procedure, but usually it is more efficiently and easily done in the laundry.

## Chemicals

Attendants doing spot treatment should be made to understand how various chemicals react with fabric. For example, chlorine bleach affects the cotton content in a blended material more than the synthetic portion. The higher the cotton content, the lower the amount of bleach that needs to be used. Dirt that settles on uniform collar linings, under the arm, or anywhere else on the fabric, particularly on polyester, should be treated as soon as possible after the uniform reaches the laundry room. Set-in dirt and grime require harsher chemicals that could reduce the life of the fabric. In the laundry area, a stain removal chart should be posted, clearly outlining which chemicals work on which stains and how this will affect various fabrics. Clear instructions should also be posted on how much cleaner to use and when and how to rinse the fabric before loading it into the washer with other materials.

### Guest Laundry

In the laundry and dry cleaning department, attendants should take special care when spot treating items belonging to guests. Guests in upscale or deluxe hotels may send designer garments worth hundreds or even thousands of dollars to be cleaned. If the cleaning product discolors or destroys the fibers, the property must bear the cost of replacement as well as the unpleasant prospect of explaining what happened to the guest and risking losing the guest's business and perhaps that of the guest's company as well. Cleaning procedures for such garments should be reviewed with the laundry manager or supervisor. If there is any question regarding how effectively the garment can be cleaned, the laundry manager should return it to the guest with a polite note explaining that the garment could not be cared for properly in the property's laundry.

### Proper Laundering Procedures

Once the loads are properly sorted and spot treated if necessary, the attendants begin the wash cycles. Washers are operated according to the manufacturer's instructions. Since the bulk of loads will be the same each day—usually bed linen, terry items, F&B linen and, in some cases, uniforms—the laundry manager can program computerized models to the proper settings, or develop a chart that indicates which settings should be used on manually set models. Attendants should run full loads, except for biohazards or special departmental requests. Partial loads waste labor hours and cleaning products. They also add unnecessary wear and tear to the washers, which usually are **calibrated** (or adjusted to sit properly on the floor) to run at peak efficiency when they are fully loaded.

Polyester/cotton fabrics require a gradual cooldown rinse and a gentle final spin to prevent wrinkling. Many fabrics will last longer if washed in warm water rather than hot. However, concern over bloodborne pathogens is raising new issues for executive housekeepers in all areas of hospitality and health care. Some now advise that any fabrics that come into direct contact with the guest, including sheets, terry items, and robes, be washed in hot water with a disinfectant/detergent. This may reduce the life of the fabric; however, it virtually eliminates the possibility of contamination of another guest. If bleach-based disinfectant/detergents are used, the property should use only white linens and terry items.

If the property uses washer/extractors to produce a product that is as dry as possible after the wash cycle, the load is placed in the dryer. Some properties use separate washers and extractors. In these cases, attendants must move the load from the washer to the extractor, then to the dryer. Dryers, too, can be preprogrammed or preset to prevent the loads from overdrying or underdrying. Excess heat can easily damage fabric, particularly synthetics. Cooler temperatures are particularly important for polyester fabrics, including uniforms. Dryer vents should be cleaned daily to prevent a lint buildup, which can hamper efficiency and, more important, pose a fire hazard. Laundry attendants should leave all dryer doors open when the laundry closes for the day to prevent a heat buildup, which could result in combustion.

After being dried, items that require ironing are put into the ironer. Other items are fed into the roller/folder. Some states require that items be ironed because the high heat used in ironing is considered part of the sanitizing process. Some executive housekeepers suggest doing this even when there is no regulation to reduce the possibility of transmitting any germs or viruses.

In states that do not require this or for permanent press or polyester/cotton fabrics that do not require ironing, attendants, the inspector, or supervisor should check items carefully as they go through the roller/folder to make sure they are thoroughly clean. Roller/folders do not use heat in their operation. However, they add to the productivity of the laundry. Using a simple, inexpensive folding machine, one attendant can do about 70 sheets per hour. *Two* attendants folding sheets by hand can do only 55 to 60 sheets per hour. Using the folder, two attendants can do double that volume. Large, automated folders increase the labor savings further. Attendants must take care when setting counters and lengths for the items being folded. Adjustments must be made for the varying sizes of product to be folded, which can range from table napkins to king-sized sheets.

Once items are folded, they are stacked on rolling carts and are ready for distribution. Some executive housekeepers advise that bed linen, particularly polyester/cotton blend sheets, be allowed to rest on the shelf rather than going from the dryer directly onto the bed. The storage period allows the fabric to rest and cool down properly, thereby prolonging its useful life.

All laundries organize the clean, folded items in some way. Some executive housekeepers request that enough linen for one floor or section be stacked on each main rolling cart. Others request that sheets be grouped together by various sizes; for example, all kings together, then queens, and so on, and the same for bath towels and washcloths. Larger laundries may prepackage complete sets of linens for each room in a bag color-coded according to sheet size. This simplifies handling and storage and also saves time for the room attendants; however, this does add several steps in the handling (see Chapter 11). The system should be tailored to the demand of the property and capacity of its laundry.

## REDUCING WASTE AND LOSS

Linens, towels, and uniforms represent a major investment for any property. The laundry can play a key role in protecting this investment. Proper cleaning procedures, provisions for reusing rag-out items, and accurate record keeping can cut waste and reduce loss.

As mentioned earlier, laundering fabrics at the right temperature and using the appropriate cleaning agent will go a long way toward extending the life of the fabrics. Formulations should be checked monthly or at least every other month to make sure they are cleaning properly, as should the equipment.

Bleach–based detergents or disinfectant/detergents should be used only as needed, not for all laundry loads unless water quality makes it necessary, as it frequently does on shipboard. While using bleach and the hottest water setting can cut fabric life as much as 30 percent, they may be necessary to keep laundry free of germs. Some eco-friendly detergents can be used for loads in which there is little concern about germ growth or bacterial buildup.

Occasionally, room attendants mix in clean, torn linen with dirty linen when loading items down the laundry chute. If this happens frequently, floor supervisors or the executive housekeepers should discuss it with the individual room attendant or during regular departmental meetings. A combination of all these problems signals the need to re-engineer laundry operations (see Tales of the Trade 10.2).

### Tales of the Trade 10.2
### The Damp Sheet Saga

An 800-room Texas hotel, in a damp, humid climate, had 10,500 sheets on hand when it opened. The 800 rooms had a total of 1,200 beds, and 75 rollaways stored in the floor linen closets. Colored queen-sized sheets were used on both the outsized twins and the queen-sized beds.

Par for this property was five, which meant 6,375 sheets, or 1,275 beds times five, were taken out of storage, unwrapped, and put into service. The balance, 4,125, was stored on pallets in the only space available, the basement.

The linen loss for the first year the hotel was open was extremely high. Since the hotel was new, this could not be attributed to wear. Control systems were not set up until after the hotel was in operation and, as a result, there was considerable pilferage.

Damage was frequent too, and often unexpected. Management and department heads were not familiar with the problems caused by the climate or proper linen handling procedures. A concrete floor in the soiled laundry area under the chutes stained more than 100 sheets before the problem was discovered, and this resulted in their premature discard. The room attendants sometimes got trash and laundry chutes confused, which stained more sheets that could not be bleached.

A laundry workers' strike left the bins full of soiled linens standing around long enough to allow mildew to grow. The extreme dampness in one part of the storeroom, undiscovered until it was too late, caused several dozen more sheets to be damaged beyond repair by mildew.

The second year, controls were implemented and the figures were far different. Repairs were made and procedures were introduced to offset the effects of the climate. The sewing room caught up and was able to make repairs. However, the same number of sheets was purchased.

Two years later, normal wear factors began to show. Occupancy for the hotel was up 23 per-

*TABLE T10.2*   *The "Damp Sheet Saga"*

| Items | Year 1 | Year 2 | Year 3 | Year 4 | Year 5 | Year 6 |
|---|---|---|---|---|---|---|
| Sheets— | | | | | | |
| On hand | 10,500 | 12,159 | 15,176 | 16,006 | 15,497 | 17,193 |
| Purchased | 3,600 | 3,600 | 3,600 | 3,600 | 4,000 | 4,000 |
| | 4,100 | 15,759 | 18,776 | 19,606 | 19,497 | 21,193 |
| Loss | −1,941 | −583 | −2,770 | −3,109 | −2,304 | −1,890 |
| | 12,159 | 15,176 | 16,006 | 15,497 | 17,193 | 19,303 |

cent and frequently hit 90 percent or above. All linen was subject to maximum use and wear. New room attendants were hired. They were not accustomed to handling linens properly and losses were up to 2,770. The next year the bulk of the first sheets wore out, while occupancies continued to be high. Occupancy forecasts for the following year were high and the executive housekeeper ordered an additional 4,000 sheets. That same year, the head of the sewing room died and no replacement could be found to equal the quantity and quality of her work. With the prospect of repairs remote and business growing, the executive housekeeper ordered another 4,000 sheets.

The result was that the hotel was extravagantly oversupplied (which is still better than under supplied) (see Table T10.2). Six par would have been sufficient. At that level, the hotel would have been able to match its worst losses, 3,109 in a single year, and still have inventory to cover the loss. Most housekeeping managers recommend that linen controls be strictly enforced before considering additional purchases, which can devastate the budget and lead to storage problems.

## MANAGING DRY CLEANING OPERATIONS

Dry cleaning operations require specialty equipment and expertise. For these reasons, they must be economically justifiable, essential for cleaning staff uniforms or a service guests view as necessary. Upscale hotels that attract business travelers whose expense accounts will cover the cost of dry cleaning may have sufficient business to run the dry cleaning operation as a profit center. Larger properties in which a large percentage of staff uniforms and/ or draperies must be dry cleaned may be able to cut cleaning bills by having dry cleaning equipment on site.

To run the dry cleaning operation at a profit, the executive housekeeper must first determine all of the costs involved. This can be done easily on a computer spreadsheet. Factors to consider include:

- The initial cost of the equipment, if it is newly installed
- The cost of chemicals, labor, and energy

These costs are then divided by the number of occupied rooms over a certain period to determine how much should be charged to cover costs and make a profit. A well-run dry cleaning operation in a 1,000-room hotel can contribute $400,000 to $600,000 in revenues each year.

Environmental impact is another factor that must be weighed. Federal regulations on dry cleaning chemicals are becoming much stricter. They now stipulate that dry cleaning plants must limit hazardous chemicals to 25 percent of the chemicals in use. Though harsh dry cleaning chemicals have proven cleaning ability, some executive housekeepers say they are too harsh for certain fabrics. Alternative products can clean a wider range of fabrics, including furs.

George Martens, laundry manager of the upscale Fontainebleau Hilton, uses two new 35-pound **dry-to-dry** cleaning machines. Instead of coming out of the equipment wet with dry cleaning chemicals, the product is cleaned and dried in the same machine. "This dry-to-dry system means employees are exposed to fewer hazardous chemicals and fumes. Also they do not have to handle the product when it is still wet with the dry cleaning chemicals and breathe in the fumes. In the dry-to-dry system, the fabric is dry and there are no fumes," explains Martens. To make sure the dry cleaning plant conforms to federal safety regulations, Martens checks for leaks weekly, both manually and with specially designed **sniffers,** which detect fumes that signal leaks. Proper pumps and storage canisters make sure used fluids are disposed of safely with a minimum of handling. Employees must wear masks and gloves when disposing of the dry cleaning fluids.

## WORKING WITH A CONTRACT LINEN SERVICE

Properties that do not have space for laundries large enough to meet their needs must use off-premise linen services. "Japan has some of the most expensive real estate in the world. As a result, every new hotel contracts out laundry service. The cost is much cheaper (than adding space for an on-premise laundry)," says Toyohiko Tashiro, executive housekeeper of the upscale Tokyo Hilton. The same holds true for hotels in cities such as New York City, where few properties can afford to sacrifice guest rooms or other revenue-generating space to set up ample laundries. Although laundry procedures take place off-premise, the executive housekeeper still is responsible for ensuring the property has an adequate supply of clean linen, that the linen is cleaned up to the property's standards, and that the pricing for the laundry service is cost effective.

### Calculating the Cost of Contract Services

The starting point in hiring a contract laundry service is to estimate the property's linen demand. This is especially important if the property will rent the linen from the contract company rather than buying its own. Most linen services buy exactly what the institution requests, thereby eliminating the need for the property to buy the linen outright. If the type of linen requested is highly unusual, the service may require a substantial deposit. Par must be set for contract laundry needs, as well as the on-premise laundry.

The executive housekeeper uses higher par levels when making this estimate. The three-par average for properties with an on-premise laundry must be expanded to at least five par: one set on the bed, one set in soil, one set in the service's laundry, one set on the way to service, and one set on the way back.

Typically, linens washed in an on-premise laundry last longer. Sheets may last 400 to 800 washings when done on premise. That life expectancy drops to 250 to 300 washings when done off-premise. The general rule is that overall linen replacement is reduced at least 15 percent in an on-premise laundry.

Outside linen services usually charge extra for such tasks as sorting, special folding, separating sheets and pillowcases, separating stained and repaired linen, and extra deliveries. Although the housekeeping department will not have to budget for a full laundry staff, management still must allocate staff hours for sorting linen before it is picked up by the service, counting items or weighing the bins that come from and go to the service and inspecting the quality of the work done.

Since studies indicate that the hotel's monthly occupancy rate is almost directly reflected in corresponding changes in linen supply consumption, many executive housekeepers who use services recommend negotiating a flat-rate monthly charge based on 100 percent occupancy. This guaranteed maximum charge is multiplied by the hotel's actual occupancy rate to determine the exact charge of the linen supply services at the end of each month. Both the linen supplier and the property realize substantial savings by eliminating the time-consuming practice of counting linen. Many services now weigh linen rather than count it to save labor hours. Hotel employees must be ready with bins when a pickup is scheduled and must weigh in clean linens upon delivery.

## LINEN CONTRACTS

A carefully written and detailed contract can help ensure the linen service will deliver properly cleaned product on time with a minimum of waste and loss. A linen contract should cover:

1. The number of days and the number and time of deliveries per week
2. Handling procedures for guest laundry
3. Whether the service will do mending and stain removal, or whether these must be done on-premise
4. Whether the service is using the best quality supplies
5. Specifications for the fold required on towels, sheets, and other foldable items
6. Whether uniforms will be returned on hangers

7. Insurance coverage, including what adjustments would be made on mechanical damages and how the claims and shortages would be settled

8. The basis for billing, whether weekly or monthly

9. Availability of emergency service on Saturdays, Sundays, and holidays

10. How to establish an accurate count of linens going in and out of the service's laundry

11. The type of equipment to be used for pickup and delivery, and whether the property must provide any specialty items to coordinate with this equipment effectively

12. Provisions for unscheduled emergency deliveries, including timing and surcharge

"It is hard to find a good contract laundry service. It is very important that the executive housekeeper provide very detailed information and be as specific as possible when going out for bids. We review our contracts every year, and then place the contracts up for bid every year. The executive housekeeper shouldn't automatically use the same company every year and just let the increases pile up," says Miriam Albano, the executive housekeeper for the luxury 500-suite RIHGA Royal Hotel in New York City.

At least three bids should be obtained. All bids must be presented in writing, with any provisions for add-on costs clearly outlined. The executive housekeeper should check any references supplied by the company. In some cases, those references may also be helpful in obtaining proper after-sales service. A consultant working with a large casino hotel noted problems with irregular linen deliveries at the property. However, a smaller property nearby used the same service and reported no problems. The consultant, executive housekeeper, and general manager were able to point this out during discussions with the linen supplier and gained a valuable edge in negotiating delivery time.

After-sales service and support are critical. The contract service must provide timely service, limit discards and loss to a reasonable level, and deal with special problems. Regular inspections and meetings with the service will prevent problems from reaching levels that could leave the hotel under-supplied, resulting in rooms waiting to be made up and resold.

After the contract is awarded, Albano closely monitors both quality and inventory. She recommends:

- Regular visits to the contract laundry service's plant. She personally visits the plant, which is 50 miles away, once a month

- Checking discards

- Checking formulation of laundry chemicals. She does this to determine whether the service is using the chemicals specified by the hotel in the contract, and whether they are working up to the hotel's standard of cleanliness

- Conducting a monthly inventory to control loss. Linen usage should be reported. Discards should be totaled as well. If discards are running substantially above projections, the executive housekeeper should schedule a meeting with the laundry service to find out why

## CREATING QUALITY ASSURANCE PROGRAMS

Whether laundry is done on-premise or by an outside contractor, all items being laundered must be cleaned properly. It is rare that one person is assigned to inspect wash full-time in an on-premise laundry. All laundry attendants should be trained to inspect the items they are handling as they load them into or take them out of the machines, or as they stack or hang clean product. Spot inspections must be scheduled for linen as it is delivered by a contract service, to make sure the proper amount and type of linen is being delivered and that it has been cleaned to the standard set forth in the contract. Having effective reporting procedures is a helpful tool in monitoring cleaning levels and productivity levels in the laundry.

### Proper Reporting Techniques

Regular visual spot checks of laundry will determine whether spots and stains have been removed. The laundry supervisor or manager, in addition to the executive housekeeper, conducts regular checks during each shift to make sure the laundry is cleaned properly. Whole loads that are discolored are easily detectable.

Other forms can be helpful in controlling both quality and productivity. They include:

***Laundry procedure reports.*** Frequently used by outside contractors, these forms tell the executive housekeeper at a glance what is being done by the service (see Figure 10.6). These forms chart water quality, procedures being followed, quality control

| LAUNDRY PROCEDURE REPORT<br>Form 4640 (5-86) | DATE | |
|---|---|---|
| Plant Name | Time In | Time Out |
| Address                          City/State | Elapsed Time | Industry Segment |

**A. WATER CONDITIONS** | **PREVIOUS REPORT**

Hot Water Temp. _____
Cold Water Temp. _____
Water Hardness: ☐ Satisfactory  ☐ Unsatisfactory ☐
Incoming Water Alkalinity _____
Iron Present ☐ YES  ☐ NO
Chlorine Present ☐ YES  ☐ NO

PREVIOUS REPORT:
_____
_____
☐ Satisfactory  ☐ Unsatisfactory
_____
☐ YES  ☐ NO
☐ YES  ☐ NO

**B. WASHROOM PROCEDURES** | | **PREVIOUS REPORT**

| | | |
|---|---|---|
| Work Classification/Sorting Properly | ☐ YES  ☐ NO | ☐ YES  ☐ NO |
| Are Correct Amount of Supplies Being Used | ☐ YES  ☐ NO | ☐ YES  ☐ NO |
| Are Proper Inventory of all Supplies Being Maintained | ☐ YES  ☐ NO | ☐ YES  ☐ NO |
| Are Machines Being Overloaded | ☐ YES  ☐ NO | ☐ YES  ☐ NO |
| Are Machines Being Underloaded | ☐ YES  ☐ NO | ☐ YES  ☐ NO |
| Are Monthly Inventories Taken | ☐ YES  ☐ NO | ☐ YES  ☐ NO |
| Are Correct Formulas Being Used | ☐ YES  ☐ NO | ☐ YES  ☐ NO |

**C. QUALITY CONTROL EVALUATION/OBSERVATION** | | **PREVIOUS REPORT**

| | | |
|---|---|---|
| Colored Garments | ☐ SATISFACTORY  ☐ UNSATISFACTORY | ☐ SAT.  ☐ UNSAT. |
| White Garments | ☐ SATISFACTORY  ☐ UNSATISFACTORY | ☐ SAT.  ☐ UNSAT. |
| Sheets/Pillow Cases | ☐ SATISFACTORY  ☐ UNSATISFACTORY | ☐ SAT.  ☐ UNSAT. |
| Terry Items | ☐ SATISFACTORY  ☐ UNSATISFACTORY | ☐ SAT.  ☐ UNSAT. |
| White Table Linen/Napkins | ☐ SATISFACTORY  ☐ UNSATISFACTORY | ☐ SAT.  ☐ UNSAT. |
| Colored Table Linen/Napkins | ☐ SATISFACTORY  ☐ UNSATISFACTORY | ☐ SAT.  ☐ UNSAT. |

**D. EQUIPMENT CONDITIONS** | | **PREVIOUS REPORT**

| | | | |
|---|---|---|---|
| Are Drain Valves Leaky | ☐ YES  ☐ NO | WASHER #_____ | ☐ YES  ☐ NO  WASHER #_____ |
| Are There Steam Leaks | ☐ YES  ☐ NO | WASHER #_____ | ☐ YES  ☐ NO  WASHER #_____ |
| Are Hot Water Temps. Correct | ☐ YES  ☐ NO | WASHER #_____ | ☐ YES  ☐ NO  WASHER #_____ |
| Are Low Water Levels Correct | ☐ YES  ☐ NO | WASHER #_____ | ☐ YES  ☐ NO  WASHER #_____ |
| Are High Water Levels Correct | ☐ YES  ☐ NO | WASHER #_____ | ☐ YES  ☐ NO  WASHER #_____ |
| Are The Washer Controls Working | ☐ YES  ☐ NO | WASHER #_____ | ☐ YES  ☐ NO  WASHER #_____ |
| Are The Charts in Good Condition | ☐ YES  ☐ NO | WASHER #_____ | ☐ YES  ☐ NO  WASHER #_____ |
| Are All Gauges Working | ☐ YES  ☐ NO | WASHER #_____ | ☐ YES  ☐ NO  WASHER #_____ |

COMMENTS:

Customer Signature                    Pennwalt Signature

| COPIES TO | Copy 1 (white)<br>HOME OFFICE | Copy 2 (canary)<br>LAUNDRY MANAGER | Copy 3 (pink)<br>EXEC. HOUSEKEEPER | Copy 4 (goldenrod)<br>SALES ENGINEER |
|---|---|---|---|---|

*Figure 10.6   A laundry procedure report helps both the executive housekeeper and contract company evaluate performance. Note that copies of this report go to four different people.*

evaluations, and equipment conditions. They also have room for comments. For example, the service may point out that the hotel's linens have not been properly sorted before they reach the service's laundry, resulting in extra labor and extra charges. These reports should provide the executive housekeeper with a detailed assessment of the service's operation and performance. If not, the executive housekeeper should suggest that different categories be included in the report that would provide the additional information needed to assess performance. Many laundry managers use similar forms to track the performance of on-premise laundries.

| WEEKLY LAUNDRY PRODUCTIVITY REPORT | | | | | | | | | | | | | | | |
| --- | --- | --- | --- | --- | --- | --- | --- | --- | --- | --- | --- | --- | --- | --- | --- |
| Week From: _____ To: _____ | | | | | | | | | | | | | | | |
| | VOLUME PRODUCED | | | | LABOR HOURS USED | | | | | | | | | SUMMARY | |
| | Flatwork | Dry Fold | Presswork | Washing Extracting Tumbling | Flatwork | Dry Fold | Sort-Shake | Presswork | Washing | Extracting | Tumbling | Pre-Sorting | Soiled Linen Pick-Up | Linen Room Linen Dist. | TOTAL Laundry Poundage | DAILY Occupancy Rate |
| Sunday | | | | | | | | | | | | | | | | |
| Monday | | | | | | | | | | | | | | | | |
| Tuesday | | | | | | | | | | | | | | | | |
| Wednesday | | | | | | | | | | | | | | | | |
| Thursday | | | | | | | | | | | | | | | | |
| Friday | | | | | | | | | | | | | | | | |
| Saturday | | | | | | | | | | | | | | | | |
| Totals This Week | | | | | | | | | | | | | | | | |
| Totals This Month To Date | | | | | | | | | | | | | | | | |

Total Pounds Produced to Date: _____     Pounds per occupied room _____

Pounds Per Productive Hour to Date: _____

Uniform Cost Accounting System for Institutional Laundries

This form designed by Institutional Division, American Institute of Laundering

**Figure 10.7**  *This daily laundry report shows the number of laundry poundage done per occupied room. This helps in computing the cost per occupied room figure that has become so vital in measuring fiscal performance.*

**Productivity reports.** If all employees are not performing up to expectation, the overall quality and quantity of the work being done suffers. Productivity reports such as the one shown in Figure 10.7 enable the laundry manager or executive housekeeper to track the amount of work being done and the amount of labor hours required to do it.

**Equipment checks.** If one machine is malfunctioning, the hotel's linen needs may not be met. All machinery should be inspected daily to make sure it is functioning properly. Any need for repair should be reported immediately.

Other information can be helpful in establishing quality assurance programs for the laundry. Some executive housekeepers and laundry managers post guest comment cards that mention the quality of the laundered items—both favorably and

unfavorably. These are discussed with staff. Consistently good comments may result in awards or rewards; consistently unfavorable comments spark discussions on how to correct the problems. The laundry manager or executive housekeeper also should track special requests from the F&B department. If red and green napery are in heavy demand each Christmas and red and white are needed for Valentine's Day, these linens should be clean and available before the need becomes so critical that regular runs have to be stopped to accommodate the specialty items.

When the laundry is running too much overtime or constant shortages and other departments request too many costly rush jobs, the executive housekeeper and laundry manager should take stock of why such problems exist and how they should be solved. The following checklist of operational strategies was developed by Pellerin Milnor Corp., in Kenner, Louisiana and published in *Laundry News*.

**Operating hours.** Can the laundry's operating hours be adjusted to be more consistent with the flow of product into the laundry? Is there work ready for attendants when they arrive so that they can begin work immediately?

**Communications channels.** Can a better, more systematic means of expecting runs on particular items such as tablecloths for a special banquet be set up? Is it possible to receive these items in more manageable lots? Can those who collect F&B linen presort it? Is there clear communication on what is needed or is the laundry's schedule continually interrupted to deliver clean linen? Can seasonal items, such as towels for the pool, be handled more efficiently?

**Persistent shortages.** When was the last time a physical inventory of linen was taken? In facilities operating on a 3-par or less level, this should be done at least every 30 days. Is there a systematic means of replacing worn or missing linen? Is theft contributing to this problem and can it be pinpointed? Would a higher-grade linen be more cost-effective because of its longer lifespan and its ability to retain its appearance?

**Personnel.** Are personnel working to their maximum efficiency? Is training and regular retraining focusing on increasing productivity? Are employees using laundry equipment to maximum capacity? Are goods being full-dried longer than actually needed in the tumblers?

**Overtime.** Would another full-time employee, especially one who could be cross-trained in other areas, eliminate the need for overtime? Are there other employees within the facility who have been overlooked as potential extra help, such as room attendants who finish assignments early or those on swing shifts? Is there a pool of accessible part-time help available or should a part-time position be created? How cost effective will it be to hire extra personnel, whether part-time or full-time?

**Equipment.** Is each piece of equipment at its optimum operating condition? Check the original specifications of the equipment. Is the equipment

under a periodic, preventive maintenance schedule through the equipment supplier?

**Up-to-date formulas.** When was the last time chemical formulas were reviewed? Because of the continual improvement of chemical supplies, it may be possible to vastly reduce chemical consumption or the running time of the equipment. In some cases, loads may be running twice as long as necessary.

**Space.** Does the positioning of equipment match the flow of the laundry? If not, is it possible to realign the equipment to improve work flow and increase work space? Are there too many carts in the area being only half-used? Is there any area outside the laundry to use as a holding space for soiled goods? Areas to consider would be easily accessible from the laundry and free of safety hazards and would minimize the threat of theft. Will larger capacity equipment fit within the existing space? Would new equipment with more functions or more automated or computerized features increase productivity?

**Linen usage.** What is the peak possible linen usage? Itemize each type of linen classification, noting individual weights and total daily poundage. If the laundry is to operate with the same number of employees for an ideal number of daily work hours, how many pounds of goods must be processed per hour?

**Cost per pound.** To date, what is the laundry's actual cost per pound of goods?

**Downtime costs.** If equipment is down even 10 percent of the time, it can add as much as one hour to the laundry's daily operation.

**Labor costs.** Is the equipment automated so that attendants can do other tasks? Does the washer-extractor have the automatic means for correcting out-of-balance loads? Are formula changes easily made? Is it possible to add a liquid supply system to further reduce labor requirements?

**Accurate sizing.** Will the equipment enable processing of peak possible linen usage? Is tumbler capacity accurately matched to that of the washing equipment? Does the equipment have the capacity for any future growth of the facility?

*Utility savings.* Can reducing finishing times cut fuel costs? Can converting to washer-extractors reduce water usage significantly?

These questions not only point to common problems, but also make an effective checklist to determine when a laundry requires renovation to keep pace with the property's demands.

## SUMMARY

As with every aspect of housekeeping, managing laundry operations must be tailored to the needs of the property, the needs of clients, and the makeup of the staff. The executive housekeeper must work with the laundry manager or contract service supervisor to look for ways to consistently improve the quality of the work being done while controlling costs.

In on-premise laundries, the laundry manager and executive housekeeper must also look for ways to motivate staff and reduce employee turnover. Incentive programs should be expanded to include the laundry. Cross-training should be made available to those who want to build a career beyond the laundry.

Lines of communication should be open. Information about safety considerations and cleaning procedures should be clearly posted in the laundry and dry cleaning plant.

Getting the most out of laundry operations requires a knowledge of:

- Linen demand
- Equipment
- Cleaning chemicals
- Productivity levels
- Proper washing and drying procedures
- Par levels
- Delivery and storage
- Environmental regulations pertaining to laundries, and more particularly, dry cleaning plants
- Costs of operation
- Linen contracts

## Review Questions

1. What factors are considered when calculating linen usage?
2. Name the basic equipment needed for an on-premise laundry for a 500-room hotel.
3. Where should laundry rooms be located in the property and why?
4. What are par levels and what factors influence the level of par?
5. Describe the flow of soiled linen through the laundry.
6. What are the correct procedures for handling biohazards?
7. What should be covered in a linen contract?
8. Describe some ways to reduce costs stemming from discards.
9. What is rag-out and what procedures will help reduce it?
10. What is a laundry procedure report and how is it used?

## Critical Thinking Questions

1. In a new hotel, new room attendants often confuse the laundry chute and the trash chute or fail to sort soiled linen properly. How should this be resolved?
2. Performance of the local contract linen service is slipping. However, no other local company has commercial capacity. How can this situation be resolved?
3. Despite repeated requests from the housekeeping department, banquet stewards do not remove crumbs and bits of food from napery before delivering it to the laundry. As a result, pest problems are developing. How should this be resolved?

# 11

# Controlling Linens, Uniforms, and Storage

## Chapter Objectives

To meet demand for linens and uniforms but still control costs, the executive housekeeper must:

- Calculate linen need
- Develop the correct procedures for linen selection
- Develop the correct procedures for uniform selection
- Establish proper inventory and control methods
- Set up effective distribution systems for linen
- Establish repair and replacement schedules
- Set proper par levels
- Keep proper records that track usage information
- Utilize storage areas to the best advantage

A property's investment in linens and uniforms can easily represent hundreds of thousands of dollars. It is the housekeeping department's responsibility to protect this investment.

This responsibility begins with selecting the best products. Whether the executive housekeeper specifies or purchases, he or she must be aware of which fabrics will perform best for the property. Housekeeping managers need to know what to order and how much to order. Once delivered, they must determine how best to distribute these essential supplies to the staff who depend on them to do their jobs—and how best to store the reserve not required for daily operations. Effective controls of linens, supplies, and storage play a key role in the department's overall efficiency as well as its financial performance.

## MANAGING LINEN SUPPLY

Linen supply is critical to the efficient operation of the property. Without clean towels and sheets, rooms cannot be made up. Without clean napery, restaurant and banquet tables cannot be set. The executive housekeeper is responsible for ensuring that this key aspect of departmental operations runs smoothly.

In lodging industry terminology, linen refers to far more than cloth made from flax fiber. It encompasses sheets, towels, pillow cases (sometimes called **pillow slips**), washcloths, fabric table cloths, fabric placemats, fabric napkins, and cloth bath mats.

Managing linen supply effectively involves:

1. Obtaining the appropriate linens for the size and category of the property, whether through purchase or rental
2. Calculating linen demand
3. Establishing proper inventory controls
4. Setting up a workable system of distribution
5. Creating a replacement schedule

Bedding, mattresses, and pillows are the basis of the primary product the property has to sell. They must be of the best quality the budget will allow. Since they represent such a large investment, they must be properly stored and properly cared for when not in use.

### Selecting Linens

All the linens required for any type of institutional use should at least meet the American Standards

Institute's Minimum Performance Requirements for Institutional Textiles and any federal or local government requirements. If budget permits, the executive housekeeper should specify linens one rung above this minimum standard, not only for increased guest comfort but also for increased durability and ease of maintenance (see Tricks of the Trade 11.1).

---

**Tricks of the Trade 11.1**
**Supplying the Small Hotel**

*The Problem:* Small, independent hotels cannot take advantage of volume discounts.

*The Solution:* Lois Theis, executive housekeeper of the 60-room St. James Hotel in Redwing, Minnesota, found a supply solution that enhanced this small, historic hotel's guestroom decor and budget performance.

"Linens were very costly for us. We do have a seamstress, a local woman who charges very reasonable rates. I discussed the situation with her and she said she could custom make our sheets. Now, instead of plain hotel sheets, we have custom-made ones with a wide band of lace trim on the sheet and pillowcase edge," says Theis. The same seamstress is scheduled to begin making draperies as well. Replacement will be slow, Theis admits, but there is no immediate pressure to replace the bed linens. After the existing linen is replaced, Theis will have no problem with repairs or replacement. Guests will be treated to hand-made, 100% cotton sheets at half the cost Theis was paying for linens from a supply house.

Theis also is having the hotel's signature quilts made locally. "We used to buy them from other sources. This saves us $200 per quilt," says Theis.

---

**Cost per use,** a calculation which weighs various factors to determine the real cost of an item, is a helpful tool in deciding which linen best suits the bottom line. Some experts suggest weighing durability, laundry costs, and purchase price. From these three features, the true cost of an item can be determined.

The cost per use is obtained by:

1. Adding the original cost of the article to the total laundry cost during its life expectancy

2. (Then) dividing that figure by the life expectancy, or total number of launderings that might be expected for the item

$$\text{Cost per use} = \frac{\textit{Life Expectancy} + \textit{Original Cost}}{\text{Wt} \times \text{Laundry cost/lb.} \times \text{Life Expectancy}}$$

For example, a tablecloth or bedsheet weighing 1.4 pounds, which has a life expectancy of 250 launderings and costs $3.50 when new, is processed in a laundry that figures their cost is $0.10 per pound. Cost per use is derived in the following manner:

$$\text{Cost per use} = \frac{(1.4)(.10)(250) + 3.50}{250}$$

$$= \frac{35 + 3.50}{250} = \frac{38.50}{250} = 0.1542$$

In the above formula, it should be noted that the institution invested $35 in laundering the item during a period of 250 uses. The investment of the original cost of $3.50 is rather insignificant when compared to the investment of $35 spent laundering it 250 times. This points to the fact that it is the number of launderings an article can sustain through normal processing that is the most important factor in determining the true cost of an item or its cost per use.

## Durability

The longevity and cost effectiveness of linens depends, to a great extent, on their durability. The executive housekeeper must consider the following when assessing durability:

1. Fabric construction
2. The weight of the fabric
3. How strong the fabric is
4. How much surface wear the fabric can withstand

**Construction.** In the process of weaving, woven yarns are interlaced at right angles to each other. The lengthwise yarns are called the **warp.** The crosswise threads are referred to as the **filling** or **weft.** The lengthwise sides or edges of a fabric are called the **selvages.**

**Thread count.** The number of threads that are interlaced in a square inch constitutes the thread count. For example, the most commonly used sheet

**TABLE 11.1**  *Durability of Three Types of Napery*

|  | Visa(R) | | 100% Cotton | | 50/50 | |
|---|---|---|---|---|---|---|
|  | **New** | **50 Wash** | **New** | **50 Wash** | **New** | **50 Wash** |
| Tear | 6400 × 6100 | 5500 × 5150 | 3900 × 4000 | 1650 × 2150 | 5400 × 5100 | 2350 × 2100 |
| Tensile | 275 × 208 | 269 × 210 | 121 × 94 | 77 × 96 | 136 × 140 | 107 × 114 |
| Flex | 6720 × 6906 | 6625 × 5851 | 739 × 528 | 108 × 184 | 5304 × 7705 | 544 × 416 |
| Weight (oz/yd$^2$) | 6.18 | 6.55 | 6.06 | 7.33 | 5.76 | 5.50 |

*Note:* Numbers are units of measure of strength of warp and filling yarns customarily used in textile testing methods.
**Source:** Milliken & Co. Laundry Services, P.O. Box 1926M-301, Spartanburg, SC 29304.

in a hotel has a 180 thread count. This means the sheet is made from approximately 94 threads per inch running in the warp, or lengthwise, direction and 86 threads per inch in the fill.

**Weight.** The weight of the fabric is specified in one of two ways: either ounces per square yard or yards per pound. When the weight is specified in yards per pound, it is important to know what the width is. Wide fabrics weigh more per lineal yard than narrow fabrics of similar construction.

**Tensile strength.** Tensile strength is the number of pounds required to break a strip of fabric or other piece of textile, 1 inch wide and 3 inches long (see Table 11.1).

An **abrasion test** is helpful in determining durability. An abrasion test measures the degree to which a fabric resists surface wear. Institutional linens, including uniforms, are very often subjected to more surface wear than strain. The abrasion test determines how many rubs the material will withstand under certain circumstances until the yarn weakens.

## Bed Linens

Bed linens selected for any property must be comfortable for the guest, durable enough to withstand hundreds of washings, and be fairly easy to maintain. Except in a small percentage of deluxe properties where 100 percent cotton or even fine linen sheets may be used, most hotels and motels use sheets and pillow cases that are a blend of cotton and polyester. In smaller properties, bed linens are more likely to be no-iron percales that come out of the dryer with few wrinkles. Properties with roller/folders and ironers in the laundry have a broader choice of which bed linens to purchase or rent (see Chapter 10).

Sheets are available in muslin or percale. **Percale** is made of a finer-combed cotton fiber than **muslin,** which has only been **carded,** which means the yarn or fiber was separated and straightened rather than combed. All sheets list a thread count, often preceded by a "T." A T/130 or T/128 muslin sheet is less densely woven and thus lighter and less apt to wear as long as a T/180 percale sheet.

Blend sheets seem to pick up tensile strength as they are laundered. Those with polyester warp threads may actually be *stronger* after 75 washings than when they were new. Some laundry experts speculate that new polyester sheets made from new no-iron fabrics can withstand 500 or more washings. Proper laundering techniques can extend the life expectancy of some of these sheets to 800 washings. Even using the 400 to 500 washings as an average life expectancy, this new generation of polyester sheets wears longer (see Chapter 10).

Size is another important factor in sheet selection. Sheets are available in these standard sizes:

- Twin: 72 wide inches by 104 inches long, a size used more commonly in residence halls, and an increasingly small percentage of older U.S. and overseas hotels; also used for rollaways.
- Double: 81 inches wide by 104 inches long
- Queen: 90 inches wide by 115 inches long
- King: 108 inches wide by 115 inches long

Blend sheets are still measured before hemming. Because they do not shrink, they may be several inches shorter than cotton sheets. Sheets are finished in two ways: **flat sheets,** which are simply hemmed, and **fitted sheets,** which have elastic at the head and foot ends to conform to the shape of the mattress. Fitted sheets are rarely used in lodging because:

- The corners often rip due to added stress at these points.

- They take up almost twice as much room in storage; they also must be inventoried separately and stored separately on the room attendants' carts.
- They are less versatile; flat sheets can be used for the top or bottom sheet.
- They slow down bedmaking; they also stay fresh looking and may go unchanged by accident or deliberately.

Top and bottom hems are generally the same width, unlike sheets for home use which have a deeper top hem. Being able to put the sheet in either direction assures even wear. If pillow cases are made from bed sheets, the hems should be 2 inches to 3 inches wide. The case should be 2 inches to 4 inches longer than the pillow.

Sheets come packed one, five, or 10 dozen to a case. A wide color selection is offered by several manufacturers, but white, off-white, and beige continue to be the most popular choices. Some deluxe hotels use highly distinctive patterned or colored sheets that coordinate with a distinctive decor, but the care required in laundering to keep the patterns and colors looking like new makes these sheets too time-consuming and expensive to maintain for most properties.

## Blankets

The key factors to consider when selecting blankets are:

1. Warmth—in hot climates, a light covering may be "warm" enough
2. Moisture—the construction and fibers should be porous and/or absorbent enough to transmit any moisture buildup to the surrounding air so the blanket does not feel wet or clammy
3. Weight—a lighter blanket is usually less constricting and more comfortable
4. Durability—including how many washings the nap can withstand without wearing or abrading (this greatly diminishes the blanket's warmth). Also taken into account is how much it shrinks, especially since most blankets shrink up to 10 percent

All blankets should be impervious to damage from mold or mildew, moths and perspiration. They also should not be treated with any special finishes or colored with dyes or inks that could cause allergic reactions.

The key factors in selecting are:

- Weave
- Type
- Fabric
- Size

*Weave.* A woven blanket is made in much the same way as a fabric sheet, except that the fill yarn is twisted slightly to increase the bulk and, consequently, the number of air spaces it holds provide warmth. The selvage usually is made with heavier and more closely spaced warps for longer wear. The weave should be uniform. If not, the blanket may ripple and pucker after laundering. The following are the most common weaves for blankets:

*Type.* There are three basic types of blankets commonly used in hotels:

- *Standard.* Standard blankets are manufactured with tight construction and napped on both sides. Needle-punch and electrostatic blankets are warmer pound for pound than woven blankets of the same fiber.
- *Sheet.* **Sheet blankets** are used for air-conditioned evenings and as extra covers for cold winter nights. Their tight construction makes them less porous than blankets with large air pockets.
- *Thermal.* Loom-woven with a leno weave, thermal blankets have many large air pockets. Used under tightly woven covers such as sheet blankets, they are as good an insulator as standard blankets of the same fiber weighing three times as much.
- **Construction.** This refers to the size, fiber and yarn, binding and napping.
- *Size.* The proper size for the blanket, after shrinkage, is the length of the mattress plus the thickness of the mattress, usually 7 inches, plus a minimum 6-inch allowance for tuck-in, and the width of the mattress plus twice the 14-inch thickness, plus a minimum 6-inch allowance for tuck-in.
- *Fiber and yarn.* Crimped fibers of an irregular cross-section and rough surface make warm blankets because they form many air spaces.
- *Binding.* All blankets are either **whipstitched,** which means that stitches are overcast over the edge of the fabric rather than sewn in a straight line side by side, or bound with nylon. Though nylon feels better against the skin, it will fray after repeated use. The cost of replacing nylon binding is making blankets with four whipstitched sides more popular and less expensive.

**TABLE 11.2**  *Key Characteristics of Popular Synthetic Blankets*

| Type of Weave | Advantages, Disadvantages | Comments |
|---|---|---|
| Tight weave | +Gives strength/−loose weave more air, warmer | Comparatively inexpensive |
| Twill | +More fill yarns to surface, making it warm | Most durable |
| Leno | Firm, strong | Adjacent warps twisted around each other, filling passing through |
| Double cloth (channel cloth) | Used for electric blankets | Two individual sets of warp and filling woven into two layers of fabric; fifth set for wiring |
| Needle-punch | | Process converts fibers into blankets without yarn-making or weaving |
| Electrostatic or flocked blankets | Many air cells add warmth | Layer of foam on each side of nylon knot scrim; charged fibers stand on end; insulation from foam cells |

• *Napping.* Heavy napping tends to weaken woven construction other than needle-punch. If the nap wears, the thermal properties of the blanket are greatly reduced. To lessen **pilling,** which means the abraded fibers gather into small balls, or shedding, blankets are treated after they are napped. Acrylic blankets can be sprayed with a solvent. Polyester blankets can be sprayed with a special adhesive. Then they are heat-treated to bond the ends of the nap fiber.

The choice of fiber frequently depends most on guest preference, but also on the category, location, and age of the hotel. Some deluxe hotels in the United States still provide fine woolen blankets. Fine grades of wool, such as wool from Merino sheep, are still standard in luxury European hotels. However, wool has some costly drawbacks. Unless it is the finest grade, which is expensive, it can be scratchy and irritating to the skin. It also is a weak fiber and can lose 25 percent of its strength when wet. It must be laundered with extreme care.

Most properties use blankets made from synthetic fibers which do not shrink, and which are mildew- and mold-resistant. These blankets generally come with a manufacturer's assurance of the uniformity of fiber length and **denier,** or width. Table 11.2 assesses key characteristics of the main types of synthetic blankets.

**Size.** Most properties have only two sizes of blanket: a 72-inch for twins or doubles; a 108-inch for king- or queen-sized beds.

## Bedspreads and Bed Covers

Because of its size, the bed visually dominates the guest room. This makes the choice of bed cover a critical aesthetic decision. From a practical point of view, the bed cover must not only be attractive, but durable, easy to position on the bed, and strong enough to withstand institutional laundering.

Washable, quilted bedspreads are still the mainstay for the lodging industry. They show no wrinkles and have a plush appearance. For king-sized beds, often it is preferable to use a coverlet, which extends slightly below the mattress, in combination with a **dust ruffle,** a bed skirt which is positioned between the mattress and box spring. This coverlet is lighter and less cumbersome than a full bedspread for the room attendant to handle when changing the bed linen (see Figure 11.1). Duvets, soft quilt-like bed covers, are also popular because they are lightweight and frequently do not require a bed skirt. If problems arise, the supplier should be contacted immediately.

In historic hotels, bed and breakfasts, or some deluxe hotels, a comforter, also known as a **puff,** may also be used on the bed—either as a bed cover in combination with a skirt or dust ruffle or more frequently in combination with a good-quality blanket.

Washability is a key consideration in selecting bedspreads or other covers. The bed cover must be able to handle a wide range of spills, from coffee with cream to ink.

**Figure 11.1**  *Comforters add a touch of residential elegance to the deluxe rooms of the Hotel Inter-Continental New York. The benefit for the housekeeping department is that comforters are easier to handle than heavier, full-length bedspreads. (Courtesy of the Hotel Inter-Continental, New York)*

Before purchasing, the executive housekeeper should test a sample spread for washability:

1. Wash one spread in mild detergent, using warm water and avoiding bleach.
2. Dry the spread in a low-heat, slow tumbling cycle.
3. Compare the spread to other new spreads that have not been washed. Acceptable shrinkage is 2 percent.
4. Examine the spread for color-fastness.
5. If the spread is quilted, check to see whether the quilting threads are easily broken or if the filler is breaking up.

Because spills may soak through quickly, the executive housekeeper should also make certain the backing material is easy to clean. A colored muslin backing is preferable to white because stains are less evident. If budget permits, a reversible spread with stain-concealing patterns on either side may be a good solution. The spread should be taken out of inventory when the backing becomes obviously stained.

## Mattress Covers

Mattress covers protect the mattress from spilled liquids as well as bodily fluids. Generally, vinyl plastic covers designed for hospital use are preferred. They can be machine washed and dried at any temperature, including heat high enough to sterilize them. Most are stainproof, nonallergenic, noiseless, and flameproof. Made like a contour sheet, they stay in place and are relatively easy to change. As further protection, the executive housekeeper may buy a flame-retardant mattress cotton felt covering. The heat will not come through this covering, so the mattress's component parts will not send off toxic fumes. Polyester felt pads are also available and, like any mattress cover, should meet federal standards for flame retardancy. Another option is to use 100 percent cotton bedding treated with Teflon™ and a special chemical so that it will not support flame.

Another type of mattress cover is a quilted polyester pad. The advantage of these is that they add a soft layer between the mattress and sheets. They are held in place by elastic bands which slip under the mattress and hold them flat. They must be changed after check-out.

## Pillows

Selecting a pillow with the right construction and firmness to please every guest is virtually impossible. The executive housekeeper's goal should be to find a comfortable pillow that will satisfy the majority of guests. Pillows may be made from synthetics, **down** (extremely soft feathers with downy feathers attached), or down and feathers.

Pillows made from synthetic fibers are far and away the most popular choice in the United States. They are washable and dryable. They are also hypoallergenic. Down and down/feather pillows must be cleaned in special machines. They are expensive, but may be a justifiable expense for hotels with a large European clientele, for whom down pillows are expected. However, some guests are allergic to down pillows.

## Testing Pillow Performance

The critical tests of pillow performance are:

1. Shape retention. When placed in the center of the arm, the pillow should balance evenly. If it folds, it indicates that the filling is thin and bumpy.
2. Resilience. When both hands are pressed into the center of the pillow, the pillow should spring right back into shape. It should be buoyant and provide comfortable support for the head. The filling should not shift or settle in one place.

## Mattresses

As with pillows, it is hard to get guests to agree on an ideal mattress. Each guest has a different opinion on how firm the mattress should be. Firmness levels range from medium to extra firm or super firm. Experts usually advise selecting a firm mattress with a certain amount of resilience from the coil springs and a soft surface. Bedboards and extensions should be stocked in the housekeeping department and made available.

Mattresses properly constructed of urethane foam that is sufficiently thick and dense, and covered by a quality fabric, can be as comfortable, lighter in weight, and less expensive than an innerspring mattress. When using foam mattresses, it is important to support them with a box spring or flat wire foundation. Because they are more flexible, they can be turned and rotated more easily by room attendants. Table 11.3 illustrates the dramatic cost savings of proper mattress rotation.

Mattresses may last from an average of three years to 20 years. Cost also varies. While an expensive mattress may cost several hundred dollars more than its inexpensive counterpart, its longer life expectancy may more than justify the initial capital outlay. Manufacturers generally provide a warranty that covers the mattress for a certain period. Usually, more expensive mattresses also carry a longer warranty.

Flame resistance or retardancy is a major concern in selecting mattresses. All bedding in the United States must pass a federal government test for flame retardancy. Some cities and states require even more stringent tests. Labels must state whether the mattress meets the government flammability standard, which means they must not ignite when in contact with a cigarette. In many cities and states, only Class A materials can be used in lodging. Class A means that flames spread slowly or not at all across the fabric's finished surface.

## Bath Linen

A few deluxe hotels offer specialty towels such as **huck** towels, small hand towels made of carded cotton, rayon or a combination of both. Huck towels sometimes require ironing. Terry cloth towels made from polyester blends or polyester and cotton remain the most popular choice in the lodging industry. As with sheets, polyester blends used in towels actually prolong the life of the towels and reduce shrinkage. A dense weave improves absorbency. Towels with a velvety plush on one side and looped terry on the other are used by some upscale hotels. While this type of towel may be softer, it is not as absorbent. The more the towel weighs, the more expensive it may be to launder and dry. This may be a small consideration, says Othmar Hehli,

***TABLE 11.3***   *Cost Savings from Mattress Rotation*

| Number of rooms | Number of beds | Cost of beds @ $200 ea | Annual cost of sleep equipment | | Annal savings with rotation | | Total (12 yrs.) |
|---|---|---|---|---|---|---|---|
| | | | With avg. life (8 yrs.) | With +50% more life (12 yrs.) | First year (less cost of system) | Following years—11 (each yr.) | |
| 50 | 75 | $ 15,000 | $ 1,875 | $ 1,250 | $ 550 | $ 625 | $ 7,425 |
| 75 | 113 | 22,600 | 2,825 | 1,883 | 829 | 942 | 11,191 |
| 100 | 150 | 30,000 | 3,750 | 2,500 | 1,100 | 1,250 | 14,850 |
| 125 | 188 | 37,600 | 4,700 | 3,133 | 1,379 | 1,567 | 18,616 |
| 150 | 225 | 45,000 | 5,625 | 3,750 | 1,650 | 1,875 | 22,275 |
| 200 | 300 | 60,000 | 7,500 | 5,000 | 2,200 | 2,500 | 29,700 |
| 250 | 375 | 75,000 | 9,375 | 6,250 | 2,750 | 3,125 | 37,125 |
| 300 | 450 | 90,000 | 11,250 | 7,500 | 3,300 | 3,750 | 44,550 |
| 500 | 750 | 150,000 | 18,750 | 12,500 | 5,500 | 6,250 | 74,250 |
| 1,000 | 1,500 | 300,000 | 37,500 | 25,000 | 11,000 | 12,500 | 148,500 |

director, operations for Radisson Seven Seas Cruises. He estimates that heavier, better quality towels may withstand 15 to 20 percent more washings than thinner ones.

As with sheets, white is the most practical color choice for towels. White towels are generally easier to wash: they also may be bleached when necessary. Because of its fresh, clean appearance, white is always acceptable, whatever the decor. There is no reordering problem due to difficulties in color matching or changes in color fads.

Coordinating towel color with the bathroom does have the advantage of providing a more residential look. The only proviso is that the colors selected not be too trendy. Strong or unusual colors may not be popular for long, and the color may be discontinued by the time the executive housekeeper reorders the bath linen. It may also make the guest bathroom look tired and dated.

For longevity, the best choice is a terry towel with wide side stitching that reinforces the vulnerable edge where the towel usually frays first. Selvages on the ends as well as the side also add to the towel's life expectancy. Selvage edges should always be hemmed.

The toweling type of bath mat intended for step-out use, as opposed to the vinyl mats to be used in the shower, are both expensive and heavy. A good one weighs more than 2/3 pound. Shower curtains should be mildew-proof and machine washable. The most common ones are made of either a woven nylon or a nonabsorbent, germ-resistant, heavy-duty nylon that does not flap when the shower is turned on. A shower curtain has no hem or seams.

**Table Linen**

Table linen should reflect the character of the food-service activities and the level of service desired. The executive housekeeper, F&B director, and perhaps a linen committee are involved in selecting the table linen. Table linen will be required for all foodservice areas, including room service.

Using white napery throughout the property reduces the overall inventory required and makes for easier laundering and stain removal. However, with pressure on F&B outlets to look and operate more like their free-standing competitors with their strongly themed decor, napery has become a design element. It may be necessary to stock several colors and patterns. If this is the case, it is best to key colors to certain outlets. A specific color should be used only for banquet table linens, making them instantly distinguishable from the smaller cloths used in the restaurants.

Most napery is of two types: **damask** and **momie.** Damask is a closely woven twill weave. It sometimes is called **jacquard,** the name of the loom on which it is produced. This lustrous, reversible textile can be made from linen, cotton, silk, or synthetics. Damask is measured by threads per square inch and is available in single damask and double damask. Single should have a minimum thread count of 140 threads per square inch; double, 195.

Damask releases soil faster than momie cloth. Damask linens made of modified, texturized polyester have some practical benefits. While regular polyester "loves oil and hates water," as one industry expert puts it, this special polyester "loves water and hates oil, so it rejects soil easily." Modified, texturized polyester can take up to 400 washings without fading or losing its **band,** or edge finishing. It can be starched and ironed with creases for outlets that require crisp table linens or napkins presented with fancy folds at the table. No-irons have very little shrinkage; cotton shrinks about 5 percent.

Momie cloth is a plain weave that wears well and is almost always used in color. It is far less expensive than damask because of the looser weave and cheaper yarns used. Usually a blend of polyester and cotton, momie cloth is fairly durable and does not pill.

## CALCULATING LINEN NEEDS

Once the type of linen has been selected, the executive housekeeper must determine how many linens to buy or rent. This calculation is tied to the property's occupancy forecast for the coming year and a **profile of business** for the coming year, which would forecast volume for the restaurant outlets as well as banquet and function sales. Tracking past usage is helpful, particularly in resorts or properties with extensive fitness or spa facilities where extra towels are required.

### Assessing Linen Demand

The amount of linen used by a property depends on:

- The property's category
- Location
- Number of rooms
- Number of beds
- Clientele, including whether most of the occupancy is family business or single travelers
- The volume of F&B operations
- The number of functions and variety of recreational activities offered

Calculating linen demand involves more than just counting the number of beds, bathrooms or restaurant tables. There must be an adequate supply of replacement linen, even when linen is being laundered. By tracking linen usage and demand over several months, the executive housekeeper can establish par for the property.

### Setting Par Levels

Par is set not only for the guestroom linen, but also for the F&B outlets and kitchens, and should include:

- Bed linen, including pillow slips or cases
- Terry cloth items, which includes all terry bath mats, bath towels, face towels, and wash cloths. In deluxe hotels this would also include the terry bathrobes provided as an amenity in guest rooms.
- Restaurant linen, including table covers and napery
- Banquet linen, including napery and other table covers
- Kitchen linen, including kitchen towels, **bar mops**—which are the cloths used to clean the bar area, chef aprons, chef caps, chef coats, chef pants, uniforms, and bartender coats.

As discussed in Chapter 10, the general rule of thumb for properties with on-site laundries calls for three par: one on the bed (or in use); one in soil, and one on the shelf; hotels that rent linen require five par.

Resort hotels generally have the highest par levels. At family-oriented resorts, it is more likely both beds in the room will be used each night of the guests' stay and both sets of linens will need to be changed. In addition, families frequently require an extra bed, whether a rollaway or a crib. Travelers in warm weather resort destinations require extra sets of towels for swimming. Resorts with complete recreational facilities also make towels available in locker rooms for guests who use fitness and on-site sports facilities. Typical par for pool towels is nine to cover pool usage, as well as towels used in the locker rooms by guests who shower and wash their hair.

Robin Diaz, executive housekeeper at the 266-room Mohonk Mountain House resort in New Paltz, New York, suggests the following pars for resorts:

- Blankets—1.5 par
- Sheets—3 par
- Pillow cases—6 par
- Hand towels, bath towels—4 par

• Wash cloths—8 par

Diaz does not set par for beach towels. Instead, she uses occupancy forecasting. If the hotel's average number of guests is 550 at peak season, she multiplies this total times three to determine the number of beach towels needed. She has computerized linen expenditures on a spread sheet so that she can track costs over the last three years and monitor usage.

Some resort hotels set par for wash cloths as high as 10 or more. Executive housekeepers point out that the higher par is needed not only because guests freshen up more often after exercise or a day at the beach, but also because guests may use the wash cloths to clean off golf shoes, wipe off golf clubs, or clean hiking or biking gear. If the terry items are attractive, the easily packable wash cloth may be the most frequently pilfered item. Hotel management is not about to begin interrogating guests over this small a matter; instead, a certain level of linen pilferage is figured into the budget.

Deluxe hotels may not equal the volume of linen required at a resort, but may need more kinds of linens Most five-star hotels now provide thick terry robes in each guest room. Some, especially those with a large number of Japanese guests, also provide **yukatas,** which are like cotton kimonos. Since the towels and wash cloths are thicker than those used in economy hotels, this means each wash load will include somewhat fewer items. More rooms are equipped with king-sized beds, which means larger sheets and, frequently, oversize pillows and pillow cases.

The linen inventory form shown in Figure 11.2 indicates what factors must be taken into account when calculating linen demand, not only what is actually needed but what is required for inventory and what needs to be replaced due to shrinkage or unaccountable loss.

## Determining Linen Demand for Other Departments

The executive housekeeper uses forecasting and housekeeping department records as useful tools to determine the department's demand for clean linen, terry, and uniforms. However, the housekeeping department must also figure in the linen needs of the F&B department and other departments that require clean linens.

The banquet department, working with the sales department, gives the executive housekeeper

a list of functions planned over a certain period. Some functions are planned a year or more in advance. This information typically will include what color napery will be used. The executive housekeeper then makes allowances for this demand when ordering. Even if the hotel purchases most of its own banquet linen, the executive housekeeper should develop working relationships with some commercial laundries that rent linens. Some meeting or function planners may request unusual color schemes. Since it is not cost effective to stock napery in every color, these special request colors should be rented only for the function.

## MANAGING INVENTORY

Each property must have efficient procedures for storing, stocking, and tracking linen supply. The goal of these procedures is to make sure clean linen supplies are available when needed by attendants or the F&B department and that inventories are sufficient to cover projected need.

### Storing Linen

Once linen has been laundered, dried, and folded (see Chapter 10), it must be stored until it is needed. In fact, executive housekeepers generally recommend that all linen rest on storage shelves for at least a day before use, a tip that is particularly helpful for permanent press fabrics which will release some wrinkles as they rest. Linens may be stored in a **central linen room,** also called a **main linen room,** and/or floor linen closets. All linen should be stacked so that it is easily identifiable for anyone who loads carts (See Tricks of the Trade 11.2).

---

**Tricks of the Trade 11.2**
**Making It Easier to Find Sheets**

*The Problem:* Attendants lose time trying to distinguish different sheet sizes in the laundry or when stocking carts.

*The Solution:* The executive housekeeper may select a different color for each sheet size. For example, all king size sheets would be white; all queens, beige, and so on. Or the professional housekeeper may ask the manufacturer or supplier to permanently mark on the sheet the name

RIHGA ROYAL HOTEL
ROOMS LINEN INVENTORY
MONTH OF:

| ITEM | Beginning Inventory | Purchases | Total | Current Inventory | Loss | Discards | Unaccount- able Loss | Unit Value $ | Loss $ | Discards $ | Unaccount- able Loss $ | Ending Inventory Value - $ |
|---|---|---|---|---|---|---|---|---|---|---|---|---|
| King Sheets | | | | | | | | | | | | |
| Queen Sheets | | | | | | | | | | | | |
| Twin Sheets | | | | | | | | | | | | |
| Pillow Cases | | | | | | | | | | | | |
| Total Flat | | | | | | | | | | | | |
| Bath Sheets | | | | | | | | | | | | |
| Bath Towels | | | | | | | | | | | | |
| Hand Towels | | | | | | | | | | | | |
| Washcloths | | | | | | | | | | | | |
| Bathmats | | | | | | | | | | | | |
| Bathrugs | | | | | | | | | | | | |
| Bathrobes | | | | | | | | | | | | |
| Total Terry | | | | | | | | | | | | |
| Blanket - King | | | | | | | | | | | | |
| Blanket - Queen | | | | | | | | | | | | |
| Blanket - Twin | | | | | | | | | | | | |
| Total Blanket | | | | | | | | | | | | |
| Bedspread - King | | | | | | | | | | | | |
| Bedspread - Queen | | | | | | | | | | | | |
| Bedspread - Full | | | | | | | | | | | | |
| Bedspread - Twin | | | | | | | | | | | | |
| Total Bedspread | | | | | | | | | | | | |
| TOTALS | | | | | | | | | | | | |

*Figure 11.2  Calculating linen needs involves not only tracking demand but monitoring loss because of shrinkage or even rag-out. (Courtesy RIHGA Royal Hotel, New York)*

of the hotel, date of purchase, and the size of the sheet using ink applied at 400°F.

The **central linen room,** which is the hub of housekeeping operations, is the main storage area for linen (see Figure 11.3). This space also may contain other housekeeping supplies, such as guest supplies, guest amenities, and guest loan items. It may also double as an office for the housekeeper. As you learned in Chapter 5, keys and carts may be issued in the central linen room. If it also serves as the uniform room, uniforms are issued in this space. All of the department's working records would be housed in the linen room unless the executive housekeeper has a separate office, which in some cases is adjacent to the linen room. Central linen rooms in larger hotels may also contain the sewing room and even storage for extra furnishings. The lost and found is located either in the main linen room or in the security department.

Many new hotels do not have a central linen room per se. There may be some storage area for clean linen near the laundry room, provided the area is not too damp; however, most of the linen would be stored in floor linen closets. The floor linen closet is a storage area for the linens and housekeeping supplies required to service a particular floor. In many cases, these so-called closets are large enough to hold adequate floor pars as well as room attendants' carts and more.

Either within the central linen room or in another storage area close by, there should also be a

*Figure 11.3  Central linen rooms must have adequate shelf space and good ventilation; they also must keep all linen within easy reach for the attendants and provide enough open space for easy movement of carts and rolling shelves. (Courtesy of the Hyatt Regency, Reston, Virginia)*

**reserve storage** for excess linen that will not be needed until periods of peak occupancy and for new linen that has not been put into inventory. All storage areas, even those that hold linen for just 24 hours, must have:

1. Adequate shelf space so that linens can be stacked neatly, not shoved together so tightly that they wrinkle or tear
2. Proper ventilation and virtually no humidity, to make sure the room stays dry to prevent mold and mildew from forming on the linens
3. A lock to prevent pilferage and loss
4. A double sink, table, and stain charts for spot treating linens

Room, banquet, and F&B linens should be stored on separate shelves for easier distribution. It is best to segregate F&B linen according to both its size and the outlet for which it will be used. Banquet linens should be clearly identified because they are a different size and shape than linens for restaurant tables.

### Stocking Linen

There are three basic approaches, with myriad refinements, to stocking linen. One is to place all linen in a central linen room where carts are restocked; a second is to stock the carts in floor linen rooms; the third is to stock the attendants' carts directly.

*The central linen room system.* Each room attendant brings his or her cart to the main linen room at the end of his or her shift. Rolling carts filled with clean bed linen and towels are taken to the central linen room, usually during the shift, although this could be assigned during the graveyard shift. Then, the attendants' carts are cleaned and restocked with linens and guest supplies for the next day.

This system has several advantages:

1. All the linens are in a central area.
2. All carts have the same amount of linens.
3. Linen inventory can be reduced because the linen room attendant knows the entire stock level and exactly how many linens are in circulation.

*Floor linen rooms.* If floor linen rooms are of adequate size, the room attendants may leave their carts in the floor linen rooms at the end of the shift. As with the central supply system, the floor linen

room is restocked each day. The difference is that, instead of holding a complete inventory, the floor linen room holds only a **floor par,** the amount of linen needed to service the rooms on that particular floor.

The advantage to this system is that the supply in the floor linen room can easily be adjusted to projected occupancy. In some hotels, floor pars are set according to occupancy projections. After consulting the day's occupancy forecast, the executive housekeeper and laundry manager determine how much linen is required for each floor linen closet to bring stock up to par. Since most of the linen in the closet is being used each day, there is no risk that some linen will sit at the bottom of piles collecting dust or soil while supplies at the top of the pile are used so often they wear out ahead of schedule. If there is excess linen on the floor because occupancy is low on a given day, the excess can be stored in the main linen room or, if available, a linen storage area in the laundry.

*Stocking carts.* Using this system, attendants bring their carts to the laundry area or wherever linens are stored about 30 minutes before the end of their shift. They clean the carts, then load the linen on them for the next day (see Tales of the Trade 11.1).

---

**Tales of the Trade 11.1**
**Solving the Storage Problem**

The 876-room Westin Plaza and 1,253-room Westin Stamford, which share a single site in Singapore, needed an efficient laundry distribution system that would keep both buildings supplied, according to Irene Lim, director of property management for both hotels.

The housekeeping department opted for a system that essentially pre-portions linen and towels. Each floor has its own par stock. Rather than simply filling a rolling rack with towels and room linen, the laundry attendants put all the clean room linen and towels for each floor into a container that looks like a **bus box,** the containers used by buspersons to clear dishes in restaurants. The boxes are placed into rolling carts that are taken to the floors during the night shift. The entire cart is raised and hung in place on the wall of the floor linen room. This means there is no need for large amounts of storage space. The floor linen rooms stock only the essentials.

When room attendants receive their morning assignments, they simply slide the boxes onto specially designed attendants' carts. Other boxes are stocked with amenities and cleaning supplies. The trim attendants' carts can carry everything required.

The primary advantages to this system are that it eliminates the need for a central linen room, an important plus at a time when back-of-the-house space is shrinking, and insures each attendant will have an adequate supply at the start of the shift. Any attendant can use any cart because they all are stocked in exactly the same manner, another factor that increases efficiency.

## Tracking Linen Supply

Linens in use should be tracked daily. The linen room attendant or linen room supervisor, the employee who has responsibility for the flow of linens to their various destinations within the property, must keep a careful count of the linens sent to and received from the laundry each day. Some properties require room attendants to share in this responsibility. Room attendants' assignment sheets list the number of linens they were issued at the start of the day's shift. As each room is finished, they have to tally the number of soiled linens, by type, removed from the rooms. At the end of the shift, these numbers would be totaled and given to the linen room attendant or supervisor, who then reconciles all attendants' figures with the total linen supply issued at the beginning of the shift.

Supervisors may be assigned to do daily counts. They first count the linen issued on their floor or floors at the start of the shift and total it, then track how much soiled linen was being sent to the laundry. All daily count sheets should have a column showing how much linen was discarded and pilfered. If room attendants do the daily counts, the supervisors should spot check these totals.

Inventories of linen in circulation can be taken as frequently as every week or 10 days, but a monthly cycle is more usual. This weekly or monthly inventory should be a **physical inventory,** not just a computer calculation but an actual count taken by employees of the linen on hand. This inventory count includes the linens in circulation, total discards, and total loss. It also would be helpful to note how much of the inventory is in poor condition or in actual need of repair. A semiannual or annual inventory should also be scheduled, to check both the linen in circulation and all reserve supplies. Physical inventories should be coordinated with the on-premise laundry. It is best to conduct physical inventories during the night shift or whenever the smallest amount of linen is in transit within the property.

Tracking linen supply helps the executive housekeeper determine whether current par levels are sufficient, whether loss and pilferage are under control, and how well the linens are performing. This information is invaluable in setting a replacement schedule.

## CREATING A REPLACEMENT SCHEDULE

Using inventory reports, the linen controller or the executive housekeeper can track usage patterns and determine when the linen inventory needs to be replenished. Under ordinary circumstances and with proper laundering and handling, most sheets that are used daily will last two to three years. If sheets rag out well before this, the executive housekeeper should review laundry procedures, check chutes for loose metal that may be tearing sheets, and schedule a meeting with the vendor to discuss the problem.

The full inventory is ordered only when a new hotel opens, or when an older hotel is renovated; renovations require an entirely different set of linens. For regular re-orders, enough linen is ordered to bring the total supply back to par. Linen orders typically are placed once a year, but deliveries may be arranged on a quarterly basis. These periodic drop shipments are beneficial because the vendor stores the linen until the pre-arranged delivery date.

## Overseeing the Sewing Room

Space should be set aside in the linen area for a sewing room, where linens are repaired and uniforms can be repaired or altered. If there is absolutely no space available nor budget for a full-time seamstress, the executive housekeeper should ask department employees whether any staff members would be willing to sew at home at a predetermined pay rate. Usually, the property supplies the fabric and thread or reimburses the staff member who buys these items and submits a receipt.

Basic sewing room equipment includes:

- Sewing machines able to handle various thicknesses of fabric and blindstitch, so stitching does

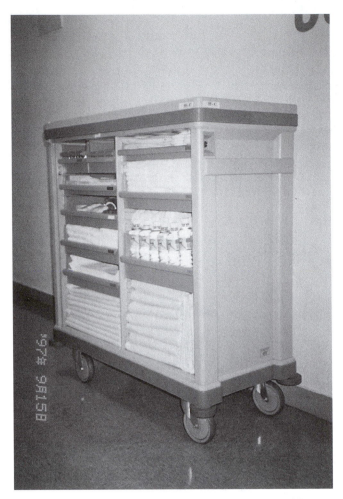

**Figure 11.4** *One solution to the distribution problem is to pre-portion linen, amenities, and supplies into specially designed boxes that simply slide directly onto the cart. This minimizes the need for a large central linen room. Floor linen rooms need stock only essentials. (Courtesy of the Shangri-La Hotels & Resorts; Hostar International's ProHost cart)*

**Figure 11.5** *Sewing machines used in housekeeping department sewing rooms must be able to handle various thicknesses of fabric as well as blind-stitch. Machines that can overedge, zigzag, and sew buttons offer labor-saving advantages. (Courtesy of the Shangri-La Hotels & Resorts, Hong Kong)*

not show on the other side (see Figure 11.5). New sergers or computerized machines are more expensive, but they are easy to operate, very accurate, and do double duty. Without them overedgers may be needed as well as zigzag machines for mending, darning, and button sewing.

- Heat patching machines for neat repairs of holes in linens
- Grommet and gripper tools

Repairs should be made with 100 percent polyester thread, which gives strength to seams, will not shrink, is elastic enough to give, and is colorfast. Nylon thread should be used for button sewers or, occasionally, blindstitch machines.

Repair tags should be clearly written or have a list of typical repairs that can be checked off. The seamstress should be trained to look over the garment carefully to check for other damage.

## MANAGING THE UNIFORM SUPPLY

Whether simple or ornate, the purpose of the uniform is to identify the employee wearing it as a representative of the property. In some properties, each department orders, stocks, and issues uniforms for its own employees. In others, the housekeeping department is responsible for all uniforms. When this is the case, an area should be set aside in the linen room for uniforms or a dedicated uniform room should be created. There should be ample room to store clean uniforms, place soiled uniforms until they are taken to the laundry, and issue replacement uniforms.

## SELECTING UNIFORMS

There are literally hundreds of different styles of uniforms from which to choose. Before making the selection, the executive housekeeper should:

1. Obtain input from the employees who will have to wear the uniforms
2. Consider the uniform's suitability for the tasks various departmental employees must perform
3. Consider the image of the hotel
4. Weigh construction, fabric content, and ease of cleaning
5. Consider the value of the uniform

### Obtaining Employee Input

Selecting uniforms without consulting the employees who must wear them can be a costly error and serious threat to departmental morale (see Tales of the Trade 11.2). Employees will have to wear the uniform every working day, and they will have to be comfortable in it in order to do the job properly. A uniform that does not allow the necessary range of movement is prone to tear as employees stretch and reach.

---

1. *Pockets in waitstaff uniforms should be straight and should be positioned on the side so that checks will not crumple when the employee bends over.*
2. *Waitstaff's jackets should have two roomy inside pockets for pencils and checks. Snaps under a collar or on a belt prevent puckering.*
3. *Beltless, zippered dresses with short, loose sleeves or loose-fitting tunics or smocks with elastic-waist slacks are suitable for the physically demanding job of housekeeping employees, and also may work well for waitstaff.*
4. *Skirt and pants lengths should be easily alterable.*
5. *Men's uniforms should have reinforced side slots that expand the openings for easy access to pockets. Waistbands should be reinforced.*
6. ***Convertible collars*** *fixed with* ***permanent stays*** *are the preferred neckwear.*
7. *Avoid decorative cuffs and embroidery. They are subject to wear, fray easily and may cost more to clean.*
8. *Except in cases in which uniforms function as costumes, the style should be classic rather than trendy.*
9. *Customizing uniform jackets with a hotel logo and trousers/slacks with a noticeable fabric stripe will dissuade pilferage.*
10. *Minimize detailing Anything that could easily catch or tear is a drawback.*
11. *Uniforms have to look good on all employees, regardless of stature.*

**Figure 11.6** *Ten tips on uniform selection.*

discarded. Employees were involved in finding a compromise. The black dresses were retained, but colorful aprons printed with famous French Impressionists' artworks were added. The waitstaff liked the compromise version's style and comfort, and it eventually became a signature for the restaurant.

Once the general manager has approved a budget for uniforms, the executive housekeeper, working with the purchasing department, a uniform committee, or departmental employees, can survey what is available. Vendors, industry publications, and trade shows all have ample information about current styles. Vendors invited to make bids should be required to provide sample uniforms employees can try on and "try out" (see Figure 11.6). Bell staff should bend over and pick up heavy suitcases. Room attendants should actually clean a room or two, bending, reaching, and stretching to see if the uniform has enough give, which means the fabric will stretch slightly. Eliza-

### Tales of the Trade 11.2
### Uniform Wars

One general manager recalls how the failure to seek out employee feedback regarding uniforms nearly led to a staff revolt. In an effort to get some fresh thinking on the uniform question and bring extra flair to the hotel's image, the general manager asked local design students to create some fashionable uniforms. Employees were not consulted; rather they were simply presented with their new uniforms. Frustrated coffee shop waitstaff protested the new designs, telling management their uniforms, which were inspired by the traditional French maid's outfit with a black dress and white apron and cap, were inappropriate. The waitstaff maintained they looked too much like room attendants.

The new uniforms represented an outlay of thousands of dollars and could not simply be

beth Powell, director of housekeeping for the upscale ANA Hotel, Washington, D.C., offers this advice: "The previously purchased room attendants' uniform was no longer available, so a 'similar looking' uniform was purchased without a try-out period before I came here. The uniform skirts simply aren't long enough. They rise too much when attendants reach and that makes the attendants uncomfortable. Next time, the room attendants definitely will be involved in selecting their own uniform."

Uniforms must also be appropriate to the department, as well as to the category and type of hotel. Just as restaurant waitstaff may not want to wear uniforms that make them look like room attendants, the room attendants do not want to be hampered by the jacket-and-tie uniform of the front desk. Uniforms for coffee shop waitstaff would be less formal than the suit or even tuxedo required for a renowned fine dining outlet. Although some uniforms are actually costumes, as is the case in some Las Vegas casino hotels or restaurants with unusual themes, the general rule of thumb is that the uniform should not detract from the personal dignity of the wearer.

## Assessing Fabric and Construction

As with linens, most uniforms are now 100 percent polyester or fabric blends. Both knits and texturized woven fabrics offer the advantages of having a neat appearance, wrinkle resistance, and good draping qualities.

Chefs and cooks of the old school used to insist on 100 percent cotton uniforms because they were more porous and absorbent than polyester or blends. New blends have a "breathability" that makes them cooler than their forerunners and more easily washable.

More and more properties today use disposable chef's hats called **toques.** Working over hot stoves, chefs perspire heavily. This means they may need several changes of toques during their shift. Wall dispensers for the toques make it easy for them to change without leaving the kitchen area. Disposable aprons also are available. These come in handy as an alternative to fabrics because grease and accidental soiling could quickly ruin fabrics. Also, these aprons may be more sanitary than fabric aprons.

Wool uniform jackets may be appropriate for front desk staff in luxury hotels and for department managers in properties where they are required to wear uniforms (see Figure 11.7). Wool jackets may

**Figure 11.7** *Proper office attire is standard for executive housekeepers. Some hotels provide "uniforms"—usually a blazer and trousers for men or a blazer and skirt for women; others set down parameters for what type of attire is suitable. In either case, executive housekeepers are expected to look the part of a departmental manager. (Courtesy of the Shangri-La Hotels & Resorts, Hong Kong)*

be worn by waitstaff, the wine steward, or the maître d' in a very fine restaurant. The concierge staff may also wear wool uniforms, though this is becoming a rarity. Wool is more common in European hotels. Although it lasts a long time, provides warmth, and conveys a look of quality, it does require dry cleaning. Lighter weight wool blends or lightweight fabrics would be preferable in a warm climate or at resorts.

## Obtaining Value for Money

Whether uniforms are rented or purchased, the goal is to obtain value-for-money pricing. It is rarely economical to buy the cheapest uniform available simply because of cost. The best choice is a uniform that is comfortable, can withstand regular washing or dry cleaning, and requires only minimal repairs. Uniform costs can range from a few dollars for a golf shirt, to full room attendants' uniforms priced from $15 to $22 or more and on to custom uniforms or even designer suits for executive staff which can total hundreds of dollars.

Value also includes reliability, both of the product and the vendor. Most reputable uniform companies provide some type of guarantee of satisfaction on their products. They also make provisions for after-sales service and should be able to supply uniforms to fill in during emergencies. How well the vendor can respond to such emergencies will be one of the deciding factors in awarding the contract.

## Setting Par Levels for Uniforms

Par must be set for all staff uniforms. Three is a reasonable uniform par. One uniform is in use, one is in the laundry, and a third is in inventory. Par levels are higher for kitchen staff who may require changes of uniform during a shift. No par level is set for aprons for kitchen staff. Supply is calculated by tracking usage daily, weekly, and monthly over a certain period. For reasons of hygiene, kitchen staff must be assured of a clean apron whenever one is needed.

# ESTABLISHING UNIFORM CONTROLS

In a large hotel where all employees wear uniforms, there should be a uniform clerk, a person whose primary responsibility is to issue, inventory, and order uniforms. In a smaller property, the responsibility for uniform control could be assigned to a sewing room employee or a supervisor.

## Issuing Uniforms

Some properties, such as very large hotels or older hotels, have purpose-built **uniform rooms** where clean uniforms are stored and issued, and where soiled uniforms are turned in. The trend now is to use a multi-purpose housekeeping area which may combine traditional linen room/uniform operations into one space.

The equipment required for issuing uniforms includes:

- Racks where uniforms may be hung; in complex operations these may be automated, much like those in commercial dry cleaning operations
- A cart where soiled uniforms are placed
- Operational supplies, such as daily inventory report forms, repair tags for uniforms, gloves for the attendant, and biohazard bags for uniforms stained with blood or bodily fluids

At the beginning of the shift, each employee turns in his or her soiled uniform from the previous day. The employee should be trained to point out any needed repairs. Only after the soiled uniform is returned is a clean one issued. This system is called an **even exchange** (see Tricks of the Trade 11.3). As a further control, some larger properties assign each employee an identification number. This number is either sewn into the uniform on a tag or marked indelibly. Employees must give this number when requesting their uniform. This way, no employee can take another's uniform and no nonauthorized personnel will be issued uniforms.

---

**Tricks of the Trade 11.3**
**Benefits of Even Exchange**

*The Problem:* Inventory control procedures are too lax.

*The Solution:* The 415-room ANA Hotel, Washington, D.C., had what Director of Housekeeping Elizabeth Powell calls a "loose even exchange" system when she joined the hotel in 1993. Employees were supposed to turn in one soiled uniform before being issued a clean one, "but too many exceptions were being made." Though there was some loss, the larger problems were that it was hard to control the inventory and repairs were not being flagged.

Powell addressed the problem on two levels. She worked with department heads to get their support for a strict even exchange program. The new policy was that employees could be refused clean uniforms if they did not bring in the soiled one for exchange. She also enlisted the support of the employees. "We call them our 'internal customers' and we treat them that way," says Powell. If more than four employees are waiting for clean uniforms, she calls in another employee to assist the office coordinator who doubles as the uniform attendant. She also seeks their input on new uniforms. Loss has been eliminated. Three is a workable par level and the system is so organized that "even exchange now takes about 60 seconds."

The uniform clerk or uniform room attendant should spot check uniforms for needed repairs before placing them in the soiled linen cart. Any uniforms stained with blood or saturated with bodily fluids should be handled with gloves, placed in a biohazard bag, and taken directly to the laundry for evaluation. If a uniform is torn, the attendant writes up a repair tag, which notes the name and/or number of the employee to whom the uniform belongs, what repair is needed, the date, and the date by which the repair must be completed. If uniforms are rented, those that need repair are tagged or bagged separately from uniforms that simply require cleaning. Uniforms that are beyond repair are discarded.

The complexity of the uniform issuing system depends on the setup and management style of the hotel. In some hotels, special uniforms, such as those for the doorman, costumed waitstaff, or front desk staff, are tagged with the individual wearer's employee identification number and/or name. It is preferable to use a three- or four-digit employee number rather than a name for identification. This prevents confusion and prevents one employee from taking another's uniform.

All employees receive a certain number of uniforms the day they begin work. At the time of issue, they should be asked to sign for the number of garments received on the day they start. When they leave their positions, their final paychecks may be withheld until they have returned all of the uniforms (see Figure 11.8). Ideally, new employees should be issued new uniforms, but this not always practical because of the problem with turnover.

On the day a new employee is hired, the employee should be made aware that he or she is responsible for the uniform after it is issued. The human resources department should explain whether the employee or the property will clean the uniforms. If employees are expected to clean them, they must be reimbursed.

## STOCKING AND STORING UNIFORMS

Some uniforms must be hung on racks to maintain a neat appearance. Those uniforms that must be hung to avoid wrinkling should be hung in groups by department and by size within each department's section of the rack. Some uniforms may be folded and placed on shelves. Shelf tags would indicate to which department each stack belongs. The stacks should be grouped by size within each department's area. Any uniform altered to fit an individual must be tagged with the employee's number or name.

All components of special uniforms, from top hats to special stockings, should be stored with or at least near the uniform. The uniform attendant or clerk should have a list or a series of diagrams describing or depicting the proper uniform for each department, including all the accessories that are part of the uniform.

### Tracking Uniform Inventory

The one-for-one trade of soiled uniforms for clean ones provides a built-in daily check of uniform inventory. After all uniforms are issued for a particular shift, the uniform attendant will be able to tally key inventory information, including:

- How many total uniforms were issued
- How many uniforms are being sent to the laundry
- How many uniforms require repair
- How many uniforms represent biohazards and may be temporarily or permanently out of inventory
- How many uniforms were sent to the dry cleaning plant or commercial dry cleaner
- How many uniforms were condemned

As discussed earlier in this chapter, chefs' aprons and toques would not be turned in to the uniform room, but (if not disposable) placed in soiled linen carts stationed near the kitchen. The laundry manager could track usage of these items. These daily usage reports are essential for determining how many uniforms are required, how frequently uniforms need repair, and whether there is a problem with loss or pilferage.

A physical inventory of uniforms should be conducted on a monthly or, more typically, a quarterly basis. All departments should be notified weeks in advance of a uniform inventory because this process requires coordination and cooperation. Unlike linen, uniforms are never a totally static commodity. The goal is to take inventory at a time when the fewest uniforms are in use.

---

## WYNDHAM HOTELS & RESORTS                    UNIFORM ISSUANCE

I, _____ have received the following hotel property:

1. Uniform: _____ Size: _____ # Issued: _____ Value: $ _____ Issued by: _____

2. Uniform: _____ Size: _____ # Issued: _____ Value: $ _____ Issued by: _____

3. Other (specify): _____ Value: $ _____ Issued by: _____

4. Other (specify): _____ Value: $ _____ Issued by: _____

5. Lock/Locker #: _____    6. Keys: _____    7. Bank: $ _____

I understand that I am solely responsible for the above items and must provide proof of return to the Human Resource Officce upon termination of my employment. Failure to return these items, or any other Wyndham Hotel property issued to me, will result in deductions from my pay.

Signature of Employee: _____

Department: _____    Date: _____

### UPON TERMINATION EACH DEPARTMENT MUST COMPLETE BELOW:

As of this date, the above items # _____ have been returned in satisfactory condition.

Signature: _____

Department: _____    Date: _____

### FOR HUMAN RESOURCE USE ONLY:

Final paycheck: # _____    Check Date: _____    Pay Period: _____

Date received: _____    Amount: _____    Employee Signature: _____

WHITE - Human Resources        MANILA CARD: Housekeeping

HR:150

**Figure 11.8** *Uniform issuance form should include a clear statement of the employee's responsibility for the uniforms. (Courtesy of Wyndham Hotels & Resorts)*

### Buying versus Renting Linens and Uniforms

Despite the size of the capital outlay required for the initial purchase and subsequent replacement, most executive housekeepers prefer to purchase linens, particularly if the property has an on-premise laundry. Owning the linen provides more control regarding inventory and supply. Even when occupancy jumps unexpectedly, there will be sufficient linen supply on hand. Also, par levels can be lower because inventory is always available.

Whether renting or buying linens, the executive housekeeper should provide as many details as possible during the bidding process. This would include:

- Total linen order, with a breakdown of each category of linen that will be required. This will be based on forecasts, room count, and estimated linen usage.
- Construction of the fabrics to be used, including thread counts for sheets and napkins
- Size of the linens required
- Type of fabric, such as whether cotton only is acceptable or whether blends will be satisfactory

- Weight of towels

This information is required in order to compare bids. One hotel manager recalls a case in which a linen vendor submitted a bid thousands of dollars below the other bidders. Close examination of the details of the bid revealed that this firm was quoting a price based on sheets with a lower thread count than the other firms.

## ORGANIZING AND MAXIMIZING STORAGE SPACE

The broad range of supplies and equipment for which the housekeeping department is responsible means that finding adequate storage space is a continuous challenge. An accessible storage space must be found for everything from day-to-day operational needs to ride-on space vacs and extra furniture. Generally, the ideal solution must give way to the most practical solution.

Solving the storage challenge requires both innovative thinking and an understanding of the property's physical plant. It also requires detailed knowledge of local fire regulations, so that storage does not interfere with any exit routes in case of fire or disaster. Suggestions for new storage areas should be discussed with the engineering department and security department as well as the general manager.

## Analyzing Storage Needs

The amount of storage space allotted to the housekeeping department probably will have been determined by the operator and architect long before the property opens and, also, long before the executive housekeeper is hired. Generally, storage space is divided into two categories: easily accessible storage for equipment and supplies required for day-to-day operations, and reserve storage for extra furnishings or equipment that is used periodically.

The housekeeping office, linen room, uniform room, and floor linen closets should provide adequate space for storage of most operational needs. Heavy machinery is usually stored in a separate back-of-the-house storage area so as not to block shelves or supplies. In the lower levels of the property, or in the **outbuildings** of a sprawling resort, the housekeeping department will be assigned several rooms for reserve storage. Storage rooms must be as free from dampness as possible if they are storing new, unopened linens, television sets, electronic equipment, minibars, or wood or upholstered furniture. Reserve storage should be inventoried on a regular basis, not only to check for pilferage but also to make sure all items are still in good condition.

Storage units should bear some identification of their contents. Where appropriate, par levels should be listed for the items in the storage unit. The executive housekeeper should keep a complete record of the total inventory of the department, as well as what can be found in all storage areas. Computerized tracking makes this job far easier. Computer forms should have columns for inventory in use, inventory in storage, par levels, and some usage information. Some also carry a pricing column which can track the investment represented by the inventory.

## Overlooked Space Needs

As you have seen in this chapter, as well as earlier chapters, linens, uniforms, guest supplies, and cleaning supplies and equipment require priority placement when allotting storage space. But space must also be found for less frequently used items.

The following five categories are often neglected when planning storage:

1. Space for outdoor furniture or seasonal equipment during off-season
2. Space for items waiting to be repaired
3. Accessible storage for outside and inside maintenance supplies, ranging from mowers and rakes to ice-melting products and wood for fireplaces
4. Storage for rollaway beds and cribs
5. Storage for meeting room equipment, unless provided for in the meeting space, as well as chairs, projectors, and lecterns

## Reducing Inventory

There is a point, beyond par, at which extra inventory is really *excess* inventory. It is costly to keep these items in storage, and they may take away storage space needed for other supplies and equipment. Employees who take inventory should be trained to note which items are obsolete or unnecessary. These items should be culled from inventory and, if still functional, sold or auctioned off to employees at low prices, donated, or discarded.

Another option for reducing inventory is to arrange with the vendor or supplier to store the property's order at their company or plant until it is needed. The property would need to store par plus a certain percentage to cover emergencies, such as unexpectedly high occupancies or missed deliveries.

Bulk purchasing can reduce storage for some operating supplies. One large container takes up less space and is easier to store than five small ones. Storage capabilities are a factor in selecting some equipment and furnishings. Those that fold, telescope, or stack will require less space.

## Finding Storage Space

Dead-end corridors offer economical and accessible storage space. Since the terminus of the corridor already has three solid walls, the space only needs a door or other front enclosure and, perhaps, shelving to be transformed into a useful storage area. This approach may offer a workable solution for adding floor linen closets. The front doors would have to be designed to look consistent with the surrounding guest corridors. The interior could accommodate cleaning supplies, guest supplies and

When insufficient storage space interferes with the ability to do the tasks assigned, the executive housekeeper should request action from the general manager. In some cases, there may be unused or under-used storage allotted to other departments. It is important that all other options be researched and noted before any demand for additional storage is made.

## SUMMARY

Housekeeping managers must be as familiar with fabric construction as with proper storage techniques for furnishings. Selecting, distributing, controlling, and storing linens, uniforms, and myriad other essentials for lodging operations is a challenging yet vital part of the professional housekeeper's job.

In some cases, experience is indispensable in determining just what percentage over par must be kept in reserve or whether a crawl space would provide workable adjunct storage. But, experience must build on fundamental knowledge such as:

- A basic understanding of fabrics
- What factors to consider when choosing linens and uniforms
- How guests and staff influence these decisions
- How to calculate par levels
- Whether to rent or purchase linens and uniforms
- Workable inventory control methods
- Tracking repair and replacement needs
- Analyzing all aspects of managing these inventories, from delivery to distribution and storage
- Finding storage space
- Reducing unnecessary inventory

### Review Questions

1. What is meant by thread count and how does it impact linen performance?
2. Describe three key considerations in selecting linen.
3. Describe three different linen distribution systems.
4. What is floor par?
5. Describe three key considerations in selecting uniforms.
6. What is the average life expectancy for:
   a. Polyester sheets

***Figure 11.9*** *For optimal use of small storage space, look for ways to use wall space as well as floor space. Wall hooks make the equipment in this area easy to reach and easy to keep organized. (Courtesy of Rubbermaid Commercial Products)*

amenities, the floor par of linens and, perhaps, attendants' carts.

When looking to expand storage, it also is helpful to consider vertical spaces (see Figure 11.9). Shelving extends vertical storage capabilities for lightweight items. Drapery rods, ladders, and other elongated items can be hung horizontally on pegs on the walls. The dead space under tables or over countertops can greatly expand storage space if used creatively. Heavy equipment must be stored on the ground.

b.  Housekeeping uniforms

c.  Towels

7. What is a repair tag and how is it used?

8. What three steps should be taken before semi-annual or annual physical inventories of linens and uniforms?

9. What are the main responsibilities of the linen room attendant and uniform clerk?

10. What is reserve storage?

## Critical Thinking Questions

1. Extra equipment from other departments frequently is crowded into the housekeeping department's storage areas. How can the executive housekeeper resolve this?

2. Discuss the advantages and disadvantages of stocking linen in a linen room versus stocking it directly on the carts as in the Prohost system.

3. The property's high-quality, expensive towels are aging but still may be usable for a year or two. Techniques used to soften and fluff them are discoloring the property's signature white towels. What are the executive housekeeper's best options?

# 12

# Preparing and Managing Budgets

## Chapter Objectives

To write an effective and realistic budget, the executive housekeeper must:

- Understand different types of budgets
- Use income statements and forecasts
- Calculate labor expenses
- Assess capital equipment needs
- Obtain input from other department heads on fiscal issues
- Set realistic budget goals
- Use technology effectively
- Assess when to cut costs and which costs to cut
- Avert deficit spending

Guest satisfaction is one measure of the housekeeping department's performance. The other measure is the bottom line. As a department head, the executive housekeeper must find a way to deliver the services that will enhance the guest's stay without draining profit.

Creating and working within a budget are key aspects of the executive housekeeper's responsibilities as a department head. The housekeeping budget is a major part of the property's overall budget, accounting for as much as 30 percent of total expenses in a small property and 10 percent to 15 percent in a highly diversified mega-hotel. By using occupancy and sales projections and assessing what is required to clean and to maintain standards, the executive housekeeper must map out the department's financial needs for the next year.

## BUDGETS AND BUDGET PROCEDURES

The housekeeping budget typically is presented as part of the rooms division budget. The rooms division budget is usually the largest in the property, and the housekeeping budget is one of its biggest categories of expense. For that reason, the executive housekeeper's ability to control costs has a significant effect on whether the rooms division meets its financial goals.

When beginning to put together the budget, the executive housekeeper needs:

- Data on labor costs and productivity
- Cost analyses for supplies and equipment
- An outline of any major repairs or capital equipment needed in the coming year

The budget process usually begins six months in advance of the new **fiscal year,** the 12-month period for which the property plans the use of its funds. It may take nine months or more to plan budgets for a year in which a major renovation is scheduled. At the start of the budget process, the general manager or rooms division manager reviews the annual **profit and loss** (P&L) statement with the executive housekeeper and other department heads. This may be done one-on-one or as part of an intensive planning session with all department heads. The P&L statement lists all sources of income, called **revenue,** and all **debits,** items which are paid out or actual losses. Debits are then subtracted from income. If income is higher than debits, the property posts a profit. If debits are larger than income, the property reports a loss, called a **deficit.** Revenue and losses are expressed as **gross,** a total before any adjustments such as taxes are figured in, or as **net,** the figure that remains after everything is figured in. The results of the P&L give management a basis from which to start planning the next budget.

Most managers customize the budget process somewhat. However, there are two basic approaches to preparing budgets. The more traditional method uses historical cost patterns to project future costs. The other, called **zero-based budgeting,** requires that department heads literally start from zero and project forward to determine what their departmental needs will be.

The more traditional approach is to calculate expenses based on historical spending patterns and the **profile of business** for the coming year. The profile of business, also called a **profile of sales,** is a forecast of business based on occupancy projections, projections for group business and function sales, special events planned for the city, special holidays or holy days observed in the area, and special sales promotions or sales packages planned by the property itself, the management company, or chain.

Using this information, each cost is defined as a percentage of overall revenues using the following steps:

1. Determine what the occupancy will be
2. Determine how much revenue this occupancy will generate
3. Assign a standard percentage or percentage range to each cost

This percentage is based on the executive housekeeper's calculation of expenses. The exact percentage depends on historical performance. If the percentage used in the past was insufficient and the executive housekeeper can demonstrate consistent, justifiable overruns, the percentage most likely will be raised. If past experience shows the percentage was too large or overruns were not justified, the percentage will stay the same or be lowered.

For zero-based budgeting, each item is justified on the basis of projected need or use, not on past performance. The executive housekeeper uses the profile of business as a starting point. This detailed look at the forecasted workload of the next year enables the executive housekeeper to calculate expenses and determine the **cost per occupied room.** It is computed by adding up total departmental expenditures and dividing this figure by the number of occupied rooms. Cost per occupied

room has become a standard measure of fiscal performance because it measures expenses directly against the income generated by occupied rooms (see Figure 12.1).

Cost per occupied room should include not only standard labor and supply costs, but any costs included in the housekeeping budget. For example, if extra labor hours are needed to prepare the property for an inspection by the management company's corporate inspector, it will boost the cost per occupied room for that period. A veteran staff may be entitled to more vacation time. Scheduling staff to cover all these weeks of vacation can add as much as $10 to the hotel's average cost per occupied room during major holidays when several staff members may be off at one time.

Accurate record keeping is another essential part of the budget process. Detailed records enable the executive housekeeper to monitor spending patterns and identify areas in which costs are running ahead of or behind the actual budget (see Tricks of the Trade 12.1)

---

**Tricks of the Trade 12.1**
**The Budgetary Benefits of Technology**

*The Problem:* Finding a way to simplify expense tracking.

*The Solution:* Kristine Hall, executive housekeeper of the 538-room Hyatt Regency Union Station, St. Louis, Missouri, created a computerized "checkbook" system for each account. Expenses are subtracted from the total budget, just as they would be in an individual's checking account. Hall knows not only how much has been spent, but how much is left in the budget after each expenditure.

Louis Fozman, executive housekeeper of the 426-room Adolphus Hotel in Dallas, Texas, worked with the property's controller to design a program that tracks daily payroll and breaks it out by job category. "I can easily monitor productivity and see where we are spending our labor hours," he says.

---

Budgets are broken down further into **operating budgets** and **capital improvement** or **capital equipment budgets.** The operating budget includes the estimated expenses for all goods and services that will be used within one year's time. This

| HOUSEKEEPING DEPARTMENT - COST PER OCCUPIED ROOM | | | | | | | | | | | | | | | | | | | | | | |
|---|---|---|---|---|---|---|---|---|---|---|---|---|---|---|---|---|---|---|---|---|---|---|
| ROOM NIGHTS | | | | 4th Qtr. Ave.CPOR | Year-end CPOR | Budget CPOR | +/- % | | | | 1st Qtr. Ave.CPOR | | | | 2nd Qtr. Ave.CPOR | | | | | 3rd Qtr. Ave.CPOR | | |
| | | 1995 | | | | | | | | | | | | | | | | | | | | |
| Expense Line/Month | JAN | FEB | MAR | | | | | APR | MAY | JUN | | JUL | AUG | SEP | | OCT | NOV | DEC | | | | |
| | | | | | | | | | | | | | | | | | | | | | | |
| Housekeeping Labor-Fixed | | | | | | | | | | | | | | | | | | | | | | |
| Housekeeping Labor-Variable | | | | | | | | | | | | | | | | | | | | | | |
| Total Housekeeping Labor | | | | | | | | | | | | | | | | | | | | | | |
| | | | | | | | | | | | | | | | | | | | | | | |
| Decorations | | | | | | | | | | | | | | | | | | | | | | |
| Laundry | | | | | | | | | | | | | | | | | | | | | | |
| Household Cleaning | | | | | | | | | | | | | | | | | | | | | | |
| Uniforms | | | | | | | | | | | | | | | | | | | | | | |
| Linens and Blankets | | | | | | | | | | | | | | | | | | | | | | |
| Robes | | | | | | | | | | | | | | | | | | | | | | |
| Uniform Cleaning | | | | | | | | | | | | | | | | | | | | | | |
| Cleaning Supplies | | | | | | | | | | | | | | | | | | | | | | |
| Window Cleaning | | | | | | | | | | | | | | | | | | | | | | |
| Contract Cleaning | | | | | | | | | | | | | | | | | | | | | | |
| Plant Maintenance | | | | | | | | | | | | | | | | | | | | | | |
| Guest Amenities | | | | | | | | | | | | | | | | | | | | | | |
| Other Suite Replacement Costs | | | | | | | | | | | | | | | | | | | | | | |
| Housekeeping - Other | | | | | | | | | | | | | | | | | | | | | | |

**Figure 12.1**  *All department expenses are tracked, totaled, then divided by the number of actual occupied rooms in order to calculate cost per occupied room (CPOR), one of the most important financial measures used in the lodging industry now. (Courtesy of the RIHGA Royal Hotel, New York)*

includes the cost of labor. The capital improvement budget, or capital budget, covers outlays for items that will last several years, which includes equipment such as vacuum cleaners or shampooers and FF&E.

## CALCULATING EXPENSES FOR THE OPERATING BUDGET

The starting point for the operating budget is to find out just how much money is needed to run the housekeeping department. All operating costs are analyzed.

### Calculating Labor Costs

Labor is the largest single cost within the housekeeping department. It can also be one of the most highly variable costs. Overtime, absenteeism, or unexpectedly high turnover can drive up labor costs significantly and put the housekeeping department well over budget.

### Tracking Labor Needs

Technology makes it possible to track labor costs on a daily basis with only minimal data entry. The number of hours each employee works is logged into the housekeeping department's computer each day. Using this information, combined with information on the hourly rate each employee earns, the computer provides daily updates on whether the department is on, below or above its targeted

budget for labor costs. Since day-to-day occupancy can be well above or below forecasted rates, the executive housekeeper can track variances and identify patterns in labor hours and costs.

Employee productivity dramatically impacts labor needs. Computer spreadsheet programs are used to create a **productivity report** (see Figure 12.2). This report shows how many assignments each employee completed during each shift worked in a particular period. After data are collected for several months, patterns of productivity emerge.

Some factors to consider when analyzing productivity and labor costs include:

- Are there regular periods during the year when labor costs exceed the budget? The executive housekeeper should analyze labor costs for the previous three to five years to determine whether these periods are regular upswings in the property's business cycle or isolated instances. If they occur each year, the budget must be adjusted accordingly to provide for extra staff or overtime during these periods.

- Are there cyclical periods when the department is overstaffed? Resorts typically have periods of high occupancy, low occupancy, and **shoulder seasons,** periods when occupancy averages are building toward seasonal highs or ebbing toward seasonal lows in occupancy. But even urban hotels may have slower periods during certain times of the year. Failure to adjust schedules to cut back on labor can be costly. Executive housekeepers in unionized properties, where the number of staff positions and hours is determined by contract,

Mar97

232 The Professional Housekeeper

# HOUSEKEEPING DEPARTMENT
## HOUSEKEEPING ATTENDANT PRODUCTIVITY
### MARCH, 1997

| DATE | # OF SUITES OCCUPIED | # OF CREDITS CLEANED | AM # | SHIFT HRS | PM # | SHIFT HRS | PRODUCTIVITY |
|---|---|---|---|---|---|---|---|
| 28-Feb | | | | | | | |
| 1-Mar | | | | | | | |
| 2-Mar | | | | | | | |
| 3-Mar | | | | | | | |
| 4-Mar | | | | | | | |
| 5-Mar | | | | | | | |
| 6-Mar | | | | | | | |
| 7-Mar | | | | | | | |
| 8-Mar | | | | | | | |
| 9-Mar | | | | | | | |
| 10-Mar | | | | | | | |
| 11-Mar | | | | | | | |
| 12-Mar | | | | | | | |
| 13-Mar | | | | | | | |
| 14-Mar | | | | | | | |
| 15-Mar | | | | | | | |
| 16-Mar | | | | | | | |
| 17-Mar | | | | | | | |
| 18-Mar | | | | | | | |
| 19-Mar | | | | | | | |
| 20-Mar | | | | | | | |
| 21-Mar | | | | | | | |
| 22-Mar | | | | | | | |
| 23-Mar | | | | | | | |
| 24-Mar | | | | | | | |
| 25-Mar | | | | | | | |
| 26-Mar | | | | | | | |
| 27-Mar | | | | | | | |
| 28-Mar | | | | | | | |
| 29-Mar | | | | | | | |
| 30-Mar | | | | | | | |
| 31-Mar | | | | | | | |
| TOTAL | | | | | | | |
| | | | | | | MONTHLY PRODUCTIVITY | 0.00 |

*Figure 12.2 Productivity is important in calculating the amount of labor hours to be budgeted. (Courtesy of the RIHGA Royal Hotel, New York)*

may use these seasons for deep cleaning to keep staff busy and productive.

- Have call-offs, no-shows, or absenteeism affected labor costs? High absenteeism translates into costly over-staffing or overtime.
- Will the union contract expire during the next budget period? The human resources department, which tracks pay rates for competing properties, should be able to provide some guidelines on typical raises in recently negotiated contracts. Even if a strike seems likely, the budget must provide for raises.
- Has productivity declined or improved? If overtime is running too high because existing staff

does not finish the assigned tasks each day, the executive housekeeper must determine whether the workload is too heavy or whether existing staff needs to be more productive. If the majority of staff members can regularly finish the assigned tasks of the day before the end of their shift, the executive housekeeper could consider raising their quota and eliminating a position or adding deep-cleaning duties, as explained in Chapters 5 and 6.

- Has overtime been excessive? Short staffing or unexpectedly high occupancy can push overtime costs well beyond the budget. If these situations occur frequently because of a tight labor market or because of the property's shifting local market or business base, the executive housekeeper must address them in the budget.

Has occupancy forecasting been accurate? The executive housekeeper should track the occupancy forecasts, the actual occupancy, and the number of hours worked by the housekeeping department staff. If actual occupancies have been running well ahead of or behind projections and labor costs have varied as a result, the executive housekeeper should work with the head of the rooms division to identify the problem.

## Forecasting Labor Costs

To determine the salary section of the labor budget, the executive housekeeper should consider the following:

1. Using forecasted occupancy and sales, and, if pertinent, historical data, the executive housekeeper can define the basic workload for the coming year.
2. This figure is then divided by the established quotas or average productivity in public areas to find out how many labor hours will be needed to do the work. Salaries for administrative personnel must also be figured in, typically using historical salary data or salary averages from surveys or competitive properties as a basis for computation.
3. The total of labor hours needed is then multiplied by the correct rates of pay to determine the forecast for departmental salaries. Because of the high turnover that characterizes housekeeping and the discrepancies of forecasting, this total serves as a guideline for salary, not a precise fiscal target.

## Calculating Costs Other than Salaries

Though actual salaries will account for the bulk of the labor budget, the executive housekeeper must also figure in the department's share of benefits. One rule of thumb states that a benefit package for an employee can average 20 percent or 30 percent of his or her salary. Training costs must also be added in, particularly if the property typically has a large number of new hires each year (see Figure 12.3).

Large numbers of new hires not only depress productivity figures, they also strain the budget. Additional training costs must be figured in; so must the training time. Most new hires are not ex-

pected to do a full quota of rooms until their second week on the job. This means overtime for existing staff or calling in part-times or swing shift workers to cover the gap.

Turnover also puts pressure on the budget. Not only must lost training costs and costs for other benefits be factored in, the added costs of recruiting, hiring, and training a new employee must be considered.

Departments fortunate enough to have a large number of long-term employees benefit from their experience, but may have correspondingly higher labor budgets. Veteran staff members earn higher wages, but also receive proportionately larger shares of certain benefits. If the property has a salary investment plan, the employer may be matching a certain percentage of the employee's contributions from salary. The higher the salary, the higher the amount of matched funds. In some cases, it would be better to take advantage of these veterans' skills and lessen the stress on the budget by promoting them to salaried positions.

Unless the property has a **freeze** on wages, which means no raises will be given during a specific period, the budget must include an estimate for raises. The human resources department can offer guidelines based on raises recently given at competitive hotels or in similar union contracts. Raises for **exempt personnel,** that is, staff paid a fixed salary each week as opposed to those paid hourly, should be estimated in the same percentage terms as those allotted hourly employees or union members. In some cases, the percentage is lowered slightly as salaries increase.

The impact of vacation time, no-shows, call-offs, and absenteeism also must be considered when making up the labor budget. Contingency funding should be created if the department requires one or two on-call people each day to cover for no-shows. Vacations should be encouraged during low periods so that extra help does not have to be called in nor overtime paid. Considering all of these factors results in a realistic, workable labor budget.

## Calculating Supply Costs

The same business profile information that enables the executive housekeeper to create a budget for labor also serves as the basis for budgeting for supplies (see Chapters 9 and 11). Projected occupancy for the budget period will determine how many linens, how many cases of guest amenities, toilet tissue and facial tissue, and how many cases of cleaning and laundry supplies will be required for the

**THE ADOLPHUS**                     DAY:_____
DAILY REPORTED HOURS                 DATE:_____

|  |  | DAILY | MTD |
|---|---|---|---|
| OCC ROOMS |  |  |  |
| ROOM ATTENDANTS |  |  |  |
| AVERAGE ROOMS |  |  |  |

| JOB CODE | JOB CATAGORY | DAILY HOURS | MTD HOURS |
|---|---|---|---|
| 17 | Room Attendant |  |  |
| 18 | Back of House |  |  |
| 19 | Clerk |  |  |
| 20 | Evening Floor Manager |  |  |
| 21 | Lead Night cleaner |  |  |
| 22 | Office cleaner |  |  |
| 23 | Evening Lobby Attendant |  |  |
| 24 | Day Lobby Attendant |  |  |
| 25 | Evening Room Attendant |  |  |
| 27 | Turndown Attendant |  |  |
| 28 | Floor Housemen |  |  |
| 95 | Night Cleaner |  |  |
| 96 | Carpet Shampoo Person |  |  |
| 97 | Day Floor Manager |  |  |
| 98 | Evening Dispatcher |  |  |
|  | **SUB TOTAL** |  |  |
|  | **MANAGERS HOURS** | 17.13 |  |
|  | **TOTAL HOURS** |  |  |

|  | DAILY HOURS | MTD HOURS |
|---|---|---|
| TRAINING |  |  |
| PROJECTS/GEN. CLEAN |  |  |
| OVERTIME |  |  |
| LIGHT DUTY |  |  |

**Figure 12.3**  *Training, overtime, and benefit costs must be calculated when writing the labor budget. (Courtesy of The Adolphus Hotel, Dallas, Texas)*

period covered by the budget. The supplies budget will also include uniforms, in-room stationary needs, departmental forms, glasses for guest rooms, and items such as room attendants' cards. New properties will even have to include rags, since the property must buy them at first.

Historical data can help define trends in usage and ways to conserve. The consumption of supplies should be fairly standard and should be linked with the rate of occupancy. Sudden rises in consumption without corresponding increases in occupancy must be analyzed carefully. Undersupply can result from factors as varied as overuse of certain clean-

ing fluids to pilferage and loss. In these cases, training or better security controls are needed—not a bigger budget.

Determining usage patterns also is useful in writing zero-based budgets. Although the executive housekeeper cannot assume that because a certain percentage was spent last year, the same percentage will be needed next year, he or she can look for patterns of spending to find out where cost efficiencies can be realized.

The supplies budget is based on occupancy projections and the profile of business. When doing the budget for supplies, the executive housekeeper should budget to make sure minimum and maximum supply levels are set (see Chapter 9). This will help avoid undersupply, which leads to costly special deliveries, and cost overruns due to oversupply. Inventories should always be checked before final supply figures are budgeted.

### Estimating Expenses for Contract Services

Historical data and current pricing trends are the only bases for estimating expenses allocated for contract services. To compute this figure, the executive housekeeper should: (1) determine how much was paid out to contract services each year for the last three to five years; and (2) calculate that figure as a percentage of expenses. Contracts should be bid each year, even if current service providers have performed well. This provides an opportunity to shop for the best price and contract terms.

The purchasing department usually tracks pricing trends for various services. Bids should be checked against these averages. If all the bids seem too high, perhaps because of impending strikes or shortages, the executive housekeeper has the option of inviting other companies to bid or evaluating whether the task could be done in-house more cost-effectively.

## CALCULATING EXPENSES FOR THE CAPITAL BUDGET

Capital equipment and FF&E do not last forever. The executive housekeeper uses the capital equipment budget to plan for the major repairs and, eventually replacement, of these items. Included in the capital equipment or capital improvement budget would be some smaller items such as vacuum cleaners (unless they are replaced each year or so, in which case they would fall under the operating budget), all large equipment, from wet-dry vacuums to buffers and polishers, laundry equipment and tables, and all FF&E items, including the bedspreads or bed covers, draperies, and all in-room furnishings.

Even in a small property, the housekeeping department requires a substantial amount of equipment to accomplish daily tasks. Before preparing the capital budget, the executive housekeeper must assess the condition of each piece of capital equipment, that is, equipment that will last more than one year. The task is made much easier if equipment repair orders and service records are computerized and kept up to date.

## ASSESSING CAPITAL NEEDS

Assessing capital needs begins with a review of the equipment already in the department, unless the budget is for a new hotel (see Tales of the Trade 12.1). A complete inventory should be maintained which lists:

- The age of each piece of capital equipment, and its projected life expectancy
- The condition of each piece of equipment, including how many times the item was repaired in the last year and how much repairs cost
- How much preventive maintenance was required for each piece of equipment and how much it cost
- Purchase and replacement cost
- What features replacement units may offer and whether these features would pay for themselves in terms of reduced cost of operation

### Tales of the Trade 12.1
### Budgeting for a New Hotel

Hired as executive housekeeper months in advance of the October 1990 opening of the 500-suite RIHGA Royal in New York City, Miriam Albano had only projections and the combined pre-opening staff's expertise to use in writing the first budget for this luxury all-suite hotel.

"The first step in budgeting for any new hotel is to evaluate the guest rooms to determine how long they will take to clean. We had a model suite available, so we did a time and motion study. From this, I calculated quotas and determined how many room attendants would be needed," says Albano, who has worked for several hotel chains including Westin Hotels & Resorts and ITT Sheraton.

Although the hotel was not unionized at the time, Albano used union scale to calculate the initial payroll budget. Projections from the marketing director and trends reports on occupancy in New York City provided the bases for calculating supply costs in the first operating budget. "I do my own purchasing so I can negotiate prices myself. By the time I wrote the budget, I knew exactly what worked, how much we needed and what it would cost," points out Albano.

Budgets for new hotels are substantially higher because every item the department needs must be purchased, from vacuum cleaners and carpet shampooers to caddies and cleaning rags.

"The market is the most important thing to consider when writing a budget for a new hotel. That means the labor market, the guest market and the city market," advises Albano.

Repair records are particularly important. If several vacuum cleaners have gone out for repair repeatedly during the last six months, it probably is time to replace them. The same applies to any piece of equipment that has become so unreliable that it prevents attendants from doing their job properly. It generally is best to replace all units of a certain age at one time. This opens up opportunities to negotiate better prices for a larger order and keeps morale problems from developing within the staff when the new equipment is delivered. However, if the budget is extremely tight, the executive housekeeper may have to replace only the units in the worst condition.

Requests for capital budget should be supported with hard data that shows why the item is needed and why the cost is justified. If the problem is that equipment is out for repair too often, the executive housekeeper should show documentation on how often the vacuums broke down, how costly the repairs were, and how many labor hours were wasted sharing the working units.

Another critical factor to address is return on investment (ROI), how long it will take the equipment to generate enough savings through increased productivity or reduced operating costs to cover the initial purchase price. For example, a highly automated, but expensive, automatic spreader/folder may take a big bite out of the year's capital equipment budget. But the labor saved by buying this machine may mean the machine has an ROI of two to three years and can actually be a cost-saver in terms of reduced labor hours before the fourth year of operation.

Any major capital expenditures, such as creating a dry cleaning operation or a renovation, require long-range planning. These purchases sometimes are allocated special budget categories created for these projects.

## Assessing Repair and Maintenance Needs

Property-wide renovation does not come out of the housekeeping budget but, rather, from the property's general fund. However, the housekeeping budget typically covers some guestroom renovation and necessary repairs or replacement of FF&E items. In some hotels, this is covered under a separate budget labeled as the repair and maintenance (R&M) budget. This budget may fall under housekeeping or maintenance/engineering. If it is prepared by the director of maintenance or engineering, there must be ample input from the executive housekeeper.

Prior to writing the renovation budget, the executive housekeeper should walk through the property with the general manager or assistant manager and point out what items need repairs. This would be based on the daily reports of attendants and supervisors, as well as the executive housekeeper's own observations. Follow-up memos should document what action the rooms division manager or assistant manager recommended. This documentation may be a useful tool in getting this part of the budget passed, especially if the property's management philosophy usually stresses repair rather than replacement.

All of this information can be used to create detailed **room classification records,** a report of the condition of each guest room. Typically, Class A rooms require no capital expenditure. Class B rooms require only partial refurbishing, such as new bedspreads, lamps, chairs, tables and draperies. Class C rooms require major refurbishing. The general manager should be shown a sample room in each category and asked for input.

## Planning for Renovation

As mentioned earlier, major renovations require either special budgets or special budget sections. These budgets require more detailed planning and time to prepare. Renovation budgets are usually discussed in special meetings with other department heads and the general manager, rather than as part of the regular budget process, (see Tales of the Trade 12.2).

**Tales of the Trade 12.2**
**Budgeting for Renovation**

Like many top luxury hotels, the 500-suite RIHGA Royal Hotel in New York City renovates constantly to meet changing guest demand. About 100 of the suites undergo a softgoods renovation each year, so that over five years all of the suites are renovated. Complete renovation of the public areas is less frequent.

Miriam Albano, the property's executive housekeeper, writes a separate budget specifically for renovation. "First our general manager sets a target cost for each suite. Then we talk with various interior designers to get bids. The interior designer selected for the project will do a mock-up suite, which we then cost out to determine the exact project cost. We multiply that by the number of suites and use that as one basis for the capital budget for the renovation," explains Albano.

She creates a separate column for labor in the renovation budget. If the general contractor will do liquidation and installation, the housekeeping department staff only strips and cleans the rooms. If the hotel is responsible for liquidation, the housekeeping department must budget for enough labor to remove all existing softgoods and any other items to be replaced, then strip and clean.

Renovations are scheduled during the slower summer months so that overtime can be minimized and there will be a sufficient number of attendants to clean guest rooms. If necessary, Albano can increase hours for the department's small core of part-time employees who usually work only two to three days per week. "Labor costs definitely go up during renovation," she notes.

Supply costs decrease. The suites are not cleaned and made up until after the renovation is over. If all goes according to schedule in a hotel such as the RIHGA Royal, that may mean they are out of inventory for only a month.

As with any capital expense relating to FF&E, there must be a budget column for labor. Some companies do both purchasing and installation, which minimizes the labor hours of hotel staff. In other cases, staff must be assigned to strip each room before renovation begins, remove all furnishings and design elements that will not be reused, and clean the room once the new FF&E is in place. The labor budget covers any work to be done on-premise, including any draperies that will be made in the property's sewing room or any shelving or other architectural elements that must be fabri-

cated by or installed by the property's carpenter(s). Overall, this budget plus the operating budget must provide for adequate staff and supplies to both clean rooms available to be sold and keep the renovation process moving along.

## Communicating with Other Departments

No part of the housekeeping department's budget is written without input from another department. The rooms division, front desk, sales, human resources, purchasing, engineering, and even F&B may all provide necessary input into the housekeeping budget.

## Rooms Division/Marketing Department

The rooms division and marketing department provide the occupancy forecasts and profile of business that are cornerstones of both labor and supply budgets. But, they also provide other information useful for budgeting. For example, guest profile information helps determine how many rollaways and cribs are needed, whether more of a certain kind of pillow should be purchased, and whether more, or less, should be spent on guest amenities.

The executive housekeeper and rooms division manager also should discuss any plans for renovation or introduction of new services to the hotel. Creating executive floors would add extra cleaning time for these larger rooms with more amenities. Introducing in-room fax machines also adds time to cleaning or requires specific new supplies for cleaning screens and keyboards. Even a small decision, such as purchasing in-room coffee makers, means a few minutes more cleaning time and, perhaps, transport time to racks or carts destined for the central dishwasher. Any additional services should be discussed and their impact fully weighed before the budget is finalized.

## Human Resources

Before beginning work on the labor section of the budget, the executive housekeeper should plan a meeting with the director of human resources to discuss salary trends, union contracts, and any other major concerns regarding labor supply.

Key questions to ask include:

• Are housekeeping department salaries competitive with hotels of the same category in the area? Exit interviews may already have determined whether salaries are too low.

- Will new hotel openings in the area affect salary scale? Properties in markets with a lot of frenzied building frequently find themselves in the midst of a bidding war for experienced employees. This possibility must be addressed in budgeting, either in the form of planned raises or for a larger training allotment for new hires.
- Will union contracts be renegotiated during the new budget? The human resources department should track typical raises negotiated in recent contracts for union employees in hotels of the same category. Is the hotel planning to downsize? If so, the housekeeping labor budget must be cut.

## Purchasing

For properties in which there is a dedicated purchasing department, the executive housekeeper plans discussions with the director of purchasing before writing the budget for supplies and capital equipment. Topics to cover include:

- What kinds of price increases are expected for the budget period?
- Are any shortages projected that will affect the budget? Manufacturers changing to new product lines or impending strikes may threaten to reduce supply. Extra inventory may have to be ordered, or contingency funds set up for emergencies.
- Have any new purchasing contracts been signed that will reduce costs?

## Sales

The sales department provides information on advance group bookings and functions. When planning the budget, the executive housekeeper should work with the director of sales to determine:

- What is the forecast for group business and function sales? Growing group and function business will increase labor costs, particularly on the night shift. If the property uses a contract cleaning service or laundry service, this extra volume of business will have to be addressed. In either case, the budget must reflect the rising costs.
- Will the department need to purchase or rent items specifically for certain groups?
- When are the bulk of the events planned? If several large groups overlap, this, too, will require more money for labor.

The sales director also may point out any need for repair or replacement in FF&E. Shabby rooms are not saleable. Enlisting support from the sales manager may be critical if the property's owner is hesitating about approving more money for repair or replacement.

Input may be required from other department heads as well. The director of maintenance or engineering can supply valuable information about which capital items are beyond repair. Records of work orders may indicate which items have been out of service too often, and which have reached the end of their life expectancy.

The executive housekeeper in a large property should also obtain input from the F&B department, regarding any special needs that will arise during the budget period. All of this information is discussed with the property's general manager. The general manager can point out any major changes in the property's operation that will affect the housekeeping budget, as well as any overall changes in staff size or market.

## BUDGET GOALS

Sound budgets are more than mere totals of columns of necessary expenditures. The housekeeping department budget must be written with the property's overall performance expectations in mind.

As a department head, the executive housekeeper participates in weekly or monthly meetings that discuss P&L statements. It should be clear from these meetings whether current departmental budgets are sufficient and also how well the property is expected to perform in the future. This provides the necessary context for evaluating what is included in or cut out of the housekeeping department's budget.

The property's anticipated bottom line is a critical factor in budgeting. **Accountability,** being held accountable for each item in the budget, serves as a good guideline for determining what is essential.

### Setting Realistic Goals

Whatever the overall financial condition of the property, the executive housekeeper must prepare a realistic budget. For example, if occupancy is projected to dip during the next year, the executive housekeeper must create a smaller, tighter budget that can be met even if occupancy plummets. This is not the time to ask for hefty raises, but to look for opportunities to increase efficiency and reduce costs. However, forecasts for a record-breaking year are not an invitation to overspend. Large, capital purchases may be budgeted, but only if the request is justified by need.

## Prioritizing Budget Items

In the past, some general managers of large or upscale properties boasted they had not been on a guestroom floor in three or more years. However, the recession of the early 1990s brought these managers back to financial reality and made them far more involved with day-to-day operations. The majority of general managers who operate successful, service-oriented properties now are well aware of the needs of guests and each hotel department.

The basic budget presented to the general manager by the executive housekeeper should have no surprises. The general manager should already know if there are salary problems to address or if extensive repairs are required. However, budget requests should be prioritized (see Figure 12.4a and b). This practice enables the executive housekeeper to write an honest budget and still make clear what the department's needs are. The budget breakdown should include:

*Priority 1.* This includes total salaries, supplies, and capital equipment required by the housekeeping department to complete basic cleaning, operational, and administrative tasks. These are the items the department has to have in order to function.

*Priority 2.* This section lists "nice to have" items, such as specialty vacuums, more automated equipment for the laundry, departmental computers and so on. Many of the items listed as Priority 2 may require a fairly large initial capital outlay, but would significantly cut labor hours or other costs within several years.

*Priority 3.* This is essentially a wish list of items that would make departmental work flow more smoothly, though the benefit may not be felt immediately.

Any such ranking must be presented clearly. The general manager should be able to see even at a glance which items are essential, good to have, or merely on the wish list.

## The Dangers of Over-Budgeting

Some general managers or controllers are so used to inflated budgets that they routinely cut the requested budget by 30 percent to 50 percent. This opens the door to unlimited problems, ranging from supply shortages to insufficient labor. The best course for both executive housekeeper and general manager is to submit a realistic budget, substantiated by proper records and other necessary documentation.

Over-budgeting can lead to other problems, such as over-spending. Buying too much equipment or supplies only not erodes the department's P&L, but also takes up a disproportionate amount of storage space. Too much capital equipment increases the cost of operations and servicing. This bloats the budget further, sparking a cycle of over-spending that may lead to drastic cutbacks.

There also is the issue of trust. A general manager who knows that the executive housekeeper is honest about budget needs is far more likely to give serious considerations to the amount requested. Although documentation will always be required, the executive housekeeper's recommendations will carry far more weight when they are proven to be reasonable.

"I basically tell department heads, 'This is your budget.' They have to tell me how much they need to spend to run their departments. They also know best what they can do without and what they can cut. I want them to be realistic. I don't want a situation in which the executive housekeeper says the department can get by without something just to turn in a lower budget, then come to me the week after the budget is approved and request approval of cost overruns," says Kevin Cameron, general manager of the 111-room Radisson Airport Hotel, Providence, Rhode Island, an educational facility of Johnson & Wales University.

Creating contingency funds should not be confused with over-budgeting. The housekeeping department requires small contingency funds to cover emergencies. For example, if several large conventions are slated for the year ahead, extra money must be budgeted to cover not only extra labor, but swing shift or on-call personnel to make sure all cleaning assignments are completed. Extra supplies must always be on hand in case occupancy rises suddenly. Labor and supply contingencies must reflect projected need. No property needs a six-month supply of facial tissue "just in case."

## MAKING BUDGET CUTS

Even realistic budgets may be too high. Executive housekeepers should understand their staff and the guest market well enough to know what budget items can be cut without cutting service standards. Labor, supplies, and capital equipment needs must

```
               CAPITAL IMPROVEMENT BUDGET—500 ROOM HOTEL

  Priority I                                                         Total


  (1)  Re-do guest rooms
  # 04-06-08-10-12 on 10 floors = 50 rooms @ $2,000 each ...................... $100,000.

  (2)  Replace corridor carpet
  floors 3-5-7 = 2,000 yards @ $30 yd. .......................................   60,000.

  (3)  Lamps
  guest rooms 35 @ $15- ......................................................      525.
  public area 6 @ $50- .......................................................      300.
  Assorted shades 50 @ $65- ..................................................    3,250.

  (4)  Bed spreads
  100 doubles @ $250 each ....................................................   25,000.
  25 kings @ $400 each .......................................................   10,000.

  (5)  Mattresses, Springs, Frames
  100 sets Doubles M & S @ $200- .............................................   20,000.
  50 sets Kings M & S @ $250- ................................................   12,500.
  25 double frame @ $25- .....................................................      875.
  10 king frame @ $50- .......................................................      500.

  (6)  25 TV sets $250- .......................................................    6,250.

  (7)  Room attendant carts (New Style) 6 @ $125. each .......................      750.

  (8)  50 pr. sheer curtains @ $75 each ......................................    3,750.

  (9)  10 room vacuums @ $90 each ............................................    9,000.

  (10)  New shampoo machine 1 @ $4400 each ...................................    4,400.

                                                         Total   $257,100.
```

(a)

**Figure 12.4**  *This capital budget shows three different priorities. Priority I is what is essential for the hotel; Priority II is what would be helpful to the more efficient operation of the department; and Priority III is what will be needed within two years.*

be weighed to determine what is expendable or where savings could be realized.

## Cutting Supply Costs

Supply costs are easier to cut than labor. "If the budget is being cut because occupancy is expected to drop, the property will not need as many supplies. The executive housekeeper can cut back linen orders, laundry supplies, amenities, and room supplies to reflect the lower occupancy and lower consumption. Precautions still should be taken to maintain minimum inventories to cover unexpected rises in occupancy," says Erma Young, executive housekeeper of the Holiday Inn International Drive Resort, Orlando, Florida.

Consumption can be controlled to a certain extent as well. The supplies budget can be reduced

```
CAPITAL IMPROVEMENT BUDGET—500 ROOM HOTEL

Priority II                                                        Total

(1)   Pool lounges replace 10 @ $95 each...................... $    950.

(2)   Recarpet banquet rooms 1-200 yds @ $35 ...............      7,000.
                            2-500 yds @ $35 ...............     17,500.
                            3-350 yds @ $35 ...............     12,250.

(3)   Banquet chairs 200 @ $60 each.........................     12,000.
                                              Total    $ 49,950.


Priority III

(1)   Lobby add new tables 6 @ $800 each....................      4,800.
      Lobby add new chairs 12 @ $400 each...................      4,800.

(2)   Recover 4 sofas 100 yards @ $25.......................      2,500.

(3)   Banquet chairs 100 @ $60..............................      6,000.
                                              Total    $ 18,100.
```

*(b)*

*Figure 12.4*   *(Continued)*

by instituting a policy of not restocking soap or amenities until it becomes necessary. "There is a list in each attendants' closet and one on the notice board showing the stock on hand, unit price and daily consumption of guest supplies and amenities. By making attendants aware of how much was being wasted, we have reduced our costs significantly," says Margit Abendroth, executive housekeeper of the Colombo Hilton in Colombo, Sri Lanka.

For items that are intended as giveaways, the executive housekeeper may be able to work out an agreement with the sales and marketing department in which part of the cost would be covered by the advertising/promotions budget. Depending on the length of stay, the property could save as much as 25 percent on laundry chemicals and energy costs by not changing towels and sheets daily (see Chapter 14). The executive housekeeper also should make sure loss control measures are effective, and that the department is not overspending on supplies because of high loss or pilferage.

*Capital equipment.* Capital expenses are among the first items to be cut. But only nonessential items should be deleted. The necessities for cleaning the property and keeping it up to standards should not be cut, even in a tight budget. Vacuum cleaners that no longer work properly or run up costly repair bills must be replaced. Holes in upholstery or carpet must be repaired. However, the department may be able to survive one more year without beepers, a new calculator, or a computer.

When looking for ways to cut the budget, the executive housekeeper must weigh the total cost of the equipment. Energy- and labor-saving features may mean that an expensive piece of equipment will actually reduce overall costs within two years.

Generally, executive housekeepers prefer to make small cuts in several areas rather than eliminating a large budget category. Reducing frequency of some deep-cleaning tasks and rejuvenating some equipment or FF&E can result in significant savings. During certain seasons, exterior window washing may be stretched from every four weeks to every six or eight weeks. Thorough carpet cleaning and pile lifting may postpone the need for carpet replacement. Any such budget cuts must be made only if they will not drag down the overall standards of cleanliness nor detract from the image of the property.

## Finding Better Pricing

The alternative to cutting the budget is to find better pricing. As soon as the executive housekeeper knows the budget must be cut back, he or she should try to identify where discounts or volume purchasing could reduce overall costs most.

Regardless of price, no item should be purchased unless it meets the department's needs. Overbuying is also a fiscal mistake. Even if vendors offer so-called "sales," the purchase is no bargain unless it can be justified on the basis of need.

## Reducing Labor Costs

Increasing productivity is almost always preferable to massive staff cuts. Raising quotas by one to two rooms each day can eliminate one or two full-time positions. The department saves not only the actual salary, but also the corresponding contribution to the benefits package. Incorporating one or two general clean assignments each day may help eliminate the need for an extra swing-shift employee. Cross-training may open up possibilities for combining several positions. The attendant who starts cleaning public space at 5 A.M. could shift to rooms at 9 A.M. This could help cut overtime costs, especially in emergency situations.

Some hotel companies have mandated cutbacks of mid-level managerial positions, such as inspectors or supervisors. This does pare down the housekeeping payroll. However, the executive housekeeper will need to allocate more time and money for training existing employees to become self-supervising or take part in team cleaning with a team leader. Some executive housekeepers are experimenting with a different approach that adds a measurable productivity factor to the supervisor's position. The supervisor's position may be redefined to include some cleaning tasks as well as inspection duties (see Chapter 5).

Cutting a substantial number of room attendants is not an option. If rooms are not properly cleaned, the property will have a substandard product to sell. The predictable result is that business will suffer further. Cuts should be made in supervisory or administrative staff first.

"Cut costs in areas that hurt the guests least, the employees 'second least.' It's better to ask for volunteers who would be willing to take a few days off without pay than cut the hours. If the situation gets really bad, though, nothing except customer service is sacred," says Kevin Cameron, general manager of the Radisson Airport Hotel, Providence.

Once all the labor, supply, and capital equipment expenses are determined, they usually are merged into the rooms division budget. Rather than submitting a separate departmental budget, the housekeeping budget is broken out as **line items,** individual entries, within the rooms division budget. The general manager can then approve or deny each line item request. If the general manager cuts an item or items considered essential by the executive housekeeper, he or she should plan a special meeting to discuss this point. Should the general manager still maintain this is a necessary cutback, there should be a frank discussion of how this will affect the department's performance. This should be followed up with a written memo summarizing the discussion and placed with the budget file.

## MONITORING THE BUDGET

Once the budget has been approved, or at least the operating portion of it, the executive housekeeper is responsible for making sure the department operates within its financial guidelines. Typically, budgets have built-in checking systems. In many properties, the executive housekeeper is also required to write a budget for each month as part of the annual budget. Each month, the executive housekeeper can compare actual performance to the budget forecast.

Frequent checks on actual costs against budget projections will make sure the department is either on budget or can institute controls before the bottom line is out of reach (see Figure 12.5). Since housekeeping is a **unit producer,** which means that all costs are related to the actual number of units serviced, expenses may have to be recalculated depending on the property's actual performance. Forecasts are not always accurate. Labor and supply budgets will have to be adjusted based on quarterly, weekly, three-day, and actual occupancy. If occupancies are running higher than expected, extra spending may not be questioned. However, if occupancies drop below projections, the executive housekeeper must have a plan ready in advance to

**HOUSEKEEPING—VARIABLE COST—REPORT**

**PERIOD # ________**

| ROOM NIGHTS | | | | REVENUE | | | |
|---|---|---|---|---|---|---|---|
| Budgeted | Forecasted | Actual | VARIANCE | Budgeted | Forecasted | Actual | VARIANCE |
| | | | | | | | |

| Allocation | Money Budgeted | | E.C.A. from Forecasted Revenue | Money Spent (Orders Placed) | E.C.A. from Actual Revenue | VARIANCE |
|---|---|---|---|---|---|---|
| Direct Supplies —Glassware— | | | | | | |
| Direct Supplies —Linen— | | | | | | |
| Direct Supplies —Cleaning— | | | | | | |
| Direct Supplies —Soap— | | | | | | |
| Direct Supplies —Paper— | | | | | | |
| Direct Supplies —Guest Supplies— | | | | | | |
| Transfer Account | | | | | | |

***Figure 12.5*** *The Inter-Continental Miami tracks its expenditures by vendor. At the same time, purchases can be checked against budget. (Courtesy of the Miami Inter-Continental, Miami, Florida)*

cut labor and supplies in order to maintain target profits (see Tricks of the Trade 12.2).

## Tricks of the Trade 12.2 Effective Budget Monitoring

*The Problem:* Simplifying budget monitoring.
*The Solution:* The must-have information for cost controls in the housekeeping department at the JW Marriott Hong Kong includes:

- Regular recap of linens, guest supplies, cleaning supplies and office supplies, to prevent overstocking.

- Daily, weekly productivity reports
- Daily, weekly calculation of departmental cost per occupied room

## Instituting Budget Controls

The best way to stay on budget is to monitor actual costs on a regular basis. Computer technology makes it possible to obtain daily updates on how much the department has spent on labor and supplies during any given period. Most executive housekeepers check these figures daily to identify problem areas at a time when small adjustments will correct the situation. Daily, weekly, and monthly expense reports for both labor and supplies should be reviewed and assessed.

| | INCOME STATEMENT | | | | | | | | | | |
|---|---|---|---|---|---|---|---|---|---|---|---|
| | Monthly Actual | % | Monthly Budget | % | Monthly Last Year | % | Y-T-D Actual | % | Y-T-D Budget | % | Y-T-D Last Year | % |
| **SUITES REVENUE/EXPENSE** | | | | | | | | | | | |
| ####Suites Revenue | | | | | | | | | | | |
| Suites Revenue | | | | | | | | | | | |
| | | | | | | | | | | | |
| ####Executive/Administrative | | | | | | | | | | | |
| ####Front Office Staff | | | | | | | | | | | |
| ####Uniform Service | | | | | | | | | | | |
| ####Reservations | | | | | | | | | | | |
| ####Housekeeping - Fixed | | | | | | | | | | | |
| ####Housekeeping - Variable | | | | | | | | | | | |
| ####Health Club | | | | | | | | | | | |
| ####Payroll Taxes and Benefits | | | | | | | | | | | |
| ####Contract Labor | | | | | | | | | | | |
| ####Decorations | | | | | | | | | | | |
| ####Newspapers | | | | | | | | | | | |
| ####Telephone and Telex | | | | | | | | | | | |
| ####Postage | | | | | | | | | | | |
| ####Operating Supplies | | | | | | | | | | | |
| ####Suites Promotion | | | | | | | | | | | |
| ####Travel and Related | | | | | | | | | | | |
| ####Pinnacle Sedan | | | | | | | | | | | |
| ####Cable Television | | | | | | | | | | | |
| ####Video C/O - Mess. Retrieval | | | | | | | | | | | |
| ####Wall Street Shuttle | | | | | | | | | | | |
| ####Reservations "800" Number | | | | | | | | | | | |
| ####Travel Agent Commission | | | | | | | | | | | |
| ####Reservations Systems | | | | | | | | | | | |
| ####Laundry | | | | | | | | | | | |
| ####Household Cleaning | | | | | | | | | | | |
| ####Uniforms | | | | | | | | | | | |
| ####Linens and Blankets | | | | | | | | | | | |
| ####Robes | | | | | | | | | | | |
| ####uniform Cleaning | | | | | | | | | | | |
| ####Cleaning Supplies | | | | | | | | | | | |
| ####Window Cleaning | | | | | | | | | | | |
| ####Contract Cleaning | | | | | | | | | | | |
| ####Plant Maintenance | | | | | | | | | | | |
| ####Other Suite Replacement | | | | | | | | | | | |
| ####Housekeeping - Other | | | | | | | | | | | |
| ####Miscellaneous | | | | | | | | | | | |
| | | | | | | | | | | | |
| **Total Suites Expense** | | | | | | | | | | | |
| | | | | | | | | | | | |
| **Net Income/(Loss) - Suites** | | | | | | | | | | | |

**Figure 12.6** *Income statements should show a breakdown of financial performance. This statement has listings for revenues and expenses. (Courtesy of the RIHGA Royal Hotel, New York)*

Each department's budget performance is also assessed on a monthly basis when the P&L statements are published. The general manager usually discusses the P&L during a regular meeting with department heads, and points out any areas where large discrepancies are developing.

Some hotels use **income statements,** a listing of all income received by the property during a certain period and all expenses incurred, as another type of control (see Figure 12.6). The budget, which is only a plan or guideline, can be measured against actual income and expenses outlined in the income statement. The results of the income statement will be essential in calculating cost per occupied room. To analyze expenses in further detail, the executive housekeeper would compare figures with the income statement specifically done for the rooms division. Using this, the executive housekeeper can clearly see how cost controls in the department affect the financial performance of the largest division in the hotel.

### Averting Deficit Spending

Since perfection in forecasting is rarely possible, it might very well be construed as only a minor matter if as many as half the accounts are showing overruns, if the other half of the accounts have been underspent by an equal amount. This situation is certainly not ideal but because of the flow of business may be the reality.

**Deficit spending**—spending that exceeds income—should be addressed as quickly as possible if they are not simple matters of cyclical spending.

Some resorts may do much of their purchasing immediately after the high season when cash flow is still strong. That may result in large outlays for the period, but these will be absorbed over the budget period. The deficits that signal the need for action are those that will not be absorbed by year's end.

When a deficit appears likely, the executive housekeeper should:

- Call a meeting with all assistants and supervisors to discuss the causes of the deficit and try to find a realistic approach for eliminating deficits on overspent accounts.
- Review productivity records to make sure every employee is performing up to expectations. If not, retraining may be in order, as may a performance evaluation.
- Make sure all tasks being done by the housekeeping department are necessary. Some tasks may not need to be done as often as they have been; others may be eliminated without affecting guest service levels.
- Make sure the department is not over-staffed. If action is required, the executive housekeeper can institute some of the cost-saving techniques outlined earlier in this chapter.

Variances should be discussed. If labor hours are going up correspondingly with occupancy, few general managers will hold the executive housekeeper responsible for these overruns. Although the department is spending more, the additional spending is a direct result of additional revenue. Unjustified variances should be assessed and solutions sought.

## SUMMARY

This chapter emphasizes that creating a realistic budget that provides for the labor, supplies, equipment, and contract services needed to maintain a clean, safe environment for staff and guests is a primary responsibility of the executive housekeeper. Understanding P&L statements, business profiles, and the property's financial goals are essential skills for today's executive housekeepers. Even in properties in which the executive housekeeper does not write the budget, he or she still will be responsible for making sure costs remain within the budgetary guidelines.

As a department head, the executive housekeeper will be actively involved in regular meetings with the general manager to review P&Ls and budget performance. He or she must be informed about the property's financial goals in order to better direct his or her department. The executive housekeeper must use this information to monitor costs and explain any variances.

Accountability is an integral part of being a departmental manager in a hotel. In this managerial role, the executive housekeeper must know how to:

- Read financial statements
- Use occupancy forecasts and business profiles to calculate expenses
- Work with other department heads
- Prepare operating and capital budgets
- Institute budget controls
- Reduce spending without reducing service
- Keep proper records
- Justify new purchases
- Prevent cost overruns
- Deal with fluctuations in occupancy and income

## Review Questions

1. What is an operating budget?
2. What is a capital budget?
3. What is the difference between a budget and an income/profit and loss statement?
4. How are the occupancy forecast and business profile used in budgeting?
5. What is a zero-based budget?
6. Describe some typical methods for monitoring budget performance.
7. What is a cost overrun?
8. What is deficit spending?
9. What forms or other data would typically accompany a request for capital equipment?
10. What is return on investment and what role does it play in the capital budget?

## Critical Thinking Questions

1. Budgets will be tight for the next year. Would it be preferable to put a cap on raises and reallocate the money for new vacuum cleaners that would increase productivity and increase cleaning quality or use inefficient existing equipment and give higher raises?
2. One-time-only special events buoyed occupancies to an all-time high the previous year. An optimistic sales director and general manager prepare the budget with hopes other events can be

found to repeat this performance. However, actual performance falls dramatically short of these projections. How should the executive housekeeper respond to the demand for 5 per-cent across-the-board cuts without sacrificing service?

3. A strike is likely. How should this be addressed in the labor budget?

# 13

# Overseeing Safety and Security

## Chapter Objectives

To meet the challenges of safety and security, executive housekeepers must be able to:

- Set up procedures for working safely with chemicals
- Develop procedures for dealing with bloodborne pathogens
- Understand and comply with health and safety regulations
- Create risk management programs
- Track and report accidents and injuries
- Establish programs for fire prevention
- Reduce risk of injury and accidents to staff and guests
- Develop loss prevention programs for staff
- Manage the problems of suspected employee theft
- Create loss prevention and damage control policies for guests

Safety and security are issues of key concern in any workplace. In the lodging industry, these issues have direct impact on day-to-day operations, especially in the housekeeping department. Each day, attendants must deal safely with everything from cleaning chemicals to fabrics or surfaces that may contain viral or bacterial contamination. All housekeeping staff members must interact politely with guests, but in a way that poses no danger to themselves. Housekeeping staff members must learn to cope safely with the physical demands of their jobs.

Proper training, retraining, and continual monitoring are necessary in order to keep both employees and guests safe. The executive housekeeper must write and/or enforce a health and safety pro-gram that complies with local and federal regulations. Prevention is the key to avoiding the human suffering involved with accident and injury, as well as the costly aftermath of absenteeism and possible legal battles.

Because the housekeeping department has access to every area of the hotel, the executive housekeeper must make security and loss prevention primary concerns. The security department usually develops the overall loss prevention program for the hotel and a security program that will deal with special issues such as bomb threats or preparations for high-profile VIPs and dignitaries. The executive housekeeper works with the head of security to adapt these programs in a way that meets the needs of the housekeeping department and the guests. Disaster plans must also be developed in conjunction with the security department. Since these regulations regarding safety and security change frequently, executive housekeepers need to set aside time to attend classes, schedule training sessions, or study training materials or videos.

## KEEPING STAFF SAFE

The lodging industry, like all industries, poses certain occupational hazards for employees. Attendants face hazards posed by improper use of chemicals or equipment, as well as muscle strains or injuries related to falls. Executive housekeepers have proven that implementing and enforcing proper cleaning and safety procedures can drastically reduce accidents and work-related illness. As with any procedures, the initial training should be clear and thorough. Training should be reinforced regularly during departmental staff meetings and, periodically, by floor supervisors or inspectors. Warning signs, charts on chemical usage, and diagrams that show how to bend or reach should be displayed where they are needed to remind staff of correct procedures. Since safety should be of paramount concern to the hotel's management as well as its staff, any repeated failure to comply with safety procedures should be handled as a disciplinary problem (see Chapter 4). Safety committee meetings can help encourage staff input.

Staff safety covers a broad range of issues in the housekeeping department, from health threats posed by slips and falls to those posed by chemical misuse or disease. The executive housekeeper must develop procedures that address each of these areas of concern. This is an essential part of a **risk management program.** This program basically addresses what could go wrong in the property and attempts to find ways to prevent these things.

Even in the most vigilant housekeeping departments, accidents do occur. Housekeeping managers must set up clear procedures for reporting accidents and on-the-job illness and detailing what will be necessary before the employee returns to regular duties.

## Working Safely with Chemicals

Room attendants, public area attendants, and laundry attendants spend most of their working day in contact with chemical cleaners. Many housekeeping managers have shifted to pre-mixed chemicals that can be dispensed through a hose attachment or other connection directly into the bottles that will be stocked on the room attendants' carts. As a safety precaution, most housekeeping managers now recommend that anyone dispensing chemicals wear gloves and eye protection to prevent contact with skin or any splashback into the eyes. Pre-mixed chemicals offer another advantage. Since they are mixed by the manufacturer according to the manufacturer's own specifications, the dilution is standardized. This reduces the possibility of improper dilution that could result in an overly harsh chemical mix which, in turn, could lead to chemical burns or skin irritations.

All bottles for cleaning and laundry chemicals should be clearly labeled. They also should be color coded so that staff members who are not fluent in English (or the mother tongue of the country) can recognize at a glance for what purpose the product is to be used. For example, glass cleaner may be color coded in blue, toilet cleaner in green, and so on. The same color coding system should be used throughout the property to avoid any confusion if employees are assigned to different areas. Any bottle that contains a potentially hazardous chemical should carry a clearly visible "warning" label and should be color coded in red or some other color that stands out from the usual cleaning supplies.

Most manufacturers will produce **secondary containers** that are color coded and have all information in one or more languages. It is preferable to use bottles on which this information is **silk screened,** not just stamped on the surface. Silk screening is a method of essentially stenciling the letters onto the surface through a fine screen that makes them almost impermeable. Other printing could wash off or wear off, eliminating valuable safety information. Preprinted labels are available. The staff member simply writes in the name of the material, checks off the hazard on a checklist, checks off the appropriate protective equipment, and writes in the name of the manufacturer. A clear plastic cover protects the label.

Cleaning chemicals and laundry agents, even those made with neutral substances, include a list of primary ingredients and any necessary caution or warning information on the bottle or package. Also listed on the packaging may be information on what hazards the contents pose and what should be done if the contents are used improperly, causing illness or injury. Hotels generally buy cleaning chemicals in volume and these must be dispensed into smaller secondary containers, any container that is not the original packaging.

## Posting Safety Sheets

The Occupational Safety and Health Administration (OSHA), the federal agency which creates and enforces safety regulations for the workplace, requires that materials safety data sheets (MSDS) be available at least for each hazardous material.

Most executive housekeepers keep MSDS sheets for every chemical and laundry agent used in the property. These sheets will describe any hazard posed by the product, including dangers presented when mixing it with other substances, and will indicate what course of treatment may be recommended if the product is taken internally, inhaled, or placed in direct contact with skin or eyes. OSHA requires that the MSDS be readily available and easily accessible. The rule of thumb is that it should take no more than four to five minutes to locate sheets for each product. Most executive housekeepers compile an MSDS binder with an index for each chemical or group of chemicals. Some suggest storing this binder in the housekeeping department; others recommend storing it in the security department, particularly if security is called when there is an accident on the job.

## Eco-Sensitive Chemicals

MSDS sheets are required even for "natural" or eco-friendly cleaners. "The executive housekeeper should check the MSDS to determine whether the product contains an eye or skin irritant. For instance, some environmentally friendly chemicals use a citrus-based ingredient. This can be an eye irritant," points out Linda Hunkins, president of Amboy Associates, San Diego, California, a consulting firm that specializes in helping companies with OSHA compliance.

The other problem is that, because products are labeled as environmentally sensitive, some employees feel they no longer have to be careful. "Employees begin trying to mix these chemicals to solve certain cleaning problems. That can sometimes be hazardous," Hunkins says. Some executive housekeepers say that eco-friendly chemicals have reduced the incidence of skin rashes, but caution is still necessary. Hunkins recommends that the same training and precautionary measures used for traditional chemicals be used for environmentally sensitive chemicals as well.

## Handling Bloodborne Pathogens and Biohazards

The increasing incidence of the HIV virus and full-blown AIDS (auto-immune deficiency syndrome) in the general population and the spread of viral strains such as Hepatitis B have broadened the scope of safety procedures for the housekeeping department. The executive housekeeper must set up the proper training and procedures for dealing with these bloodborne pathogens and other biohazards. All departmental employees, especially the supervisors and managers, must be made to understand what is to be done when blood, bodily fluids including vomitus, urine, or feces or other hazards such as needles or syringes are found on property.

## Biohazard Training

The best way to prevent problems in dealing with hazardous materials is to allow only specially trained individuals to deal with them. In larger properties, several members of the security department are trained as a biohazard team which is called in to handle and dispose of hazardous materials. In smaller properties, the assistant executive housekeeper, the executive housekeeper, the head of security, and even the general manager may be trained in biohazard removal and disposal. Regardless of property size, the executive housekeeper should at least be familiar with the proper procedures regarding biohazards. The AH&MA, the IEHA, and many educational/training companies have produced videos and other training information specifically addressing proper procedures for biohazards.

According to Dalia Peña, director of housekeeping at the deluxe 1,620-room Wyndham Anatole Hotel, Dallas, Texas: "We teach staff members about handling bloodborne pathogens as part of their first day of training. We show them a video that describes what to do and what not to do when encountering blood and other bodily fluids." New hires are trained to call the biohazard team which has the training and equipment to remove the blood-stained or fluid-soaked items safely and dispose of them properly. The focus is that this knowledge is essential to on-the-job safety. The executive housekeeper must decide whether attendants will be permitted to handle towels or linens lightly stained or soiled with blood or bodily fluids. If so, all attendants must be issued tight-fitting plastic gloves, such as surgical gloves or, preferably, heavier weight gloves that are not too cumbersome. Even if the hotel does not require that attendants wear gloves at all times (which is advisable), the attendants must wear gloves when dealing with biohazards. All carts, both for room attendants and public area attendants, should be equipped with special red bags to be used only for hazardous material.

Once soiled items have been properly removed, the biohazard bag should be taken to the laundry, not put down the laundry chute. The bag could tear in the chute and contaminate other linen. As stated in Chapter 10, the laundry manager or supervisor should immediately assess any biohazard bags brought to the laundry. The decision must be made as to whether the linen can be sanitized and sterilized or disposed of. Soiled items such as mattresses or carpeting have to be chemically sanitized or, if badly soiled, disposed of—usually by burning.

Many executive housekeepers are leaning toward a policy which forbids attendants from handling any hazardous material. When attendants see any materials or surfaces stained or soiled with what they suspect is blood or bodily fluids, they are instructed to call the housekeeping department. In larger hotels, they may be instructed to call security as well.

Biohazard kits should be available in the housekeeping department and, if applicable, in the security department. They should contain plastic jumpsuits, gloves, head covers, foot covers, and protective eyewear such as goggles, as well as tape which covers any areas where one piece of clothing ends and another begins. Outfitted with this protective gear, the biohazard team will come to the area and remove the items. If the items are not removable, the executive housekeeper and chief engineer must decide whether cleaning or replacing the contaminated items is the correct course of action.

Security should always be called if needles or syringes are found. Attendants should never handle these, even with gloves. The security department should be familiar with local regulations regarding disposable of needles and syringes. In some areas, they are routinely taken to the police station. In others, they may be disposed of at hospitals or other medical facilities. Because of the threat of contamination, needles and syringes should not be disposed of in the regular trash. At the Tokyo Hilton, Tokyo, Japan, executive housekeeper Toyohiko Tashiro points out that even toothbrushes and razors must be disposed of separately and treated as industrial waste. Since these too may contain blood or bodily fluids, they must be handled with gloves. Precautions are necessary even if blood is dried. Many experts suggest risk of HIV contamination ends when the blood or fluid is dried; Hepatitis B, on the other hand, can survive up to seven days. They recommend that, to be on the safe side, executive housekeepers use the seven-day figure for measuring the period of possible contagion.

When training staff to deal with these hazards, information presented in the training sessions should be accurate and objective. The executive housekeeper or trainer should discuss the staff's fears or concerns, and point out how following the correct procedures will prevent the transmittal of disease. However, employees also must be made to understand that following these procedures is mandatory. Certain employees may not want to wear gloves or follow correct procedures because they believe nothing will happen to them. Safety procedures regarding biohazards apply to each employee. Employees should be made to understand that following these procedures is a factor of job performance. Failure to adhere to these procedures will result first in a verbal warning, then a written warning and, ultimately, suspension or dismissal.

## Chemical Hazard Training

All housekeeping staff also should be well trained in how to deal with the chemicals they use each day. Staff should learn about proper use of chemicals and any dangers posed by mixing them with other substances as part of their initial training. As part of standard training, housekeeping employees should be trained to:

- Make sure spray nozzles are aimed away from their faces before spraying

- Hold the bottles a safe distance from their faces to avoid any chemical contact with their eyes and to avoid inhalation of an excessive amount of fumes

- Wear eye protection when squirting toilet cleaner into the toilet bowl, because the splashback from this procedure is a frequent cause of minor eye irritations

- Wear gloves when cleaning toilets, as this reduces rashes from the harsher disinfectants required to clean toilets, and also lessens any possibility of contracting disease or infection

- Clean toilets with a short-handled swab or mop so that the attendants' hands are never in direct contact with the toilet bowl

Attendants should also know which chemicals not to mix. One executive housekeeper recalls an incident in which a laundry attendant mixed bleach with a **rusticant,** also called a rust remover. The mixture exploded, sending several employees to the emergency room with severe injuries. Bleach should not be used in the same area as ammonia. This can create lethal fumes. In most properties, only supervisors or housekeeping managers are permitted to use bleach. Some housekeeping managers are shifting to hydrogen peroxide for certain disinfecting needs because it has no fumes and is less harsh if it comes into contact with skin.

Chemical disposal requires expertise. One or two employees in the housekeeping department and/or maintenance should be specially trained in chemical disposal procedures. Manufacturers provide the necessary information on what type of container should be used for hazardous chemicals and those that could become unstable. The information tells whether the material should be sealed in the container and for how long and in what type of area it should be stored. Some containers, for example, cannot be stored near any vent that permits steam to escape or heat to build up. Most loading docks have areas restricted to hazardous chemicals.

Some fluids, such as certain harsh fluids used in dry cleaning operations, also require special handling because they cannot be drained into the local sewer system. The executive housekeeper must keep a set of local regulations on hand to determine what wastes will require special disposal procedures.

The executive housekeeper can use OSHA regulations, advice from chemical and equipment manufacturers, recommendations from physical therapists, input from staff members, and knowledge gained through experience in what works best to develop a comprehensive and effective health and safety program for the housekeeping staff.

## PREVENTING ACCIDENTS

Keeping employees safe on the job must be a primary concern. OSHA reports contend that only 2 percent of on-the-job accidents are unavoidable because they are caused by natural catastrophes or freak situations (see Table 13.1). This should mean the other 98 percent of accidents are avoidable, at least in theory. Studies also show that 93 percent of accidents could be eliminated by a combination of proper training, adequate supervision, and employee vigilance. Substantiating this conclusion is the finding that an overwhelming 78 percent of all accidents are caused by the individual's failure to note or heed a reasonably obvious indication that an accident is possible. Continuous training and close supervision can help employees avoid on-the-job carelessness and make proper safety and precautionary procedures a regular part of the work routine (see Table 13.1 and Figure 13.1).

## COMPLYING WITH OSHA REGULATIONS

OSHA regulations are the starting point for any health and safety program because compliance with these regulations is mandated by law. Fines range from a few hundred dollars to thousands of dollars, depending on the seriousness of the violation.

Basically, OSHA makes it mandatory for all employers to keep their places of business "free from the hazards that are likely to cause death or serious harm to employees." Inspectors may make legal entry either to conduct a complete examination of the premises or respond to a complaint made by any employee or union. The law specifically forbids giving the employer any advance notice of a scheduled inspection and prohibits the employer from retaliating in any way against the complainant. Conducting periodic OSHA check-ups helps ensure the department will go through any inspection successfully (see Figure 13.2).

## CREATING A HEALTH AND SAFETY PROGRAM

Effective health and safety programs go beyond mere compliance with OSHA regulations. Health and safety programs should be designed to prevent accidents, thereby reducing injuries, absenteeism, and insurance costs. The by-product of these programs is better productivity and improved morale.

Some key points to be covered in a comprehensive health and safety program include:

- Setting up a safety committee with a balance of line employees and executives. Limiting committee membership to six months to a year permits broad involvement and constant input of new ideas. Accident-prone employees who are otherwise good workers may be good candidates for this committee.

- Developing thorough safety training programs for new hires. These should be reviewed regularly to keep them current as chemicals, equipment, and regulations change.

- Creating retraining programs that emphasize simple ways of avoiding accidents. This can be reinforced each week during staff meetings or on a daily basis when assignments are made.

- Eliminating open invitations to accidents such as slippery walks, loose handles, and cracked glass.

- Enforcing the existing safety rules.

- Continually analyzing accidents by person, place, and occasion. If a few workers are responsible for the majority of accidents, they should be retrained and closely supervised after retraining.

- If the same accident keeps happening in the same place, the cause should be identified and corrected.

- Making sure everyone knows what to do in case of an accident.

*TABLE 13.1*

| BASIC ACCIDENT CAUSES | |
|---|---|
| **10%**<br>**PHYSICAL** | **88%**<br>**SUPERVISORY** |
| I    Physical Hazards<br>  a. Mechanical<br>  b. Electrical<br>  c. Steam<br>  d. Chemical | I.    Faulty Instructions<br>  a. None<br>  b. Not enforced<br>  c. Incomplete<br>  d. Erroneous |
| II.    Poor Housekeeping<br>  a. Improperly piled<br>  b. Congestion | II.    Inability of Employee<br>  a. Inexperience<br>  b. Unskilled<br>  c. Ignorant<br>  d. Poor judgment |
| III.    Defective Equipment<br>  a. Machines<br>  b. Tools<br>  c. Equipment | III.    Poor Discipline<br>  a. Disobedience of rules<br>  b. Interference by others<br>  c. Fooling |
| IV.    Unsafe Building Conditions<br>  a. Fire protection<br>  b. Exits<br>  c. Floors<br>  d. Openings | IV.    Unsafe Practice<br>  a. Chance-taking<br>  b. Short cuts<br>  c. Haste |
| V.    Improper Working Conditions<br>  a. Ventilation<br>  b. Sanitation<br>  C. Light | V.    Lack of concentration<br>  a. Attention distracted<br>  b. Inattention |
| VI.    Improper Planning<br>  a. Layout of operations<br>  b. Layout of machinery<br>  c. Unsafe practices | VI.    Mentally Unfit<br>  a. Fatigue<br>  b. Excitable<br>  c. Temper |
| VIII.    Improper Dress<br>  a. No goggles—gloves—masks<br>  b. Unsuitable—long sleeves—high heels | VII.    Physically Unfit<br>  a. Defective<br>  b. Weak<br>  c. Fatigue |

## Operating Equipment Safely

The housekeeping department's health and safety program must also address the problems posed by specific areas such as the laundry. Unlike the room attendants, laundry attendants must work safely with heavy power equipment. Some key aspects of the laundry operation that should be addressed in a health and safety program include:

- Power-marking machines must be equipped with guards to prevent injury to fingers.
- Washing machines and drying tumblers must be equipped with interlocking devices that will prevent the inside cylinder from moving when the outer door on the case or shell is open, and will also prevent the door from being opened while the inside cylinder is in motion. These are referred to as **lock-out, tag-out** precautions. They are essential safeguards that prevent any other employee from accidentally over-riding equipment that has been shut down for repair, safeguards built into the equipment that will prevent hair or limbs from being caught in machinery, and safeguards that will shut off equipment automatically if a limb is trapped.
- Extractors must be equipped with an interlocking device that will prevent the cover from being opened while the basket is in motion. It should

A simple, back-to-basics approach to safety procedures can be very effective in minimizing accidents. Veteran executive housekeepers say that monitoring adherence to simple safety procedures can reduce the number of accidents by half.

1. Attendants should wear the proper protective gear, including gloves and protective eyewear. Inexpensive filter masks can vastly reduce accidents associated with fumes.
2. Attendants should make sure vacuum cords are rolled up when vacuums are not in use. This reduces the danger of tripping over the cord.
3. No employee should run. This presents the dangers of tripping and falling.
4. Wet floor signs should always be used, even if the floor is damp and will dry quickly. Failure to use them endangers both staff and guests.
5. Long hair should be tied back. Generally, no dangling jewelry should be worn. These items can easily be snagged or caught in machinery, thereby posing a hazard.
6. Shoes with nonskid soles should be mandatory safety equipment.
7. Carts, caddies, or baskets—not arms—are the only recommended carrier for supplies.
8. Employees should not place their hands into any area they cannot see, including the area between the seat cushion and the side of the chair, on high shelves, and behind furniture that is near a wall. Items ranging from needles to razor blades and broken glass may fall into crevices. Shattered glass has been found even on high shelves of closets near bathrooms.
9. Two people must be assigned to any task that requires a ladder: one to climb on the ladder, the other to hold the ladder.
10. Glass should never be placed in the trash. It should go in a special container which is impervious to cuts or rips.

**Figure 3.1**  *10 Tips for Preventing Accidents*

also prevent the power operation of the basket while the cover is not fully closed and secured.

- Power wringers must be equipped with a safety bar or other guard across the entire front of the feed or first rolls.
- Steam pipes that are within 7 feet of the floor or working platform, and with which the worker may come into contact, must be insulated, covered with a heat-resistant material, or otherwise properly guarded.
- Each power-driven machine must be provided with a means for disconnecting it from the source of power. Starting and stopping devices for machines must be located so as to be operable from the front. It is important that these safeguards be checked regularly to make sure they are function-

Amboy Associates, of San Diego, California, created the following "15-Minute OSHA Compliance Walk-Through." Though not intended as a substitute for a comprehensive safety audit, it does indicate what an OSHA inspector might look for during an on-site inspection. This addresses only areas covered by OSHA, not hazardous waste, which is regulated by state and/or federal environmental agencies or departments of natural resources. What follows is a sampling of questions an OSHA inspector may ask.

Manager Interview

1. Is there a written Hazard Communication Plan (HAZCOMM)? Employers are required to have a written plan that describes how the training, labeling, MSDS management, and other requirements of "Right to Know" will be met. Linda Hunkins, president of Amboy Associates, a consultant and publisher of information products on OSHA compliance, says failure to have a written HAZCOMM was the leading cause of violations and fines for the fiscal year that ended September 1995. Some critical issues that must be covered in the HAZCOMM Plan include:
   - Where the written HazComm Plan will be kept
   - Who ensures that the written inventory of hazardous materials is current and accessible to all employees?
   - Who collects MSDS sheets for all hazardous materials, (which would include nearly all cleaning and laundry chemicals) and where this collection will be kept.
   - What labels are used on all secondary containers and who puts them on.
2. Has the employer certified its Hazard Assessment of Personal Protective Equipment (PPE) Needs? Employers must conduct a hazard assessment and certify it has been done.
3. Is there a formal disciplinary policy relating to safety?
4. Are there written training records? These records must document the date, subject, attendees and trainer. Training records for handling bloodborne pathogens must be even more detailed. They should include the qualifications of the trainer and a very detailed discussion of what was covered, advises Hunkins. A training sign-sheet is also a helpful piece of documentation.
5. Do any employees wear respirators, including dust masks? If so, there must be written procedures covering use, fit testing, cleaning, and maintenance of respirators and masks. Employers must also test the fit of each respirator and train employees on how to use and check them.
6. Did staff size exceed 10 employees at any time during the past year? If yes, there must be a **written** Emergency Action Plan. Also, employers with more than 10 employees must maintain the OSHA Form 200, an occupational illness and injury report. This form must be posted each February 1 for 30 days.

**Figure 13.2**  *The 15-Minute OSHA Compliance Walk-Through (Courtesy of Amboy Associates, San Diego, California)*

7. Can it be anticipated reasonably that any employees will be exposed to human blood this year? Has any employee been assigned responsibility for first aid. If "yes" to either of these questions the property must have a written bloodborne pathogen exposure control plan. Hepatitis B vaccinations must be offered and employees must be trained in protective equipment use and procedures.

**Figure 13.2** (continued)

ing properly. Also, safety precautions should be posted in visible areas near the equipment.

## PREVENTING INJURIES

The physical demands of professional housekeeping can place a great deal of stress on the body, particularly the back. Back injuries account for many lost days of work.

Even with high quotas and downsized staffs, housekeeping departments can instruct all employees in how tasks should be done correctly to prevent strains and other injuries. Tasks such as flipping mattresses must be done by two people, not one. Rather than straining to reach areas such as the fluorescent light over the bathroom sink, or actually climbing up on the sink, attendants can use a clean johnny mop sprayed with glass cleaner or all-purpose cleaner. This johnny mop should be set aside for this purpose only and never used in the toilet.

Proper equipment such as high dusters, long-handled dusters specifically designed to reach high places, should be provided to public area attendants. If strains and back injuries are becoming significant problems, the executive housekeeper may choose to call in expert help, such as a local physical therapist, to work with the department in developing safer methods for accomplishing the tasks necessary in cleaning (see Tales of the Trade 13.1).

### Tales of the Trade 13.1
### A Small Hotel with Big Ideas on Safety and Security

Like most hotels, the 60-room, upscale St. James Hotel in Red Wing, Minnesota does not have major problems related to health and safety or security. Executive housekeeper Lois Theis has developed innovative, cost-effective programs aimed at prevention to keep it this way.

She conducts regularly safety meetings with her own staff to discuss the causes of on-the-job accidents. Working with them, she developed a list of check points aimed at preventing certain types of accidents and injuries. This list was also filed with the hotel's safety director.

As in many housekeeping departments, minor back injuries were a common complaint. Theis asked a physical therapist to come to the hotel and to develop better procedures for tasks that strain the back. Flipping mattresses was a particular problem. The therapist positioned two attendants on one side of the queen-sized mattress. Working together they pull the mattress to the edge of the bed, then stand it on end. One attendant supports the mattress while the other moves to the opposite side of the bed. When in position, the attendant on the far side gives the okay to lower the mattress slowly and they work together to lower and position it.

Vacuuming was also a literal pain in the back. The therapist pointed out that attendants were stretching too far and standing incorrectly. The correct practice is to have feet pointed in the same direction as the vacuum and follow the vacuum closely, rather than pushing it far out from the body. Theis says both recommendations have reduced back strains. To prevent other muscle strains, the department does the series of stretches illustrated in Figure 13.3 each morning and again after lunch. "We all eat together so this has become part of our routine. It takes only 5 to 10 minutes. I won't accept any excuse for not doing it," says Theis, who has worked at the historic hotel for 17 years. Potential accident sources are clearly outlined in employee training information.

## ESTABLISHING PROCEDURES FOR HANDLING ACCIDENTS AND ILLNESS

Even the most vigilant housekeeping operation does experience accidents. Every employee in the housekeeping department must know exactly what to do when an accident happens.

As soon as the accident occurs, the employee must call the supervisor or the housekeeping department to report it. All accidents, even minor cuts, scrapes, or abrasions, must be reported and documented. In some larger properties, the em-

**HOUSEKEEPING**

Do these at home and during work.
All movements are done slowly and released slowly.

1) Tuck chin
   Keep shoulders down.
   Slowly turn head to left, then to right.
   Look straight ahead.
   Tip each ear to shoulder
   Repeat 3 times each direction.

2) Stand.
   Place hands on low back.
   Arch back over your hands.
   Slowly return to upright.
   Repeat 5 times.

3) Place right hand on left shoulder.
   Right elbow stays neck high.
   Keep right shoulder down.
   Push right elbow closer to left shoulder.
   Hold position where shoulder
      stretches, 1 minute.

4) Tuck chin.
   Clasp fingers behind head.
   Move elbows backward.
   Stretch chest muscles.
   Hold 1 minute.

5) Stand with back against wall.
   Tuck chin.
   Flatten low back toward wall
      (roll top of pelvis backward).
   Hold 5 counts.
   Relax, repeat 5 times.

6) Place straight arm behind you with palm up.
   Place on a waist high surface.
   Hold position 1 minute.
   Repeat with opposite arm.

7) Cock wrist back.
   Spread fingers apart.
   Keep elbows straight.
   Place open palms on wall or tabletop.
   In no stretch, slowly lean straight
      elbow toward fingertips.
   Hold when hand/forearm stretch, 1 minute.

© Physical Therapy of Red Wing

*Figure 13.3* *Knowledge of correct procedures can reduce risk of injury.*

ployee calls security, which is responsible for all first aid. In case of severe injury or loss of consciousness, any staff member who finds the injured worker enters an emergency code on the nearest in-house hotel phone which registers at the front desk. If the hotel has certified paramedics on staff or employees with certified first aid or **cardiopulmonary resuscitation** (CPR) training (if appropriate), those employees will be sent directly to aid the injured worker until an ambulance arrives.

Treatment will depend on the type and severity of the injury. First aid kits should be stored in the floor linen rooms and regularly checked to make sure they have the correct supplies, including a full allotment of bandages and a disinfecting agent for cuts and abrasions. **Eyewash stations,** equipment that flushes the eye, usually are set up in the laundry if the property has one. If there is no on-premise laundry, eyewash stations are located in the linen room or some area with a sink. Protective eyewear should prevent most injuries to or irritation of the eye. However, since employees sometimes forget such safety regulations or are inconsistent in adhering to them, eye injuries can happen. All employees should be thoroughly trained in the use of eyewash stations.

To comply with OSHA regulations, medical and/or first aid facilities must be no more than 10 to 15 minutes from the property or the property must have someone trained in first aid on the premises. Some hotels have a doctor on call to deal with both staff and guest illness or injury. Staff should be updated regularly as to who to notify in case of medical emergency. Emergency numbers should be displayed in the housekeeping department office, the laundry and the linen room.

## Proper Reporting Techniques

Most accident reports are made directly to the supervisor. It is then the supervisor's job, or that of anyone who took the report, to file the proper paperwork. The accident report should list the name of the employee, the date and time of the accident, the location where the accident happened, a brief description of what happened, and the resulting injury. The documentation also should state briefly what treatment was offered or actually administered. Two copies of the accident report should be filed: one in the housekeeping department or the security department, whichever has responsibility for tracking accident reports, and a second in the employee's file in the human resources department.

If the employee had to consult a physician, the physician's report should be attached to the accident reports and placed in the departmental and personnel files. In some cases, the employee may be treated, released, and able to return to work the following day. In cases involving longer recuperation, the employee must be re-examined and given a written approval by the physician to return to work. These reports, too, should be placed in the files. To prevent any recurrence of the illness or injury, and to prevent any legal problems, the executive housekeeper may not persuade or pressure the employee to return to work before the employee is re-examined and declared fit for work by the physician.

On-the-job illness, such as the onset of a minor cold or flu, may merit early dismissal or a lowered quota or fewer assignments but is not reported. However, if an employee feels suddenly dizzy, headachy, or nauseous, the incident should be reported. These symptoms may stem from a chemical hazard or gas leak and should be investigated further. If either is suspected, the employee should be seen by a physician.

## Light Duty

**Workmen's compensation,** the money paid to workers injured on the job during the period when they are not able to work, is a costly business for any lodging operation. In some situations, it is the only option open to both parties because of the severity of the injury. In these cases, workmen's compensation may provide much-needed income to a valued employee and help insure the employee will have a regular income until he or she can return to work. However, in less serious cases, the executive housekeeper may have a less costly alternative. **Light duty,** tasks which are not physically demanding, can serve as a cost-effective bridge between regular assignments and workmen's compensation. Typical light-duty work would include answering the department phone, doing filing or, if the person is computer-literate, entering nonconfidential data on the computer. If the housekeeping department has no extra light-duty work, the employee may be assigned to light duty in another department. Light duty may also be used if an employee has a cold or minor flu. Though few employees could clean at top efficiency when not feeling well, they may be able to do some light clerical work. This prevents an unnecessary call-off for that day and keeps the employee productive.

## FIRE PREVENTION

Statistics show that a hotel fire breaks out once every 34 hours somewhere in the world. Most are small fires that are easily controlled. The general underlying causes of these fires are difficult to ascertain, and a number of imponderables have to be taken into consideration. Among these are the guests' unfamiliarity with their surroundings, high personnel turnover, negligence, and indifference. The large proportion of fires caused by the guests is most striking: experts estimate more than 40.7 percent are attributable to cigarettes!

Despite the variety of causes, the housekeeping department can work with other departments to reduce the risk of fire and plan for what to do in case of fire to minimize injury and loss of life.

## The Housekeeping Department's Role in Fire Prevention

The housekeeping department plays a major role in preventing fire. Cleanliness is fire's natural enemy since it provides nothing for the fire to feed on. Storage areas should be kept free of clutter. Also, there should be minimal use of combustibles. Any combustibles, such as oily rags, should be stored in proper containers away from heat. Equipment should be regularly checked and maintained. For example, a frayed electrical cord could lead to sparking that results in a fire. Room attendants should be trained to check that in-room irons are turned off and allowed to cool down before storing them.

Equipment checks should be made daily. At least once a month, the head of the housekeeping department should request that all personnel search for, note, and report any observed violations of the property's fire safety program. Areas to check include:

- Smoke alarms and overhead sprinklers (both of which often repay their cost in lower insurance premiums), must be checked regularly to make sure they are in proper working order.

- Electrical lines. Worn or frayed cords should be replaced immediately, as should worn plugs. Overly long lamp cords should be avoided, and any broken switchplates should be repaired or replaced. Electrical outlets should be checked to ensure they are not overloaded.

- Ducts for heating, air conditioning, and ventilation, especially the exhaust ducts over kitchen ranges, which should be cleaned thoroughly and inspected regularly. If these ducts contain the type of dampers that close automatically when their sensors detect fire, the dampers should be checked regularly to make sure they are working.

- Smoking regulations in areas where smoking could cause a hazard should be strictly enforced.

- Trash collection areas, which should be cleaned regularly.

- Fire retardant coatings, which can be removed through frequent cleaning. The coating must be renewed regularly on some surfaces. Fire-retardant coatings should be added to all surfaces possible, including plastic plants.

- Noncombustible items, including metal wastebaskets, nonflammable blankets and spreads, fire-retardant mattress covers, and fire-retardant draperies.
- Waste accumulation in the bottoms of stairwells and elevator shafts is a common cause of fire. These areas should be cleaned regularly.
- Portable fire extinguishers should be inspected monthly and recharged regularly.

In addition to these daily checks, the executive housekeeper should train staff to be familiar with OSHA's fire protection checklist and immediately report anything that fails to comply. Room attendants should check that both information on what to do in case of fire (see Figure 13.4), along with a clear diagram are posted in every guest room.

## Fire Disaster Plans

Every employee should know what to do in case of fire. This should be spelled out clearly in the employee handbook and instructions should be posted in various locations throughout the hotel. It also should be written down as part of the property's **Emergency Action Plan,** a plan which outlines exactly what to do, where to go, and whom to notify if an emergency arises.

The executive housekeeper may also participate in writing an **emergency response plan.** This requires extra training, but would detail what action the employee could take to control the fire or emergency. This could include which equipment to shut down, how to use a fire extinguisher, and even which doors to open or close.

To ensure orderly evacuation in case of fire, regular fire drills are mandatory and give properties a chance to assess their **fire disaster plans,** plans which outline which procedures to follow in case of fire, how employees should exit the building, and where each department should reassemble. Whether in a drill or a fire, housekeeping supervisors managers must bring along the daily sign-in sheet. The executive housekeeper should take a head count when departmental employees are reassembled outside of the property to make sure all employees are accounted for.

"It is important to train employees to *respond* rather than react," says Dalia Peña, director of housekeeping services for the Wyndham Anatole,

**Figure 13.4** *This straightforward red-and-white card is placed by room attendant on top of the stationery folder at the Four Seasons in Boston so that guests will know exactly what to do in case of fire.*

Dallas, Texas. The important factor is not to panic or cause anyone else to panic. The proper steps are:

1. The staff member who spots the fire pulls the alarm or reports the fire
2. Room attendants place their carts in a guest room, if possible, and close the door; carts should not be left in corridors because they can be potentially dangerous obstructions to people trying to leave the building.
3. Laundry attendants should be trained to shut down machinery.
4. Employees go to the nearest fire exit and try to help guests.

These procedures are to be followed *only* if they can be carried out without risk to the employee.

***TABLE 13.2***  *Housekeeping Hazard List*

| Potential hazard | Safety instructions |
| --- | --- |
| Exposure to chemical solvents | Material data sheets posted for employee review.<br>All chemicals used are clearly marked.<br>Protective gear used per manufacturer's instructions.<br>Aware of first aid techniques indicated for chemicals used.<br>Changes in skin condition reported immediately to supervisor. |
| Muscle injury | Use proper lifting techniques.<br>Get help if load is too heavy.<br>Two people will assist in turning mattresses. |
| Stumbling/Tripping/Slipping | Keep passageway clear of obstacles.<br>Put out warning sign while vacuuming first floor.<br>Wipe up all wet spots immediately.<br>While cleaning bathtubs, put a hand on opposite side. |
| Vacuum shock | Do not vacuum a wet carpet.<br>Unplug vacuum before working on it. |
| Broken glass—cuts | Sweep up large pieces, do not pick up with hands. Vacuum up tiny pieces.<br>Place glass in container in storage room. |
| Infectious waste/linen bags | Large red bag for bloody linen or any linen with body fluid or waste. |
| Needle control | Put needles in sharp container. Use gloves and much caution. |

*Source:* Eureka, Inn, Eureka, California.

"The first priority in an emergency action plan is to prevent the loss of human life," says Linda Hunkins, of Amboy Associates.

## KEEPING GUESTS SAFE

The housekeeping department's safety plan should address the issue of guest safety as well as employee safety. Any on-premise guest accident has rippling repercussions: the immediate pain suffered by the guest; the negative word-of-mouth publicity the guest could disseminate about the incident; and, possibly, a lawsuit. Preventive action to avoid guest accidents or injuries usually takes only a little time and a small investment. Failure to institute these procedures, should an accident or injury occur, can impact business for months or even years to come.

### Reducing Risks in the Guest Rooms and Public Spaces

One of the most frequent complaints on guest comment cards regards slips and falls in the guestroom bathtub. As in homes, the property's guestroom bathroom is one of the key danger spots. The wet, slippery surfaces pose a constant threat.

Manufacturers of bathtubs have worked to improve the nonslip finish on tubs. Most tubs are manufactured with a slip-resistant surface, comprising small, inconspicuous circles or rectangles. However, abrasive chemicals must not be used on these tubs because it can remove the finish.

If the manufacturer's original slip-resistant finish does wear off, an acid-etching product can be applied to reduce slipperiness. Though not expensive, the process lasts only about two years and can be done only twice before the surface begins to show through. Another option is to install a new bathtub liner with a slip-resistant surface. This has become common practice in the lodging industry and, though priced at several hundred dollars per bathtub, is less expensive than removing and replacing all bathtubs in the property.

These slip-resistant finishes are preferable to rubber mats or strips of slip-resistant material that can be attached to the tub bottom with adhesive. Mats must be cleaned daily to avoid the buildup of bacteria. The stick-down strips must be removed and cleaned daily, as well. Shower stalls also should feature a slip-resistant bottom.

Grab bars should be installed in tubs and showers, as well as in the stalls of public rest rooms, employee showers, and showers in pool and spa areas. A vertical grab bar on the right side of the front end of the tub allows a bather to raise himself or herself more easily and avoid slipping. Guest rooms designed specifically for those with physical disabilities will require a series of grab bars. Provisions of the Americans with Disabilities Act (ADA) must be complied with in all new build properties.

Floors can pose another threat of falling. Ceramic tiles can be evaluated in terms of their slip resistance. The American Society for Treating Materials keeps a list of the manufacturers whose products have been tested and comply with the standard set for slip resistance. Marble floors frequently must be treated with a coating or a polish with a slip-resistant rating. Some risk management experts recommend measuring friction on polished marble surfaces before treating them to determine the proper coating. Special machines are available for this purpose. Positioning "wet floor" signs wherever areas have been cleaned and remain even slightly damp is essential to protecting guests from slips and falls and reducing the property's liability. Hairdryers must be **hard-wired,** using a plug or connector that cannot be pulled out. This prevents the hairdryer from falling into the tub or the sink. Most experts also recommend using metal waste baskets or the new generation of flame-resistant plastic to reduce the risk of a fire starting in and spreading from the waste basket.

Pool areas should be slip resistant. Whirlpools, whether in rooms or in the spa area, should have specially designed grates that keep long hair from getting caught and pulling the person under the water.

## LOSS PREVENTION

The executive housekeeper should work with the security department to devise a loss prevention program for the housekeeping department. Loss prevention also figures into the overall risk management plan. This program must cover two areas: loss of guests' belongings and loss of hotel property. Although elimination of guest pilferage of small items is an ultimate goal, it is virtually an unattainable one. It is difficult to prevent guests who want souvenirs from taking home a washcloth or pen. The aim of a loss prevention program is to control loss and prevent it from becoming a costly problem in terms of inventory, supply, guest relations, and insurance.

## Preventing Theft of Guests' Belongings

Safeguarding guests' belongings is crucial to a loss prevention plan. All housekeeping employees must be made to understand, from their first day on the job, that if they remove any of the guests' belongings from a room and, if it is proven, the theft will result in immediate dismissal.

Policies regarding theft of guests' belongings should be clearly stated in the employee handbook and reinforced during staff meetings. Although a variety of in-room information and even posted signs urge guests to place jewelry, money, and other valuables in the in-room safe or hotel safe, many find this inconvenient. Instead, they may leave these items in plain view.

Executive housekeepers offer several options. If the hotel has a large security staff and the items left in the room are worth a substantial amount of money, the attendant may be instructed to call a supervisor and contact security. A security guard would then be assigned to guard the room while the attendant is cleaning. The in-room safe should be cleaned only after check-out. Attendants should call security if any valuables are left after checkout. These should be placed in the lost and found.

## Installing Computerized Locks

New computerized door locks play an important role in heightening security. Instead of inserting a metal key in the lock, guests or staff members insert a plastic card in which the code is embedded. The computerized locking system scans the code and if the code is recognized, opens the lock. This system keeps a log of which codes were used to the enter the room. The security department or housekeeping department can track how many people have been in the room and at exactly what times. Printouts are available with entries that can cover several weeks or more.

The fact that housekeeping management and the security department can easily find out who entered each guest room and when it was entered serves as a deterrent to theft. More often than not, executive housekeepers say this system is beneficial in protecting room attendants from unsubstantiated accusations of theft. Frequently, guests simply misplace objects. When they cannot find the missing item, they may incorrectly accuse housekeeping staff. However, if the complaint is registered at 10 A.M., and the log shows no hotel employee has entered the room since 1 P.M. the previous day, it may be a good indication the guest has misplaced it. Rather than confronting the guest, the usual practice is to contact security and report the missing item. The executive housekeeper, assistant housekeeper, or a supervisor may then search the room along with the guard.

Since the logs from the locking system may be examined if a suspected theft is reported, it is essential that housekeeping employees do not allow any other staff member or guest to use their keys. Use of computerized locking systems also means there is no need to give room attendants or house attendants a master key. Usually, only the executive housekeeper, the department head for engineering and/or maintenance, the general manager, and perhaps the rooms division manager will be issued master keys. Master keys should not be used by any other staff member, except in an emergency. This should be noted in writing on the log as soon as possible after the emergency is handled.

## Key Controls

Even with a computerized locking system, attendants should sign keys out and in at the beginning and end of their shift, as discussed in Chapter 5. This system helps deter theft. The computerized codes are changed at the end of each shift so no employee can enter a room after the shift to steal anything.

As a matter of personal safety and security, room attendants should never allow anyone to enter a guest room without first ascertaining that the person has actually rented that room. If someone claims to have rented the room and forgotten the key and asks the attendant to let him or her in while the room is being cleaned, the attendant should politely ask the person's name and explain that the front desk must be contacted to verify that the person has rented that room before the person can enter the room. The attendant should then call the front desk, give the name, and await confirmation. If the individual becomes overly persistent or abusive, the attendant should immediately call security or dial the **emergency code** which registers at the front desk. This not only deters thieves, but also helps protect room attendants from personal attack. An employee should never clean a room while the guest is in it. Training should include information on staff safety and security (see Tricks of the Trade 13.1).

### Tricks of the Trade 13.1

**The Problem:** Is it safer to have the door open or closed during room cleaning?

**The Solution:** Either approach can enhance staff safety, as long as it is supported by proper training. Robin Diaz, executive housekeeper for the 266-room Mohonk Mountain House in New Paltz, New York, uses an open door policy for cleaning guest rooms in this historic resort. "We train the room attendants to block the doorway with the cart while cleaning the room. Having the door open helps protect the room attendant from accusations of theft and also from the threat of personal attack." On a day-to-day basis, the open door policy makes the room attendants feel less isolated, Diaz says.

Ed Conaway, executive housekeeper for Grand Heritage's 280-room U.S. Grant Hotel, strictly enforces a closed door cleaning policy for room attendants. "Our room attendants frequently are on the floor by themselves. I require that the door be closed during cleaning so that no one can sneak into the room. Sometimes when I'm on the floors and see an open door, I'll walk up and tap the attendant on the shoulder. That demonstrates clearly how easy it is for someone to move a cart slightly and quietly enter the room while the attendant is cleaning. That usually makes the point and I rarely have to remind anyone again. Our policy is clear: if the room attendant feels unsafe or uncomfortable because someone is lurking in the area, the attendant should leave the area immediately and report it," says Conaway.

Another deterrent is the package pass, a special pass which allows the employee to leave the property with a package after the contents are inspected by security (see Figure 13.5). The package pass cannot stop all theft, because employees may sneak out doors other than the employee exit. However, the pass program does make it more difficult for theft or pilferage to become widespread.

## Lost and Found

Any item, including cash, that remains in the guest room or is found in any other area of the hotel, and is obviously not a tip, is still the property of the guest. Proper lost and found procedures will prevent many wrongful accusations and curb guest complaints about possible theft (see Figure 13.6.)

**PROPERTY REMOVAL AUTHORIZATION**

Date_____

Please permit _____
*Employee's Name*

Employed in _____Dept.

to take with *Her* ☐ _____Package(s) containing_____
*Him* ☐ *Number*

_____

Which has been inspected and O.K.'d by: _____
*Dept. Head*

Time out _____ ☐ A.M. _____
☐ P.M. TIMEKEEPER or SECURITY OFFICER
LV 1857

**Figure 13.5** *Package pass severely limits the possibility of employee theft.*

After check-out, the attendant and supervisor should carefully check the guest room or suite for anything the guest may have left behind. Security should be called if the items are extremely valuable or illegal. In all other cases, the items are turned over to the supervisor or, in small properties, to the executive housekeeper or general manager.

These items are tagged with the name of the person who found them. It they were found in a guest room, the room number, date found, and name and address of the guest will be noted. The employee should be given a receipt for the item. Security or housekeeping will call the guest and ask him or her to identify the item. If the person identifies it correctly, the item is mailed back at the hotel's expense. Items not claimed within 60 to 90 days may be given to the employee who found them or donated to a charitable organization in the employee's name.

## Procedures for Suspected Employee Theft

An executive housekeeper would be miraculously fortunate to complete his or her career without having an employee accused of theft. As a manager, the executive housekeeper must develop clear, consistent policies for handling this very real personnel problem.

Unless the employee is caught in the act of stealing *and* there is a witness present who will corroborate what has happened, the suspected theft

**BALLY'S**
LAS VEGAS
**LOST AND FOUND REPORT** N⁰ 61572

DATE FOUND:_____ DATE TURNED IN:_____

LOST OR FOUND ARTICLE:_____

ROOM NUMBER:_____ LOCATION:_____

CHECK-OUT DATE:_____

| | NAME | BADGE # |
|---|---|---|
FOUND BY:_____ _____
TURNED IN BY:_____ _____
RECEIVED BY:_____ _____
RECEIVING OFFICER:_____ TIME:_____ DATE:_____
MAILING INSTRUCTIONS:_____
NAME:_____
ADDRESS:_____
CITY:_____ STATE:_____ ZIP:_____
SPECIAL INSTRUCTIONS:_____
REV 3/97 LV 977

**Figure 13.6** *Room attendants should receive verbal and written instructions on what to do with lost-and-found items to prevent problems with suspected theft.*

must be reported to security immediately. Security will make a report on what was stolen, on what date and approximately at what time, who reported the theft, and any other pertinent data. Since the employee must be considered innocent until proven guilty, he or she must continue working while security investigates the complaint (see Tales of the Trade 13.2).

If the item or amount stolen is extremely valuable or if there is any indication that illegal drugs were involved, the security department will call in the police. The outcome of the investigation will determine the next step. Should charges be brought and the employee found guilty in court, the employee can dismissed with cause.

---

**Tales of the Trade 13.2**
**To Catch a Thief**

An attendant who specialized in turndown service became notorious among executive housekeepers at one city's upscale hotels. The attendant's work was generally good, and the attendant's attendance was generally reliable. So, when guests complained that $10 to $20 was missing from various rooms on various nights, the executive housekeeper did not initially suspect the hardworking attendant. A further investigation by security showed all losses were reported from rooms this attendant had turned down. However, nothing was proven and the amounts were so small no investigative effort was undertaken.

Only by networking did the executive housekeeper determine how extensive this attendant's history of petty theft was. "The problem is that, since the amounts were small and we were never able to prove anything, this person's name was never logged into the police records. We should have contacted the attendant's previous employers before hiring this person," notes one executive housekeeper. Since there was no proof, the employee could not be fired. However, the executive housekeeper did lay off this person during staff cutbacks.

Firing an employee because of a suspicion is illegal. In situations such as this, the executive housekeeper can shift the employee to public space duties or eliminate the position through downsizing. Careful hiring practices, which may include testing (as discussed in Chapter 3) or other checks, may prevent more serious problems.

---

Gaming has brought substantial income to Nevada, but it also has generated exacting regulations. All prospective housekeeping employees at Bally's in Las Vegas must obtain a sheriffs card before starting work, notes Kay Weirick, director of housekeeping services for Bally's. Each person who applies for a sheriff's card, whether he or she will work in a gaming area or another area of the hotel, is fingerprinted at the sheriff's office. These fingerprints are cross-checked by police to determine whether the person is a convicted felon. "This really helps us in hiring, for any number of reasons," says Weirick.

All prospective employees must interview first with the union, then with personnel. The housekeeping department conducts a third interview. A drug test is also required before being hired. "The drug test not only shows whether the person has used illegal drugs but also may show whether the person is taking certain types of medication that may require us to provide a certain type of emergency help if something happens on the job," notes Weirick. The results of drug testing may be beneficial for many properties. For example, a condition such as diabetes would not prevent the person from being hired. However, some applicants may be unwilling to say they are diabetics for fear they will not be hired. Knowing that a person is taking prescribed medication is important in health and safety programs, and may be necessary to save the person's life if an emergency arises.

## SAFEGUARDING THE HOTEL'S INVESTMENT

The executive housekeeper also must work to prevent loss and damage to the hotel's property and departmental inventory in order to control bottom-line costs. Locks and inventory tracking are basic but effective methods of loss prevention.

### Providing Locks and Limited Access

Loss prevention starts with locking up as much equipment and supplies as possible. Keys should be issued only to those who absolutely must have access.

Linen and supply closets should be locked at all times. Only the floor supervisor and housekeeping managers should have keys. As stated in Chapter 11, linen inventory can be monitored and controlled to help prevent loss. Larger hotels with purpose-built linen rooms usually lock the room it-self, but also have locks on supply cabinets. Only supervisors and top management have keys. One innovative inventory system provides extra supplies for each room in a locked bin. When keys are is-sued to the attendants, they also receive keys for the storage bins. Anything that is removed is easy to track.

Employees should be made to understand that pilferage of such items, whether by staff members or guests, erodes the bottom line of the property and may affect profitability levels needed to cover raises and incentive programs. Amenities also should be given in limited amounts. Each atten-dant should receive only a small number of extra bottles of shampoo, conditioner, moisturizer, bars of soap. Attractive amenities such as fine soaps or specially formulated shampoos should not be placed on the top of room attendants' carts where guests or anyone else in the corridors can easily pilfer them.

Employees should be trained to use only the employee entrances and exits. Another deterrent is the package pass, which is a special pass that al-lows the employees to leave the property with a package after the contents are inspected by secu-rity. The package pass cannot stop all theft, because employees may sneak out of doors other than the employee exit. However, the pass program does make it more difficult for theft or pilferage to be-come widespread. Package passes should be re-quired for any employee leaving the building.

All employees must clock in and out, and no employee should be able to **swipe,** that is, draw a plastic, encoded card through a computerized de-coder slot, use a time card for another employee, or punch another employee's own card in a stan-dard time clock. If an employee does not clock out, the supervisor should bring it to the employee's at-tention the following day and note that this is a violation of policy. Anyone who sees an employee leaving the property through any door except the employee entrance/exit should redirect the em-ployee to the proper exit. If the employee ignores the direction, the action should be brought to the attention of the executive housekeeper and dis-cussed with the employee.

## PREVENTING THEFT AND DAMAGE OF GUEST BELONGINGS

Most executive housekeepers find it is much more difficult to limit pilferage by guests than by em-ployees. A certain amount of loss is factored in

when calculating inventories for supplies such as wash cloths and amenities.

### Limiting Theft of Guest Belongings

Pens, sewing kits, even small linens may be ex-pected and acceptable categories of guest pilferage. The executive housekeeper's goal will be to prevent or at least control theft of more major items. There are measures the executive housekeeper can take to limit guest theft:

- Hard wire televisions and video cassette record-ers into the outlet, rather than just using a plug.
- Patrick Shea, general manager of the 80-room Econolodge, Minneapolis, Minnesota, says his property is experimenting with a warning state-ment on remote controls that indicates the use of the remote control could damage any television other than the one in the hotel. The goal is to reduce theft of remote controls from guest rooms.
- Limit the number of entrances as much as pos-sible, and lock all but a main entrance at night. This is harder in motels in which each room opens directly to the outside.
- Install dead-bolt locks on guestroom doors. They are harder for thieves to open.
- Use good quality but plain linens and towels. They may be less attractive "souvenirs" than those with beautiful monograms or custom colors.

One newly transferred general manager was shocked to see his hotel's plush, monogrammed towels displayed in the bathroom of a house a real-tor was showing him. Pilferage of the towels cost the homeowner the sale of his house. Executive housekeepers also report higher theft rates for ex-pensive feather pillows.

- Track losses. One executive housekeeper in an upscale convention hotel noted pilferage rates were high after certain groups checked out. These groups represented valuable business for the ho-tel. Now, before these groups check in for their annual functions, housekeeping staff removes and stores knick-knacks and items that are ex-pensive to replace, leaving only the most basic supplies in the rooms.
- Bolt down lamps and clock radios. Theft-proof devices should be used for artwork, while other items such as small sculpture can be glued down, even in specialty suites.

To discourage guests from packing up the plush bathrobes used as amenities, the deluxe Loews

Ventana Canyon resort near Tucson, Arizona, places a simple note in each guest room stating that the robes are provided for the guest's use while on property and that such robes are available for sale in the hotel's gift shop.

The executive housekeeper should work with the security department to develop an overall security plan to prevent pilferage. As part of this plan, identification is required for all employees. Also, no one should be able to take an item out of the building, supposedly for repair, without proper paper work which is signed and authorized.

## Limiting Damage to Guest Belongings

The executive housekeeper's provisions regarding damage to guest belongings should focus more on minimizing loss than prevention. No plan can prevent clients in a hospitality suite from spilling drinks or food on the carpet or keep an enraged guest from punching a hole in the wall or throwing a lamp through a window. These are unfortunate realities for many executive housekeepers who must then deal with the aftermath.

*Hospitality suites.* When there is extensive damage to a hospitality suite, it should be evaluated by the executive housekeeper, the head of maintenance, and the sales manager. The general manager also may be involved. The general manager and sales manager will have to weigh whether to ask the client to pay for the damages and risk losing that client's business, or writing it off. If the damages requires carpeting or expensive furnishings to be replaced, the hotel's management usually asks the client to pay for replacement.

Hospitality suites booked for special events, particularly sporting events such as football games or festive occasions such as New Year's Eve, often sustain heavy stains and sometimes minor damage such as broken lamps. Design elements used only for decoration should be removed and stored. Extra attendants should be scheduled to do the cleanup. Food and beverage stewards assigned to work the suite should be trained to report any major spills to housekeeping immediately. Prompt cleaning may prevent soiling that would lead to the need for deep cleaning or replacement.

*Fires.* Guest smoking is a major cause of fires. Despite concerted efforts to prevent this kind of damage, fires begun by careless smoking continue to damage hotels and result in loss of life. In the case of small fires, burned or charred items should be removed and repaired or replaced. Any items damaged by smoke should be cleaned if possible or replaced. Since the sprinkler system will have been triggered, the carpet will be very wet and extractors will be required. **Ionizers,** which remove smoke odors, should be set up to remove any lingering smoke odor. More serious fires usually leave the room a total loss and everything will have to be replaced.

*Accidental damage.* Small incidents of damage ranging from the lingering odor of smoking in a no smoking room to small burns, ink stains on fabric, or small tears are routine challenges for the housekeeping department. Guests are rarely held liable for this kind of damage, although some hotels now will add a $100 "charge" for smoking in a non-smoking room. This loss must be factored into the housekeeping budget (see Chapter 9). Historical records of loss and repair costs will provide a guideline.

## Disaster Plans

Although the security department writes the disaster plan, which outlines where to go in the hotel in case of natural disasters such as hurricanes or earthquakes and what to do in cases ranging from these disasters to bombings, often with the help of a consultant, the housekeeping department must develop a contingency plan for dealing with the aftermath.

All employees must know where to go in such cases. Supervisors and managers must take a head count as soon as possible. The executive housekeeper should devise cleanup plans that may have to be carried out without power and water, and with very little staff The goal, as in all cases, will be to protect human life, then to control damage. In areas where flooding, hurricanes, or wind damage are frequent, the executive housekeeper may research companies that specialize in boarding up windows and disaster cleanup to determine who should be called if needed (see Tales of the Trade l3.3).

---

**Tales of the Trade 13.3**
**Dealing with Natural Disasters**

Both Rita Genslé, executive housekeeper of the Inter-Continental Miami, Florida, and Nancy Gibel, executive housekeeper of the Clarion Hotel and Comfort Inn & Suites, Miami Springs, Florida, have been at their posts during hurricanes.

In Genslé's case, employees were sent home before the hurricane hit. The hotel had a full house but only core managerial staff. Everyone in the hotel was directed to areas without windows. Fortunately, only some banquet rooms sustained damage. "We were lucky because the air conditioning worked so we could use that to help dry out the carpets," Genslé says. Extractors pulled out excess water and prevented serious damage from mildew. "We all worked round the clock," she adds.

Gibel's hotel sustained even less damage after the hurricane than the Inter-Continental, but shutoff of electrical power proved far more challenging than the hurricane itself. The hotel's emergency generator provided only low-level power. Toilets could not be flushed and no water was available for cleanup. "We had to schedule deep cleaning of the rooms to eliminate the odor," said Gibel. "We also disinfected them several times before selling them."

## SUMMARY

Safety and security issues represent a major challenge to the housekeeping department. Developing sound plans and procedures for safety and security helps to avoid unnecessary danger for workers and guests. It also helps the property to prevent loss and financial drain.

The security department is a valuable resource and working partner in developing security and health care safety plans. The executive housekeeper, however, must provide input gained from proper reporting and tracking. Safety compliance issues, including meeting federal, state, and local regulations, must be adhered to.

There is no substitute for understanding the basic issues outlined in this chapter which are involved in safety and security planning:

- Chemical hazards
- MSDS sheets and appropriate treatment
- Threats posed by biohazards and appropriate handling procedures
- OSHA regulations and compliance

- Fire safety programs
- Health or safety programs
- Loss prevention programs
- Damage control programs in guest rooms and suites
- Disaster plans

## Review Questions

1. What are MSDS sheets and how are they used in a health and safety plan?
2. Describe proper disposal techniques for blood-borne pathogens.
3. What is PPE and to whom should it be issued?
4. What is OSHA and how does it affect the provisions of a health and safety plan?
5. What is a Hazard Communication Plan and what key elements should it contain?
6. Describe proper procedures for staff when a fire is discovered.
7. What is light duty?
8. What is risk management?
9. Describe proper key controls for master and emergency keys.
10. Name four occupational hazards of housekeeping.

## Critical Thinking Questions

1. The housekeeping department is already understaffed and unemployment in the city is under 4 percent. The executive housekeeper sees two housekeeping employees stealing liquor. How should this be handled and what disciplinary action would ensue?
2. A VIP guest reports an item was stolen from his room. A printout shows housekeeping, engineering, and the guest all entered the room before the complaint was made. Sales department records show a small meeting was held in the room. How would the executive housekeeper handle this issue?
3. Housekeeping employees do not view taking home toilet tissue, bandages, pens, and other supplies from the property as stealing. However, their pilferage is affecting inventories. How can the executive housekeeper stem the loss without direct accusations?

# 14

# Trends for Today: Using Technology, Instituting Environmental Practices

## Chapter Objectives

New technology and new business demands require executive housekeepers to expand their skills to keep pace with the needs of the industry. Executive housekeepers must:

- Acquire basic computer skills
- Use technology to increase operational efficiency
- Use technology to control labor and supply costs
- Use computers to track performance and quality
- Shift to environmentally friendly housekeeping practices
- Set up water and energy conservation programs
- Set up recycling programs
- Motivate and train employees to implement environmentally friendly housekeeping practices
- Change purchasing practices to favor eco-friendly vendors and manufacturers

Factors ranging from the demographics of the travel market to legislation are redefining professional housekeeping, but few factors are changing housekeeping practices as much as technology and the concern for the environment.

Knowledge of computer basics is fast becoming a prerequisite to being hired. Professional housekeepers who lack computer skills not only limit their own career paths, but their management capabilities as well. All aspects of operations, from budgeting to labor management are, or soon will be, computerized. Computers enable executive housekeepers to monitor costs better, conduct labor analyses, and generally track the financial performance and productivity of the department.

Most corporate executives in the lodging industry agree that controlling labor costs will continue to be a primary concern into the next millennium. That means fewer people will be doing the same amount of work. Technology, if used effectively, will help fill this gap and help the department continue to maintain proper standards.

Clean rooms will always be in demand, but guests are demanding more. One key demand they are making is for environmentally friendly operations. In response, individual properties and large lodging chains alike are going "green," generating favorable publicity. Going green requires many changes, with the heaviest burden of this decision falling on the housekeeping department.

## MAXIMIZING THE BENEFITS OF TECHNOLOGY

Technology touches every aspect of lodging operations, from energy controls and security systems to reservations and scheduling. It is becoming increasingly important that professional housekeepers become technologically aware. More specifically they will have to be computer literate. They will have to understand the basic operations of the computer **hardware,** which is the equipment itself, including the keyboard, disk drive and monitor, and **peripherals,** or **add-ons,** that may include printers, fax capabilities, and modems. They must also be familiar with the computer **software,** or the specific programs used by the property.

Software is changing how the housekeeping department operates in several key areas:

- Room status reporting
- Supervision
- Labor management
- Accounting/budgeting
- Inventory and ordering

A PMS (Property Management System) is a tool for increasing efficiency and reducing time and waste. This computerized approach to accounting and reporting ensures that all departments follow uniform financial procedures. It also provides far more detailed and reliable records for the housekeeping department. Another primary benefit of computerization is the ability to track information easily and discern trends. At this point, software companies are beginning to develop programs specifically for the housekeeping department. Previously, professional housekeepers had to work with computer experts at their property to adapt the front office systems developed for traditional accounting, reservation, and purchasing functions.

Both hardware and software may differ from one property to the next. However, being familiar with computer basics will ease the transition and reduce the time needed to learn another system. In order to carry out some of the necessary managerial tasks a professional housekeeper should know: word processing, the basics of building an informational database, and one of the more common spreadsheet programs. Professional housekeepers also must keep abreast of the latest changes in technology, from communications to security, in order to manage their departments efficiently and cost effectively.

## Rooms Status Technology

One of the most common applications of technology in the housekeeping department is rooms status reporting. Most commonly, this is accomplished by an **interface,** which creates a connection between two different systems. For rooms status reporting, the interface links the property's **central computer system** and the telephone system.

Attendants and inspectors or supervisors are given a list of dial codes and a definition of each. Attendants usually dial one code as soon as they enter a room to indicate it is being cleaned, and another code when they are finished cleaning to show that it is awaiting inspection. If staff is not self-supervised, the inspector, supervisor, or team leader would inspect the cleaned room, then dial a code that means the room has been checked and is available to sell. Self-supervised attendants enter a code that indicates the room is ready to sell.

When setting up the codes, it is important to create enough codes for all situations, for example:

- Dirty—normal cleaning will not make it ready for sale
- Attendant in room
- Out of order
- Recheck
- Clean, inspected

In its training materials, software manufacturer Remco Software Inc. also advises executive housekeepers to create a code for "empty." The reason is: "Some guests will book a room for more nights than they actually stay and leave the key without notifying the front desk. When the housekeeper finds a vacant room, he or she can phone to change the room's status from occupied to empty. This will not check out the folio, only change the status of the room. If the room is erroneously marked as empty, the status is repaired by simply retrieving and saving the worksheet for that guest. "This approach to rooms status reporting is low cost, easy to use, instantaneous, and accurate."

Another option for reporting room status utilizes the television. Since pay-per-view is already linked to the main computer, it is fairly simple to add another menu for rooms status reporting. The attendant simply uses the selector box for pay-per-view or the remote control to indicate the status of the room. This information is relayed instantaneously to the appropriate display monitors. The next technological step is the touch-screen TV, on which the attendant simply touches the screen in order to call up a menu option. Information is relayed to the main computer and is available immediately on display terminals at the front desk and in the housekeeping department. Some properties have gone one step further, installing a terminal at the attendants' stations on each floor.

The use of technology vastly increases the accuracy of room status reporting that can be transmitted within the department and within the hotel.

The front desk staff knows instantly which rooms are ready, which will be ready, and how long the wait will be. Reception staff also knows exactly how many rooms must be removed from inventory until work orders are completed. The link to the terminal in the housekeeping department enables the executive housekeeper to check how many rooms have been done at any time during the shift. If necessary, staff can be shifted from other duties to clean rooms that are needed for early check-ins. At the end of the day shift, the executive housekeeper also can check for any Do Not Disturb (DND) rooms that have not been cleaned and assign them to the night shift or have the room division call to check the status.

---

### Tricks of the Trade 14.1
### Benefiting from Other Technologies

Beepers have become important communication tools for supervisors and department managers. Supervisors on the floors can be reached easily to communicate any new priorities or special requests. Departmental decision makers can be "beeped" quickly to resolve any problems. Two-way walkie-talkie systems, long used by coordinators for meetings and functions, are also useful for housekeeping managers who must stay in touch.

Executive Housekeeper Dalia Peña, of the 1,620-room Wyndham Anatole hotel in Dallas, Texas, says voice mail and beepers are indispensable for her department. Voice mail eliminates the need for the departmental secretary to simply be a message-taker and allows for more detailed messages to be left. Beepers increase the speed of communication and help ensure that problems are addressed as quickly as possible. E-mail is speeding up intra- and interdepartmental communications. Staff not only relays messages, but actual work orders and other documents, such as financial information and reports.

---

### Supervision

Computers also can help reduce pressure on the shrinking supervisory staff. Using **hand-held data collectors,** electronic machines with tiny screens into which information can be recorded, the inspector or supervisor can automate the inspection

process. He or she can enter information on the room number or location, then begin rating the quality of the work done. The performance of each task is evaluated on a numerical scale, or the program can be set up to ask for only yes or no answers. Difficulty ratings or ratings weighing the importance of certain tasks can be introduced. For example, floor cleaning may be rated more important and more difficult than dusting picture frames. Fewer points would be deducted for a dusty picture frame than for an unclean floor. Professional housekeepers usually can work with the software company to customize the software to a certain extent.

All of the information is instantaneously relayed to the **central processing unit (CPU),** the main "brain" of the computer, and can be retrieved by anyone using the system. Though this kind of system is still fairly new and fairly expensive, costing upward of $25,000, some managers argue that one-time capital expenditures are far more cost effective than open-ended labor costs. In other words, by using these systems, fewer inspectors or supervisors are needed to check more rooms and check them more accurately. The inspectors or supervisors must respond to each prompt on the screen, rather than writing down or checking only what has been missed or done incorrectly. Instead of waiting until their inspection is completed to write up the report, they can enter each item as they check it.

A technological system that aids in inspection and supervision has other benefits, says Paul Johnson, director of environmental services for the 650-bed Cape Fear Valley Medical Center in Fayetteville, North Carolina. "With the computer, spot inspections are truly random. This can show critical areas that need improvement and increase the overall quality standards. The computer can compile data from the supervisors' reports and identify trends. They might point to a problem with dusting or floor cleaning that otherwise would go unnoticed. They also help with tracking performance information," says Johnson. This kind of system lifts the load of paperwork from supervisors and gets them back on the floors controlling quality.

### MANAGING LABOR COSTS WITH TECHNOLOGY

Technology has produced practical tools for managing the housekeeping department. Even simple software can help in creating schedules and assignments, tracking work orders, tracking labor costs, and assessing performance.

## Schedules and Assignments

To maximize the effectiveness of the system for scheduling special cleaning assignments, Johnson recommends that the professional housekeeper first create a long-range frequency chart using the computer. Some software creates a built-in calendar for each task entered, so that the work assignment is made automatically. For example, if the executive housekeeper schedules carpet cleaning quarterly in the year-long frequency schedule, the program would post a reminder note at the beginning of each quarter. Johnson advises that the executive housekeeper review this frequency chart regularly and update it as needed. Any changes in frequency should be documented so that the following year's schedule can be adapted accordingly.

Daily work assignments can be individualized to each employee. More important, workloads that include daily special assignments can be spread out over the work week. The assignment sheets should be made out for each attendant and should indicate for which room numbers he or she will be responsible. Using data supplied by the night clerk or the front desk, each attendant's listing would indicate:

- Whether each room is already checked out
- Whether a room is due to be checked out that day
- Whether there are rooms blocked for groups which need to be ready early
- Whether the room has VIP status
- Whether the room has any other special requirements and cleaning priority

*Scheduling.* Computerization also helps the professional housekeeper plan staff schedules. Occupancy and sales projections, historical performance data for a certain period, and analyses of month-to-date labor costs all can be used to set schedules farther in advance. Some professional housekeepers now try to post schedules one week to 10 days in advance to reduce call-offs.

Even so, schedules are driven by occupancy and are subject to last-minute changes. By accessing information from the night clerk's report, the professional housekeeper can determine how many check-out rooms will be on certain floors, and schedule accordingly. This information can be updated instantaneously from the front desk.

*Tracking work orders.* Another function performed by computers is that they can issue work orders and track their progress. Some software enables the professional housekeeper to create a **proactive work order,** which requires that the work order elicit a response—in this case, that the work has been completed. Newer properties are using E-mail to relay work orders. These systems also track completion. Either way, it is a simple matter to find out when the order was issued, how long before the work was done, and whether there were subsequent problems.

*Tracking labor costs.* A computerized timekeeping system is an important tool in labor management. This provides a total of labor hours worked each day and daily overtime analysis. The professional housekeeper can use this information in scheduling, but also for staffing forecasts and productivity analyses (see Figure 14.1.) Analyzing the results of the rooms status report will show how long each attendant spends in each room. This can be used to determine whether quotas are accurate. Most systems also track wages so that the executive housekeeper can track salaries. The executive housekeeper can look at trends in payroll costs either to plan a budget or control departmental costs. He or she also can use computerized salary information to find discrepancies in pay. Veteran employees may have started at a much lower rate than those recently hired. These inequities need to be addressed. Unless the executive housekeeper is the only person in the department permitted access to the computer, files regarding budget and finance and personnel files on departmental employees should be protected with some kind of **lock-out code,** a password of the computer that only allows people who know that code to access specific information.

*Assessing performance.* Supervisors' reports, on-time performance, and contributions to the department all can be **logged** directly into an employee's personnel file. Logging in is the process of putting information on the computer.

## ACCOUNTING AND BUDGETING WITH TECHNOLOGY

Since bottom-line performance is so important, all executive housekeepers will have to be able to track and explain all departmental spending—from labor

**ЯR**
RIHGA ROYAL HOTEL
NEW YORK

**HOUSEKEEPING DEPARTMENT**
**STAFF FORECAST & PRODUCTIVITY REPORT**

A.M. HOUSEKEEPING ATTENDANT FORECAST                                    WEEK OF_____

| DAY | SUN | MON | TUES | WED | THURS | FRI | SAT |
|---|---|---|---|---|---|---|---|
| DATE | | | | | | | |
| # OF OCCUPIED SUITES | | | | | | | |
| x FACTOR (2.1) | | | | | | | |
| = # OF CREDITS | | | | | | | |
| + TRAVEL | | | | | | | |
| = TOTAL # CREDITS TO SERVICE | | | | | | | |
| # OF HOUSEKEEPING ATTENDANTS NEEDED | | | | | | | |
| SCHEDULED PERMANENT | | | | | | | |
| SCHEDULED ON-CALL | | | | | | | |
| TOTAL SCHEDULED ATTENDANTS | | | | | | | |
| +/- ATTENDANTS | | | | | | | |

A.M. HOUSEKEEPING ATTENDANT PRODUCTIVITY REPORT

| | | | | | | | |
|---|---|---|---|---|---|---|---|
| ACTUAL # OF OCCUPIED SUITES | | | | | | | |
| x FACTOR (2.1) | | | | | | | |
| ACTUAL # OF CREDITS | | | | | | | |
| ACTUAL TRAVEL | | | | | | | |
| OTHER (2nd Service, etc.) | | | | | | | |
| TOTAL ACTUAL # OF CREDITS | | | | | | | |
| HOUSEKEEPING ATTENDANTS NEEDED | | | | | | | |
| HOUSEKEEPING ATTENDANTS ACTUAL | | | | | | | |
| +/- HOUSEKEEPING ATTENDANTS | | | | | | | |
| CREDITS SOLD | | | | | | | |
| HOUSEKEEPING ATTENDANTS IN TRAINING | | | | | | | |
| HOUSEKEEPING ATTENDANTS - OTHER | | | | | | | |
| PRODUCTIVITY | | | | | | | |

**Figure 14.1** *Computers can track labor productivity and costs with minimal data entry each day. When data on all employees is merged into one file, the executive housekeeper can easily identify costs in trends and performance. (Courtesy of The Eureka Inn, Eureka, California)*

to supplies. By logging in the required data, the executive housekeeper can analyze the department's costs per occupied room on a daily basis. He or she can correct small cost problems before they become big ones. Perhaps the simplest approach is to create "accounts" for each line item. Every time money is spent from the "account," it should be subtracted from that account's budget. Ideally, the software should enable the housekeeper to compare spending both to the monthly budgeted total and the overall annual budgeted total, since spending may vary from month to month.

The availability of so much data makes it easier to plan a realistic budget and avoid costly overruns. Spending for any line item can be reviewed at any time. If costs are running over budget, the executive housekeeper can check spending against occupancy and historical performance to find a rea-

son. It is easier to find out when and why costs are out of line and control them before radical action is required.

"It's important to keep in mind that housekeeping departments are not run according to **bearable budgets** (or costs against income they generate) they are based on frequency of service. Computerization allows the housekeeper to look at the peaks and valleys of occupancy, and budget accordingly for each time of year," notes Johnson, of the Cape Fear Medical Center.

## Inventory and Ordering

Computerized ordering and purchasing can also play a key role in cost control. More and more manufacturers and/or vendors now have on-line ordering capabilities. Traveling down the so-called "information highway," the professional housekeeper or purchasing director can access pricing and availability information in the manufacturer's or vendors' database (see Tricks of the Trade 14.2). It also is easier to compare pricing and "shop" for new products. Housekeeping departments that do their own purchasing, but do not have on-line capabilities, should generate computerized purchase orders to save time.

---

### Tricks of the Trade 14.2
### Boosting the Benefits of Technology

*The Problem:* How to use all the data that computers collect.

*The Solution:* Kristine Hall, executive housekeeper of the 538-room Hyatt Regency Union Station, St. Louis, Missouri, goes one step beyond using the computer for cost controls. She uses the data to identify cost savings. Hall logs in purchase orders for each vendor to determine with which companies she does the most business. If the volume is high, she uses this information to try to obtain better discounts based on the volume of business, which has helped lower costs, or—in some cases—improved service.

Inventory controls can be linked to ordering. Computerized tracking shows at a glance where inventory levels stood at the last time inventory was taken (see Figure 14.2). Inventory levels can be compared with last year, weighed against occupancy levels, and figured into the cost per occupied room figure. The computer can be programmed to **flag,** or indicate, items nearing minimum inventory levels.

---

## INSTITUTING ENVIRONMENTALLY FRIENDLY CLEANING PRACTICES

The "reduce, reuse, recycle" credo of the environmental movement is playing a growing role in lodging operations. Concern for the environment is on the minds of many travelers, and most properties do not want to risk alienating guests with policies that show a callous disregard for the environment. Instituting sound environmental practices is more than a marketing buzz word, it is a business-building decision. Many government agencies, such as state departments of natural resources, and private corporations will only book room nights

and meetings at properties with a demonstrated commitment to environmentally sensitive management. Although the environmental movement is rolling along at a much faster pace in Europe, where recycling and waste management are becoming legislative priorities, most properties in the United States are taking their first steps toward going green.

Many major lodging companies already have introduced basic environmental programs. These programs help with training, finding vendors of environmentally friendly cleaning products and providing marketing support materials for the guest rooms. Groups such as the "Green" Hotels Association, Houston Texas, and the International Hotels Environmental Initiative, London, as well as consulting firms such as HVS Eco Services, Mineola, New York, all help properties establish an environmental program. Some state environmental protection agencies or departments of natural resources are also good sources of information. The federal Environmental Protection Agency's WAVE (Water Alliance for Voluntary Efficiency) recently funded a free water-efficiency clearinghouse: Waterwiser (at American Water Works), 6666 Quincy Ave., Denver, Colorado, 800/559-9855.

### Mapping Out a Program of Environmental Controls

Determining how extensive the property's commitment to environmentally friendly operations will be depends on its location, chain affiliation, guest preference, the level of staff, and management commitment. The decision to shift to environmentally friendly operations is felt throughout the hotel. Yet, no single department feels the impact more than the housekeeping department (see Table 14.1).

Introducing environmentally sound cleaning practices involves:

- Rethinking cleaning practices to find ways to reduce chemical, water, energy, and paper usage

- Reviewing the contents of cleaning chemicals to make sure they are biodegradable and environmentally safe. Some executive housekeepers have gone one step further to look for cleaning compounds that will be less harsh on skin and, if possible, odor-free.

- Buying exclusively from vendors that follow environmentally friendly practices such as conservation and recycling

## THE ADOLPHUS HOTEL
ROOMS LINEN SUPPLIES INVENTORY
ACCOUNT #01-1210
DATE: MARCH 1997

| DESCRIPTION | PREVIOUS MONTH QUANTITY | RECEIVED QUANTITY | CURRENT MONTH QUANTITY | USAGE | UNIT | PRICE | CURRENT MONTH EXTENSION | USAGE EXTENSION |
|---|---|---|---|---|---|---|---|---|
| BATH MATS-BEIGE | 906 | | 906 | 0 | EA | 3.65 | 3,306.90 | 0.00 |
| BATH MATS-WHITE | 660 | | 480 | 180 | EA | 3.42 | 1,641.60 | 615.60 |
| BATH TOWELS-BEIGE | 200 | | 100 | 100 | EA | 4.49 | 449.00 | 449.00 |
| BATH TOWELS-WHITE | 624 | | 624 | 0 | EA | 4.37 | 2,726.88 | 0.00 |
| BLANKET KING | 8 | | 8 | 0 | EA | 16.45 | 131.60 | 0.00 |
| BLANKET QUEEN | 18 | | 18 | 0 | EA | 19.45 | 350.10 | 0.00 |
| BLANKET TWIN | 8 | | 8 | 0 | EA | 23.55 | 188.40 | 0.00 |
| BODY WRAPS-MENS | 130 | | 122 | 8 | EA | 10.29 | 1,255.38 | 82.32 |
| BODY WRAPS-WOMENS | 126 | | 119 | 7 | EA | 13.53 | 1,610.07 | 94.71 |
| HAND TOWELS-WHITE | 600 | | 240 | 360 | EA | 1.71 | 410.40 | 615.60 |
| MATTRESS PAD KING | 24 | | 24 | 0 | EA | 16.15 | 387.60 | 0.00 |
| MATTRESS PAD QUEEN | 24 | | 24 | 0 | EA | 13.80 | 331.20 | 0.00 |
| MATTRESS PAD DOUBLE | 24 | | 24 | 0 | EA | 12.45 | 298.80 | 0.00 |
| MATTRESS PAD TWIN | 60 | | 60 | 0 | EA | 11.87 | 712.20 | 0.00 |
| PILLOW CASES-WHITE | 1512 | | 1512 | 0 | EA | 1.51 | 2,283.12 | 0.00 |
| ROBES-ADULT WHITE | 194 | | 100 | 94 | EA | 30.15 | 3,015.00 | 2,834.10 |
| ROBES-CHILDS 0-3 | 5 | | 1 | 4 | EA | 22.00 | 22.00 | 88.00 |
| ROBES-CHILDS 4-6 | 2 | | 0 | 2 | EA | 24.00 | 0.00 | 48.00 |
| ROBES-CHILDS 7-14 | 3 | | 0 | 3 | EA | 27.00 | 0.00 | 81.00 |
| SHEETS KING-BEIGE | 247 | | 247 | 0 | EA | 11.25 | 2,778.75 | 0.00 |
| SHEETS KING-WHITE | 633 | | 633 | 0 | EA | 11.38 | 7,203.54 | 0.00 |
| SHEETS QUEEN-WHITE | 534 | | 354 | 180 | EA | 8.75 | 3,097.50 | 1,575.00 |
| SPA TOWELS - RIBBED | 0 | | 0 | 0 | EA | 3.11 | 0.00 | 0.00 |
| TWIN FITTED | 60 | | 60 | 0 | EA | 6.20 | 372.00 | 0.00 |
| TWIN FLAT | 120 | | 120 | 0 | EA | 7.10 | 852.00 | 0.00 |
| WASH CLOTHS-WHITE | 3600 | | 2400 | 1200 | EA | 0.72 | 1,728.00 | 864.00 |
| TERRY JACKETS | 14 | | 14 | 0 | EA | 21.00 | 294.00 | 0.00 |
| TOTAL LINEN $$ | | | | | | | 35,446.04 | 7,347.33 |
| | | | | | | OCC RMS | | |
| | | | | | | CPOR | | |

CC: ROOMS DIVISION MANAGER
LAUNDRY MANAGER
CONTROLLER

**Figure 14.2** *Computer tracking tracks both inventory levels and expenditures. (Courtesy, The Adolphus, Dallas, Texas)*

- Finding outlets for reuse of consumable supplies, ranging from outmoded equipment to partially used bottles of amenities
- Creating training programs for staff

### Getting Started

Some lodging companies have training films and information packages to help the housekeeping department shift to environmentally friendly practices. Programs can range from intensive efforts to encourage environmental concerns, which would involve overall operations, to a few simple operations.

For those properties that do not have this kind of material available, Patricia Griffin, head of the "Green" Hotels Association, suggests starting "with baby steps". "Even if the general manager is not committed to environmentally sensitive programs, there is a lot the housekeeping department can do on its own. For example, if it is impossible to change suppliers and the hotel is using harsh chemicals, the attendants can just use less. Bleach may not be needed for every job, or a greater dilution may work just as well. Any department can start a reuse program. Before equipment, towels, or even scrap paper is thrown out, the executive housekeeper should ask if anyone on staff could use the items at home. But, he or she has to be fair.

No one wants employees arguing over who takes what. Starting an environmental program can be as simple as not ordering a toothpick with a ruffle on it," advises Griffin.

Griffin recommends that the housekeeping department analyze its operations before starting a program. Determining how much glass, aluminum, paper, and cardboard goes into the trash will help management decide what kind of recycling program to start. Also, an attendant can easily do a water audit, says Griffin. "All that's needed is a two-gallon bucket, a watch with a second hand and a milk jug. When water pressure is high, usually in the middle of the night, the attendant should position the bucket under a sink faucet and let the water run at full force for 15 seconds. Then the water can be measured in the milk jug. The total of the gallons that flowed out in the 15 seconds is then multiplied by four to calculate gallons per minute. If the gallons per minute are more than 2.5 from a sink or 3.0 from a shower, the property needs a water conservation program."

## Location

Legislation on environmental issues varies greatly, depending on geographical location. The professional housekeeper should contact the appropriate local, county, or state agencies to find out what constitutes compliance with existing environmental laws and codes. Most veteran housekeepers advise going one step further. They suggest working with sources within the management or franchise company or with local environmental groups. This way, the professional housekeeper will be able to find out what legislation is pending and how it will affect compliance in the future.

Location plays a major role in determining how extensive the environmental commitment *must* be. Resorts in deserts or along beachfronts legally cannot or may simply choose not to use harsh cleaning chemicals. Most are unwilling to risk any seepage into the water supply. Cruise line operators also must be environmentally sensitive. Othmar Hehli, director, operations for Radisson Seven Seas Cruises, foresees a day when dry cleaning machines that use Perchloroethylene will not be permitted on cruise ships.

## Chain Affiliation

Some lodging companies have made a corporate-level commitment to the environment. Chief executives of a dozen major lodging companies are ac-

**TABLE 14.1**  *The Pressures to Go Green*

Based on 141 surveys from housekeepers, an environmental consulting firm, HVS Eco Services, found that:

- 65 percent feel their property is sensitive to the environment
- 89 percent would like to see the environmental sensitivity of their property improved
- 92 percent would be willing to make changes in the way they do their work if those changes make their property more environmentally sound
- 57 percent would be willing to volunteer time each week to make their property more environmentally sensitive
- 54 percent follow environmental practices at home

The program they would choose as being the most important to start or improve:

- 45 percent—Environmental education program for employees
- 36 percent—Recycling program
- 14 percent—Energy conservation program
- 5 percent—Water conservation program

tive on the council of the International Hotels Environmental Initiative. They include: Forte Hotels, Inter-Continental, Hilton International, also based in the United Kingdom; ITT Sheraton; Marriott; Holiday Inn Worldwide (HIW), all headquartered in the United States; France's Accor, Radisson/SAS, Radisson Hotels International's European division, based in Brussels; and Mandarin Oriental, The Taj Group, Omni Hotels Asia/Pacific and Renaissance Hotels, all based in Asia and the Pacific. Other chains have written broader guidelines that allow properties to go green on a more individualized basis.

One of the mega-companies, HIW, which is involved in promoting environmental awareness, has, as a basic feature of its program *Conserving for Tomorrow*, a stipulation that towels will only be changed every third night or upon check-out unless guests request more frequent service. This is becoming a fairly standard environmentally friendly move, and one that can generate significant cost savings. Craig Hunt, HIW's executive senior vice president and head of HIW's environmental program estimates that the 82 hotels involved in a one-year test of this program saved more than 200,000 gallons of water and prevented more than 100,000 gallons of detergent from entering the waste water system. Significant savings also were realized in terms of energy costs for laundry operations and saved labor hours.

"When you consider the labor savings, reduction in chemicals, energy and water savings, this program could easily save $30,000 a year for a 100-room property or $100,000 for a 500- to 600-room property," points out Hunt. HIW's program also has energy-saving and recycling components. Suppliers are required to use recycled products and to provide environmentally friendly cleaners and detergents.

### Guest Involvement

Research conducted by HVS Eco Services in New York indicates that 70 percent of the respondents said they would be likely or very likely to stay in an environmentally friendly property. This is good news because several key programs require guest support.

To appeal to guests' desire for environmental concern, attendants must check the in-room literature on environmental programs and promotional materials; they must make sure the room contains a tent card, plaque or other materials explaining any program that requires guest participation. The in-room door hangers should explain clearly and concisely what action guests should take—such as what to do when they want linens changed. Guest should be required to take some sort of positive action to indicate their choice. They may be asked to turn the plaque with a certain side facing up, hang up a doorknob hanger, or leave towels on the floor. And, it must be pointed out to guests that they can request clean linens at any time during their stay (see Tricks of the Trade 14.3).

**Tricks of the Trade 14.3**
**Listening to Guests**

*The Problem:* Guests still want linen changed daily.
*The Solution:* Implement environmental programs in areas that do not affect guests so directly. Above all, listen to the guests. Linen reuse, or any environmentally friendly program, can be suggested and encouraged by the property's management, but it is difficult to make it man-

**Guests' Environmental Priorities**

Housekeepers and other managers thinking about starting environmental programs should consider these facts from a recent study conducted by Virginia Tech:

• 70 percent of those questioned say they are likely to extremely likely to stay in a hotel with a pro-active environmental strategy

• 91 percent believe that properties should use energy-efficient lighting where possible, while 87 percent think lighting should be turned off when guests are not in their rooms

• 86 percent think lodging properties should provide recycling bins for guests' use

• 67 percent believe that for guests staying more than one night, bed sheets should not be changed daily, unless specifically requested

*Figure 14.3* Technology enables executive housekeepers to analyze inventories, current costs per room, and par levels, then weigh all this against last year's performance. (Courtesy of The Adolphus Hotel, Dallas, Texas)

datory. "Guests from some cultures did not like the idea of using some towels or sheets more than one day. They considered it poor service. Since we have many international guests, we must provide the level of service they expect, such as replenishing soap and other amenities on a daily basis," comments Rita Genslé, executive housekeeper of the deluxe Inter-Continental, Miami, Florida.

A small card explaining recycling programs should also be placed in each room (see Figure 14.4). If the room is equipped with a mini-bar, the card should be placed near the unit. Typically, guests are asked to place empty, recyclable cans or bottles on top of the dresser. Attendants remove them during regular cleaning and put them in the appropriate recycling receptacles. Attendants should be instructed never to go through trash in search of recyclables to avoid any risk of being cut. Lodging companies report guests are very receptive to the new environmental programs. "We've had absolutely no guest complaints," says Hunt. "In fact, we've received many compliments, and that's

**SAVE OUR PLANET!**

Dear Guest:

Every day tons of detergent and millions of gallons of water are used to wash towels that have only been used once.

PLEASE DECIDE FOR YOURSELF.

A towel on the rack

means

"I'll use it several times".

A towel on the floor

means

"please exchange".

10% of Profits Donated to The Sierra Club
© 1994 "Green" Hotels Association™
P. O. Box 420212, Houston, TX 77242-0212
713/789-8889, Fax 713/789-9786

**Figure 14.4** *Enlisting guest support for environmental programs can be as easy as providing a tent card or door hanger explaining the hotel's environmental programs. Instructions should be clear and concise. (Courtesy of "Green" Hotels Association, Houston, Texas)*

very gratifying. I think the guests truly enjoy playing a role in helping the environment."

## ENCOURAGING STAFF INVOLVEMENT

Shifting to environmentally friendly housekeeping practices usually does not require intensive retraining. Most of the executives housekeepers who work in "green" properties say that motivating staff to support a program of environmental responsibility requires more planning than actual retraining.

"Managers involved in our **Conserving for Tomorrow** effort have found that they do not need monetary incentives to get staff involved. In most cases, the staff wants to participate in a program that will benefit the environment," says HIW's Hunt.

Some staffs need more motivation (see Tales of the Trade. 14.1). The benefits of implementing the idea can be extended by passing along a small percentage of the savings to the employee for the next 12 to 24 months. Other traditional methods of motivation work well, too, such as naming an environmentally friendly employee of month and providing recognition in the form of a special badge, small award, or even a certificate for a free lunch.

### Tales of the Trade 14.1
### Boston Park Plaza: An Environmental Success Story

"In 1991, we had very little knowledge of what (environmental) impact we could have. Launching into our environmental program really opened our eyes as employees," says Lewis Ware, then director of housekeeping for the 977-room Boston Park Plaza in Boston, Massachusetts, a model of environmental policy.

The program was launched after the hotel conducted an extensive survey testing guests' attitudes toward environmentally friendly operations. The responses were overwhelmingly in support of going "green," says Ware, who since has been promoted to senior assistant hotel manager. "My biggest challenge initially was how to sell this idea to the 155 employees in my department. Their first question was, "Are we going to get paid more?" I had to say "no," but I did come up with the idea of bringing some of

the revenue from recycling back to the department," adds Ware.

Ware proposed using the proceeds from can and bottle recycling to set up an employee fund. He told employees they would decide how the money was to be used. "I said they could have a party or whatever, but one employee stood up and said the attendants had so many problems with the vacuums, we should use the money to buy new ones. I asked management if they would match the funds we generated through the can and bottle recycling to help us buy what we called our 'eco vacuums.' They agreed," says Ware. Ware discussed various aspects of the changeover to environmentally friendly practices during daily departmental meetings. Since the hotel is unionized, Ware also invited union representatives to a meeting before the program was launched to explain the program and answer any questions. The union had no objections. More intensive training was done at monthly and bimonthly meetings. Some manufacturers were invited in to help train the employees in how to use their products correctly.

Substantial savings also were realized by streamlining the variety of cleaning products used and installing a water reuse system in the laundry. Less harsh chemicals also reduced the incidents of skin rashes and nausea, says Ware. Another payoff for the propertywide commitment to the environment: The hotel was named the President's Environment and Conservation Challenge Award winner for 1992, the nation's highest environmental honor.

The "Green" Hotels Assn., Houston, Texas, suggests:

- Allowing employees to take home flowers used to decorate meeting or function rooms
- Allowing employees to take home extra prepared food after functions, assuming that it has been held at safe temperatures.
- Giving an extra four to eight hours of paid vacation to employees who carpool, ride a bus, bike, or walk to work.

The Miami Inter-Continental, Miami, Florida, won an environmental award from the International Hotel Association, Paris, and American Express, New York City, for its extensive environmental commitment. One feature of its program was to offer employees furnishings and equipment that were no longer suitable for hotel use at a very low cost or through a special auction. This program underscored the hotel's commitment to reducing its waste and demonstrated to employees the direct benefits of reusing rather than throwing things away.

Generally, experts warn against setting up monetary awards that may have to be cut back if times get tough. Kim Moffitt, of HVS Eco Services, suggests sharing the benefits of environmentally friendly practices with staff by earmarking a portion of the department's saved operating costs for morale-boosting items. One hotelier suggests explaining how it will affect the attendants' daily work. "We told them, on average, they'd be making fewer beds each day. That's something every attendant can grasp—and appreciate. We've had a lot fewer sore backs."

Dalia Peña, director of housekeeping services for the 1,620-room Wyndham Anatole Hotel in Dallas, Texas, permanently assigns some room attendants who are sensitive to smoke or had other allergies to floors designed for guests with similar maladies. The no-smoking policy on the floor, combined with the use of in-room air filtering systems that remove dust, smoke, pollen, mold spores, and other impurities, creates a healthier working environment for these attendants.

Many executive housekeepers already assign non-smoking attendants to no-smoking guest rooms. Some executive housekeepers even use assignment to no-smoking or environmentally friendly rooms as a reward for good performance. Frequently, matching employees with preferred work environments results in fewer reports of on-the-job illness related to air quality, fewer call-offs because of allergies, and improved productivity.

### Troubleshooting

Patricia Griffin, of the "Green" Hotels Association, stresses that any training programs and implementation of environmentally friendly cleaning practices must take into consideration the multicultural makeup of most housekeeping department staffs. "Some studies estimate that as many as 60 percent of the employees who work in the lodging industry's housekeeping staffs and other entry level jobs may not be able to read English. On most staffs, the majority probably do not speak English as a first language." All supplies should be color-coded to indicate what the product is, and training materials should be bilingual.

Some staff members also may have trouble adapting to new products and new cleaning routines. Some solutions are:

- Call the manufacturer for answers and/or on-site retraining for problems using environmentally friendly products or problems with effectiveness
- Train supervisors to give pointers or reminders as they check rooms
- To reinforce new systems or routines, issue weekly reminders or updates during departmental meetings

It should be made clear that learning the new procedures will take time and problems will arise, but that these procedures must be ones to which all will adhere. Professional housekeepers in properties with successful programs say it is important that support for the environment begins with top management. A half-hearted commitment by an executive housekeeper can only undermine staff response. Staff should be involved as early as possible in planning environmental programs. The goals should be discussed during a special departmental meeting and reinforced during training sessions. The supervisor or executive housekeeper should remind the staff that being environmentally friendly also improves working conditions. Less harsh chemicals decrease the risk of skin rashes and other chemical reactions. Also, these programs prevent attendants from having to breath in harsh fumes.

## DETERMINING THE COSTS

For the housekeeping department, going "green" should result in cost savings rather than added expenditures (see Tales of the Trade 14.2). However, the executive housekeeper has to look at all the costs involved before determining whether the program is producing its maximum financial result.

**Tales of the Trade 14.2**
**How a UK Resort Went Green**

British lodging industry magazine *Caterer & Hotelkeeper* offered an independent hotel a free environmental audit and analysis, courtesy of hospitality consultant Business Green. Ian J. Aston, managing director of the 78-room Derwentwater, Hotel, Keswick, in the United Kingdom's lake district, took advantage of the offer.

Like Boston Park Plaza, replacing small amenities bottles with refillable dispensers helped the Derwentwater's housekeeping department realize substantial savings. Aston estimates this single change has reduced labor hours "by half a chambermaid." Water-efficient shower heads reduced water consumption 45 percent. The changeover in cleaning products also has saved the housekeeping department time and reduced waste. One company's highly concentrated cleaning solutions are delivered in containers that are wall mounted. This unit is connected to the water supply. On demand, there is a pump action which automatically mixes the concentrate with water and dispenses the correct dilution directly into pump spray bottles.

Like many other operators, Aston says his property has had trouble finding environmentally friendly products for every cleaning problem. In trials conducted by the property's housekeeping department, some "wholly green" products "were found to be ineffectual, particularly over a period of time." The systems Aston now uses "are not 100 percent environmentally friendly, but they are a vast improvement over what used to be available."

One of the best motivators for staff members has been showing them the difference in energy bills on a monthly basis. Housekeeping attendants can see how much of a difference it makes when they turn off lights. Fluorescent lighting and low-energy equipment also make a difference. As a further incentive, Aston offers £50 ($83) to an employee whose suggestion is used.

Some factors to consider include:

1. Are the environmentally friendly cleaners cost competitive with products used previously? If not, could another vendor provide the same quality for a better price?

2. Buying in bulk saves on packaging. But, are the bulk chemicals being used up before their expiration date? If not, will the vendor agree to a buy-back arrangement? Also, how many labor hours does it take to repackage the bulk cleaning products?

3. Are the cleaning chemicals living up to the manufacturers' claims? If attendants have to use a product several times to get results or still revert to harsher chemicals, costs will escalate, and the goal of using safer products will be compromised.

4. How has the program impacted scheduling and labor costs?

5. Is the department credited with its fair share of saved energy and water costs stemming from the launch of the environmental program?

6. How much has the program cost in terms of training and any extra initial inspections?

Ideally, environmental programs should not only help save natural resources but also save on the bottom line. Even simple efforts such as having attendants turn off lights after cleaning guest rooms and setting back heating or air conditioning levels to minimum settings can save a property 5 percent or more on energy costs. These programs do carry start-up costs, ranging from training to slight losses in productivity initially to purchasing new supplies such as extra bags for attendants or in-room tent cards. Long-term savings should more than justify these costs.

## Instituting Environmentally Friendly Cleaning Methods

For many housekeeping departments, the changeover to eco-friendly cleaning practices begins with very basic programs. The advantage to this approach is that it requires only a small investment in retraining, a low budgetary investment, and low risk if the program does not work as expected. Some programs that usually produce the best results with the least operational risk include:

- Conservation
- Waste reduction
- Reduction of energy/water usage
- Recycling

## Conservation/Waste Reduction Programs

Most environmentalists say that, of reducing, reusing, and recycling, reducing, is the most important goal. For the lodging industry, it may also be the most cost-effective basis for environmentally friendly management programs.

Giving guests the option of not having towels changed daily is becoming one of the most widespread eco-friendly housekeeping practices in the lodging industry. Except for printing support materials that explain the programs to guests and a short training session for staff to help them track when to change linens in stay-over rooms, the program requires very little investment. And it has a big payoff in terms of saved energy, water usage, and supply costs.

Some properties automatically change the linens in stay-over rooms after the second day; others, including HIW, change them after the third day. This decisions depends on guest preference and the standards set by the property.

Though this program is fairly simple, it is not fail-safe. Before setting it up, the executive housekeeper must:

1. Work with both attendants and supervisors to set up a system that insures the linens get changed on the correct schedule

2. Work with the laundry manager to make sure heavy linen volume can be handled if the hotel has a lot of checkouts on one day

3. Set up a control system, usually through guest comment cards, to try to insure that guests both understand the program and are satisfied with the result

Loews Hotels, an upscale operator, has launched its pilot EarthSmart program and may eventually include it in all of the chain's 14 hotels worldwide. In addition to using fluorescent bulbs which last longer and reduce energy usage, providing recycling containers and offering guests the option of not having sheets and towels changed daily, the Loews EarthSmart program also includes key features such as:

- All-natural bath, hair, and skin care products in permanent wall dispensers. This saves on packaging but also frees up housekeeping staff from having to resupply amenities daily. The acrylic dispensers are easy to clean.

- Air filtering systems that remove dust, smoke, pollen, mold spores, and other impurities from designated EarthSmart rooms. These systems are no substitute for daily maintenance and deep cleaning, but they help limit dust buildup and, perhaps, extend the periods between general cleaning.

- Specially designed shower heads to conserve water and remove chlorine and other impurities. These could help control staining from water with high levels of iron or lime.

- Unbleached cotton robes that serve as a guest amenity. These robes are easy to launder.

***Training and inspection.*** Assignment sheets should have space to note when linens need to be changed. In hotels with short average stays of 1.1

nights, such as city center business hotels, this is not much of a problem because linens must be changed upon check-out. But in convention properties where average stay is commonly three days, or resorts where it may be a week, attendants will need written instructions on assignment sheets indicating which rooms require a full change of linen on a particular day. Some companies are experimenting with making beds differently. If sheets are folded one way, it means they are clean. Folded a different way, it means they have not been changed. It is important that attendants be reminded to check guest instructions each day, as mentioned in the previous chapter on troubleshooting. Inspectors and/or supervisors will require extra training. They also may need extra time, at least at first, to ensure that the linens have been changed when they are supposed to be.

***Laundry.*** Planning for linen reuse programs also should involve the laundry manager. Don Hartley, general manager of the 248-room Holiday Inn Brentwood, near Nashville, Tennessee, installed a light that resembles a stop light in the laundry. "It turns to green when we plan to change the linens in every room. We try to do this on a slower day when we know the laundry can get it all done. Using the light helps the laundry staff prepare. When we're full, we turn the light to red," explains Hartley.

***Followup.*** The only way to find out whether the linen reuse program is working for guests is to track comments and complaints. Particular attention should be paid to guest comment cards after this program is instituted. As mentioned earlier, some housekeepers take a more active approach, either leaving a printed, signed note requesting guest input or actually calling guests to see whether they understand the program and whether they are satisfied with it.

## Waste Reduction

Ideally, nothing should be discarded. However, practical concerns about bloodborne pathogens and the very real pressures to maintain the housekeeping department's standards and schedule make this ideal a difficult one to achieve. A more realistic approach would be to look for ways to minimize waste and encourage conservation. The Intl. Hotel Environmental Initiative (IHEI) reports that even little changes mean a lot to the environment. IHEI notes that the Omni Hong Kong's "simple decision" to replace small, individual jam jars with large, refillable jars made a dramatic impact on the property's level of waste. It saved some 85,000 small glass jars from ending up in the trash.

Waste reduction has been a goal of professional housekeepers long before the environmental movement began. Faced with tight budgets and finite levels of supplies and equipment, executive housekeepers are masters at prolonging the useful life of a variety of items. Some basic approaches to waste reduction include:

1. Assessing reuse possibilities before discarding anything. As discussed in Chapter 11, linens that are no longer suitable for use in the guest rooms can be made over into rags. Only refillable containers should be used.

2. Having suppliers refill pails of cleaning solutions, thereby reducing the need for storage bottles

3. Using cloth bags, both as in-room laundry bags for guests, and linen bags on attendants' carts

4. Providing glass glasses or recyclable, wrapped plastic glasses for in-room use

5. Recycling or reusing paper waste. As a rule, many lodging companies require that both sides of the paper be used for memos and departmental communication

6. Providing wall-mounted dispensers for liquid soap and shampoo in the guest bathroom offering large, mounted refillable amenity containers, or replacing amenities only on an as-needed basis, rather than routinely restocking each day

For fiscal and environmental reasons, properties are looking for ways to reduce waste overall. Reusing and reupholstering furniture should take priority over replacement. FF&E that cannot be reused can be auctioned off to employees or donated to charity. Charities and homeless shelters are good sources for a variety of reuse programs, ranging from partially used bottles of amenities to old draperies and even carpeting. Local health regulations should be checked first. Items such as mattresses usually cannot be donated or resold.

## Reduction of Energy/Water Usage

The housekeeping department is also in a good position to control guests' energy usage and staff's water usage. Some environmental programs for the housekeeping department recommended by HVS Eco Services to help the housekeeping department to save energy include:

- Clean light fixtures and lamps daily. Dusty lamps and fixtures reduce the efficiency of the lighting system.
- Clean skylights regularly to maximize natural light and minimize the need for electric lights.
- Shift more cleaning functions to daytime hours when less lighting is needed. Night cleaning should be conducted in blocks so that lighting is used in one area at a time.
- Reset in-room air conditioning or heating to minimal settings after the room is cleaned each day and turn off the lights.
- Leave on only one lamp at turndown.
- Disconnect refrigerators in vacant rooms and leave the door open.
- Close faucets tightly and report any leaks
- Turn off lights in back-of-the-house areas when work is completed.
- Remove any furniture or other obstacles that directly obstruct the air flow to the heating, ventilating, and air conditioning (HVAC) equipment. HVAC equipment should not be used to expedite carpet drying.
- Do not iron linens. Linens folded immediately after drying usually do not require ironing.
- Dry at the lowest temperature possible.
- To decrease water usage, HVS Eco Services advises the following:
- Avoiding letting water run until it is very hot.
- Wash only full loads of laundry, except for biohazards which should be washed as soon as possible.
- Use only one rinse for linens and other thin laundry.
- Make sure water pressure is not set too high on laundry equipment. Most laundry equipment will function properly at 35 pounds per square inch (PSI).
- Reuse water when possible. Water recycling equipment saves the so-called gray water, or lightly used rinse water, then recycles it as wash water for the next loads. Some manufacturers claim this cuts water heating fuel costs by 50 percent to 70 percent, and results in recycling of up to 80 percent to 90 percent of laundry waste water.
- Lower water temperatures.
- Budget for aerators for sinks and shower heads, and use fill diverters for toilet tanks. Fill diverters,

available through the "Green" Hotels Association, cost less than $1 and save three-quarters of a gallon of water per flush.

***Energy Controls.*** Conserving energy begins with the simple flick of a switch. Before leaving checked-out rooms, the room attendant should make sure electrical appliances such as the television, radio, and coffee maker are turned off. If windows were opened to air out the room, they should be closed. Lights should be turned off. Room attendants also should turn off individually controlled air conditioning units. For centrally controlled heating and air conditioning, the room attendant should make sure the system is set on the standard minimum temperature outlined in the hotel's policy.

Some heating and air conditioning Systems use **infrared sensors,** some of which "read" movement to determine whether someone is in the room. If no movement is detected for a certain period, the system automatically returns the heating or air conditioning to preset minimums. When someone re-enters the room, this system automatically restores the heating or air conditioning to a comfortable level.

Other systems interface with the hotel's computer. When a guest checks out, the room's lights and television are turned off and air conditioning and heating are returned to minimum settings. As soon as the next guest checks in, the computer returns the settings to more comfortable levels. However, this system does not adjust settings during the guest's stay.

The housekeeping staff should be made to understand what is being controlled automatically and what needs to be adjusted. Some properties are experimenting with air and water purification systems as well. New on the market are vacuum cleaners with a special filter system that essentially purify as they clean. "Green" Hotels Association members can receive lists of products and suppliers. HVS sells its Eco Tel Product Index for $5.

## Recycling

The biggest challenge recycling poses for the housekeeping department is in terms of collection and storage. Cans, bottles, and newspapers must be removed from guest rooms and transported to areas where they will be held until pickup. Usually, a leakproof bag is provided for the attendants' carts for aluminum and glass recyclables. Newspapers should be stacked neatly in the corridor so that the house attendants can remove them promptly (see Tricks of the Trade 14.4).

---

**Tricks of the Trade 14.4**
**Storing Recyclable Wastes**

*The Problem:* Corridors are filled with newspapers all morning.

*The Solution:* The Boston Park Plaza trains house attendants to pick up the recyclable newspapers at the same time they remove soiled linen. Separate snap-on bags are provided for this purpose on the cart. This means the papers are picked up almost as each guest room is cleaned, so there is no mess in the corridor. Lewis Ware, the hotel's senior assistant hotel manager and former director of housekeeping, had special recycling bins constructed and placed in the back-of-the-house corridors. This speeds up pickup of all recyclables because they do not have to be taken all the way to the basement. Except for this one extra step, recycling did not mean any added work for room attendants or house attendants.

---

The executive housekeeper needs to coordinate recycling activities with the head of the maintenance department. Some city center properties in large cities may qualify for daily pickup by recycling trucks, but most properties must create a storage area for recyclables. Covered containers are preferred, if possible, so that recyclable cans and bottles do not attract pests. If frequency or cost become problems, several properties in one area or several other businesses could work together to obtain a volume discount from one hauler.

## Environmentally Friendly Supplies and Equipment

Today, as major manufacturers begin to offer full lines of environmentally friendly products, executive housekeepers should be able to find products that meet most cleaning challenges. The HVS ECO-TEL Product Index, a source guide listing manufacturers of eco-friendly products and services, lists supplies for cleaning as well as laundering. Compounds include all types of general-purpose and glass cleaners, polishers, and degreasers. Members of the "Green" Hotels Association can consult the association for help in finding environmentally friendly products and services.

As with any new product, the executive housekeeper should request an on-premise trial. Tests should be conducted over a week to ten days to see how the products perform over time. If there are a few, specialized cleaning challenges that the products cannot meet, the professional housekeeper can work with the manufacturer to find something that will be more effective. There may be a somewhat harsher product that will be used on an as-needed basis. Lewis Ware, of Boston Park Plaza, was unwilling to use bleach. He switched to a cleaner with a bleaching agent that only supervisors may use.

## SUMMARY

The job description of the professional housekeeper is constantly changing and expanding, and the individuals in the profession must change their career skills to meet these demands. Just two decades ago, only a small percentage of the lodging industry was experimenting with computers. Now, computers are seen as an operational necessity, not only in the front of the house but the back of the house as well. They are vital management tools and, as managers, professional housekeepers must learn to use them. As managers, professional housekeepers must also respond to changing markets. The travel market of today not only wants a room that looks like home and but also one that fits with the travelers' lifestyles. A commitment to the environment is part of a growing number of people's lifestyles. Implementing environmentally friendly cleaning practices, from towel reuse to recycling, makes the property more marketable and, hopefully, more profitable.

But eco-friendly cleaning practices also make the property a better working environment for employees, especially if training and motivation make them feel part of a team. Less harsh chemicals are often less irritating to skin and, sometimes, have fewer fumes. Air and water filtration produce cleaner air and water for employees as well as guests. Reuse and conservation programs help the bottom line, which should benefit employees where they need it most—in job security and salary.

To integrate these trends into the everyday operation of the lodging industry, and particularly the housekeeping department, the professional housekeeper will need to address new priorities such as:

- Using property management systems as a way to track room status
- Doing budgeting and accounting using computer software
- Scheduling, staffing, and assigning tasks using computer software
- Forecasting and identifying trends using computer software
- Using technology to speed up operations and control labor hours
- Becoming environmentally aware
- Conserving water and energy
- Finding effective, eco-friendly chemicals
- Revising cleaning procedures to maximize the effectiveness of eco-friendly cleaning products
- Training staff in eco-friendly practices
- Bringing the benefits of eco-friendly practices to the bottom line

### Review Questions

1. What is the difference between computer hardware and software?
2. Describe the basic steps in reporting room status by telephone.
3. What is a PMS?
4. What is on-line purchasing?
5. Describe two benefits of an electronic timekeeping system in computerized labor management.
6. What is recycling and reuse?
7. Describe three procedures that can be implemented in the housekeeping department to conserve water.
8. Describe three procedures that can be implemented in the housekeeping department to conserve energy.

### Critical Thinking Questions

1. Hurried guests are not careful about separating out recyclables. What can the housekeeping department do to resolve this?
2. To save on laundry costs and linen, and for environmental reasons, the executive housekeeper would like to introduce a linen reuse program that calls for changing sheets and towels in stayover rooms every other day. The general man-

ager prefers traditional service. How could the executive housekeeper justify the proposal?

3. Computerization of the housekeeping department means someone will be needed to do data entry, but the department has no budget for hiring another employee. How would the executive housekeeper address this?

# APPENDIX A

## Traditional Care Techniques

As part of the move toward more natural cleaners, some executive housekeepers have gone back to time-honored substances and cleaning methods. Traditional approaches to some key cleaning challenges are included here. Some challenges have various options. The listed and numbered options are not expressed in any order of preference.

Even though the substances mentioned here are natural, care must be taken in their use. Also, surfaces should be rinsed well. After cleaning, all traces of residue from food products should be cleaned up thoroughly to prevent pest problems.

## Copper

1. Rub with half a lemon dipped in salt, rinse with warm water, and polish with a soft cloth.
2. Wash with warm water, then rub with a paste of salt, fine sand, and vinegar using a clean, flannel cloth; wash again in warm water. After cleaning, rub the item with a little oil to remove tarnish.

## Brass

1. Rub with equal amounts of flour and salt moistened with vinegar to remove tarnish.
2. Rub on Worcestershire sauce to remove tarnish, then wash off.

## Chandeliers and Mirrors

1. Wipe with a cloth wrung out of a solution of water and alcohol; polish with a newspaper.
2. Blast chandeliers by blowing away dust. Camera shops have several compressed air products for cleaning cameras that work well.

## Crystal or Glass

1. Apply a paste of dry mustard and oil to remove deposits ringing a vase.
2. Apply a construction sand and water solution to remove discoloration.
3. Shake crushed eggshells and soap and water in a vase or bottle; rinse well.

## Furniture: Bruises

1. Wet the dent or bruise with warm water. Fold a piece of brown paper several times, then soak it in warm water. Lay it on the dent or bruise. Apply a warm, *not hot*, iron to the paper until the moisture has evaporated. If the bruise is not raised to the surface, repeat the process.

## Furniture: Marks

1. Rub gently with 0000 steel wool dipped in oil and then cigarette ash.
2. Rub with linseed oil.

## Furniture: Scratches

If the wood is dark, rub it with a walnut half.

## Ink Removal

1. For carpet, soak with milk and keep applying and soaking up the ink stain. When the stain is completely removed, wash the carpet with soapy water and rinse with clear water. Let the carpet dry.
2. Use gentle soap, lemon juice, and starch in solution to clean the spot.

## Lace

1. Hand wash lace gently in lukewarm water; do not wring it out, simply squeeze it. Rinse in diluted sugar water (1 pint water and 3 lumps sugar), squeeze it gently and pin it on to a cloth to dry. If it is still limp, press it between pages of waxed paper with a warm iron.

## Leather

1. Clean with a brush dipped in a weak solution of soda water and water, then rinse dry. To revive the luster, apply egg white with a sponge.

## Marble: Cleaning

1. Use toothpaste to remove rings.

## Marble: Polishing

1. Polish with milk.
2. Sift together 1/2 pound baking soda; 1/4 pound powdered pumice, and 1/4 pound chalk; add water and rub well into the marble; let dry; wash off with soap and water and dry.

## Mildew

1. For portable items, cover spots of mildew with a mixture of soap, starch, and salt; expose the item to the sun.

2. Soak items with mildew overnight in milk; then place in the sun to dry.

## Rust (specifically iron rust)

1. Rub the item with lemon juice and salt. If the rust is stubborn, let the item stand one hour or apply the mixture a second time, then rinse in water. (Use a weak dilution of ammonia in the rinse water if all else fails.)

## Wallpaper

1. Rub gently with uncooked oatmeal using a clean cloth. Cover the entire area with dropcloths to catch any residue.

# 15

# Capitalizing on Opportunities for the Future

## Chapter Objectives

To maximize future opportunities, professional housekeepers should:

- Expand educational skills
- Hone managerial skills
- Expand computer skills and technological understanding
- Be able to anticipate the changing needs of the guest of the future
- Anticipate the capabilities of new products and design elements

The students of today will be the professional housekeepers of tomorrow. In what kind of world will they work? What types of jobs will be available? Where will their career paths take them?

As in most professions, the changes affecting the housekeeping profession are dramatic and ongoing. In order to meet these challenges, professional housekeepers must anticipate how the industry will evolve. As discussed in Chapter 14, computer literacy is fast becoming a requirement for housekeeping managers. The advanced technology of both systems and equipment, as well as the managerial demands for up-to-the-minute data on rooms and costs, will require more than a basic understanding of how to turn on a terminal and type on a keyboard.

Perhaps the strongest message for the professional housekeepers who will define the future of the profession is that their jobs will become even more managerial. In emergency situations, they may be called upon to clean a guest room, but their day-to-day job will be to manage labor effectively and run their department efficiently. This strong focus on managerial skills requires more than on-the-job training. It will require more education, and more continuing education.

For those who acquire these skills, their career paths will expand as opportunities arise for professional housekeepers. The ability to manage one of the property's largest and most important departments successfully will broaden career opportunities both within the property and in other industries.

## THE CHANGING ROLE OF THE PROFESSIONAL HOUSEKEEPER

The image of the professional housekeeper as "the lady with the key" is gone forever. The man or woman who heads the modern housekeeping department is far more likely to spend time initiating cost control programs and coping with human resource issues than scrubbing tile or vacuuming corridors. One source predicts, "Professional housekeepers will be spending more and more time with the property's top management and less and less time on the floors. Management skills will be far more important than technical training."

### New Skills for New Responsibilities

The skills required of an executive housekeeper are changing as the job evolves. Some research done as recently as the early 1990s showed that executive housekeepers in all aspects of the profession averaged a little over 13 years of education. This profile will be very different within five to 10 years. As the executive housekeeper's position crosses "the threshold of management" in mid-tier and larger properties, it will be expected that the person who holds the post has an associate's degree or beyond. For those seeking jobs in deluxe or very large properties—those with more than 500 rooms—a four-year degree will be essential. However, in the housekeeping profession, experience is still an important asset when looking for jobs at large or high-profile properties. In the near term the skills any professional housekeeper should add to his or her resume include:

1. **Computer literacy.** Computer skills are essential to modern management. Familiarity with lodging technology, from property management systems to in-room air purification systems is also a plus. More than a passing knowledge of business technology will also be helpful, as rooms continue to evolve toward mini-office concepts, complete with in-room fax machines, sometimes with printers. All this technology has to be cared for, and the executive housekeeper who understands these systems at least well enough to develop proper cleaning techniques and schedules will have an advantage (see Figures 15.1a and 15.1b).

2. **Financial skills.** Though the professional housekeeper is not expected to be an accountant, he or she is expected to develop and balance a budget and help the property meet its financial goals.

3. **Human resources management.** Many professional housekeepers who enroll in continuing education studies or apply for advanced degrees are adding courses in human resources. Since labor continues to be one of the largest departmental costs, and labor problems one of the areas most vulnerable to costly litigation, any professional housekeeper with some expertise in handling labor issues has an advantage when applying for a post.

4. **Management skills.** Even those who have no aspirations of becoming a general manager will need to know the basics of lodging operations.

Preparing for the longer term, professional housekeepers should consider broadening their skills and management capabilities. Beth Risinger, head of IEHA predicts significant changes in the role of the professional housekeeper. "In the future,

the position of executive housekeeper may evolve toward a title such as general operations manager. The person who fulfills this role may be responsible not only for the cleanliness of the property but also for the grounds, engineering and maintenance, laundry and safety and security. In health care, we may see this general operations manager also be responsible for food distribution."

However broad these responsibilities become and however strong the management emphasis is, housekeeping cannot be reduced to a series of numbers on a spreadsheet. "A bureaucrat sitting at a desk cannot manage housekeeping operations. The job of the executive housekeeper or director of housekeeping is definitely evolving more toward being a business manager than being someone who supervises the attendants. But the housekeeping manager still has to make sure the attendants are coming to work and that the job of cleaning the property is getting done correctly," comments one veteran industry watcher.

## JOB OPPORTUNITIES

The skills necessary to succeed as a professional housekeeper open the door to lifelong career opportunities. These opportunities exist both within and beyond the lodging industry, in the United States and around the world.

***Opportunities in the United States.*** Industry experts quoted by *HOTELS* magazine predict rooms growth in the United States will continue to be only about 2 percent per year for the next several years. Mid-tier to upscale hotels that average 0.75 to 1 employee per guest would require 150 to 200 employees for each 200-room hotel. Adding 550 properties a year would create 80,000 to 100,000 new jobs, 10 percent of which would be managerial.

Executive search expert Stephen J. Renard, Renard International, predicts job growth for executive housekeepers will be fairly stagnant in the near term. One factor hampering overall job growth is that the title of executive housekeeper is being eliminated in some properties, especially those in the economy tier. The duties are being combined with the responsibilities of the rooms division manager, points out Renard.

Professional housekeepers will find more opportunities at the upper end of the lodging market. "The larger hotels and deluxe properties will continue looking for executive housekeepers," says

*(a)*

*(b)*

**Figure 15.1**  *(a) Upgraded city center hotel suites are evolving toward mini-offices/ entertainment centers in the living space, and a comfortably residential, distinct sleeping area. This creates new demands on the housekeeping department's staff, as well as its equipment and supply needs. (Courtesy of The Westin Bangkok, Bangkok, Thailand) (b) Attendands assigned to specialty rooms, such as this business suite in the Westin Bangkok with its sophisticated technology, should be trained to clean in a high-tech environment. (Courtesy of The Westin Bangkok, Bangkok, Thailand)*

Renard. These properties cannot afford any slippage in standards, nor can they risk guest dissatisfaction over the standards of cleanliness. Most of the job opportunities will be in existing hotels, since new construction and the lingering effects of the overbuilding in the 1980s are limiting hotel growth in the upper tier.

Renard points out that there is also fairly steady turnover at the executive housekeeper level. "Most younger people don't stay in the job very long; they move on to the front office and the rooms division." For those who choose to stay in the profession, there will be good, career-long opportunities. "Executive housekeepers are like good wine. The more mature they get, the more valuable they are. There is more demand now for executive housekeepers in their 40s or 50s than in their 30s. Because of the nature of the labor force, the executive housekeeper must take on the role of mother or father to the staff. That's easier for a mature person. Also, since the labor force continues to be primarily made up of adult immigrants, it is more likely they will be willing to take orders from someone their age or older," Renard comments.

Operators know that good executive housekeepers may be difficult to find. Some hotels have had to search months to find the right executive housekeeper. Others have had to launch an international search to find the person with the right qualifications.

*International opportunities.* The bulk of the job growth for executive housekeepers in the near term will be outside of the United States, Renard says. Although professional housekeepers may be able to find jobs almost anywhere outside of the United States, the Middle East and Europe would be good places to start looking in the near future.

Asia remains the hot bed of hotel development. Its volatile young economies are attracting business travelers from around the region and around the world. These business travelers have sparked a major wave of new construction in gateway cities throughout the region, particularly in Malaysia and Indonesia, and a secondary push for resort building along the region's beautiful beaches. Although their economies are just stabilizing, Latin American countries are becoming a target for hotel development. Many major cities have seen little or no new hotel construction for decades. Now, lodging companies are seeking to get a foothold before their competitors do. Most of this first wave of construction will be in the upscale markets, creating new managerial job opportunities. Whatever the location, international travelers demand international standards of cleanliness. Experienced executive housekeepers are in demand.

Renard points out that fluency in a second or third language will be beneficial to those seeking overseas' positions in countries where English is not used extensively. An understanding of local culture is also important, as is an understanding of the likely makeup of the property's labor force. In many countries, immigrants make up the prospective labor pool for entry-level jobs in the lodging industry. Knowing how to tap this market and manage a multicultural staff will be essential.

The professional housekeeper also needs to make sure his or her skills and experience would translate well to the working environment of the country. Different management styles and varying levels of technical knowledge will be required in different countries.

## International Management Styles

Throughout the world, the job of the professional housekeeper is becoming more and more managerial. But management styles and technical requirements differ. "The management style in North America is much less formal. Managers and staff are on a first-name basis. This makes the management style more personal and it ensures better communication," comments Marion Hansen, the German-born executive housekeeper of Ocean Pointe Hotel and Spa, Victoria, British Columbia, Canada.

Ocean Pointe's General Manager Rick Stolle, who has worked in the United States, Canada and Europe, agrees that executive housekeepers will have to take a different approach in Europe. "In Europe, managers manage more by dictate. In North America, the staff wants to know *why* something has to be done a certain way. Training also differs. In Europe, training is fairly standardized. Employees (usually even attendants) have taken some training at a technical school or (for managers) at a hotel school. Apprenticeship programs also provide a great level of training. But there is still something of that 'upstairs/downstairs' attitude (that those who work in service-oriented jobs are "servants"). In North America, people are trained to be *of service*, not to be servants. At this hotel, we hire for attitude. It's a lot easier to teach skills. It's almost impossible to change attitudes," comments Stolle.

Still, experience in Europe can expand a housekeeper's technical knowledge, especially in historic hotels and hotels with general managers trained at some of the world's most famous hotel schools. In Asia, there are many opportunities for executive housekeepers who want experience in opening new hotels and managing departments at high-end, five-star operations.

## Career Paths of the Future

As you learned in Chapter 2, career paths for executive housekeepers are broad, and they continue to expand. Most experts predict the responsibilities of the executive housekeeper's job will continue to grow, perhaps to encompass all maintenance functions as well. More and more, the executive housekeeper will be the pivotal point of control for protecting the investment in the property's physical plant and all of the capital assets it contains.

At some point, the housekeeping staff may include a blend of robotic cleaners for rote functions and employees for work that requires expertise and innovation. Executive housekeepers will need to address these problems and take advantage of the technology of the future to build a more efficient operation.

Executive housekeepers may find themselves working under the sea or, in the next millennium, in a hotel being planned by a Japanese firm on the moon. They will work in rainforests and, perhaps, even on the tundra. Wherever people travel, hotels will be built and they will need executive housekeepers.

One thing that will not change, say most industry watchers, is the need to remember that guest satisfaction is the key. Even with virtual reality and high-tech teleconferencing, people will continue to travel and will want to feel "at home" even in a hotel. And, for most, a clean, comfortable guest room is vital to achieving this home-away-from-home feeling.

## The Future of Salary and Benefits

In the future, salaries will improve gradually. Again, Renard predicts those willing to work abroad may see a more meaningful paycheck. Although the raw salary figures may be the same or slightly less than in the United States, they are far more meaningful because in many countries the executive housekeeper does not have to pay tax. For example, a $36,000 net salary that is a salary from which nothing more will be deducted, means a better income than a $40,000 salary from which

taxes, insurance, and other deductions will need to be made.

Professional housekeepers also will share in the lodging industry's movement toward providing better benefits. Insurance, paid sick leave, and paid vacations are becoming standard for many chains, management companies, and independent hotels. Years ago, these were rare. Attaining managerial status enables the professional housekeeper to participate in programs beyond these basics. Included in the executive housekeeper's compensation package may be any or all of the following:

1. **Insurance.** In the past, companies bore the cost of health/hospitalization insurance for their employees. Now, it is more likely health insurance will involve contributions both from the company and employee. Most companies make some kind of health insurance available; comprehensive plans may include dental insurance and/or optical insurance. Some companies also make life insurance available at low rates or through plans in which the employee and employer both make contributions.

2. **Investment plans.** As lodging establishments compete for the best managers available, they have begun offering menus of investment plans like those of their corporate competitors. These may include:

   • **A retirement fund.** Few companies have pensions, which provide for regular, life-long income for the company's retirees. The amount of the pension payment is based on the employee's pre-retirement salary. Pensions largely have been replaced by retirement accounts that blend investments deducted from the employee's salary with a matching percentage contribution from the employer. These are generally tax-free and have the advantage that they reduce taxable income because contributions are deducted before the tax is taken out of the salary. Many companies have a variety of investments in which these funds may be placed, and employees can change their investments quarterly to take advantage of the best returns in various investment markets.

   • **Stock option plans.** Large, publicly held companies, including lodging companies or their parent companies, sometimes offer **stock options** to their highest ranking employees. This means the employees are able to buy a certain number of shares of the company for a certain price. For example, an employee may be entitled to buy a certain number of shares for five years at the prevailing price when the agreement is made.

- **Profit sharing plans.** When a company offers a profit-sharing plan, a certain set amount, usually based on a percentage of the employee's income, is deducted on a pre-tax basis from each paycheck. Some or all of this amount is then matched by the company. The combined total is invested. Some plans let the employee choose among different options for investing the money; others pre-determine the investment—usually some low-risk investment market.

3. **Paid vacation/leave.** The hours for managers in the lodging industry can be long and it is not unusual for even top management to work some weekends or holidays, when the situation demands. Although the 9-to-5, 40-hour work week may not be a reality in the lodging industry, top managers can expect *fairly* regular work hours and regular time off.

   Many companies make provisions for **compensatory time.** For example, if an executive housekeeper has to work on a holiday, he or she may be able to take off another day during the week with pay as compensatory time. Top managers can expect to have paid vacations, and may even be able to negotiate more weeks of paid vacation as part of their compensation package when they are hired. The employer may also offer various types of special leave, from maternity leave to part-time leave to allow for continuing education.

4. **Housing and maintenance.** Renard points out that many properties outside of the United States still provide special compensation packages for **expatriates,** staff members who are citizens of other countries, that includes on-premise living quarters for senior management. Although this may be only a studio apartment or the equivalent of two standard rooms plus limited kitchen facilities, it is rent-free and there is no charge for daily cleaning or maintenance. Properties throughout the world also may provide for an executive dining room in which the executive housekeeper and other top managers eat free or at reduced cost. Free laundry and dry cleaning services also may be a privilege afford to senior managers.

5. **Hardship benefits.** Working internationally is not generally viewed as a *hardship*. However, a post in a culture that is very different and requires substantial commitment and adjustment may offer some highly attractive benefits. These may include housing, tax-free compensation (if the local government permits; the individual still may be expected to pay tax to the country of which he or she is a citizen), daily transportation to and from work, **per diem** (literally "for each day") allowances covering basic needs from meals to dry cleaning and even partial tuition payments so that the employee's children can attend a local school that teaches in their native language—though this is becoming rarer. The rule is that the harder it will be to find a qualified person to fill the position, the more elaborate the salary and benefits arrangement will be.

6. **Memberships and education.** It is still common for companies to pay for memberships in clubs or associations that will help executives in their business endeavors. This applies to industry associations. However, because hotels and motels often rely on the good will of the community to generate meeting and function business, this may also include memberships to civic and fraternal organizations. Companies frequently will bear all or at least a substantial part of continuing education costs.

7. **Entertainment and expense allowances.** Like other managers, executives housekeepers incur entertainment and other incidental expenses that benefit business. Companies provide for some type of expense account for the executive housekeeper. All expenses must be justified.

8. **Miscellaneous.** Depending on the business interests of the company itself, parent company, or subsidiaries, the executive housekeeper may be able to obtain discounts on products and services ranging from airfare to free or reduced-rate stays at sister hotels.

## The Labor Issue

Labor is one of the biggest challenges facing executive housekeepers. Finding workers, controlling labor costs, and maximizing staff efficiency (without sacrificing standards) will continue to be tough assignments for anyone who heads up a labor-intensive housekeeper department.

## THE SHRINKING LABOR MARKET

Professional housekeepers in the United States and other parts of the world already feel the impact of the shrinking labor market. Lower birth rates in generations after the baby boomers of the 1950s have reduced the actual labor supply. The *Kiplinger Washington Newsletter* forecasts total births will continue to edge downward and young people will comprise an even smaller proportion of the population by 2020. This has put pressure on the lodging industry and other industries that rely on unskilled labor for myriad tasks.

***Entry-level labor.*** Most experts predict that immigrants will continue to make up the backbone of the entry-level labor pool for housekeeping departments and other departments requiring unskilled labor. Kiplinger predicts that by 2060, minorities will make up 50 percent of the U.S. population, up from the current 20 percent. Executive housekeepers need to respond to this in several ways:

1. New waves of immigration will have to be anticipated. Since even entry-level positions require training and information, the professional housekeeper must make sure someone on staff speaks English and the language of the new immigrants well enough to translate.
2. As more cultures blend within the department, the executive housekeeper will have to find ways to minimize any cultural friction.
3. It will be important to understand the culture and traditions of new immigrants. This would range from religious considerations to how familiar the people are with accepted housekeeping practices.
4. The executive housekeeper will need to find the most effective means for reaching and tapping these new labor pools. Some industry watchers say flexible scheduling may be a workable solution to the labor problem. The pressure for workers to have more than one job or for families to have more than one income has generated a new work force. However, this is a labor pool that requires flexibility to work hours around the primary job or around school or family schedules.

***Skilled labor and management.*** The lodging industry will continue to experience a defection of managers to higher paying industries. Studies done in the United Kingdom showed many people leaving the hospitality industry after less than 10 years to take higher paying jobs with more regular hours in other industries.

The recent movement toward better salaries and compensation in the lodging industry may stem this tide in the future, but it will be a gradual process. The lodging industry and related fields must show some long-term commitment to human resources programs, even during cyclical downturns in business.

## Staff Cuts

During the recession of the early 1990s, many industries, including lodging, learned to accomplish more with fewer employees. This was a lesson well learned and will shape staffing requirements for this decade and beyond. In the housekeeping department, those in mid-level management were found to be most expendable. Inspectors' or supervisors' positions were either eliminated wholesale or vastly reduced in many properties. Other properties that retained supervisory staff responded to pressure to control labor costs by raising quotas for both supervisory staff and attendants. This seemingly small change sometimes reduced overall staff by one to two positions.

Executive housekeepers are setting up training programs that empower room attendants to be self-supervising or utilizing technology to help the existing supervisory staff check more rooms efficiently. They continue to refine training and experiment with different approaches such as team cleaning to find ways to increase each employee's productivity. Renard points out that some of the supervisory staff cuts may be restored as occupancy and profitability return.

A very few deluxe hotels provide the exception to this less-is-more attitude toward staffing. Guests who can afford to pay several hundred dollars per night to stay at the high-end international chains such as Four Seasons, Regent, Ritz-Carlton, Inter-Continental, Peninsula, Shangri-La or premium properties in broader-based lodging chains, expect flawless service. They may also expect their rooms serviced twice daily. Meeting these expectations requires enough staff to clean and maintain these well-appointed hotels. Quotas often are lower because rooms are larger and have more design elements than their streamlined, business-class competitors.

Some properties may even have valets or butlers for guests staying on concierge or executive floors. Part of the housekeeping staff, the butler or valet unpacks bags, brings refreshments for the guest, and cleans the guest rooms assigned to him or her. Several deluxe lodging chains have experimented with butler service. A typical quota would be one butler for seven rooms.

Any executive housekeeper who has valets or butlers on staff needs to create flexible assignment procedures. Though cleaning rooms remains a basic requirement of the job, the butler or valet also must be able to respond to numerous and highly individualized guest requests. These may range from the expected, such as sewing on buttons and caring for clothes, to the unexpected. In one case, a guest had packed only brown shoes but was invited to a black-tie reception. A quick-thinking valet contacted members of the hotel's senior management, asking if any had black shoes in the guest's size. One person did, loaned the guest his shoes, and made the guest a loyal customer.

Though the cost of the butlers/valets is offset somewhat because the rooms to which they are assigned would require attendants in any case, market demand for such a service generally has not been strong enough to justify any extra labor costs. More typically, the executive floors are serviced by top performers from the housekeeping staff who also are trained to deal with VIPs and a concierge or guest services representative assigned specifically to the upgraded floors.

As professional housekeepers become more comfortable using computers, they will increase their productivity. This is especially important at a time when the number of assistant housekeepers or executive assistant housekeepers is generally being reduced. Computerization allows the executive housekeeper to track departmental productivity and expenses at the push of a button. Although executive housekeepers now must interact more with top management each day and attend more meetings with other departmental managers, they also use time management skills to make sure they still have adequate time to be on the floors, to understand the needs and performance abilities of their staff, and to insure that cleaning standards are being maintained properly.

### Contract Cleaning Services

Although most professional housekeepers prefer to have staff perform as many functions as possible, the reality of labor costs may mean more work is being done by outside contractors. Executive housekeepers will have to find better ways of controlling costs and performance by these outside services, and coordinate the activities of several different services.

As the contract cleaning industry grows, prices will become more competitive, as will the range of services offered by each company. The shrinking physical plant of the property, necessitated by ris-

ing real estate and construction costs, may limit how much equipment, storage, and back-of-the-house space is available for housekeeping activities. With no space for any but the most compact laundry, the professional housekeeper of the future may have to look to outside contractors to provide all dry cleaning services, some special laundry services and more.

Generally, core cleaning operations will remain in the housekeeping department. Some properties are experimenting with hiring off-premise cleaning contractors to provide backup service to the housekeeping department. Attendants on staff would clean guest rooms, while the service's employees would be cleaning the public areas, back of the house, or specialty areas such as outdoor banquet venues.

For security reasons, it is unlikely that operators would have any outside service clean guest rooms. It is equally unlikely that any operator would risk slippage in standards by entrusting room cleaning to an outside contractor However, at least one analyst suggests that hiring outside contractors to clean public areas and the back of the house may be a workable solution in cities in which operators face tough demands from unions or need to provide heavy benefits packages. Hiring outside contractors may be equally appealing in labor markets in which employees are hard to find. Rather than constantly searching for qualified employees and competing for staff by raising salaries to unjustifiable levels, the executive housekeeper can hire a cost-effective cleaning service to do all but core functions. Blending staff and contract cleaners will pose ample managerial challenges for the professional housekeeper of the future.

## THE NEW LOOK OF THE LODGING INDUSTRY

The role of the executive housekeeper of the future also will change in response to changes in guest demand, changes in the physical plant of the property, and changes in the types of products that will be available (see Tales of the Trade 15.1). Preparing for these changes, rather than responding to them, will be more effective and far less costly.

**Tales of the Trade 15.1**
**The Room of the Year 2020**
One or two executive housekeepers may be preparing to meet the challenges of cleaning the

first hotel on the moon (a Japanese company is already exploring that possibility), but many professional housekeepers will find significant changes here on earth.

Gerald Allison and Howard Wolff, directors of the award-winning architectural firm of Wimberly Allison Tong & Goo, with offices around the world, envision the hotel of the future this way:

The front desk will be a thing of the past. And so will keys. Guests will be taken directly to their assigned rooms, where they will access the room with a device that recognizes their handprint or thumbprint. All of their preferences and any special requests would be in their computerized file and would have been noted when the reservation came in via modem from their home or office.

Once inside, the guest room will be a home away from home and an office away from the office. Not only will it have all the necessary technological amenities for doing business, it will have the latest in creature comforts: sensor-driven heating and air conditioning systems that will remember what temperature each guest likes the room to be; adjustable lighting; even windows with so-called "smart glass" that darkens in bright sunlight and lightens when it is dark outside. Instead of fumbling for light switches, guests will simply don a headband with electrodes to control the lights, entertainment system, and heating and cooling systems. Some interior designers say chairs will become entertainment centers, with capabilities for providing virtual reality experiences. Televisions will come out of the armoire and be housed in special areas behind wall panels. Fabrics will be inherently fade resistant. More laminates will be used, as wood becomes rare.

The hotels of the future may be "starscrapers," up to 800 feet tall. They may be in fully enclosed artificial environments. Some eco-friendly resorts may be built under the sea. One rustic prototype has been operating for several years.

Beth Risinger, of IEHA, sees the housekeeping department changing along with the hotel. "Robots will be cleaning the rooms of the future, not humans," she predicts. Rising labor costs and difficulty finding staff will make a case for at least experimenting with robotic cleaners.

Other experts say dust and smoke will be removed automatically as part of the function of the air purifying systems. Fabrics may be "self-healing," minimizing damage from burns—if anyone still smokes then. Some plumbing fixtures may even be self-cleaning. But there still will have to be a manager who makes sure the robots are doing their "job" and the bottom line is healthy.

## The Changing Guest Profile

People will continue to travel and continue to stay in hotels, motels, inns, and even tent camps around the world. Who will travel, what they will demand from the lodging industry, and how long their stay will be, all will have an impact on the housekeeping department of the 1990s and beyond.

Market-driven is a term that now seems to drive the lodging industry. Responding to guest demand faster and better than competitors gives a property a marketable edge. If all guests want in-room fax machines, the first property to provide them at no extra cost or a small extra cost may capture a larger market share.

Executive housekeepers need to understand the property's market profile in order to anticipate special requests and special guest needs. How well the professional housekeeper anticipates and meets these demands will have a direct impact on how satisfied the guests will be.

## Business Travelers

Business travelers are the bread-and-butter business of the hotel industry. And, at least for the foreseeable future, this will continue to be true. **Video conferencing,** which functions like a conference call but with video display of all the parties on the line, may have an impact on business travel. But, as the advent of the phone and fax have proven, technology has not yet erased the need for face-to-face business meetings.

The change that will affect professional housekeepers is how much the business traveler will demand. Guest rooms oriented to the business travel market more and more will include some kind of mini-office component. Instead of just dusting dressers and armoires, nightstands and tables, the attendants will have to be trained to work around more equipment: extra phones, in-room fax machines and, say some hoteliers, even personal computers if the price keeps coming down. This may also mean that the housekeeping department will have to add its own audio-visual expert who can plan deep-cleaning operations and advise on what chemicals can be used for interim cleaning, rather than continue relying on a staff member in the audio-visual department.

New brand concepts may offer business travelers more than technology. They also may include a microwave, a better stocked mini-bar, or even a mini-refrigerator. These have only a small effect on cleaning time, but as room attendants point out, minutes add up. Time and motion studies are usually done before properties open to determine quotas. But the fast-changing pace of the industry means they should be done whenever several new amenities are introduced or during renovation as soon as a model room is available.

## Family Travelers

Family travel is expected to continue to increase. This includes not only travel to traditional vacation destinations, but also weekend stays added on to one or both parents' business trip. In fact, many lodging companies are adding child-friendly services to business and conference properties to encourage parents to prolong their stays and boost weekend occupancy.

For the professional housekeeper, this new market will mean higher per-room occupancy and, in some instances, slightly longer average cleaning times. Families will need not only the two double beds in the guest room, but also more rollaways and cribs, and FF&E that will make it comfortable to relax in the room. More in-room video entertainment features are being added, as are microwaves and minibars.

Family business has an impact throughout the housekeeping department: from providing more towels, pillow, and blankets for multiple occupants to supplying more bottles of amenities. It also may necessitate a change in scheduling. Single business travelers generally leave their rooms early to make the most of their business day. Families need extra time, simply because there are more people. Room attendants and supervisors should note by what time the majority of rooms are vacant. This can be tracked on the computer and schedules adjusted accordingly.

## Senior Travelers

The **Kiplinger Washington Newsletter** predicts that people who are 45 to 65 years old will comprise 25 percent of the U.S. population by the year 2020, up from 20 percent now. A study on mature travelers presented during a recent International Hotel Association (IHA) conference on the potential of the senior travel market in Europe indicated that not only will there be more seniors traveling, but that this travel segment will have more discretionary income than other sectors, more time to spend traveling, and more willingness to spend that time filling shoulder and off-peak seasons.

For the executive housekeeper, this increase in senior travelers may mean more rooms with double occupancy. From university-sponsored tours to special-interest tours, some senior travelers enjoy group travel, and that often means two guests per room. Some senior citizens also appreciate safety amenities, such as more grab bars placed throughout the room rather than only in the bathtub or shower enclosure. However, results of the IHA seminar clearly warn against stereotyping senior travelers. The strongest message is that properties catering to senior travelers will need to provide extra staff training to better understand and provide service for the mature travel market.

## Disabled Travelers

Long an overlooked travel market, people with disabilities are finding barriers to travel gradually being removed. Most of the changes required to service guests with disabilities must be made to the infrastructure of guest rooms: wider doorways to accommodate wheelchairs, more grab bars, signage for the visually impaired, and special phones or similar equipment for the hearing impaired. Typically, properties will provide several rooms specially equipped to meet the needs of disabled travelers. Signaling a new trend, some properties are now being designed so that every guest room is at least accessible to those in wheelchairs.

Executive housekeepers say these rooms do not have much effect on either quotas or cleaning time. Attendants assigned to these rooms should regularly check that any special equipment is in proper working order.

## International Guests

As recently as the early 1980s, an executive housekeeper in a large, business-oriented Paris hotel was dismayed to find the majority of the hotel's Japanese guests saw no need to lock their guest rooms when they went out each day. She quickly contacted a representative of the group and explained proper security measures. Despite the growing internationalization of travel, cultural differences still exist and staff must be trained to anticipate and respect them.

"Expected standards of cleanliness have risen all over the world," says Rick Stolle of Ocean Pointe Hotel and Spa, which attracts 50 percent of its clientele from British Columbia and Alberta, Canada; 30 percent from the U.S. Pacific Northwest; 6 percent from the Pacific Rim; 6 percent from Europe; and 8% from other areas. "I do think North Americans are still the most demanding in terms of cleanliness."

A clean bathroom is a special priority for North American travelers. Says one veteran housekeeper, "Most North Americans don't mind a little dust in the corners, but if there is the slightest bit of dirt in the bathroom they will complain." Lyn Aoki, director of housekeeping for the Sheraton Waikiki, Honolulu, says the hotel's Japanese guests are very particular about housekeeping standards. "Typically, our lowest ratings on guest comment cards come from Japanese guests," she says. Asian and European guests expect such in-room amenities as coffee- and tea-makers. They also may expect some other touches of home, such as robes, slippers, and toothbrushes for Japanese guests or down or feather pillows for Europeans. The executive housekeeper should work with the marketing and sales staff to make sure any special requests or other special cultural considerations are noted prior to check-in. This will give the executive housekeeper time to order anything that is needed, make sure these requests are noted on the daily assignment sheets, and discuss any special cultural considerations with the staff.

## Guests with Special Needs

Properties seeking to maximize their markets are looking to cater to every market niche. People with special needs are part of that market mix. Non-smoking rooms soon will outnumber smoking rooms; they already do in many hotels. The newest trend, as discussed in Chapter 14, is to provide environmentally sensitive rooms, some with purification systems, and low-allergen rooms for allergy sufferers. Ocean Pointe Hotel and Spa and some properties in Europe still have special rooms for people traveling with pets. At Ocean Pointe, there is a C$75 ($59) surcharge for rooms in which pets are permitted. Stolle says this covers the cost of cleaning the room thoroughly enough to sell to guests without pets.

Some of these specially equipped guest rooms will take longer to clean. They also may have more specialty equipment, such as purification systems, that will require more monitoring. But, in most cases, they require a change in the type of FF&E and chemicals used rather than a change in cleaning practices.

## Maximizing New Equipment Potential

The future holds not only an evolving type of property, but also new products and equipment for maintaining that property. Interior designers and lodging company executives alike predict that more money will be spent on the infrastructural elements, components of the physical structure such as walls, flooring, and so on, and less on the FF&E which must change to meet current taste and style.

For the executive housekeeper, this will mean dealing with upgraded surfaces both in public areas and guest bathrooms. The 1-inch square tile previously used for guest bathrooms and public restrooms is being replaced by larger tiles with more style. There will be more granite and marble in upscale hotels, bigger and more pampering guest bathrooms and more business amenities—even in resort hotels. Flexibility will be the key in economy properties, where some companies are experimenting with built-in casegoods to free up more floor space. There will be more lighting and more flexible task lighting, or different levels of lighting designed for different purposes, such as bright lighting for reading or working, dimmer lighting for relaxing or watching television.

Professional housekeepers will have a range of new products to clean these changing rooms. In the face of legislative pressure and the pressure of public opinion, chemicals for general cleaning purposes will continue to become more environmentally friendly. The counterbalance, also spurred by public opinion, will be the need for more germicides and laundry equipment capable of sanitizing and sterilizing. Issues ranging from concern over bloodborne pathogens to OSHA compliance will make protective gear such as gloves and goggles an essential part of the working uniform.

There are now commercial vacuums on the market with small air filters. This is probably just a first step in making equipment more environmentally sensitive and more beneficial to the environment. Housekeeping departments already have various small machines or chemicals that can remove various smells, from cigarette smoke to smoky fires, from rooms. This equipment may become more sophisticated, removing allergens or cleaning the air as well.

Professional housekeepers will need to expand their technological knowledge to keep up with advances in equipment. Robotic equipment seems to be the wave of the future. It addresses two key concerns: If it performs as the manufacturers claim it will, it will reduce labor, and it will perform consistently, without days off; without illness, and without the human foibles that can affect performance.

## SUMMARY

No amount of technology can change the fact that cleanliness is an important factor, whether in choosing a hotel room or selecting a unit in a senior living center. Nor can technology replace the need for a manager who can make sure these spaces are cleaned and maintained properly.

The job of the executive housekeeper is bound to change; perhaps even the title will be adapted in the future. Employers will certainly demand more education, more managerial skills, and a better understanding both of computers and equipment technology. Even if robotics do one day replace a portion of the staff, the executive housekeepers of the future still will need "people skills," to direct the core staff and to work effectively with other department heads.

To capitalize on the opportunities of the future, the professional housekeeper will need to address such issues as:

- Improving computer literacy
- Adding a degree or continuing education courses
- Increasing internationalization—of guests, staff, and job opportunities
- Finding and retaining labor, which will be in short supply
- Negotiating an appropriate salary and benefits package
- Capitalizing on new products and services

## Review Questions

1. Name some typical components of a managerial benefits package.
2. Name several new guest markets and discuss how they will affect the housekeeping department.
3. Discuss how new lodging products can affect the job of the executive housekeeper.
4. How important will technical knowledge be in future?
5. How will changes in the labor market affect the housekeeping department?

## Critical Thinking Questions

1. Discuss the advantages and disadvantages of using more robotics and fewer employees.
2. Discuss the advantages and disadvantages of working abroad.
3. The general manager has proposed promoting the executive housekeeper to director of housekeeping. But the executive housekeeper position will be dropped and the number of assistants will not be increased. How will this affect departmental operations?

# Glossary

**Adjoining rooms.** Two or more rooms side by side, with or without connecting doors between them. In other words, rooms can be adjoining without being connected.

**Assignment sheet.** Written instructions that detail what tasks must be done by an employee during his or her shift.

**Back-of-the-house.** The service areas not open to the public.

**Back-to-back.** Heavy check-out and check-in on the same day, so that as soon as a room is made up a new guest checks in.

**Balancing.** The duty of the staffing clerk every morning when he or she tries to assign someone to clean rooms over the quota of the day.

**Banquet house attendant.** Person who does set-ups and cleaning in meeting rooms.

**Bay.** Section of a building defined by architectural or structural elements.

**Beeper.** A portable communication device that acts as a pager. Some units emit a sound signal; others vibrate. Newer models display the number of the caller.

**Best practices.** Optimum procedures for accomplishing a given task.

**Biohazard.** A threat posed by living organisms.

**Bloodborne pathogen.** Disease-causing germ or virus carried in blood.

**Bonnet cleaning.** Cleaning system which uses a rotary machine fitted with special bonnet pads to agitate carpet cleaning.

**Booking.** Reservation that is made for a room or a function.

**Boxed beds.** Two twin beds pushed together to make a king-sized bed.

**Break down a room.** Remove the tables, chairs, stages, and other items from a function or meeting room after an event is completed.

**Bridge the beds.** Putting two twin mattresses crosswise over box springs to form a king-size bed.

**Brush up (BUP).** Tidying a room after a guest has checked out (beds having been done earlier) and replacing the bathroom supplies. Also known as a **touch-up** room.

**Budget.** The financial framework for operations which outlines all expected expenditures for a certain period.

**Buffer.** Machine used for floor care that polishes at low speed.

**Building superintendent** (sometimes called chief engineer). The person in charge of the maintenance of the building.

**Burnisher.** Machine used for floor care that polishes at very high speeds.

**Busperson.** Person who clears the table in a restaurant after each course.

**Call-off.** An absence requested on very short notice, usually less than two hours before the start of a shift.

**Canteen.** The area on a guest floor that houses the ice machine and other vending machines.

**Capital budget.** A budget or a portion of a general budget that outlines planned expenditures for capital equipment.

**Capital equipment.** Equipment that lasts a year or more.

**Card.** The process of separating or straightening wool, yarn, or fiber.

**Casegoods.** Furniture made of wood with drawers or cupboards. This term now includes most furniture except beds.

**Check-in.** The process of registering the guest, assigning the guest a room, and issuing a key. Check-in, officially, refers to the time at which the guest "takes possession" of the room.

**Check-out.** The process of vacating a hotel room (taking luggage), turning in the key, and paying the bill. Also, on housekeeping assignment sheets, a room status indicating that a guest has officially vacated; shown by the code C/O.

**Chief engineer.** The person in charge of the engineering department, which may include a crew of plumbers, electricians, and other specialized personnel.

**Closed dates.** The dates on which no rooms can be rented because of a full house.

**Color–fastness.** The ability to hold color after cleaning; indicates the fabric is unlikely to bleed or fade as a result of cleaning.

**Commercial rate.** The rate agreed on by a company and hotel for all individual room reservations. Some hotels give all business travelers a commercial rate, even if their companies do not have contracts with the hotel.

**Comp.** Complimentary; there are no charges for room and/or service(s). A **"full comp"** means there is no charge for the room or any services, including meals, telephone, valet and so on.

**Compensatory time.** Time off with pay taken in return for unpaid overtime or, less frequently in the lodging industry, work on holidays.

**Confirmed reservation.** An oral or written confirmation by a hotel that a reservation has been accepted (written is preferred). There is usually a 6:00 P.M. (local time) check-in deadline. Guests can check in later if they notify the hotel and hold the room with a credit card.

**Connecting rooms.** Two or more rooms with private connecting doors permitting access between them without going into the corridor.

**Contract furnishings.** Furnishings designed for institutional use as opposed to home use; they are purchased on a contract that includes specifications, delivery time, and so on.

**Cost per occupied room.** A calculation in which all departmental costs for a certain period are totaled, then divided by the actual number of occupied rooms for that same period.

**Covers.** The number of persons served food at functions or in a restaurant.

**Crevice tool.** A vacuum attachment that narrows to a slit-like opening.

**Crinkle sheet.** Also called a **third sheet** or a **night spread,** this distinctly woven sheet (resembling seersucker) is used to cover and protect the blanket.

**Cross-training.** Training an employee to do tasks for positions other than the one for which he or she was hired.

**Day rate.** This is usually one-half the rate of the room, for use by a guest during a given day up to 5:00 P.M. This is sometimes called a **use rate.**

**Deficit spending.** Spending that exceeds income.

**Department.** An organizational unit of the property defined by the special functions it must perform.

**Disaster plan.** A plan that outlines where to go in the hotel and what to do in case of a natural disaster such as a hurricane or a man-made disaster, such as a bombing.

**Division.** An organizational unit of the property made up of several departments.

**Do not disturb (DND).** Instructions left by the guest, usually on a door hanger provided by the hotel, that no one knock on the door or disturb the guest. Also, the code on room assignment sheets indicating the guest did not want to be disturbed and the room was not serviced.

**Double double.** A room with two double beds.

**Double locked (DL).** An occupied room in which the dead bolt has been turned to prohibit entry from the corridor.

**Dropping a room.** Term used when a room attendant services one room less than the quota.

**Dry foam extractor.** Machine that uses a dry foam cleaner and low moisture.

**Dry powder cleaning system.** A two-part cleaning system in which dry power or crystals are applied and bind with the dirt, then the powder or crystals are vacuumed up.

**Due out (D/O).** A room status indicating that guests are due to depart that day at the regular check-out time.

**Emergency Action Plan.** A plan that outlines exactly what to do, where to go, and whom to notify if an emergency arises.

**Emergency Response Plan.** More detailed than the Emergency Action Plan, this spells out what actions an employee could take to control the emergency situation, such as how to use a fire extinguisher in the case of a small fire.

**Entry-level jobs.** Jobs that do not require prior experience and for which the least amount of training and instruction are needed.

**Equipment.** Durable goods used in a lodging operation.

**Even exchange.** A system, most frequently used for uniform issuance, in which employees must turn in one soiled item before being issued a clean one.

**Exempt personnel.** Personnel who are paid a fixed salary each week, as opposed to an hourly rate.

**Face weight.** The yarn weight of carpet.

**Felts.** Table pads or mattress covers.

**Fire Disaster Plan.** A plan which spells out what procedures employees should follow in case of fire.

**Flag.** On an assignment sheet, this refers to a printed message from the reservations department noting a guest's special instructions prior to arrival or any special instructions from the management pertaining to the guest's room. When referring to lodging companies, a flag refers to a company name or brand name.

**Floor par.** The number of sets of linen needed to service the rooms on a particular floor.

**Folio.** A guest's bill.

**Frequency chart** or **Frequency schedule.** A long-term schedule, usually covering a year, which lists what tasks must be done each day, week, month, and on a periodic basis.

**Front desk.** The area where the guest checks in, where the keys are kept, and where the mail is distributed; also refers to the front desk staff who pass along information to housekeeping and other departments.

**Front office.** The area where information regarding guests is kept, such as reservations and folios.

**Front of the house.** The entire public area, including the banquet and meeting rooms.

**Furniture, fixtures, and equipment (FF&E).** All of the design elements within the hotel; sometimes referred to as furnishings, finishes, and equipment.

**General clean.** Indicates a thorough cleaning of guest rooms and baths. Also known as **deep clean.**

**General manager (GM).** The chief executive at the property level.

**Graveyard shift.** The eight-hour shift that begins at 11 P.M. or midnight.

**Gross.** In financial terms, the raw total with nothing subtracted. Gross revenues are a simple total of all revenues the property has taken in for a certain period.

**Guest charge.** Charges put on a guest's folio.

**Guest history** or **Guest profile.** A record of a guest's preferences, special requests, and patterns of stay.

**Guest loan item.** Hotel property loaned to a guest for all or part of his or her stay.

**Hard block.** A notation on a reservation that means the guest must be assigned to a particular room.

**Hard wire.** Installing an electrical appliance or piece of equipment in such a way that the appliance wires are connected directly through the wall to the building's electrical wiring without use of a plug.

**Hazard Communication Plan (HAZCOMM).** A written plan that spells out communication standards for hazardous materials. Contents of the plan are set by the Occupational Health and Safety Administration.

**Held luggage.** The guest's property is held in lieu of payment for a room.

**High duster.** A long-handled tool specially designed to clean high, hard-to-reach places.

**Hot water extraction.** Cleaning system that sprays hot water through a high-pressure nozzle flushes dirt to the surface, then vacuums dirt up and carries it away to a sink drain through a discharge hose.

**Income statement.** A financial statement listing all income received by the property during a certain period.

**Inventory.** Stock on hand. When used as a verb, it means to take a count of the stock on hand.

**Inventory record or inventory report.** A list of each supply item, showing current stock levels and, often, showing cost data.

**Job description.** A detailed report of all functions that must be performed by an employee and the manner in which they must be performed.

**Job specification.** An explanation of the minimum requirements that must be met by a job applicant.

**Johnny mop.** Short-handled mop for cleaning the toilet bowl.

**Key controls.** Loss-prevention procedures that closely track who is issued which keys at the beginning of the shift and whether all keys are returned at the end of the shift.

**Labor analysis.** An analysis which shows, on average, how many labor hours it takes to complete a task.

**Light duty.** A workload that is not demanding in terms of physical stamina or mental challenge.

**Lock-out/tag out.** Mechanized safeguards that prevent employees from accidentally over-riding shut-down functions on machinery that is down for repair.

**Make up.**    Changing the linen on beds and cleaning the bathroom while the guest is registered.

**Maximum inventory level.**    The maximum level stock should reach; no more orders should be placed until some of this overage is used up.

**Minimum inventory level.**    The lowest level stock should reach before reordering.

**Model room.**    A sample room that contains all of the furnishings, finishes, and equipment that will be installed in a new build or renovated guest room.

**Month to date (MTD).**    Accounting totals shown for a specific month as of a specific date.

**Muslin.**    A fabric that has been carded rather than fine combed; usually refers to a fabric used for sheets.

**Napery.**    Table linens.

**Net.**    When used in financial terms, the remainder after all costs have been subtracted from the total. For example, net revenues would be those revenues after taxes are deducted and all other financial commitments, including loan payments, are met.

**Nonrecycled inventory.**    Cleaning supplies or guest supplies that are used (or consumed).

**No-show employee.**    Staff member who fails to show up for work and does not call to explain the absence.

**No-show guest.**    A guest with a confirmed reservation who does not check into the room or call to cancel the reservation.

**Occupancy.**    The number of rooms actually in use.

**Occupational Health and Safety Administration (OSHA).**    The federal agency that creates and enforces regulations dealing with safety in the workplace.

**Occupied (OCC).**    An occupied room with a registered guest who has luggage. OCC is the code used on the attendants' assignment sheets.

**One for one.**    One veteran employee trains one new employee.

**On-the-job training.**    Training that teaches by having the new hire learn tasks by doing them, rather than by watching demonstrations.

**Open.**    Room available for renting.

**Operating budget.**    The financial outline of all expenditures for goods and services that will be used within one year.

**Operating supplies.**    Cleaning supplies and guest supplies consumed within one year.

**Operation.**    The functioning of a hotel, especially the activities dealing directly with serving the guests.

**Organizational chart.**    An outline which tracks the property's chain of command and lines of authority for various job titles.

**Orientation.**    The introduction of a new hire to the property and an explanation of all duties and responsibilities he or she will be expected to carry out.

**Out of order (OOO).**    The status of a room that is unrentable because it is being repaired or renovated.

**Oversold** (also **Overbooked**). Reservations have been accepted beyond the hotel's capacity to provide rooms.

**Package pass.**    A pass which indicates that a parcel being taken off-property by an employee has been inspected.

**Par.**    The number of sets of linen needed per bed or sets of towels needed per guest use.

**Percale.**    A very closely woven fabric made from fine-combed fibers; usually refers to fabric for sheets.

**Physical inventory.**    An actual, visual count of supplies and equipment on hand.

**Physical plant.**    The entire structure of the hotel; sometimes used just as **"plant,"** when referring to the entire hotel operation.

**Pick-up.**    To straighten up a room, usually after the room has been made up and the guest has checked out. Very little time is involved in a pick-up as opposed to a brush-up which may require changing linen and cleaning the bathroom.

**Piggy-back vacuum.**    A light-weight vacuum worn like a backpack.

**Pile density.**    The number and yarns and weight of a carpet.

**Pile height.**    The height of the yarns and, sometimes, the style.

**Pile lifter.**    Machine that raises the pile of carpet as close as possible to its original height.

**Pitch.**    A density indicator for carpet.

**Plugged room.** A room made inaccessible by security, due to death or theft.

**Pre-registered.** All registration is done prior to the guest's arrival; the guest simply is issued the room key without delay.

**Processing.** Filling out various insurance and tax forms; usually refers to this procedure when it is done immediately after an employee is hired.

**Productivity report.** Report that assesses how many tasks or how much work has been completed by an individual or staff during a certain period.

**Profile of business.** Forecast of all sales revenue expected in a certain period that includes an occupancy forecast as well as projections for meeting and function business.

**Profit and loss statement (P&L).** A financial statement listing profits, the income that outweighs expenses, and losses, the expenses that outweigh income, for a given period.

**Property.** A hotel's building, land, and all the facilities connected with it.

**Property maintenance.** A department in very large hotels, often a division of housekeeping, that does heavy cleaning in the front of the house and back of the house; it usually includes the night cleaning crew and may be in charge of keeping up the exterior and grounds.

**Purchase order.** An offer to buy something. When the seller accepts the purchase order it becomes a contract.

**Quota.** The minimum amount of work that management has designated for each individual or team.

**Rack rate.** The current rate charged for an accommodation, with no discounts.

**Rag out.** Term applied to discarded linen that is too frayed or torn to be reused in guest areas.

**Recycled inventory.** Supply items that can be reused, such as uniforms, linen, equipment, and machinery.

**Roll in.** Putting a rollaway bed in a guest room.

**Roll out.** Taking a rollaway bed out of a guest room.

**Rooming list.** The list of names submitted in advance by a buyer to occupy a previously reserved accommodation.

**Room status sheet.** A chart with the current count of how may rooms have been sold and how many are vacant.

**Rotary brush wet shampooing.** Cleaning system in which a rotary brush agitates the carpet pile while wet shampoo is being dispensed.

**Rotational schedule.** A schedule which rotates employees' days off.

**Risk management program.** A program that assesses what could go wrong in a property and attempts to find ways to prevent this.

**Runner.** The person who "runs" orders from the housekeeping office to employees on the guest floors; also, the person who "runs" clean linens from the linen rooms to attendants on the guest floors and returns soiled linen to the laundry.

**Rush room.** A room that takes precedence over all other cleaning assignments because the guest is already checking in and waiting to occupy the room.

**Sample.** A small swatch of material; any single piece of furniture or a fixture provided so that an evaluation can be made before the entire purchase order is written.

**Secondary containers.** Any containers that are not the original packaging.

**Section.** A room attendant's assigned area. Usually a section consists of 16 rooms.

**Segment.** A sector of the lodging industry that includes properties in the same category. For example, deluxe hotels are one segment; all-suites are another segment.

**Self-supervision.** A status which empowers attendants to inspect guest rooms (or public areas) they have cleaned and release them to the front desk.

**Service a guest room.** Term frequently used to mean "clean a guest room."

**Single.** A room with a bed for one person.

**Skip-clean.** A basis for cleaning which means a few general clean assignments are done each day.

**Skips.** People who leave the property without paying their bill.

**Sleep out.** A guest who rented a room but did not sleep in it.

**Space vac.** A vacuum with an extra wide head.

**Staff turnover.** Changes in staffing as people resign or are dismissed expressed as percentage. In Europe, "turnover," used alone, refers to revenues.

**Standards of Performance (SOP).** Measures of performance that assess the quality and quantity of tasks performed.

**Standing schedule.** A comprehensive, long-term framework for scheduling.

**Supplies.** Consumable items used in operations.

**Stewards.** In kitchens, these are the dishwashers who often are in charge of storing and transporting dishes, glassware, and tableware; banquet stewards set up and knock down banquet and meeting rooms.

**Strip a bed.** Remove the dirty linen from the bed.

**Studio.** A living area connected to one or more sleeping rooms.

**Support positions.** Jobs that directly assist a department head.

**Swab.** A nonabrasive scrubber with a long handle.

**Swing shift.** A shift that overlaps two standard shifts.

**Swing team.** A team of employees who do not have standing assignments but may be assigned to different tasks each day on as-needed basis; also, a team of employees that covers for employees with regular assignments on certain days.

**Swipe.** To draw a plastic, encoded card through a computerized decoder slot.

**Taking the count** or **Taking the AM/PM report.** Taking a physical check of guests in the attendants' section to determine the up-to-date status of each room. This is usually done twice daily.

**Team cleaning.** An approach to cleaning in which work is done by a group rather than an individual.

**Thread count.** The number of threads interlaced in a square inch of fabric.

**Tidy-up.** To straighten and clean a room after the guest's departure. Full service would have been completed earlier.

**Time and motion study.** A study which tracks a number of employees doing the same task to determine how long it takes, on average, for the task to be performed and which approach to doing the task is most efficient.

**Trouble report.** A written report indicating that a repair is needed.

**Turndown** or **Night service.** Removing the bed cover and turning down the bed, straightening the

room, and replenishing the used supplies and linen.

**Twin.** A room with twin beds.

**Unit producer.** A department or other organizational unit that bases its supply and equipment needs on the number of units that must be serviced each day. The housekeeping department is a unit producer. If 300 rooms are sold, enough labor must be assigned to clean 300 rooms, sufficient supplies must be allocated to clean 300 rooms, and so on.

**Vacant/dirty (V/D).** A room status indicating that the guests have checked out but that the room has not been cleaned.

**Vacant/ready (V/R).** A room status that indicates the room is unoccupied, cleaned, and ready for renting.

**Very Important Person (VIP).** Sometimes known as a Most Important Person or Special Attention List (SPLAT), this designation means this particular guest is to receive special attention and the very best service possible.

**Vitreous flooring.** Flooring made of stone clay product fired in a kiln to produce a hard, stone-like quality; ceramic tile is one example.

**Walk in.** A guest who requests a room without having booked a reservation.

**Walking a guest.** Sometimes called **farming out,** this means sending guests with reservations that cannot be honored because the hotel's rooms are sold out to a comparable hotel(s) with vacancies. The hotel who walks the guest arranges for transportation to and from the other hotel, makes the reservation there, and covers the cost of both transportation and room.

**Warp.** Lengthwise yarns used to make a fabric.

**Washer/extractor.** Washer with a built-in extractor that spins loads at very high speeds to remove excess moisture.

**Weft.** Crosswise threads used to make fabric.

**Wicking.** A process in which wetness or stains are drawn up from the packing through the face or pile, usually of carpet.

**Year to date (YTD).** An accounting term indicating that the totals reflect the beginning of the year to a certain date.

**Zero-based budget.** Budget that bases projected expenditures on the projected business levels for the coming period.

# Index